3/γ δ

English America and the Revolution of 1688

ENGLISH AMERICA

and the
Revolution of 1688

Royal Administration
and
the Structure of Provincial Government

J. M. Sosin

University of Nebraska Press
Lincoln and London

Publication of this book was aided by a grant from the National Endowment for the Humanities.

Library of Congress Cataloging in Publication Data
Sosin, Jack M.
    English America and the Revolution of 1688.
    Includes index.
    1. United States—Politics and government—Colonial period, ca. 1600–1775.
2. Great Britain—Politics and government—Revolution, of 1688.
I. Title.
E195.S78   973.2'4   81–16084
TSBN 0–8032–4131–3   AACR2

The paper in this book meets the guidelines for permanence and durability of the Committee on Production Guidelines for Book Longevity of the Council on Library Resources.

In memory of my mother

Contents

A Note on Dates

ALL DATES unless otherwise indicated (n.s. for new style) are in the Julian calendar, ten days behind those of the Gregorian calendar adopted by some of the states of Western Europe in 1582–83. In England, where the Gregorian calendar was not to be adopted until 1752, it had become the custom from the thirteenth century to advance the number of the year on 25 March, the date of the Feast of the Annunciation. Not until 1750 did Parliament by statute provide that year numbers would change on 1 January in and after 1752 and that the day *following* 2 September 1752 would become 14 September. In the notes to this work I have followed the practice often used by contemporaries of writing dates from 1 January to 25 March to indicate both the civil and the Julian year, as, for example, 2 February 1685/6. In France or other regions where the new style, or Gregorian, calendar was in use, this date would be written as 12 February 1686. In 1700 the discrepancy between the Julian and Gregorian calendars had increased by one day, from ten to eleven. For correspondence between England and areas in Europe employing the Gregorian calendar I have indicated both days (for example, 9/19 August) to avoid confusion.

Preface

THE WAR FOR AMERICAN INDEPENDENCE is the capstone of early American history. To scholars and laymen in America alike it is the embodiment of the sense of national identity. But this was not the first colonial revolution. Almost a century before, in 1689, colonists in Massachusetts, New York, and Maryland had risen against arbitrary rule imposed under the aegis of a distant government. These rebellions, although the subject of some historical inquiry, have been overshadowed both by the War for Independence and the more dramatic and apparently more constitutionally significant revolution in England: the deposing of a Catholic king and the establishing of responsible government by limiting royal prerogative through the supremacy of Parliament. While the uprisings in the American colonies which followed closely the Glorious Revolution in England did not result in independence, they did, nonetheless, have great significance: they helped shape the political configuration of America—the governmental structure of what a century later was to emerge as an independent nation.

Students of colonial America have devoted comparatively little attention to the Glorious Revolution. We have a handful of articles and dissertations devoted to the rebellion in particular colonies and only one book dealing specifically with the revolution as it applied to the provinces as a whole. Michael Kammen's article on Maryland ("The Causes of the Maryland Revolution of 1689," *Maryland Historical Magazine* 55 [Dec. 1960]: 293–333), has the virtue of comprehensiveness, but it fails to discriminate. It lists almost every conceivable development—social, economic, political, and psychological—as causes of the uprising at Saint Marys. These factors affected everyone in the colony, but only some, not all, of the Protestants, joined or even accepted the "Protestant" revolution against the regime of the Catholic proprietor. Theodore B. Lewis's "Massachusetts and the Glorious Revolution, 1660–1692" (Ph.D. diss., University of Wisconsin, 1967) is rich in detail and admirably researched, but accepts almost in a filiopietistic fashion the rationalizations of the Puritan opponents of royal government. In studies devoted to Manhat-

1

tan, Thomas Archdeacon ("The Age of Leisler: New York City, 1664–1710: A Social and Demographic Interpretation" [Ph.D. diss., Columbia University, 1971], and *New York City, 1664–1710: Conquest and Change* [Ithaca, N.Y.: Cornell University Press, 1976]) saw ethnic conflict, the resentment of the Dutch inhabitants displaced from power by the English conquerors, as fundamental. Joyce Diane Goodfriend, in " 'Too Great A Mixture of Nations': The Development of New York City Society in the Seventeenth Century" (Ph.D. diss., University of California, Los Angeles, 1975), has drawn different conclusions from the tax lists used by Archdeacon. Moreover, the thesis of ethnic conflict at best offers an explanation for the rebellion in Manhattan, but not for the other communities in New York, Dutch or English, and not for the other colonies in America. Alison Gilbert Olson's *Anglo-American Politics, 1660–1775* (New York and Oxford: Oxford University Press, 1973) is a brief work based on printed materials and by the author's admission is meant as a suggestive essay. The extensive chronological scope of the work limits its value for an understanding of the last two decades of the seventeenth century.

The most challenging study devoted to the entire American scene is David Lovejoy's *The Glorious Revolution in America* (New York: Harper and Row, 1972). Lovejoy saw Americans long before the Declaration of Independence as committed to republican ideology and a defense of individual rights. Such an explanation poses difficulties, for it fails to distinguish rationalizations and mere professions of belief from actual commitment to ideas as tested by consistent behavior. As this study will attempt to show, ideology did not distinguish men in Maryland and elsewhere who carried out revolutions from men who opposed them. Gershom Bulkeley, a Royalist in Connecticut, protested the overthrow of government established by the crown by an appeal to the rights of liberty and property against a revolutionary government acting without authority. So too did Royalists in Massachusetts who claimed the rights of Englishmen against Puritans exerting the same privileges in overthrowing a regime established by the crown of England. But there is also something suspect about the argument that Puritans in Massachusetts such as John Wise were moved to rebel by an ideology stressing the rights of Englishmen and a commitment to republicanism. For half a century, and but one year before direct royal government came to the Bay colony, the laws and taxes imposed on the inhabitants had been based on nothing more than the consent of the self-professed godly elect. The majority of the adult men in the Puritan commonwealth, those not full members of the Congregational churches, had not enjoyed political rights. Government in Massachusetts had rested only on the consent of a minority, those who

qualified to vote for and hold office on the basis of a religious qualification. Only when stripped of power by the crown did the commonwealthmen fall back on the doctrine of government based on the rights of
Englishmen. Had they had their way after the revolution of 1689, in
Massachusetts government again would have rested on the consent of the
godly.

My own research offers strong support for the thesis posed by David
William Jordan and Lois Green Carr (Jordan, "The Royal Period of
Colonial Maryland, 1689–1715," [Ph.D. diss., Princeton University,
1966]; Carr and Jordan, *Maryland's Revolution of Government, 1689–
1692* [Ithaca, N.Y., and London: Cornell University Press, 1974]). Instability, in great measure, resulted from the incongruity between the political station and the social status of men denied authority at the upper levels
of government. For the men who seized power in the various provincial
capitals during the spring and summer of 1689, despite their professed
fears of a plot to impose arbitrary control from London and to eliminate
representative governmental institutions, the basic question was, not
preservation of Protestantism or self-government, but who would hold
office under the mantle of the crown of England.

This book is the second of three dealing with the Atlantic English
communities and the interaction of the imperial and provincial worlds
over the course of more than half a century from the collapse of the
Puritan Commonwealth and the restoration of monarchy in England to
the succession of the first of the Hanoverian kings in 1714. In a previous
work, *English America and the Restoration Monarchy of Charles II* (Lincoln and London: University of Nebraska Press, 1980), I have traced the
development of English policy and the interaction of transatlantic politics, commerce, and kinship from 1660 to 1685 as they impinged on the
governmental structure of the colonies during a formative period. Royal
administration both before and after the Commonwealth and Protectorate regimes had been lax and ineffective for the first seventy-five years of
the English experience in America. During the seventeenth century tens
of thousands of English men and women had established, across the
Atlantic, communities and governments, scattered and diverse, little re-
strained by the government of the mother country. Almost completely
free from external restraint, these American communities had thrived
and expanded, all the while rent by tensions and animosities—ethnic and
religious—and the competition for power by strong-willed men. Only in
the last months of the reign of Charles II did the English monarchy finally
take decisive steps to bring the most recalcitrant of the colonies, Puritan
Massachusetts, under direct control.

The focus of this volume is on the years 1685 to 1696. I do not mean to imply that the origins of the Glorious Revolution in America are to be found only in the measures undertaken by James II at his accession in 1685 or that the revolutionary settlement did not extend beyond 1696. The present work attempts to assess the impact of the Glorious Revolution on the structure of American government, on the attempts by royal authorities to impose administrative cohesion, and the consequence of social and political instability in America for imperial administration. At issue were the political configuration of America, relations between church and state on the question of freedom of conscience, and, perhaps, the future of representative government.

In ecclesiastical arrangements, degree of religious toleration, ethnic composition, and form of government, the various colonies differed. Customarily, Englishmen identified political power with social status, but in America social mobility, greater economic opportunity, and fragmented political authority had a disruptive influence. Men sought political recognition commensurate with their social status, but the higher offices of colonial government were limited in number. Social mobility and economic opportunity created more aspirants for these prestigious positions than could be accommodated within the governmental structure. The potential for social disruption and upheaval existed, inherent in social fluidity, fragmented authority, ethnic and religious pluralism, and competition for power at the uppermost levels. That men commonly resorted to the rhetoric of liberty and appealed to the rights of Englishmen or the sanctity of popular or Biblical government often meant no more than that they needed to appear high-minded while pursuing their private ambitions and may well have been. Anti-Catholicism could serve the same purpose. At times men opposing each other held similar intellectual tenets and espoused the same ideology. To explain, to exculpate, to justify their behavior, men fell back on religion, the defense of local or traditional rights, and the threat of some enemy, external or domestic, like the French or the sinister Papists.

The danger in English America for disorder existed; its realization depended on events, often fortuitous, and the weakness of men. The spark was provided by the successful revolution carried out by Anglican leaders in England against the Catholic monarch during the winter of 1688–89.

In the reign of James II some men in America expressed fear that the English king seemed bent on drastically altering the governmental structure and the relationship between church and state. James and his closest advisers seemed poised to consolidate the various petty jurisdictions and to bring them under more direct control, and to curtail, possibly even abolish, locally elected assemblies and the privileges established by charters.

The revolution which drove James II from the throne in 1688 did ensure that in America locally elected assemblies would continue, but it did not put an end to attempts by royal administration to subject the provincial governments to more direct supervision, if only to coordinate English military efforts as war on a large scale, intercolonial and international broke out, the result, in part, of the overthrow of the Catholic monarch.

Revolution in 1688 had great political and constitutional consequences on both sides of the Atlantic; it confirmed some measure of representative government in America and established the theory of the supremacy of the English Parliament not only over the monarch but over the colonies as well. Kings and queens now were required to rule England and the dominions according to the laws of the legislature at Westminster. No longer could the monarch and his ministers alter the governments of the chartered colonies by rescinding or vacating patents simply by the exercise of the royal prerogative or writ of the royal courts. Action against colonial charters would now come only through legislation by Parliament. But the effectiveness of the legislature at Westminster in turn depended on organized political parties marshaling enough votes in favor of a particular proposal. In the state of parties, Whig and Tory, court and country, during the reigns of William III and Anne, not all issues were party issues, as was demonstrated early in the eighteenth century when an advisory board for plantation affairs solicited legislation to vacate the provincial charters. Colonial government was not a party question, one which took precedent over local partisan quarrels, private interests, and the needs of the government in waging war in Europe.

More critical after 1688 than the theory of parliamentary supremacy to the success or failure of any policy undertaken for the American colonies was the involvement of the English monarchy in a protracted conflict with Bourbon France. William, prince of Orange, was the leader of a Protestant coalition against Louis XIV when he crossed the North Sea in 1688 to save England for Protestantism. As king of England he was nonetheless a Dutch king committed to using the resources of the island kingdom against the Bourbons in Europe. Compelled to rely on the colonists in America to combat the French from Canada, William III and his ministers were not free to impose their authority on Massachusetts and the other provincial regimes. War in Europe and parochialism in Westminster would limit royal administration for America.

English America and the Revolution of 1688

Introduction

On 6 February 1685, Charles II, after an unexpectedly long reign as king of England, died. His tenure had been surprisingly long; in the spring of 1660, when he had arrived at the royal palace of Whitehall after years of turmoil, civil war, and exile, observers had not given him much time on the throne. In 1660 monarchy had won only by default after the failure of the Puritan experiment in commonwealth and protectorate government. The king had faced a vigorous, unruly people, subjects reluctant to accept central authority, and a Parliament packed with suspicious members and dominated by ambitious men ready to challenge the king and his ministers for control of government and the mainsprings of power. The refusal of religious zealots to accept the end of the Puritan regime, and open opposition in Westminster by opportunistic politicians appealing to fears and religious animosities had further jeopardized the restored monarchy. Partisans caught up with Whiggish and anti-Catholic rhetoric had charged the king and his Catholic brother, James, duke of York, with plotting to alter the tenuous religious and political settlement hammered out after 1660 and to impose authoritarian rule and the Church of Rome.

The financial and political weakness of the monarchy in England had prejudiced effective administration of the English settlements in America. After the hiatus of neglect under the early Stuarts and the Commonwealth and Protectorate, Charles II and his ministers had evidenced concern that the colonies should no longer remain "loose and scattered," but be brought under a "uniforme inspeccion and conduct." The king himself had pursued another goal, to promote liberty of religious conscience, at least for the various Dissenting Protestant sects, an object denied him in England by a house of Commons dominated by an Anglican squirearchy resentful of the treatment accorded them by the Puritans during the rule of the Roundheads and determined to maintain their political power and the ecclesiastical monopoly of the Church of England.

Toleration and a closer political tie to Whitehall had been the late king's goals, but in practice matters had worked out differently. Charles

9

had confirmed the separate status of almost all of the provincial regimes existing at the outset of his reign and had gone on to gratify private individuals and groups by issuing charters to sanction their efforts at colonization. By rewarding favorites and accommodating Protestant Dissenters the king had authorized the founding of six additional provinces, each diverse in its social structure and pluralistic in its ethnic and religious composition, and some bizzare in their governmental arrangements. Under Charles II the crown had sought unrealistically to bring the colonies under tighter control merely by having the crown commission or instruct governors resident in the American settlements. The king and his ministers had failed to curb local authority and to render the separate jurisdictions across the Atlantic more closely dependent on the crown.

In all but one of the provincial governments, including those sanctioned from England, an elected assembly participated in the legislative process. The sole exception was New York, taken from the Dutch and granted as a proprietary colony to the king's brother, James. But in 1683 the royal duke, succumbing to local pressure and needing financial aid, instructed his deputy at Manhattan to issue writs for summoning representatives of the inhabitants to vote money and to pass laws.

The practice followed by Charles II of granting charters for new colonies, patents requiring that the inhabitants or their representatives have some voice in government, almost ensured the failure of the king's goals. The English dominions in America had become even more loose and scattered. Hard-pressed by the opposition leaders at Westminster, Charles and his servants in government had sought to hold royal expenditures in the overseas plantations to a ridiculously low level, thus reducing officials appointed by the crown to dependence on local leaders. At the same time, through a navigation code enacted by Parliament, king and ministers sought to increase revenue accruing to the administration in England from an expanding colonial trade as the American and West Indian colonies prospered and their economy became integrated into the growing commerce of Europe.

After almost a quarter of a century, the ministers of state had accomplished little, despite warnings given as late as 1681 to the proprietors of Carolina and Maryland over the chaotic state of government and collection of the customs duties. The year 1684 had brought a direct threat to the royal revenue on the Potomac River. To the north the French in Canada and the hostile Indians allied with them posed what appeared to be a growing menace to the security of the divided, quarrelsome colonies in New England and the exposed frontier province of New York. The latter was especially weak and vulnerable. Officials at Manhattan had called for some consolidation to enable them to resist more effectively.

But the final disposition of the government of New York had had to await a decision by the crown for Puritan Massachusetts. For a generation, the "commonwealth" men, imbued with a sense of mission as the elect of God, had resisted any attempt by moderates to reach an accommodation with the ministers at Whitehall on enforcing the acts of trade and navigation, on tolerating peaceable Protestants who dissented from the established Congregationalist churches, on allowing others besides full members of the Puritan churches and the more wealthy to vote and to hold office in the Bay colony, and on permitting appeals from the courts of Massachusetts to the crown. By procrastinating, by dissembling, and by litigation the commonwealth men had hoped to outlast Charles II, as a generation before, prior to the Civil War, they had his father. Finally, Charles II and the ministers of state had acted. In 1684 the royal courts at Westminster had vacated the charter issued in 1629 to Massachusetts. But a comprehensive political settlement had not yet been decided upon when Charles II died and his brother, a convert to Roman Catholicism, became king of England.

CHAPTER 1

The Restoration Legacy

To CONTEMPORARIES and later men, the character and ambitions of James II were unclear. Was he a designing bigot—cast from the same mold as Philip II of Spain and Louis XIV of France—a monarch who calculated to impose autocratic rule, to reestablish the Church of Rome in England and in the colonies, or was he, however clumsy and tactless, a monarch who hoped to win for his fellow Catholics and other Dissenting Christians the rights Cromwell and Charles II earlier had failed to secure from zealous Puritans and embittered, suspicious Anglicans?

Initially the new king, in great contrast with the impression given by his late brother, seemed purposeful and efficient. The very day Charles died, James met with the privy councilors. They issued an order for a letter to the governors across the Atlantic continuing officers in the provinces in their posts.[1] The new court shared certain goals with the previous administration: to bring the chartered colonies under closer supervision, to curb the diverse governments in North America, and more effectively to coordinate defense against France in the Western Hemisphere. The king, a convert to the Church of Rome, was zealous in his religion. Within a few weeks he and his queen were openly attending mass at Whitehall, much to the distress of many of his subjects. But James declared that he had long enough concealed his religious sentiments in order to please his brother. He would now be "above-board." Quakers were pleased for they and other Dissenters had suffered under the Parliamentary legislation restricting political rights and religious freedom to adherents of the established Church of England. So William Penn, a leading Quaker and a friend of the new monarch, told him. Smiling, James replied that he desired "not that peaceable people should be disturbed for their religion."[2]

In the reaction against the antimonarchial excesses of opposition politicians, James II initially enjoyed a large measure of support. His government brutally suppressed an uprising in Scotland led by the earl of Argyle and a revolt in the west of England attempted by Charles II's bastard son, the duke of Monmouth. When James's first parliament met, it voted a generous grant to enable the crown to restore the Royal Navy and to pay off outstanding debts. It imposed further duties on imports, heavy taxes on tobacco and sugar, three pennies more on English colonial tobacco, six on foreign. Protests by merchants in London and Bristol engaged in the Chesapeake and West Indian trades and by spokesmen of planters on the Chesapeake had counted little. The administration hastened to assure the traders and the colonists overseas that the burden would not fall on them, but on the English consumers. The additional taxes voted and the boom in foreign trade brought the total revenue from overseas commerce to almost a million pounds a year.[3]

To safeguard this lucrative source of revenue, Parliament reenacted legislation prohibiting the planting of tobacco in England, and the Privy Council issued orders strictly to enforce the various acts of trade and navigation. These laws aimed to channel certain products of the colonies to English ports when shipped to foreign markets. Here they were subject to customs duties. English ships bound for the plantations could not leave port until security was given that they would return tobacco, sugar, and other enumerated products to England. On the recommendations of the Commissioners of Customs, orders went out for the destruction of tobacco plants in Gloucester, Worcester, Hereford, and Warwick. Tobacco grown in England greatly prejudiced the shipping of the kingdom, hindered the growth of the plantations as well as the royal customs revenue, and diminished the trade of the English port towns. Under orders from the Privy Council, Samuel Pepys, secretary to the Admiralty, instructed the commanders of the king's ships on colonial stations to seize all foreign vessels trading to the plantations, all but Spanish ships arriving at Jamaica or Barbados to buy slaves. Across the Atlantic the governors in the colonies received orders to enforce the parliamentary shipping code.[4]

In the ensuing months the new administration faced a variety of other problems relating to commerce and the colonies: complaints over kidnapping and irregularities in transporting of indentured servants to the foreign plantations and protests from officials in Dublin over the reenactment by the English Parliament of legislation making Irish ports ineligible to receive tobacco, sugar, and other enumerated produce directly from America. Closer to home, the handicraft workers and tradesmen in and about London, "his Majesty's natural born subjects," complained of aliens, "Jermines," Spaniards, and Frenchmen among them, who were driving the English artisans from their livelihood.[5]

In North America the French also posed a threat to the English dominions. During the reign of Charles II the French court had sent a full regiment of regular troops to Canada. For some years it had been evident that tension between certain of the Indian tribes (now backed by the

French) and the English (supported by the Iroquois) had been increasing. Officials in Quebec and Montreal seemed determined to curb the Five Nations, who hitherto had shielded the English. The governors sent out from Whitehall to New York and New Hampshire, two of the more exposed and sparsely populated provinces, had sought support from the stronger, more populous Puritan colonies of New England. Governor Thomas Dongan, the Catholic army officer recently assigned to Manhattan, was no exception. In his view New York needed forts and money as well as hundreds of men from neighboring East and West Jersey, Connecticut, and Massachusetts.

In the face of growing rivalry between France and England in Europe, both James II and Louis XIV apparently sought to avoid a costly war in the colonies. By the Treaty of Whitehall in November 1686 their emissaries agreed to neutrality; if war broke out in Europe, neither side was to commit hostilities in America. But in Canada, the officials of the Sun King moved against the Iroquois, the Indian confederation Dongan and other English officers thought necessary to protect the colonists. Each side then sought to blame the other, the French holding the English responsible for arming the Iroquois against them, the English protesting that the French had invaded Iroquois territory, a region under nominal English protection. Far to the north the Canadians seized three trading stations in the Hudson Bay region. The three English commissioners, Robert, earl of Sunderland, Sidney Godolphin, and Charles, earl of Middleton, appointed to negotiate with agents of the French court, urged James II for the security of his dominions in America to support the Iroquois and instruct his governors to assist the Five Nations against any French incursion.[6]

Better to meet the French threat, the English court consolidated the scattered and divided provincial governments north of the Delaware into a single Dominion of New England under an appointed royal governor, an experienced military officer familiar with the situation in New York. Edmund Andros had arrived in Boston in 1686 assigned to govern Massachusetts Bay (New England, as it was commonly called). In announcing to a colleague the consolidation of the governments of the northern colonies, William Blathwayt, long-time secretary to the Privy Council's Committee on Foreign Plantations, blamed incursions by the French. "I believe this union may make us more formidable."[7]

Other consideration had led to this administrative consolidation of colonies. For some time the ministers of state at Whitehall had been unhappy with the chartered provinces, plantations whose patents issued earlier in the century by the Stuart kings allowed them to enjoy government not immediately dependent on the crown of England. The threat of legal action by writ of quo warranto in the royal courts at Westminster against the charters of these quasi-independent colonies seemed less a long-standing preconceived scheme to impose direct control and to eliminate representative governmental institutions than a recent reaction to disparate, but highly disturbing events in particular colonies.[8] New York had become a royal province when its proprietor became king. Shortly before, in 1684, James had been willing to grant the inhabitants a representative assembly. In this he had followed the example set by his brother for all of the other provinces. As late as 1682, when Charles II had commissioned the first royal governor for New Hampshire, he had instructed him to call representatives from the towns to meet with the executive and the appointive council to enact laws and vote taxes.

But difficulties had repeatedly surfaced in certain proprietary and corporate colonies. Governmental jurisdiction had been disputed in East and West Jersey and in the lower counties on the Delaware River. In the Albemarle region of Carolina and in Maryland political instability and proprietary weakness had threatened the royal customs service. Lord Baltimore had received a warning in 1682: legal action would be taken against his charter if he did not set affairs in his proprietary right. But only two years later, over the strong objections of the king's governor in Virginia, Baltimore and the proprietary officials in Maryland under him claimed the customs revenue from shipping entering the Potomac River. Late in 1684 the presiding officer of the Maryland council, George Talbot, during a scuffle murdered Christopher Rousby, a royal customs official. At about the same time officials in New York complained to England of violations of the shipping code in East Jersey to the detriment of the royal customs. They urged that the crown place East and West Jersey and the three lower counties on the Delaware River—territories once part of New York—under the government at Manhattan and join Rhode Island to New York. Such a union would strengthen the military and financial resources of the province. Governor Thomas Dongan failed, however, to supply the ministers at Whitehall with any grounds for legal action against the corporation at Providence.

Of all the chartered colonies, Masssachusetts for more than twenty years had caused the most concern. Men determined to preserve the independence of commonwealth committed to serving God's will (as they understood it) dominated the government at Boston. For two decades they had resisted any accommodation with the crown of England. A royal patent issued in 1629 entitled them, they claimed, to exercise governmental powers, independently of England. Charles II had insisted that they allow his subjects in the colony to appeal decisions from the provincial courts to Westminster, that they allow freedom of religious conscience to all Protestants who did not abuse this liberty by disturbing the peace, and that they not restrict the right to vote and to hold office to men who were in full communion with some local Congregational church. It had been to little avail. Although a few wealthy men had been admitted to the freedom of the corporation on the basis of a high tax-paying qualification, political power remained with the visible Puritan saints. By 1683 the freemen probably numbered fewer than one of every three adult men in Massachusetts. By procrastinating, the Puritan leaders had hoped to outlast the Stuarts; they had hoped that political and religious turmoil in England would bring down Charles II as it had brought down his father more than a generation before.

Charles II had survived longer than the commonwealthmen in Boston had expected, but only narrowly. In 1684 the Court of King's Bench vacated the patent for Massachusetts. The province, in the language of the times, was now brought into a closer dependence on the crown; the king would now name a governor.

Beyond this, it was not clear what form of government Whitehall would impose on either Massachusetts or New York. The court deferred a decision to confirm an elected assembly for New York until it decided on a constitution for the Bay colony. Early in November 1684, following the vacating of the charter of Massachusetts, the Committee for Plantation Affairs in Whitehall had recommended that a governor be sent out empowered to call for an assembly in the province, but two weeks later the lord keeper directed his colleagues that in the instructions to the governor no mention be made of an assembly and that the governor and his appointed council make laws and exercise all authority until the king's further pleasure be known.[9] The duke of york, among others, was reported shocked by a scandalous, seditious sermon allegedly preached by the Reverend Joshua Moody and the Reverend Increase Mather, two leaders among the Puritan faction in New England. A few weeks after James became king, William Blathwayt reported him resolved to reduce all of the proprietary and independent governments "to an immediate dependence upon the Crown," but Edward Randolph, a colleague of Blathwayt and the Royalist official who had taken the lead in contesting the Puritans of the Bay colony, submitted a plan for the government of New England by which the townsmen of Massachusetts, Maine, and New Plymouth elected assemblymen to sit with the local councilors appointed by the crown as a provincial legislature.

It was by no means certain what the men at Whitehall had in mind for the American provinces generally or New England in particular. They seemed uncertain whether to sue out writs in the courts at Westminster against Rhode Island and Connecticut before sending off a governor to

New England, or to allow the provincial regimes voluntarily to join a general government for New England. Should they refuse, the ministers might then seek writs from the royal courts.[10]

A few men sitting on the king's council as the lords of the Committee for Trade and Plantation Affairs would influence any decision. As a group they had demonstrated their loyalty when the opposition Whig politicians had attacked the monarchy during the last years of the late king's reign. But they had little else in common. Robert Spencer, earl of Sunderland, had become a principal secretary of state under Charles II. One of the older ministers, he was most able and efficient, but often unprincipled. Nominally an Anglican, he curried favor with the king by looking to the Church of Rome. In October 1685 Sunderland succeeded his rival, George Savile, marquis of Halifax, as lord president of the council when Halifax refused to support repeal of legislation restricting office to men who repudiated the Catholic doctrine of transubstantiation. Sunderland had other opponents: two Scottish brothers, James Drummond, earl of Perth, and John Drummond, earl of Melfort. As liaison between Perth, who headed the government at Edinburgh, and the king in London, Melfort was one of the few men who could see James II at any time without going through Sunderland. The Drummonds were among the proprietors of the province of East Jersey, and as such they had insisted on the right of the proprietors to maintain a government in the province separate from that of New York. Also opposing Sunderland were the young Anglican Tories, the brothers Laurence and Henry Hyde, earls of Rochester and Clarendon. Also on the committee sat the duke of Ormonde, the earl of Craven (one of the proprietors of Carolina), the duke of Beaufort, Sir Robert Southwell (onetime clerk of the Privy Council, Blathwayt's mentor, and consultant on colonial matters), and the lord keeper, Francis North, Lord Guilford. When the last-named died, in September 1685, Sir George Jeffreys of Bloody Assizes fame succeeded him.

Through these men William Blathwayt, long-time secretary to the Committee for Trade and Plantations, and Edward Randolph, Royalist agent and customs official, sought to influence the decisions made at Whitehall on America.

At the outset of the reign when James's province of New York had become a royal colony, Blathwayt had thought the new king was resolved to bring the chartered colonies to an immediate dependence on the crown. Lord Baltimore as proprietor of Maryland had already been singled out. A writ would be sued out against his charter if he proved obstinate. But within a few weeks Blathwayt seemed less certain. Although the proprietor had been "respited," at least until "all things be more quiet,"

Blathwayt believed the king was still resolved to bring Maryland under direct royal control.[11] Despite Blathwayt's seeming assurance, James II never carried through.

It was Randolph who was most active. For years he had campaigned against the independent, Puritan-dominated provinces in America. Rather than colonies, they seemed to be little commonwealths. His efforts had finally met with some success in 1684 when the royal courts had vacated the patent to Massachusetts Bay. A few prominent men in Boston had indicated to Randolph their willingness to accept some regulation from England. Following the unexpected but perhaps temporary decision not to allow a representative assembly for the colony, early in 1685 Randolph had more unhappy news for the moderates in Boston. The king had promised the governorship to Colonel Percy Kirke, a professional soldier who had once commanded the king's garrison at Tangier. In putting down Monmouth's rebellion in 1685, Kirke earned strong condemnation for the "great carnage" in the west of England. Randolph considered the hotheaded Kirke most unsuited for the task of governing New England; it required a quiet, prudent man.

From Randolph's correspondence—and he was close to Ormonde, Beaufort, and Clarendon—it appeared that the ministers of state were not committed to suing out writs against the charters of Connecticut and Rhode Island. They might take such a legal step should authorities in Hartford and Providence refuse to submit to a general government. While urging the annexation of Rhode Island, Thomas Dongan, the governor of New York, had not supplied any grounds for legal action against the charters. Randolph himself would provide the arguments.

On 5 May 1685, Guilford, Clarendon, Sunderland, and Craven, sitting as the lords of the Committee for Plantation Affairs, took up a representation submitted by Randolph. He claimed that in New England no impartial tribunals existed to hear causes between private persons or between magistrates and inhabitants. Annexed to Randolph's representation were the petitions of residents of New England asking that the crown empower a royal governor to erect courts. At this point the lords of the committee noted that the provincial regimes against whom these complaints were raised were by royal patent exempted from any authority other than appeals to the king. They ordered Randolph to prepare a document with such particulars as would justify issuing writs of quo warranto against the charters.[12]

Involved with hearing evidence before the council concerning Titus Oates, the pathological liar whose charges against leading Catholics had helped embroil the nation in mass hysteria a few years before, the committee did not take up Randolph's particulars against Connecticut and

Rhode Island until the middle of the summer of 1685. On 10 July the full council had received complaints of offenses committed in Maryland: encroachments by proprietary officials on the customs revenue and the murder of Christopher Rousby by the presiding officer of the Maryland council. Reacting strongly, the king in council ordered Lord Baltimore to attend them at the next meeting and instructed the attorney general, Robert Sawyer, to sue out a writ of quo warranto against his charter. Another letter had arrived, one from the mayor, aldermen, and principal officers of the city of New York. Ever since James (the original English proprietor of the region encompassing New York, New Jersey, and the Delaware counties) had divided the territory, the trade of the city and, consequently, the revenue of the provincial government had suffered.

Randolph had already submitted articles charging high misdemeanors against Rhode Island and Connecticut, accusing officials there of arbitrarily taxing and fining the inhabitants, passing laws contrary to the statues of England, violating the parliamentary navigation code, and denying the king's subjects the right of appeal to the king's courts at Westminster. Connecticut stood further charged with denying inhabitants the exercise of religion according to the Anglican Book of Common Prayer and with arbitrarily fining persons for not attending the services of the local Congregational churches. As proof Randolph submitted extracts from the statutes of Connecticut and Rhode Island.

The issue was not long in doubt. On 15 July Clarendon, Rochester, Halifax, Ormonde, and Beaufort recommended that writs be prosecuted against the corporations of Connecticut and Rhode Island and the proprietaries of East and West Jersey and the Delaware counties. Only a few years before, James had passed title to the latter territory to William Penn, the Quaker proprietor of Pennsylvania. These provinces ought to be brought to a nearer dependence on the crown, the committee recommended. Two days later the full council confirmed the decision and took up the replies Baltimore had submitted to the charges brought against his administration in Maryland. He was to return in a week to hear the evidence presented by the Commissioners of Customs.[13]

Randolph wasted no time. In less than two weeks he secured the five writs and was prepared to set out for America. One point, the appointment of Percy Kirke as governor, "since the great carnage he has made in ye West," disturbed Randolph. New England needed a quiet governor, an experienced, prudent man such as Sir Edmund Andros, another professional army officer who had previously served as proprietary governor of New York but who "upon some unlucky mistakes," Randolph thought, had been "unkindly laid aside."[14]

Time was pressing. The summons from the sheriffs of London to the authorities of Connecticut and Rhode Island to answer the writs issued against them were returnable in Westminster the next court term. Randolph needed to take ship for America within three weeks if he were to serve the writs in time. Clarendon assured the eager messenger the committee would deal with the matter as soon as possible. Other business was more pressing, and the king's court was then at Windsor.

There was now some doubt whether Kirke would go. Others besides Randolph thought him unsuited for the position in Massachusetts. On 18 August, Randolph pressed his case before the Committee for Plantation Affairs: more than nine months had passed since judgment had been entered against the charter of Massachusetts and the government in the colony vested in the crown. The king could at least appoint a temporary council of men well disposed to the crown until the governor general arrived. By 2 September the ministers had agreed to send off Randolph to Boston. He had presented a list of men—moderates on the question of relations between the Bay colony and the English crown—to serve as members of a temporary conciliar administration. Evidently Randolph did not think the decision against a representative assembly made the previous November was final, for he drew up a list of New England towns whose inhabitants were to have liberty to choose one or two representatives for an assembly.[15]

One of the men Randolph suggested to serve on the council for New England was Robert Mason. He claimed the proprietorship of New Hampshire on the basis of a grant made to his grandfather half a century before by a defunct English corporation. To eliminate any source of friction—the townsmen on the Piscataqua fiercely contested Mason's claims—Randolph urged him to give up his pretensions in exchange for a small annual allowance out of the quitrents and the governorship of Bermuda. Although Clarendon apparently approved of the suggestion, nothing came of it. Mason persisted in his proprietary claims to the soil of New Hampshire.[16]

Randolph spent many weeks late that fall and early the following winter at Deal waiting to take ship for Boston to deliver notices of the writs against Connecticut and Rhode Island and to present the commission for Joseph Dudley and the other members of the royal council to administer the affairs of Massachusetts pending the arrival of a governor. Colonel Percy Kirke, the officer to whom Charles II the previous fall had promised the governorship of Massachusetts, was now clearly in disfavor. Lord Keeper Jeffreys, himself later condemned by the Whigs for his conduct at the Bloody Assizes, was satisfied that the reports of Kirke's brutality at Taunton were more than mere "flying" rumors.

Not until the following spring was the choice for governor revealed.

As Randolph had hoped, it fell on Edmund Andros. At the Plantation Office, one official, John Povey, expected the new governor would not have as much satisfaction from the position as he might ordinarily have had, for the "constitution for that government" was "without any assembly." The decision so to structure the government must have been made by a very few men, perhaps only Sunderland and the king, for Povey—he and Blathwayt had the task of drafting the commission and instructions for Andros—found a "plantation government without an assembly . . . very . . . mysterious." He was skeptical such an arrangement would answer the royal service. Andros, with the consent of the majority of the appointed councilors, had authority to make laws and to continue current taxes as well as to set such other impositions as necessary for the support of the administration. The commission to Dongan at New York contained the same provisions. Povey, familiar with the past problems involving Massachusetts, thought this arrangment "will put Sir Edmund to his utmost dexterity" with the Bay colonists who were stubborn enough to desert the country and their estates rather than place their confidence in a royal governor "tho the person be very grateful to them." Andros did not sail from The Downs until 19 October 1686. Clarendon, less well informed, was optimistic over his chances of success, for Andros presumably "understands the people, and knows how to manage them."[17]

The decision to omit a representative assembly from the government of New England was probably the work of Robert, earl of Sunderland, not a decision taken by the other ministers. The previous summer, while drafting a commission for the temporary council at Boston, the Lords of Trade and Plantations had asked the lord president to learn the king's pleasure concerning a clause for calling assemblies to make laws and to raise money. Such a provision was agreeable to the crown law officers. Sir Robert Sawyer and Sir Thomas Powis had reported that, notwithstanding the forfeiture of the charter, the inhabitants of Massachusetts retained the right to consent to laws and taxes. According to information a solicitor in London later gave to Increase Mather, Sunderland intervened with James II to strike from the commission the provision for calling an assembly.[18]

Andros faced a difficult problem with few resources at his command. By the express order of James II he must keep diligent accounts of the revenue. All money collected must be for the immediate use, support, and security of New England. The new governor before departing received authorization to draw one hundred soldiers from the camp at Hounslow Heath.

While formulating plans for the administration of the new government at Boston, the court in April 1686 directed Robert Sawyer, the attorney general, to renew the several writs ordered the previous July against Maryland, East and West Jersey, Connecticut, and Rhode Island. A month later the Privy Council met again to discuss colonial affairs. The cryptic notation entered in its register merely stated that, the king having taken into consideration the state of the plantations, the council ordered the attorney general to proceed against the charters of the remaining proprietaries, Pennsylvania, Carolina, and the Bahama Islands. But a newsletter dated 1 June 1686, possibly written by a clerk of the council or an undersecretary, and sent to William of Orange in the United Provinces of the Netherlands shed more light on the decision. The king in council at its last session had ordered writs against the charters of the colonies "in order to the recalling them and giving them other new ones. Wherein a lattitude shall be allowed to the Roman Catholics which, without doubt, will cause many consultations there, and, perhaps, some revolts."[19]

But in the proprietaries of the Catholic Lord Baltimore and the Quaker William Penn there were no penalties against Papists. Within a week Sunderland informed the attorney general that for "some particular considerations," the king had decided to suspend the proceedings against the proprietor of Pennsylvania. The law officer was to forbear any further action against Penn, but to continue the suits against Carolina and the Bahama Islands. No further action was taken during James II's reign against Pennsylvania. In remonstrating with the quarrelsome officials in Philadelphia Penn took credit for putting a halt to the writ. Had he not, "some busy bodys would have had their mouths stopped for good and all."[20]

Among the proprietors of Carolina and the Bahama Islands the earl of Shaftesbury reacted sharply when his colleague Craven informed him of the contemplated legal action against their charters. He did not know upon what ground a writ could be brought. The proprietors had spent considerable money on the colonies, and if they were to surrender their patents, he could not see how they were to be reimbursed. Shaftesbury professed himself to be as unwilling as any man to dispute the king's pleasure, but it was not within the power of any person, the monarch included, to dispose of another's property. Craven read these words to James himself.

Further complaints against proprietary officials in the Carolinas came in, alleging violations of the acts of trade, including transgressions and irregularities by the governor. At this the king in council on 24 August 1688 ordered Sir Thomas Powis to proceed by writ of scire facias against the proprietors of Carolina and the Bahama Islands to vacate their charters.[21] The action was never carried through.

The southern proprietaries were of secondary importance, for the colonies north and east of the Delaware River took precedence in the plans of the ministers of state. In the north the military menace loomed greater. Initially James's ministers contemplated two distinct governments, one for New York and another for New England.[22] A sharp rivalry now developed between Boston and Manhattan for control. Randolph, when he delivered the "superannuated" summons at Providence, suspected the Rhode Islanders were playing off Massachusetts against Dongan. Should New York acquire the two southermost provinces of New England, Massachusetts would be ruined, he speculated. The Quakers, particularly apprehensive over the prospects of coming under the jurisdiction of the Bay colony, had approached Dongan. In turn the royal council at Boston had dispatched Major John Pynchon of Massachusetts and Captain Wait Winthrop, son of the former governor of Connecticut and brother of Fitzjohn Winthrop of New London, to persuade officials at Hartford to accept annexation to Massachusetts rather than come under New York.

Unknown to the protagonists in America, the decision was not long in doubt. Acting on the assumption that the officials of Rhode Island had agreed not to stand suit over the quo warranto, the Lords of Trade on 12 September 1686 recommended that Andros be empowered to receive the surrender of the charter, to promise the inhabitants the king's protection, and to take over the government. If officials at Hartford followed the example it was hoped the Rhode Islanders would set, Andros would also accept the surrender of the charter of Connecticut.[23]

News arriving in London from southern New England seemed to indicate that officials there were procrastinating. The following spring the ministers of state again directed the crown law officers to prosecute writs ordered the previous summer against Maryland, Connecticut, and Rhode Island. And in July arrived complaints from George Muschamp in Charles Town of illegal trade in proprietary Carolina. Some proprietary officials in Charles Town had claimed that, inasmuch as the charter for the colony was issued after the enactment of the parliamentary navigation act, they were not bound by its provisions and could trade directly to Ireland and Scotland. The Committee for Plantation Affairs now ordered a review of the various patents and charters issued for the colonies.[24] Yet the administration took no action against the Catholic Lord Baltimore or the Quaker William Penn, proprietors of Maryland and Pennsylvania. Nor did it ever proceed with the proposed writ against Carolina.

By this time Andros had arrived in America and had conducted a seemingly triumphant tour of southern New England. Officials in Hartford and Providence had apparently acquiesced in the incorporation of Connecticut and Rhode Island into the dominion.[25]

The last annexation came early in 1688, probably as a reaction to the threatening military situation on the northern frontiers and a diplomatic *impasse* in Europe. An order in council issued on 27 January 1687/8 appointing the members of the Privy Council as a standing Committee for Trade and Foreign Plantations reflected a sense of urgency in Whitehall. It was now clear that Sunderland and the other English commissioners could not resolve with the emissaries of Louis XIV the dispute between the two powers over North America. Sunderland had received a plea from Dongan in Albany that New York must have support from the New England colonies and the Jerseys.[26] Alone it could not bear the burden of securing the northern frontier against the French.

For a generation the English governors at Manhattan had insisted that New York needed assistance from her eastern neighbors. With Connecticut and Rhode Island annexed to Boston, the next step was clear. In March 1688 an exultant Blathwayt announced to Randolph the joining of all the English territories in America from Delaware Bay to Nova Scotia. A new commission issued to Sir Edmund Andros annexed New York to New England. Writs of scire facias against the two Jerseys would expedite their union to the dominion. "This, besides other advantages, will be terrible to the French and make them proceed with more caution than they have lately done." On 25 March 1688 a warrant was ordered for a commission under the Great Seal of England to join the northern colonies, except Pennsylvania and the Delaware counties, into a province to be called the Dominion of New England, with Andros as governor and Captain Francis Nicholson as deputy, or lieutenant governor. Dongan was recalled.[27]

The crown specifically excluded the territories of the Quaker William Penn and did not pursue the writ against the charter of the Catholic proprietor of Maryland. By the laws prevailing in the two colonies the king's coreligionists, his Catholic subjects, enjoyed toleration and political rights.

The desire to coordinate and consolidate the military resources of the region north and east of the Delaware accounted for the creation of the Dominion of New England. Amalgamation had been achieved by executive action, by orders of the king in council. Despite Blathwayt's references to obtaining writs of scire facias, the claims of the proprietors of East and West Jersey to exercise powers of government were dubious. As the initial English proprietor, James, duke of York, had had no authority to transfer such power to others. When he succeeded to the throne in 1685, his province of New York, and perhaps the two Jerseys as well, became royal colonies, although the proprietors of East and West Jersey retained their rights to the soil as did Robert Mason. New Hampshire some years before had come under direct royal jurisdiction with a governor appointed from London as early as 1682. The ministers at Whitehall did not prosecute the writs against Connecticut and Rhode Island—a mistake, as it later turned out—but had assumed that the governing authorities of the two corporations had voluntarily surrendered. The inhabitants of New Plymouth, the remaining province, had never received sanction from the crown of England to exercise governmental powers. Plymouth had become part of Massachusetts three years before.

Despite the various orders in council directing the crown law officers to prosecute writs against the charters of the proprietaries and corporations in America, the royal courts at Westminster had vacated only the charter of the Bay colony, and this in the last year of the previous reign. In London in 1688 agents from Boston, seeking to capitalize on James II's announced policy of freedom of religion, appealed to the king to repudiate this action as illegal.

Religion had been at the heart of English political controversy for generations, and anti-Catholicism was central to the rhetoric of opportunistic politicians. For decades Englishmen had been nurtured on tales of Bloody Queen Mary, the Catholic daughter of Henry VIII, and the execution of over 300 Protestant martyrs; of her husband, Philip, and the black legend of Spain; of Guy Fawkes and the Gun Powder Plot; and, following the Restoration, of a succession of popish conspiracies to burn London and impose Catholic Tyranny. In 1685 Louis XIV gave Europeans an example of militant royal Catholicism by revoking the Edict of Nantes and coercing French Protestants by military force.

James II's hope to emancipate his coreligionists was doomed. A report unanimously submitted by a committee of the House of Commons called for the crown to enforce the laws against religious dissenters. The king chose to quash it. But many members of Parliament had signed the document, thus indicating their dissatisfaction with the monarch's views. While James's goals were not clear—toleration or the eventual establishment of Catholicism—his methods provoked controversy and resistance. What was apparent was that he sought repeal of the penal laws against Roman Catholics and Protestant Dissenters as well as of the Test Act, the statute that deprived all but communicants of the Church of England of office. When the Tories of Anglican persuasion would not consent to the destriction of their political and ecclesiastical monopolies, the king turned away from them. Sunderland now triumphed over Rochester, Clarendon, Halifax, and Godolphin, and with a small group of Catholic peers at court he played on the king's prejudices. The fallacy in the king's thinking and the measure of his bias lay in assuming that, once Catholicism was allowed to compete, it would win out over the Protestant faiths.[28]

When the Anglicans proved hostile to the king's position, he fell back to what he perceived to be the prerogative of the monarch by issuing a Declaration of Indulgence. Expressing his aversion to persecution on religious grounds and his belief in the need to allow his subjects liberty of conscience, he pledged to protect and maintain the communicants and the clergy of the Church of England as by law established in the full enjoyment of their rights. But he also declared his will that the execution of the laws restricting freedom of religion and imposing religious tests for holding office be suspended. Quakers were among the first to benefit; some twelve hundred of them imprisoned under the penal laws went free. William Penn and his family were the subjects of a special warrant signifying to the ecclesiastical authorities that they must not molest the Quaker leader and his relations.

James extended this policy to the colonies in the West Indies and in America. On 27 May 1687 the king in council ordered the governors in the foreign plantations to publish the king's Declaration of Indulgence. All civil officials responsible for enforcing the laws were commanded to obey.[29]

Spokesmen for the old Puritan element in Massachusetts, Increase Mather and Samuel Nowell, later claimed the blessing of the king's declaration of liberty of conscience in appealing to James II against what they termed the oppressive behavior of Anglicans under Governor Edmund Andros in New England.[30]

Reaction in England to the monarch's policy even among the Protestant Dissenters was mixed. William Penn, a friend and an advisor of the king, publicly supported James. He undertook a mission to Holland to convince William, Prince of Orange, of the king's good intentions. At this time William and his wife Mary, as the nephew and daughter of James, were the heirs apparent to the throne of England. William's adviser, the Whig refugee Gilbert Burnet, was contemptuous of the Quaker, viewing him as a "talking, vain man," overly opinionated and too sure of his ability to persuade others. In several interviews Penn sought to convince the prince to support James's measures, but William would agree to toleration only if Parliament repealed the penal laws. Nor would he consent to the abolition of the Test Act, a law excluding Catholics from office.[31]

Penn, on his return to England, continued to support James. In April 1687 he held forth in the Quakers' conventicle in Gracechurch Street and "magnified" the king's mercy in granting toleration. Some Presbyterian preachers also accepted the king's declaration. But other Dissenters and Anglicans were suspicious, fearing that toleration would ultimately lead to the establishment of Roman Catholicism. Would other faiths then be tolerated? The marquis of Halifax warned the Dissenters that the Catholics embraced them now all the better to squeeze them later. Such was the hysteria engendered by religious fear that some Protestants suspected that Penn was a secret Jesuit priest. Thomas Marriett, an Anglican who for a score of years had served as a justice of the peace, warned Penn that the king's Declaration of Indulgence was not to be taken seriously, for James as a Catholic was not his own master. In matters of religion the king's word "must signify noe more than ye Edict of Nantes when ye Pope pleaseth." Gilbert Burnet had taunted Penn with the same argument.[32] Many Dissenters seemed to agree.

James II pressed his campaign. After a survey of opinion among prospective candidates for a new parliament revealed that they would not vote for repeal of the Penal and Test acts, James ordered a campaign launched against the charters of the boroughs to remodel the corporations so as to ensure that men favoring his policy would be returned to Westminster. Charles II had forced some corporations as early as 1681 to accept alterations in their government. In the words of William Blathwayt, "a Second & more thorough Purge" now followed. From March to September 1688, thirty-five boroughs forfeited or, under pressure, surrendered their charters. By the terms of the new patents issued them the crown nominated new officials for the corporations and retained the right of removing them.[33] Late in April James announced his intention of summoning a parliament, reissued his Declaration of Indulgence, and the following month ordered the document read on two successive Sundays in all of the Churches at the usual time of divine services.

The Catholic king might have drawn some encouragement from the reception accorded his policy by Protestants in America. George Fox, a founder of the Society of Friends, received word from Maryland that the Quakers had great hopes that the king's orders requiring toleration would be of service. In the summer of 1688 two Puritan emissaries arrived in London from Boston. The old commonwealth element in Massachusetts, displaced from power with the abrogation of the charter and the establishment of the dominion, had seized the opportunity offered them by James's declaration for religious toleration. In July 1688 the king heard the petition and "humble" memorial of Increase Mather and Samuel Nowell. According to the two Congregationalist divines the Anglican party in Boston had misrepresented the Puritans in Massachusetts as seditious and disaffected men. Andros was denying them religious freedom. They claimed the blessing of the king's gracious declaration of liberty of conscience.[34]

The commitment of James's subjects both in England and in

America to religious toleration would soon be tested. The king had sought to bring the colonies more directly under the crown. How far had the sweeping alteration in government compromised his position in America? How firmly did the officials he had appointed control government there?

CHAPTER 2

The American Scene, 1685–89:
Outside the Dominion

THE POLITICAL HORIZONS of the great bulk of the 150,000 or so English settlers across the Atlantic were no broader than those of the inhabitants of the counties of England. Immigrants to America, although they had crossed the ocean, brought with them the strong sense of localism tenaciously held by Englishmen: a resentment against outside interference and a commitment to long-held privileges. Men were concerned with their immediate communities—the county in England, the province or even the village in America.

Englishmen in America remained committed to traditional values. Customarily, political leadership stemmed from social status, but in the colonies greater economic opportunity and social mobility than were normally present in England had a disruptive effect. They intensified the competition among local leaders for prestige and influence. The sons of the lesser gentry and merchants who crossed the Atlantic and the men who rose from the middle and, occasionally, the lower ranks continued to believe that social prestige was to be acknowledged by the exercise of political power. Economic opportunity, social fluidity, and fragmented governmental authority characterized the American scene.

In provincial America there were more men who aspired to higher political office, if for no other reason than as a mark of social status, than could be accommodated within the existing governmental arrangements. In the individual colonies political power was fragmented among several institutions. Men could advance their careers by enhancing the elected assembly, by claiming for themselves in that body the same rights and powers members of the English House of Commons had sought earlier in the century. They might seek to better their position through the patronage and authority of a governor and a council appointed either in the name of the king or of a proprietor. And if denied gratification and recognition at the provincial level, aspiring politicians could always appeal to Whitehall and Westminster to reverse an unfavorable decision. Their rivals stood fast on the privileges of the local authority.

America was plagued by political instability and friction, both brought on by the clash of strong-willed men, the pursuit of economic advantage, the incongruity between status and political power at the uppermost level of society, and the contest between those who held power and those who aspired to it as a mark of recognition, as a symbol of having arrived.

Politics, the quest for status and office, was a passion with provincial leaders. William Penn, the propietor of a Quaker colonial experiment in brotherly love, once referred to his colony as "this licentious Wilderness." He enjoined his coreligionists in America; "Be not so *governmentish*," and counseled them, in vain, as it turned out, "to avoide factions & partys, whisperings and reportings, & all animositys."[1]

The efforts of Charles II and James II to bring the colonists to achnowledge a greater degree of dependence on the crown of England and to consolidate governments added but one more dimension to the political scene in America. For some men it created an avenue to honor, recognition, and profit, but for others it posed a threat to their power, an authority based on the sanctions of some local institution. That men often resorted to the rhetoric of liberty, that they exhorted the rights of Englishmen, often indicated that they needed to appear virtuous even while pursuing their own interests. Antipopery could serve the same purpose.

The response in America to the innovations instituted under James II varied according to the particular social and political structure of each colony. Those provinces lying east and north of the Delaware River were directly affected. By the summer of 1688 they had been amalgamated into one administrative unit and their governments drastically altered.

South and West of the Delaware the impact of the new reign was much less. Here the English colonists continued to live in several distinct provinces under separate governmental jurisdictions. Three counties on the right bank of the lower Delaware initially settled by Swedes and Dutchmen had been conquered by the forces of the English crown and then granted to William Penn, the proprietor of Pennsylvania. The same legislature and executive served both the province and the lower counties. To the south, Maryland had been established as a proprietary by the Calverts, the barons Baltimore of the Irish peerage. The other colony on the Chesapeake, Virginia, was the oldest of the English provinces and the only southern colony whose government depended directly on the crown with a governor and a council appointed in the name of the king. Between Virginia and Spanish-held Florida was Carolina, the property of a proprietary board resident in England.

Two separate communities made up Carolina, one consisting of an overflow of small farmers and planters from Virginia settled along the shores of Albemarle Sound and the banks of the Chowan River just south of the Old Dominion, the other made up of recent arrivals from the West Indies and the British Isles established further to the south along the Ashley and Cooper rivers.

The Albemarle region, inaccessible to larger vessels engaged in transatlantic commerce, was home to a few thousand settlers eking out a marginal existence. It had scarcely occupied the attention of the proprietary lords, much less the English authorities. As the Quaker John Archdale, who later acquired a proprietary share in Carolina, informed a correspondent; "We have not immediate opportunities to send to England by reason there is no settled trade thither."[2] The inhabitants had to rely on New England vessels of shallow draft to carry off their tobacco and animal hides. The attempt to collect a duty of one penny per pound of tobacco imposed by the English Parliament had touched off an uprising in 1677. Generally, the proprietors had experienced great difficulty in asserting their authority in the remote backwater, even in finding a suitable man to assume authority. Finally they had sent out one of their own, Seth Sothell, to govern.

The Ashley and Cooper river community, settled only fifteen years before James II came to the throne, had escaped open revolt and violence, but here too government was unstable. The complex political institutions the proprietors formulated and the men they appointed rendered the situation difficult. A board located some thousands of miles across the ocean would have a difficult enough time, but its position was made all the more precarious by the attempt to impose an elaborate code on the colony. The Fundamental Constitutions provided for a governor, a council consisting of deputies appointed by the individual proprietors and those elected by a local assembly, provincial nobles granted patents by the proprietary board, and a local parliament elected by the freeholders.

The diverse ethnic and religious composition of the southern settlement further compounded the problem of governing Carolina. The earliest group to arrive consisted of Anglicans and Royalists from Barbados and the other English West Indian islands. Proclaiming themselves defenders of provincial liberties, these Goose Creek men had challenged the proprietary board in London. By 1682 the proprietors had embarked on a program to offset the influence of the West Indians by inducing others, English Dissenters, French Huguenots, and Scottish Covenanters, to move to America.

Society in the southern portion of Carolina was fragmented and divided. The Anglican English and the Barbadians were settled in Charles Town and along the Ashley and Cooper rivers, the French on the Santee, and the Scots further south. Berkeley County was Church of England,

Colleton was Dissenter, and Craven was Calvinist. Factionalism was intense, with prominent men sometimes supporting, other times opposing the proprietary board. South Carolina had endured a rapid turnover in governors. Joseph West had served longest, but he had given up the struggle to maintain order, throwing up his position and moving north to New England. James Morton succeeded in 1685. Despite the explicit proscription by the proprietors of three of the Barbadians for trading in Indian slaves, James Moore, Maurice Matthews, and Arthur Middleton returned to office, elected by the provincial parliament. The Carolina voters, susceptible to the punch bowl, were easily manipulated.

It was difficult to tell who governed in Carolina. The Scots from their settlement in Stuart Town disputed the jurisdiction of the government at Charles Town. During a session of the palatine court, one established by the deputy of the senior proprietor, Robert Quary disputed the appointment as sheriff of Berkeley County of the Barbadian Bernard Schenkingh as a man "notoriously evil and infamous." Schenkingh had been ejected from the grand council for drunkenous and scandalous behavior. In the fall of 1685 a warrant was issued to commit Ralph Izard for seizing some public records from Quary.[3] The proprietary board, apprehensive over a threatened suit against the charter by the crown and fearing to give royal officials any pretext for legal action against the patent, suspended Quary himself for allegedly allowing a pirate ship to land plundered goods in the colony.

Late in the summer of 1686 the proprietors commissioned James Colleton, a member of the proprietary family, as governor of that portion of Carolina lying south and west of Cape Fear. One of their number, Seth Sothell, had already gone out to the Albemarle settlements. As proprietors, the earl of Craven, the duke of Albemarle, the earl of Bath, and Sir Peter Colleton were particularly concerned that they and the officials in America acting for them give no reason to be accused of laxness in preventing traffic in pirate goods or in failing to prevent raids into Spanish Florida.[4] In the spring of 1687 George Muschamp, the royal customs collector at Charles Town, complained to London of the difficulty of enforcing the navigation code. Some shippers in the provincial capital claimed that the charter issued for the colony in 1665 allowed them to trade directly with Scotland and Ireland and permitted Scots and Irish vessels to bring goods to Carolina. The English attorney general dismissed these claims and condemned such traffic as illegal. That the charter to Carolina came after the passage of the Act of Navigation counted for nothing unless the patent contained a clause giving the colonists license to navigate contrary to the law. The palatine, Craven, on behalf of the proprietary board pleaded ignorance. Citing the Carolina charter to justify an exemption from the parliamentary navigation code was merely the "discourse" of "ignorant" and "loose" persons, not men concerned in the proprietary government. The vessel Muschamp seized had put in at Carolina only for repairs. The crown apparently took no further notice of the situation except to order Craven the following month to appoint Muschamp to the provincial council.[5]

Factional animosities in Carolina were not so easily ignored. In Albemarle Seth Sothell was earning the hostility of local planters. At Charles Town John Boone, despite being expelled from the council for dealing in pirate goods, was reelected to office. Craven, Albemarle, Bath, and Sir Peter Colleton then issued strict instructions to Governor James Colleton not to permit such proceedings. Men convicted of crimes could not be restored to office. This rule thus restricted the right of the local parliament to challenge the authority of the proprietors in imposing the Fundamental Constitutions. Craven and his colleagues professed themselves willing to alter the code if it contained anything detrimental to the populace, but they saw issues in terms of power. There would be no satisfying the men who made the greatest stir except by yielding to their ambitions.

Among those with high aspirations was the Barbadian Maurice Matthews, a man made the object of satire by his opponents for his haughty, overbearing disposition. He drew up a resolution declaring that the proprietors had rendered the Fundamental Constitutions as initially drawn up in 1669 void by subsequently attempting to alter them. The only legal foundation of government thus was the royal charter of 1665. Accepting this argument, a majority in the provincial parliament then declared illegal all proprietary instructions issued under the Fundamental Constitutions. After a committee composed of adherents of various factions failed to agree, James Colleton, "in some passion," as his enemies charged, on 14 February 1688 produced a proprietary letter sent out the previous March affirming a version of the Fundamental Constitutions issued in 1682 as the frame of government for Carolina. A deadlock then ensued.[6]

In contrast to Carolina, Virginia during these years appeared stable. The gentry controlling the colony apparently had learned a lesson from Bacon's Rebellion, the civil war which had wracked the province in 1676. The authorities in Jamestown and the leading magnates in the counties had acted quickly and decisively a few years later to put down an abortive uprising attempted by some irate planters resolved to take matters into their own hands by destroying tobacco plants and thus relieving the glut of tobacco for the market.

The marketing of the colony's staple remained a problem. There were others: a heritage of factional animosities, the political aftermath of suppressing the insurrection of 1676, and the drain on the revenue from quitrents on land available to the provincial government by a grant made to an English nobleman and former governor of the colony, Thomas, Lord Culpeper, of the region lying between the Potomac and the Rappahannock rivers, the Northern Neck.

Among the colonies south of the Delaware, Virginia was the only royal province, the only colony whose government depended directly on the crown of England. At Jamestown a governor appointed and instructed by the king presided.

The leading magnates in the Old Dominion, seeking posts as surveyors and collectors of the customs and a place on the provincial council, looked either to the governor or to the court at Whitehall. Patronage tied them to the crown and to men in England with political influence. Nicholas Spencer, a councilor and provincial secretary, maintained close contact with William Blathwayt, secretary to the committee of the Privy Council for trade and plantations and auditor general of the plantation revenue. In 1686 Spencer placed his son in service with Blathwayt. John Armestead owed his position on the council to the royal governor, Francis, Baron Howard of Effingham. Among the more lucrative posts in the colony were the offices of auditor of the public accounts and receiver general. William Byrd coveted these, but he had to contend with an Englishman, Robert Ayleway, who put forth a prior claim. Working through his commercial correspondents in London, Micajah Perry and Richard Lane, and through Blathwayt, Byrd successfully circumvented Ayleway. John Custis was another member of the council of Virginia, a collector of customs for the district of the eastern shore, and the major general of the provincial militia. Following an erroneous report of his death, his posts went to other men. In successfully petitioning the king to restore him to his offices, Custis made much of his loyal conduct during Bacon's Rebellion.[7]

Not all who had supported the royal administration during the civil upheaval in 1676 continued steadfast, however. Philip Ludwell and Robert Beverley resented the leniency shown the defeated rebels by commissioners sent from England and their own loss of power. Ludwell, married to the widow of the governor against whom the insurgents had risen in 1676, had assumed the leadership of the Green Spring faction, named after the Virginia estate of the deceased Sir William Berkeley. Beverley, clerk of the House of Burgesses, had made himself particularly objectionable to the royal commissioners charged with investigating the cause of the rebellion. Firmly entrenched in the assembly, Beverley waged a protracted campaign against Lord Howard after the governor assumed office in February 1684. Beverley was in a strong position, given the claim of the majority of the burgesses that a bill, once attested by their clerk, could not be altered. It then had the force of law. Lord Howard protested that no bill could become law until signed by him as the king's representative. The burgesses would allow him a veto as the presiding officer of the council, but not as the king's governor.[8]

The court at Whitehall had reacted sharply to this challenge. It condemned the proceedings of the burgesses as irregular and tumultuous, occasioned chiefly by Beverley, and instructed the governor to prosecute the clerk "with the utmost severity" for defacing the records of the assembly. Lord Howard was to dissolve the house so that the inhabitants might select better representatives. These orders did not arrive until the second week in November 1686, when the assembly was nearing the completion of business. The burgesses had proved as stubborn as before. Lord Howard displaced Beverley from all public offices and suspended Philip Ludwell from his collectorship as an "abettor" of faction who fomented disputes between the governor and the assembly. Allegedly, he had met privately with the leading "refractory" burgesses and encouraged them in their opposition to Lord Howard. No sooner had the governor proscribed Beverley than, further to show his contempt, Ludwell named Beverley's son to a surveyor's post.[9]

The crown upheld the dismissal of Ludwell, but the following year the planters of James City County returned him to the House of Burgesses. Lord Howard refused to allow him to take his seat.

Local politicians had contended over not only the prerogatives of the crown and the privileges of the elected assemblymen but revenue from quitrents on land for the support of government. The financial base of the provincial administration had been undermined when Charles Stuart had granted to a group of exiled Cavaliers the escheats and rents from lands in Virginia. Following a controversial term as governor, Thomas, Baron Culpeper, had relinguished his claim to some income from the colony but had retained his rights to the Northern Neck, the area between the Rappahannock and the Potomac rivers. Lord Howard, who had succeeded Culpeper, with the support of the local council, contested the arrangement, for income from the region went to the absentee proprietor rather than to support the provincial administration at Jamestown.

The protests of the governor and council of Virginia were to little avail. The crown would not go to any further expense in purchasing the proprietor's patent; it was already behind in paying Culpeper his salary and expenses as governor both of Virginia and the Isle of Wight. In 1688 James II confirmed without any limitation as to time the grant for the Northern Neck with the boundary extended to the "first heads or springs" of the Potomac and Rappahannock rivers. Culpeper died the next year, and his interest passed to his wife, Margaret Van Hesse, and their daughter, Catherine, who married Thomas, fifth Lord Fairfax.[10]

The Culpeper and Fairfax interests were not without allies in Virginia. Several prominent residents of Stafford County in the Northern Neck, among them William Fitzhugh and his partner in law, George Brent, either supported or sympathized with the proprietary cause. Daniel Parke and Nicholas Spencer had been agents for the proprietary, and when Spencer died in 1689, the Culpepers employed Philip Ludwell, who was then in England seeking the recall of the governor. The controversy over the proprietary became enmeshed in the factional politics of the colony.

One other issue pervaded political discussions in the province, the marketing of the staple crop of Virginia. Under English law, tobacco, when marketed outside the colonies, had first to be shipped in English or English colonial vessels to some port in England where a tax was imposed, a duty greatly increased by Parliament during the first year of the reign of James II. Chronic overproduction on the Chesapeake had already outrun demand for tobacco, and the additional duties, despite the assurances of the king's ministers, had apparently restricted the market in England by greatly increasing the price to consumers. To reduce the amount of tobacco and to enhance the market, the Virginia legislature petitioned the crown for an exemption from the new duties and sought to restrict the crop by imposing a deadline for planting. Hard-pressed by the burgesses to sign the bill, Lord Howard hoped the crown would disallow the measure.

In London the Commissioners of the Royal Customs gave short shrift to the arguments of the Virginia legislature: the burgesses had offered nothing new on the question of the additional duties that the merchants in England had not before submitted. The difficulties the planters faced were the result of overproduction. The Customs Board recommended no alteration in the duties imposed on colonial tobacco entering English ports.[11] So great was the crop produced on the Chesapeake, so few the ships sent out from England, and so depressed was the market that in the spring of 1687 the prominent planter and merchant, William Fitzhugh, advised a consignee in London that there was little point in shipping tobacco for sale in England.[12] The king's Commissioners of Customs continued opposed to any legislation passed in Jamestown fixing the lading of tobacco at certain designated locations and restricting planting. Their reasoning was not concrete: some unforeseen hindrance in trade might prejudice the royal revenue.

Effective legislation limiting planting needed the concurrence of neighboring Maryland. The marketing and shipping of tobacco was a complicated business, involving several separate and often conflicting interests and setting the owners of large merchantmen against the proprietors of smaller vessels in the carrying trade, the large planters against the smaller, and the merchants of the outports in England against Londoners. And as always, the crown had its financial interest. In the summer of 1687 Micajah Perry and fourteen other London merchants petitioned the crown to prohibit the export from Virginia of tobacco in bulk. Tobacco not packed in hogsheads was easy to smuggle, was more difficult to handle, and diminished the royal revenue. But the Commissioners of Customs and the Lords of Trade recommended only instructing the governors of Maryland and Virginia to seek appropriate legislation from their respective assemblies.[13]

In Jamestown the burgesses ignored the request, busying themselves instead with setting out bitterly worded complaints against the governor. Their grievances related to disallowance of bills previously passed by the legislature and fees demanded by the governor and the clerks of the provinical secretary's office for recording surveys for land. Fines and forfeitures, they insisted, ought to be accounted for to the assembly and applied to the cost of government. Lord Howard countered with the argument that such fines rightly belonged to the crown, to be appropriated by the king for the needs of administration.[14] Thus was set the conflict in Virginia between the governor and the councilors claiming the prerogatives of the crown and the burgesses elected by the freeholders.

The division within the upper levels of Virginia society led to a stalemate. Philip Ludwell, once a staunch adherent of the provincial administration under Sir William Berkeley, was then in London lobbying against Lord Howard. Better to defend himself, the governor late in February 1689 returned to England, leaving the senior councilor, Nathaniel Bacon, to preside over the administration. The situation on the Chesapeake seemed critical. Rumors of momentous events in England and tales of Catholic and Indian plots in neighboring Maryland, when they reached the ears of the gullible and the unscrupulous in Stafford County in the Northern Neck, threatened to precipitate an outbreak of violence in the Old Dominion.

Economic and political problems comparable to those plaguing Virginia also strained relations in nearby Maryland. The inability of the proprietary Calvert family to win support compounded the difficulty of resolving these issues. Maryland during its first five decades had experienced several outbreaks directed against the Catholic proprietary, the last as recent as 1681. During the middle decades of the century the province had proved a land of opportunity for some of the poorer men who managed to survive the rigors of climate and toil and to rise from the status of indentured servant to independent planter as well as for the lesser gentry and smaller merchants who had migrated to the Chesapeake during the years of commercial expansion. The increase of population and the diffusion of settlement had required the creation of several new counties, thus providing offices for the newly arrived gentry and the more successful of the former servants.

Real power lay not with local county courts or the assembly, however, but in the person of the proprietor, Charles Calvert, the third Baron Baltimore, and a narrow circle of his friends, relatives, and associates who dominated the provincial capital, Saint Marys. They determined all judicial and administrative appointments, controlled the land office and the highest court, and in the governor's council (the upper house of the legislature) passed on bills coming from the assembly.

By the end of the third quarter of the century, several developments had heightened discontent. The danger of invasion by hostile Indians created anxiety, and overproduction of tobacco lessened economic opportunity. Before 1670 all freemen could vote in elections, but in that year the proprietor restricted the franchise to men with fifty acres of land or fifty pounds in property. He also reduced the number of representatives from each county elected to the assembly from four to two. Some Anglicans, unhappy with the rule of the Catholic proprietary, had called for the establishment of the Church of England, a measure the proprietor had resisted on the ground that the population of Maryland included not only Anglicans and Catholics but Anabaptists, Quakers, and Presbyterians.

Dissatisfaction with the proprietary rule was not manifested among the rank and file of the settlers. The ordinary planters remained passive, and life at the local level remained almost entirely unaffected despite an open attack against the Calverts carried out by a relatively few men. Related to each other by blood and marriage and residing in the counties in the immediate vicinity of the capital, they had personal grievances against the proprietor and his adherents. A more numerous group of recent arrivals had enjoyed power only at the local level. They had been denied status at uppermost echelons by the policy of preferment the proprietor had followed.

Ambitious men, whose social and economic position would ordinarily have entitled them to high office, resented the concentration of lucrative and prestigious posts in the hands of a small minority of Catholic gentry, immediate relatives, and close friends of Lord Baltimore. What made the proprietor's policy more vulnerable was that, in a province in which the great majority of settlers were Protestants, the impression was created that power lay with Catholics. Baltimore denied the charge, claiming that he had appointed Protestants as well as adherents of the Church of Rome. But the fact was that the only Protestants to win high office were friends of close relatives of the Calvert family.[15]

Open opposition to proprietary rule had erupted twice within a generation, once in 1660 and again in 1681. In recent years the opposition had centered in three closely related families, Coode, Slye, and Gerard. Thomas Gerard, a Catholic immigrant, had once been close to the Calverts, but in 1660 had broken with the proprietor and supported an unsuccessful coup launched by Josias Fendall. Heavily fined and proscribed from holding office, Gerard had fled to Virginia, where he died in 1673. His daughters and their families carried on his feud with the Calverts. Anne Gerard married Nehemiah Blakiston, a lawyer and merchant of Saint Marys, while Susannah took as her first husband Robert Slye, by whom she had a son, Gerard. Robert Slye was one of the more wealthy and prominent men in the colony, a merchant with extensive holdings in land. He too had incurred the enmity of the proprietor by supporting Fendall's abortive rebellion. Two years after the death of Slye, Susannah Gerard, a forty-year-old widow, married a Welsh-born immigrant, John Coode. Wealthy widows did not remain long unwed in colonial America.

Descended from a respected family of lawyers, John Coode had not been otherwise blessed by nature. Deformed and clubfooted, he was further cursed by a monkeylike visage. In manner he was defiant, argumentative, and impious, characteristics sharpened by his addiction to strong drink. His constitution made him a chronic rebel. After attending Exeter College, Oxford, for two years and being ordained a deacon in the Church of England, he had served briefly in Cornwall. He then turned up in Maryland, where he won the hand of the widow Slye, some fifteen years his senior and a woman subject to fits of madness. Given his wife's connections, Coode soon made his mark at the local level, serving as an officer in the county militia and as a justice of the peace. In 1676 he represented Saint Marys County in the provincial assembly.

Another representative from Saint Marys was Coode's brother-in-law, Kenelm Cheseldyne, a lawyer and onetime attorney general for the province. Coode, his stepson Gerard Slye, Cheseldyne, and his other relatives, Thomas and Justinian Gerard, by 1681 had gone as far as they could without proprietary backing.

Coode was the dominant figure in this group. Prone by his personality and deformities to challenge authority and frustrated by the proprietor's favoring Catholics and near friends and relatives when awarding higher office, in 1681 the Welsh immigrant threw in with Fendall in another attempt to overthrow the Calverts. Even at this early date they charged that the Catholics were collaborating with hostile Indians to murder innocent Protestants in Maryland.

The proprietary administration had acted quickly in suppressing the revolt. Fendall was convicted and heavily fined, but Coode got off because the evidence against him was circumstantial. But along with his relatives he lost office. Gerard Slye left for London to recoup the family's fortunes and to undermine the proprietary regime. He later testified to alleged Catholic domination of the military and civil officers in Maryland. He also supported the charges made by Christopher Rousby, a collector of customs appointed by the crown, against Baltimore.[16]

The proprietor of Maryland came under attack from two other quarters. Lord Howard of Effingham, governor of Virginia, charged him with encroaching on the royal revenue when Baltimore insisted that shipping on the Potomac enter with officials on the Maryland side of the river. Baltimore had already received a warning from the ministers of state in Whitehall over irregularities in collecting customs. In addition the proprietor was engaged in a contest with William Penn over the boundary between Maryland and Pennsylvania and the division of the territory between the Delaware and the Chesapeake bays.

When Penn in 1684 left America for London to press his case, Baltimore followed. Since his son was a minor, the proprietor commissioned a board of deputies to administer the affairs of the colony. Ordinarily, precedence would have gone to William Taylor, a Protestant and the senior councilor in terms of service. Instead, the proprietor promoted his Catholic cousin, George Talbot, to the first position. Others named with Talbot were Vincent Lowe, John and Henry Darnall, Nicholas Sewall (all Catholics); and William Stevens, William Digges, and William Burgess (all Protestants, and the latter two relatives of the Calverts). The hegemony of the Catholics and the Calvert family remained intact.

The charge that Catholics in Maryland were conspiring to eliminate Protestant contenders was given further credence when, in a drunken brawl on the night of 13 October 1684, the man Baltimore named to head the commission of government, Talbot, stabbed to death Christopher Rousby, the royal collector of customs. Although apprehended by authorities in Virginia, Talbot escaped to Maryland, where officials insisted on trying him rather than return him to the Old Dominion. Protestant opponents of the proprietary regime charged that friends, relatives, and officials who controlled the provincial government and who approved of the killing protected the accused murderer. Nehemiah Blakiston, appointed in the name of the crown to fill the vacant collectorship, concurred in this charge. He added another: proprietary officials, obstructing his efforts to collect the king's revenue, were lining their own and the proprietor's pockets.

Baltimore had been warned before. Now the Privy Council ordered the crown attorney general to sue out a writ against his charter. Seeking to clear himself, Baltimore contested Blakiston's claim that the proprietary officials were interfering with the collection of the royal revenue. He also ordered the provincial authorities to turn Talbot over to the governor of Virginia for trial by special commission. In April 1686, after unsuccessfully challenging the court and the indictment, Talbot confessed to having killed Christopher Rousby, but claimed not to have acted in malice or by premeditation. As Nicholas Spencer, one of the judges, reported, "the fatal stroke" was dealt in the "height of passion." The court sentenced him to death, but Lord Howard stayed execution until he received the king's instructions. James II commuted the sentence to banishment for five years.[17]

Baltimore's control over Maryland seemed uncertain, particularly after news of the threatened writ reached America. Early in 1687 Lord Howard wrote Sunderland asking that Maryland be made an adjunct of Virginia and he allotted a proportional increase in his salary. Yet despite an order in council issued at Hampton Court for the crown law officers to prosecute a writ against Maryland, no further action followed against the proprietor's charter. Indeed, the Privy Council continued to address correspondence to Baltimore as if he and his officials were to remain in control of the provincial government. For example, the crown ordered the proprietor to use his utmost endeavors to have the colonial assembly pass a bill restricting the export of tobacco in bulk.[18]

Unable to return to America at this time, the proprietor sent a new governor out to preside over the administration. Lord Baltimore seemed to have learned nothing. The man he entrusted with the task, William Joseph, a Roman Catholic, made evident his sympathy for the privileges of the proprietor and the doctrine of rule by divine right in his opening address to the assembly of Maryland in October 1688. The proprietor's leading opponent, John Coode, was back in the house, where he joined Kenelm Cheseldyne, now elected speaker. Differences between the opponents and the supporters of Baltimore came to a head over various economic issues and the rights of the overlord as opposed to those claimed by the assemblymen. As happened in Charles Town and Jamestown, provincial government in Saint Marys became deadlocked.[19]

Much the same situation prevailed in Philadelphia and in the counties along the lower Delaware, a region contested between Lord Baltimore and William Penn. At the time James came to the throne, both proprietors had left their colonies for London, where they had contended against each other for title to the land between the Delaware and the Chesapeake bays. By the terms of the charter granted by Charles I in 1632, the Calverts had received lands uninhabited at the time by any Christians. Unknown to the authorities in England, Swedish settlers had occupied the region. They had fallen to the Dutch, who in turn had succumbed to the forces sent out by Charles II in 1664. The English crown held the territory on the west bank of the Delaware as conquered lands. In 1681 Charles II had awarded the region north of forty degrees north latitude to the Quaker William Penn as a proprietary colony; two years later his brother, James, duke of York, transferred the three counties on the lower Delaware—New Castle, Kent, and Sussex—to Penn. The Quaker proprietor initially treated all of his holdings as one administrative unit, but Baltimore contested ownership of the lower region.

By the end of 1685 the Lords of Trade apparently had resolved the dispute between the two proprietors by dividing the tract lying between the Chesapeake and the Delaware into two parts by a line from the latitude of Cape Henelopen to forty degrees north latitude.

The problem of governing the settlements on the Delaware proved much more intractable. The European populace already seated there before Penn received his patent and deeds varied considerably in ethnic origin and religious affiliation. The settlers on the lower Delaware had come from the Netherlands, England, or Sweden, and if they held to any formal religious creed, they were Lutherans or Anglicans. The immigrants who first settled the upper counties of Philadelphia, Chester, and Bucks in Pennsylvania proper were for the most part English and Welsh Quakers or German Pietists. This pluralism was a source of immediate difficulty.

William Penn, after conferring with several associates among the Quakers in England and in Ireland, had attempted a "holy experiment." He established a set of laws on the simple dictum that "good men never lack good laws" or, as he hoped would be the case in Pennsylvania, that good men would accept the proprietor's code. The charter granted by Charles II in 1681 required Penn to make laws for the colony with the approbation of the freemen. Since these laws could not be repugnant to those of England, within five years of enactment provincial statutes had to be dispatched to London for review by the king in council. As Penn appreciated, he and his officials could easily circumvent this requirement by reenacting any measure shortly before the expiration of the five-year limitation.

To bypass the wishes of the local politicians was not as easily done.

At a meeting held in Pennsylvania in the spring of 1683, the proprietor had assented to a document commonly called the Second Frame, or the Charter of Liberties. It was not a patent or charter issued by the crown and had no relation to the patent issued by the king in 1681. By the provisions of this Second Frame, the government of Penn's holdings consisted of the proprietor or his deputy, an elected council, and an elected assembly. When Penn returned to England the next year to do battle with Lord Baltimore, he vested executive functions in the council, but reserved the right to confirm the actions of the local authorities.[20]

From the outset Pennsylvania was blessed with a relatively high proportion of well-to-do merchants and landholders—men who might well challenge the proprietor—as well as an independent class of artisans and yeomen. As Penn might well have realized, two potential and possibly related sources of danger to the colony and the government existed. Reacting to the appearance in Philadelphia of William Dyer, surveyor of the royal customs, in 1685 the proprietor urged the Quaker leaders to require strict obedience to the parliamentary navigation code and to cooperate with the royal officials. Dyer had already complained of obstructions in Maryland and in East Jersey, and the crown had ordered writs of quo warranto sued out by the attorney general. To the contentious leaders in Pennsylvania, Penn urged, "For the love of God, men, and the poor country, be not so . . . noisy and open in your dissatisfactions." Decrying the disorderly conduct of the "multitude," the proprietor begged his closest confidants in the council not to "debase your Noble call by a low, mean & partial behaviour." He would have them suppress all contentions and take care that "no offence be given to the King's officers but that you treat them with respect."[21]

Penn's personal influence and his support of the king on the issue of toleration for Protestant Dissenters and Catholics probably won an exemption for Pennsylvania from royal control. By a warrant issued on 9 March 1686 to ecclesiastical authorities in the dioceses in England, Penn and his family were exempted from prosecution, and less than a week later by the terms of another royal warrant imprisoned Quakers were released. Later that spring James II exempted Penn's colony from prosecution under the writs of quo warranto planned against the other proprietary charters. As Penn's friend, a principal secretary of state, informed the attorney general, the king had thought fit "for some particular considerations" to suspend the proceedings against the proprietor's charter. Penn took the credit.[22]

Political animosity had come early to the City of Brotherly Love, the province of Pennsylvania, and the lower counties on the Delaware. By the time Penn left America at the end of 1684, three factions, somewhat amorphous and unstable, had begun to emerge. A small inner circle of the proprietor's close adherents and appointees made up one clique. Few in number, they occupied the important proprietary and provincial offices and dominated in the council. Another group, also predominately Quaker, resented the proprietary prerogatives. John Simcock and Joseph Growdon had once supported Penn, but in America they chafed under a proprietary policy they regarded as restrictive. A number of newly arrived Quaker merchants from New York, England, and the West Indies joined them in opposition. Together they challenged the political arrangements of the province by which power was concentrated in the council and proprietary offices were dominated by Penn's closest adherents.

The lower counties were home to members of another faction. Most of the settlers in Pennsylvania were Quakers, but the Swedes, Dutchmen, and Englishmen living on the lower Delaware who maintained any affiliation with an organized church were Lutherans or Anglicans. They clashed with the Quakers in the province on matters relating to defense, commerce with the Indians, and shipping. Their representatives in the provincial council and particularly in the assembly sought autonomy.

To placate as many men as possible, Penn had vested the executive function of government in the council as a whole, rather than appointing a single individual as deputy governor, with Thomas Lloyd, a graduate of Jesus College, Oxford, and the son of an affluent Welsh family, as president. Through death and emigration the ranks of the proprietary supporters decreased. Only a small number of adherents remained wedded to Penn in the face of rising antiproprietary sentiment among the prominent Quaker merchants and landowners. Disillusioned with the proprietor, Lloyd and his followers on the council gradually took for themselves the powers Penn sought to reserve for himself under the terms of the frame of government adopted in 1683.

Unable to return to the colony because of the press of events in England but fearing to break completely with Lloyd, Penn altered the structure of the executive in 1687 by appointing five "trusty and well-beloved friends," Lloyd, Nicholas More, James Claypoole, Robert Turner, and John Eckley as his deputies with the power of executing, annulling and altering laws. He reserved to himself authority to confirm their actions and his "peculiar royalties and advantages." The deputies must require the provincial councilors to attend to business. Should they persist in their "slothful and dishonourable" attendance, Penn threatened to dissolve the Frame of 1683 "without any more ado." The proprietary deputies must suffer no disorders in the council or in the assembly or allow any encroachment on the powers and privileges of the proprietor. They must admit no "parleys" or "open conferences" between the provincial assembly and the council. The board of proprietary deputies, with the approbation of the council, proposed legislation; the assembly, as provided by the royal charter, merely consented or dissented.

Penn himself was under pressure. Officials at Whitehall were insisting that appeals from the provincial courts be allowed to the crown in England. He was particularly anxious for his own rights. Next to preserving virtue, he admonished the deputies, they must have "a tender regard to peace and my privileges." Love, forgive, help, and serve one another; and "let the people learn by your example."

Penn's instructions and new appointments to the board—John Simcock and Arthur Cooke replaced More and Claypoole—failed to end factional animosities and bring stability to the government of Pennsylvania. The deputies were at odds with each other and with the proprietor.[23]

Could Penn now recognize that pious platitudes were inadequate? In the summer of 1688 he happened to meet the daughter of William Lambert, a former general in the old Commonwealth government. Her husband, Captain John Blackwell, an old Puritan, had also served under Cromwell and had had extensive administrative and financial experience in Ireland, the Bahama Islands, and in Massachusetts Bay. Then living in Boston, he seemed ideal for Penn's purpose. Involved with none of the factions, Blackwell might be the man to quiet animosities among the contentious Friends, collect quitrents and other moneys due to the proprietor, and curtail the ambitious politicians bent on limiting Penn's power.

From the correspondence later exchanged between Penn and the new deputy governor whom the proprietor commissioned in July 1688, it was clear that Penn gave Blackwell some account of the personalities he would encounter and of the unsettled state of affairs in Philadelphia. Penn expected Blackwell to be the "sweeper" of the proprietor's "fouled chimneys." He must act, if no other way was possible, authoritatively to end, or at least to suppress, animosities. He must not allow the assemblymen to debate, amend, or alter any proposal. This was not "their work." They must merely respond "yea or nay" to whatever was submitted to them, as provided by the terms of the royal charter. If the assemblymen proposed to alter this arrangement, the proprietor "must then returne to the English Governm[en]t." Penn now proposed to appoint the council and to take up the executive authority after the "old" model.

After receiving written instructions from a man he had never met, John Blackwell set out from Boston for Philadelphia. Unknown to him, the proprietor, when informing the Friends in Pennsylvania of the appointment of the deputy governor, had already undermined him. If the Quakers did not like Blackwell, they were only to nominate others, and Penn would lay him aside!

The deputy governor received a chilly reception in Philadelphia. Thomas Lloyd and the other proprietary opponents proved as stubborn and obdurate as the sixty-year-old Puritan sent out to govern them. On 15 December 1688, when Blackwell arrived at Pennbury, the proprietor's estate, he sent a note to William Markham, the provincial secretary, notifying him of his arrival and asking him to inform the councilors and commissioners of state that he expected to be in Phildelaphia the next day. The usual place of business was Penn's house in the provincial capital. It was also the residence of Markham, the proprietor's cousin. When Blackwell arrived, he found no one to greet him. The council room was in disorder with papers lying about, some scattered on the floor. At last Markham appeared; he admitted that he had received the deputy governor's notice, but had been unable to act without the direction of the other members of the executive board.

When the commissioners of state finally did put in an appearance, Thomas Lloyd complained that he should have received formal notice of Blackwell's coming. Moreover, Blackwell could not govern the colony, he insisted, until the commissioners gave up their office to him. Even after Blackwell produced his commission from Penn, Lloyd refused to accept it as sufficient until it had passed the great seal of the colony, a seal Lloyd as keeper controlled.

This confrontation set the tone for Blackwell's turbulent and brief administration. Within weeks Blackwell notified Penn that factionalism was frustrating the functioning of government. The affairs of the colony in general and of government in particular were in "a most confused" state. The only effective way to combat the "Cabals" rested with the proprietor. Blackwell urged decisive action, for some persons had been encouraged in their hostility against Penn "by the Honey of your concessions, having tasted too much of it; more indeed than their stomacks can beare."

Government at the provincial level in Pennsylvania was at a standstill, with the proprietor limited to sending over from England pious pleas for the Friends to avoid animosities. In disgust, Blackwell resigned and left the colony. Before departing, he composed a blistering report, one manifesting deep resentment against Penn's chiding that he ought to have been more Christian in his behavior toward the Quakers. Did the proprietor mean "that if a man strike me a blow on one cheek, I should pray him to strike me a blow on the other cheek?" To Blackwell the government of Pennsylvania was unsupportable under the frame Penn had established and a people "who dispise all Dominion & dignity that is not in themselves."[24]

Penn's relations with James II had hitherto secured some protection for the contentious Quakers on the Delaware, but the fall of the proprietor's protector and the suspicion in England surrounding Penn would bring the contentious politicians in Philadelphia under the scrutiny of a new Protestant monarchy, a more skeptical administration at Whitehall.

In the Quaker proprietary, as elsewhere in the provinces south and west of the Delaware, the political situation was precarious. Government in Albemarle was weak, in Charles Town at a stalemate. At Jamestown no governor by 1689 presided as a representative of the crown — in a colony suffering from political rivalries and economic depression. Much the same situation existed in Maryland, where religious animosities and factional jealousies strained the social fabric. In Pennsylvania too, factionalism tinged with religious overtones placed the authority of government in jeopardy.

CHAPTER 3

The American Scene, 1685–89:
Annexed to the Dominion

THE MASSIVE POLITICAL REORGANIZATION undertaken by the English crown between 1685 and 1688 affected most immediately the North American colonies lying east and north of the Delaware River. Hitherto they had numbered eight separate and distinct jurisdictions, each independent of the others and related to the government of England in varying degrees. Their social and ethnic composition as well as their political arrangements varied significantly.

Within New England—the name was often used for Massachusetts Bay alone—were five separate political jurisdictions. The towns confederated as New Haven a generation before had already been merged with Connecticut. The strongest province in the region, the colony with the most cohesive population, was the former Puritan commonwealth of Massachusetts. It included the scattered settlements on the far northern frontier east of the Piscataqua River, once the proprietary of the Gorges family of England. Four small towns south of the Piscataqua in the region called New Hampshire had at one time also been part of the Bay colony. Claimed by the Mason family as part of a grant made early in the reign of Charles I, New Hampshire had been separated from the Puritan commonwealth by the crown in 1679 and established as a distinct province. The title of Robert Mason as proprietor to the soil, although accepted in London, was contested in the colony. Strong ties of commerce, kinship, and religion linked the leading families of Portsmouth and the smaller Piscataqua communities with Puritan Massachusetts. The villages making up the colony of New Plymouth, the first founded in 1620, had never received a charter from the English government. In political, social, and ecclesiastical arrangement they resembled their more populous and powerful neighbor, Massachusetts Bay.

The last of the New England colonies were Rhode Island and Connecticut. Each had received a charter early in the reign of Charles II, a patent confirming its political and civil establishments. Connecticut enjoyed a relatively cohesive social structure; in contrast, Rhode Island suffered from animosities brought on by the clash of strong personalities and competiton for town lands. Since the fundamental law of Rhode Island did not allow the civil authorities to impose any religious establishment or restrict worship, the colony had attracted a number of religious dissenters from Congregationalism, particularly Quakers and Baptists, as well as personalities not inclined to accept any discipline, ecclesiastical or civil.

New York and New Jersey had the most diverse religious and ethnic elements in their population. This heterogeneity, in conjunction with peculiar (in the case of New Jersey, bizarre) political arrangements, contributed to great political instability. Initially settled by the Dutch, the Delaware and Hudson valleys had fallen to the English and become the proprietary of James, duke of York. The king's brother had transferred title to New Jersey to two protégés who had then divided the colony between themselves with West Jersey going to Lord John Berkeley and East Jersey to Sir George Carteret. At this time James was not the sovereign, and his right to endow the two proprietors with anything more than title to the soil was dubious. Governmental jurisdiction over the Jersey communities became further confused when the Carteret family and Berkeley sold out their interests. The West Jersey proprietary was then divided into one hundred shares, East Jersey into twenty-four.

By 1685 about 120 individuals had purchased shares or portions of shares in West Jersey. Many of the proprietors in the British Isles never moved to the colony, but engaged agents to manage their property or sold off their holdings in fractions. Other proprietors actually came to West Jersey along with a thousand or so men, women, and children who between 1677 and 1682 settled along the Delaware. The population was predominantly Quaker.

Before embarking for America, the proprietors had issued a document, the Concessions and Agreements, providing for a provincial assembly of one hundred representatives, one for each of the proprietary divisions, the members to be proprietors or freeholders chosen annually by the inhabitants. Through the influence of William Penn, the duke of York was prevailed upon to relinquish any claim to the revenue in West Jersey, but in the release he issued on 6 August 1680 he settled the government only on Edward Byllynge, not on the other proprietors. A conflict then ensued between Byllynge, who claimed to be governor on the basis of the grant from the royal duke, and the resident proprietors and the inhabitants. In 1684 the provincial assembly sent Samuel Jennings and Thomas Budd to London to press their case against Byllynge with George Fox and other leaders of the Quaker community in England.

The Friends had the matter under consideration for some time, between September 1684 and July 1685, before deciding that Byllynge was entitled to the government on the basis of the grant from James. The authority to govern, unlike title to the land, they further concluded, could not be divided into shares. But they recommended to Byllynge that he confirm the Concessions and Agreements, with its provision for an elected assembly. Byllynge refused, and Jennings and Budd took the issue to officials of the king. At this point the crown ordered the attorney general to sue out a writ of quo warranto.

Edward Byllynge died on 16 January 1687, but a new figure challenged the local leaders at Burlington. A month after Byllynge died, his heirs sold his interest to Daniel Coxe, an English physician, courtier, land speculator, and promoter, vesting in him not only the ownership of a block of proprietary shares but also the claim to the government of West Jersey. In September 1687 Coxe wrote to the owners resident in the province—under the presidency of Thomas Olive they had formed the Council of Proprietors of West Jersey—of the anxiety of the London-based proprietors over the situation. The Londoners, mainly small traders and shopkeepers, made up a majority of the English holders. At their request and after consulting with William Penn and his agent, Philip Ford, Coxe assumed for himself the function of governor, a right he was willing to sell for a thousand guineas.[1]

Although Daniel Coxe never crossed the Atlantic, he aimed to build up in America vast holdings. To this end he acquired land in West Jersey, New England, New York, and Pennsylvania and shares of the East Jersey proprietary.

The political structure of East Jersey, like that of her sister province, was flawed. In 1682 the heirs of Sir George Carteret sold the proprietary title to a group of twelve English Quakers, among them William Penn and Gawen Lawrie. Six weeks later the Friends brought in a syndicate of Scots, including Robert Barclay, John Drummond (later Viscount Melfort), and his brother James, earl of Perth. The patent issued by Charles II on 23 November 1683 confirming the sale of East Jersey mentioned only the Scots by name. Some of the original London proprietors then withdrew; others divided their shares and sold fractions. Eighty-five individuals became proprietors of East Jersey, forty-five of them Scots. Among the more prominent English purchasers were Daniel Coxe and William Dockwra.

Without waiting for their authority to govern to be confirmed, the proprietors based in Britain elected Robert Barclay as governor and sent out a deputy to the colony to displace the administration previously established under Carteret. In 1685 they adopted a frame of government.

By the Fundamental Constitutions, the inhabitants of the colony who held fifty acres of land or fifty pounds in personal property elected representatives to a legislative assembly; proprietors or their appointed deputies sat in the council of East Jersey.

Several hundred Scots had migrated to join the polyglot population occupying the towns already established in the colony. Among the five thousand or so inhabitants were immigrants from the West Indies, Quakers, and Dissenters from the Puritan colonies of New England and Long Island. Many of the latter had come at the behest of the governor of New York before news of the transfer of New Jersey in 1664 had arrived in America. These townsmen claimed an exemption from rents and, at times, immunity from proprietary government.

Ethnic and religious diversity as well as conflicts over land titles and rents soon became the basis for factional strife in East jersey. The British proprietors decided to allow the shareholders resident in the colony to manage the disposition of proprietary land, but the Board of Proprietors of East Jersey—all but two of the members were Scots—soon became involved in a dispute with townsmen of Shrewsbury and Middletown who claimed to hold their property on the basis of grants from the first English governor of New York. Representatives from these townships who had formerly sat in the provincial assembly also complained over the failure of Gawen Lawrie, the deputy governor sent out from London, to call a meeting of the legislature until the spring of 1686. Unhappy with the situation in America, the British proprietors in September 1686 sent over an Edinburgh merchant, Andrew Hamilton, to investigate and commissioned a new deputy governor, Lord Neil Hamilton. The Scottish peer had a short tenure, however. When the assembly of East Jersey rejected his proposals for taxes, he left the colony.[2]

The confused state of affairs in East and West Jersey had not gone unnoticed in Whitehall. Early in the reign of James II the secretary for the Committee for Trade and Plantations had informed William Dockwra that the lords of the committee expected some responsible person to attend them on behalf of the proprietors of East Jersey, since William Dyer, the royal surveyor of the customs, had complained of the authorities there interfering with the enforcement of the acts of navigation. After considering Dyer's charges, the king in council that fall ordered Sir Robert Sawyer to sue out a writ of quo warranto.

Municipal officials and traders at Manhattan added their complaints: separating the Delaware territories and the Jerseys from New York had cost the city of New York one-third of its trade. The provincial secretary of New York, John Spragge, elaborated on this theme. Goods entering the region through New Jersey rather than at New York lessened the revenue accruing to the crown colony. Not only the two Jerseys but Connecticut was necessary for the government of New York. Spragge professed to have convinced Andrew Hamilton of the disadvantages of continuing matters as they were and proposed that the proprietors of East Jersey exchange their holdings for the Pemaquid region on the far eastern frontier.[3]

The British proprietors were not amenable to the suggestion. Having spent considerable sums of money on the port of Perth, they also resented efforts of the king's officers at New York to compel shipmasters to enter at New York rather than at facilities in East Jersey. They won their point, temporarily at least, when the crown instructed Governor Thomas Dongan to permit vessels to enter Perth without first stopping at New York, provided the authorities in East Jersey allowed persons appointed by Dongan or the collector to gather customs duties.

A precarious military situation in America tipped the balance against the proprietors of New Jersey. Dongan spent the winter of 1688 at Albany with a garrison of 450 men, many of them drawn from the militia. He had been at great expense to maintain this force and to supply some 800 Indians. With a border to maintain against both the French and hostile tribesmen, the government of New York, hard-pressed to meet ordinary expenses, could not bear this additional burden. Income from provincial revenue the previous year had come to only three thousand pounds. To annex the Jerseys was not enough, although adding East Jersey to New York would at least protect the customs revenue for New York.[4]

The British-based proprietors, led by Perth, Drummond, Coxe, and William Penn, appreciating that they might loose jurisdiction over the government, fought to save their investment. In April 1688 they offered to surrender their political authority in exchange for certain concessions from the crown: freedom for vessels to use the ports of East Jersey; trade with the Indians; rights comparable to those enjoyed by lords of the manor in England; authority to erect courts of justice; appointed officials, including the governor, to come from the ranks of the proprietors; and above all, a patent from the crown confirming the ownership of the soil to the proprietors. To the Lords for Plantation Affairs in Whitehall, these terms were unacceptable; they ran contrary to the provisons already concluded for New York and New England.[5]

In New York the position of the provincial government was weak, a result, in part, of the failure of James as proprietor and later as king to win the support of a diverse, polyglot population. The attempt to govern and to raise money for the support of the provincial administration without the benefit of an elected assembly further prejudiced the efforts of Governor Thomas Dongan.

Three distinct ethnic and religious groups resided in New York. Although the Delancey and the Bayard families played a role in the commerce of the colony, the French Huguenots were relatively few. The more numerous Dutch were a conquered people; their loyalty had been doubtful. In the third quarter of the seventeenth century England had been at war with the United Provinces of the Netherlands on three occasions. During the most recent conflict, when a naval force from Europe had captured New York, the Dutch inhabitants had shown no inclination to defend the province for the English proprietor. Some of the leading men among them had served in the subsequent administration. The bulk of the English in the colony resided in towns located on Long Island, communities originally settled under the auspices of the Puritan regimes of New England. A proprietor or king who professed the Catholic faith, demanded quitrents as a condition of holding land, and would not allow them a representative assembly had little claim on their loyalty. The Long Islanders also resented the special commercial privileges awarded New York City as an entrepôt by the provincial authorities when seeking to build up the export trade of the colony. Traditionally the English on Long Island had traded through Boston.

Among the English at Manhattan were merchants and factors who had arrived more recently from England or the West Indies. Enjoying some social and economic standing, they had not been admitted into the ranks of the ruling group appointed by James or his deputies. Taking advantage of the absence of Governor Edmund Andros in 1681 and employing the rhetoric of the Whig opposition in Westminster, these English merchants had protested in the local courts against the imposition of import duties. By using obstructionist tactics they had succeeded to the extent that a few of them had subsequently been admitted to the ranks of the officeholders.

Edmund Andros during his term of office in New York (1674–80) had also earned the enmity of a few members of the Dutch community, particularly the German-born merchant, Jacob Leisler. Of humble origins, Leisler had come to New Amsterdam as a soldier for the Dutch West India Company, had married well, but had never been fully accepted by the more prominent of the Dutch families. To the contrary, he had become embroiled in a legal dispute with his wife's relatives over an estate and in a controversy between two groups contending for control of the local Dutch ecclesiastical organization. Andros had come down strongly against Leisler and his associate, Jacob Milborne, a former indentured servant and brother to an Anabaptist preacher of Massachusetts. From this dispute Leisler had emerged embittered against the established families of the province and the English authorities. Later he openly challenged both. Several of the men subsequently associated with Leisler in an insurgent movement were close relatives of Samuel Edsall.

The English governors of New York had enjoyed good relations with the most prominent of the Dutch families, especially the Van Cortlandts, Philipses, and Schuylers. They could supply the credit the governors needed to finance their administrations, particularly during emergencies; in turn they received appointments to the provincial council and other marks of esteem.

The proprietary regime had always been in a precarious state, however, so much so that James had contemplated selling the colony. By 1683 he had apparently learned the lesson of the merchants' revolt of 1681. To provide adequate revenue for the government he authorized Andros's successor, Colonel Thomas Dongan, to call a legislative assembly. The proprietor had seemed ready to accept a bill providing for a Charter of Liberties and Privileges, as it was called, passed by this assembly when Charles II died. With the succession of the proprietor as king, New York became a royal colony. James II then chose not to confirm the Charter of Liberties, with its provision for a representative assembly, and postponed settling a government for New York, pending a final arrangement for Massachusetts. In the meantime Dongan governed according to instructions sent from England.

To Jacob Leisler, resentful of the English governors and embittered over the refusal of his more successful Dutch relations to admit him into the privileged circle, and to the sons-in-law of Samuel Edsall could now be added those aspiring politicians who had forced the proprietor's hand in the matter of the assembly. Unless they could bring about some change, the road to preferment was closed to them. The pinnacle of provincial politics was the council, appointed by the king, often on the recommendation of the governor. Among those who served during Dongan's administration were Frederick Philipse, Stephanus Van Cortlandt; Major Anthony Brockholes, the commander of the few companies of royal soldiers in the colony; John Spragge, the provincial secretary; Lucas Santeen, the collector of customs; Gervais Baxter, the commandant at Fort James on Manhattan; John Young, an aged Long Island resident; Lewis Morris, a well-to-do immigrant form Barbados; Nicholas Bayard; James Graham, a lawyer from Scotland, appointed provincial attorney general; and John Palmer, another lawyer who had been a merchant in the West Indies.

The councilors as well as the officials of the municipal government at Manhattan supported Dongan's plea for New York to regain the lost territories of Delaware and New Jersey. It must be further enlarged to encompass Connecticut and Rhode Island. By the late spring of 1686, the ministers of state appeared resolved to maintain New York as a colony separate from New England, but they had transferred Pemaquid from the jurisdiction of Dongan at Manhattan to Andros at Boston.[6]

As governor of New York Dongan faced two pressing and related problems: finding revenue to maintain his government and defending the province from the threat posed by the French and northern Indians. The ordinary sources for revenue had proved inadequate. As early as 1685 Dongan had had to borrow over thirty-five hundred pounds from local merchants on his personal credit. He had reason to complain over the manner in which Lucas Santeen, the officer sent out from England to collect import duties, performed. Early in 1687 the governor suspended Santeen, naming James Graham and Stephanus Van Cortlandt receivers of the revenue for New York and New Jersey. The crown confirmed the suspension, but sent out one Matthew Plowman to succeed as collector. Unfortunately, as it later proved, the Customs Board in London had acted too hastily. Soon after Plowman left for America, the Commissioners of the Treasury learned that he had not posted the necessary security to execute his office. Moreover, the information they now had of his character was not "much to his advantage," Blathwayt, the auditor general of the plantation revenue, confided.[7] Some provincial politicians soon found another fault in Plowman. Men in New York opposed to the royal administration made much of the fact that, like Dongan, he was a Papist.[8]

Early in 1687 James II had resolved to recall the Roman Catholic governor and to employ him in England. Dongan received orders to leave New York as soon as a successor arrived, or sooner if subsequently ordered. Yet Dongan, having pledged his own credit to raise money for his administration, could not leave New York until his accounts were settled. The revenue then available was insufficient, with Santeen's accounts nearly three-thousand pounds in arrears. Dongan then asked that thirty-five hundred pounds be remitted from England to clear the debts he had contracted with local merchants. To widen the financial base, he again recommended annexing the neighboring colonies to New York.

Despite Dongan's pleading, no aid was forthcoming. By the fall he had learned that the crown had decided to annex Connecticut to Massachusetts. The ministers of state might just as well then add New York to New England, for it could not maintain itself. Annexing the Jerseys would serve to preserve what little revenue was available to the administration at Manhattan, but would not add greatly to the money or the men needed. Whether Dongan remained in New York or returned to England the crown now left to his discretion.[9] He chose to remain for a time to help organize defenses against the French.

Despite the Treaty of Whitehall concluded in November 1686 between James II and Louis XIV, hostilities seemed imminent on the northern frontiers. Dongan had sent a militia of some 450 men to Albany, mortgaging his own estate and borrowing heavily from the Albany merchant, Robert Livingston.[10] Dongan's counterpart in Quebec, Jacques Brisay, marquis de Denonville, had arrived in Canada in 1685 bringing with him reinforcements from France. Twenty years before, Louis XIV had sent out a full regiment of royal troops for the colony. Denonville was convinced that the menace to New France posed by the Iroquois confederation with whom the Canadians had been at odds for years could be eliminated only by driving out the English in New York who supplied the Indians. Dongan saw the position of the English as essentially weak. To correct the military and financial imbalance he consistently urged unification of the northern colonies, at least bringing in the Delaware counties, East and West Jersey, and especially Connecticut, a colony he thought could provide 3,000 militiamen.[11]

It did not quite turn out as Dongan had hoped. Not Dongan's regime at Manhattan, but Andros's administration at Boston served as the nucleus for an expanded English dominion in northern America, the entire region north and east of the Delaware. By the terms of a new commission issued in 1688, Andros would govern this extensive region with the advice of an appointive council, a precarious base on which to establish government. The tenuous position was not appreciated in Whitehall. The veteran observer of colonial affairs, William Blathwayt, exulted that the union of English territories from the Delaware to Nova Scotia "will be terrible to the French and make them proceed with more caution than they have lately done."

Certain provinces marked for royal action escaped. William Penn had apparently won an exemption from legal action for the lower counties on the left bank of the Delaware and for Pennsylvania. The writs threatened against Maryland and the Jerseys were never pursued,[12] as the British proprietors of the latter colonies were negotiating to surrender their power of government. The officials of Connecticut presumably were willing to acquiesce in the wishes of Whitehall. Caught between the threat of a writ against the charter and pressure from Dongan and his supporters at Manhattan, the Connecticut leaders procrastinated, seeking time.

Edward Randolph, the royal agent who for a decade had been battling the Puritan regime in Massachusetts, had compiled a broad list of charges against the corporations of Connecticut and Rhode Island, accusing them of violating the terms of their charters by passing laws contrary to those of England, violating the parliamentary navigation code, denying appeals to England, and in the case of Connecticut, requiring attendance at the established Congregational church on penalty of five shillings fine for every absence. As proof Randolph had submitted extracts from the book of laws published in Connecticut in 1673. The ministers of state wasted little time in accepting his arguments. After reading over the evidence he had presented, they ordered the attorney general to proceed with writs of quo warranto.[13]

Randolph, as usual, had exaggerated, but his charges nonetheless contained much truth. In Connecticut, unlike Massachusetts, most men had the right to vote for provincial officials, and the government enjoyed broad, widely based support. A group of families, the "standing order," who were commonly acknowledged to possess the requisite qualities of piety, dignity, and experience, dominated the government. Among the more noteworthy were the Winthrops. John Winthrop, son of the first governor of the Bay colony, had himself been a governor of Connecticut, and his sons, Fitzjohn and Waitstill (Wait), were influential in local affairs. But men like the younger Winthrops and their friend, John Allyn, the provincial secretary, were not blind to the opportunities offered outside the "land of steady habits." They were not necessarily opposed to the Dominion of New England if it offered them opportunity. The Winthrops had been close with Sir Edmund Andros when he had served as governor of New York, and they belonged to a group of land speculators, mainly of Massachusetts, seeking approval from the crown for their claim to the Narragansett country of Rhode Island. Many of these Narragansett proprietors, initially at least, supported the Dominion of New England.[14]

Fitzjohn Winthrop had been named to the council in the commission issued by the crown to Andros. When the new governor arrived in Boston, Winthrop hurried north to attend him. James II had authorized Andros to receive the surrender of the charter from officials of Connecticut. To John Allyn, acquiescing, rather than contesting the issue in the royal courts at Westminster, was "the best we can expect. Yet some are so blind that they cannot see what is theire owne interest." The provincial secretary seemed certain that most of the inhabitants were inclined to join Massachusetts rather than any other colony. If Fitzjohn Winthrop could obtain a copy of the commission issued Andros by the king or the indulgence therein granted in matters of religion, it might encourage the men of Connecticut to submit.

Winthrop was quick to reply in a letter probably calculated to reassure the Connecticut men and to appeal to Allyn and others with ambition. It would be better to accept the king's "gratious" offer than to stand trial over the charter, a contest in no way advantageous. No one in Boston thought they could win in such a suit, and "it will be pitty that many of yo'seelues should not be continued in place of trust." Andros had authority under his commission "to call to the councill such of yo'selues as he shall think fit, and noe good man neede doubt that it will not fall to his share, but may be greatly hazarded if y^{r}selues shall wayte the issue and consequence of a tryall." The king had sought to promote the interest and prosperity of the people, Winthrop concluded, and to that end had granted an indulgence in matters of religion.[15]

Winthrop's plea may have been decisive. The government at Hartford adopted a stance which offered the royal authorities an excuse. In letters to Andros and to Sunderland (a prinicpal secretary of state and lord president of the council) the Connecticut men indicated that although they preferred to remain in their present status as a colony separate from both New York and New England, if the king thought otherwise, they would submit. They were obedient and loyal subjects, notwithstanding the misrepresentations made against them. Government under Boston was preferable to the administration of Manhattan.

Randolph took this stance as evidence that the officials at Hartford would submit to annexation, but he nonetheless urged the Committee for Trade and Plantations at Whitehall to prosecute the writ against the charter for the effect such legal action would have elsewhere in America. He felt confident the Connecticut men would not defend against a suit.[16] As it later turned out, Sunderland and the other ministers of state would have done well to follow Randolph's advice. From London, William Whiting, once an inhabitant of Connecticut but now a merchant in England who had been solicited by the authorities in Connecticut to act in their behalf, wrote to his old friend and schoolfellow John Allyn that there was no point in defending the charter. Whether it was surrendered or condemned by the courts of law made no difference: it was all one. He himself would not appear in court for the colony and could find no one else to do so. Whiting was wrong; that the crown never legally prosecuted the charter later saved the colony of Connecticut as a corporation. At the time this was not apparent, but the patent was later deemed valid and in force.

To heighten the attraction of Andros's administration for Governor Robert Treat and his colleagues at Hartford, John Saffin, a Boston merchant and a member of the Narragansett proprietors, also wrote to John Allyn. It was inevitable that all of the chartered colonies would come under the immediate supervision of the crown. Many men in Boston feared that "they that stand out longest will fare the worst at last." More important, "whatsoever the vicissitudes of affayres be than may happen in England, matters will never be againe in *statu quo* here."[17]

To threats and appeals Connecticut officials responded ambiguously. In the spring of 1687 the court at Whitehall ordered the writs
against the charters of Connecticut and Rhode Island prosecuted. William Whiting at last aroused himself. He hired a solicitor and authorized
one of the clerks of the Privy Council to appear as attorney on behalf of
Connecticut. At that point the lords of the Committee for Trade and
Plantations introduced the letters from Treat and the General Court at
Hartford. These signified, so the ministers of state claimed, a willingness
to surrender. The crown then issued instructions to Andros to annex
Connecticut and to admit Treat and Allyn to the council of the dominion.
Later that summer Whiting received orders from Hartford to defend the
charter. With only forty pounds of the colony's funds left, he thought it
unreasonable to expend his own money in behalf of a government that in
all probability would be dissolved.[18] Whiting took no action.

Andros received his orders in Boston on 18 October 1687. Accompanied by Fitzjohn Winthrop and seven other members of his council as
well as a "gard of Granadeers mounted & well equipped," he traveled to
Hartford. On 1 November he read to the assembled assistants his commission and the order the king and council has issued on 18 June. He gave
the officials of Connecticut no opportunity to debate or to ask questions.
After swearing in Treat and Allyn, he dissolved the meeting. The next day
he confirmed all of the civil and militia officers of the colony.[19]

Several members of the council of the Dominion of New
England—the Winthrop brothers and their brother-in-law, Richard
Wharton, among them—were particularly anxious to have the jurisdiction of the regime at Boston extended over the region disputed between
Connecticut and Rhode Island known as the Narragansett country, or the
King's Province. As members of the so-called Atherton Associates—
Humphrey Atherton had formed the group—these proprietors claimed
the region on the basis of a forfeited mortgage from local Indians. Although numbering some residents of Rhode Island, Plymouth, and Connecticut, the associates consisted mainly of merchants and speculators
from the Bay colony. Massachusetts men had predominated among the
commissioners appointed by the crown and headed by the former royal
governor of New Hampshire, Edward Cranfield, who in 1684 had decided ex parte in favor of the speculators and against Rhode Island. For
years the authorities at Providence had successfully disputed the claims of
the putative proprietors, citing the boundary provisions of the charter
granted Rhode Island by the crown and an agreement concluded with an
agent for Connecticut.

The regime at Providence was itself weakened by friction and discontent within Rhode Island, by animosity between Quakers and non-

Quakers, and by disputes between various towns. The contentious men of Warwick had challenged the authorities of Providence over the division of village lands. Rent by internal divisions and attacked from without, Rhode Island was in no position to withstand the pressure from authorities in London.

Shortly after the accession of James II, the Narragansett proprietors had resumed the attack on Rhode Island. They had an ally at Whitehall in the person of the former governor of Virginia, Lord Culpeper, whom they had admitted into their company. Early in the new reign, Culpeper, Richard Wharton, and others petitioned the crown for confirmation of their lands. They offered a special inducement: they were ready to pay quitrents of two shillings and sixpence per hundred acres of land and to submit to such regulations as the king thought fit. The rate conceded was what Andros as governor of the dominion would demand for the crown in New England, a region where the chartered government had not required quitrents. Fitzjohn Winthrop, Simon Bradstreet, John Saffin, Richard Wharton, and their colleagues also made a point of their loyalty to the new monarch: in the Narragansett country they had proclaimed James II with all possible solemnity.

While the putative proprietors were appealing their case against the administration in Providence to the crown, in London Edward Randolph was successfully pressing charges to justify vacating the charter of Rhode Island. By the late spring of 1686 Randolph was back in New England, where he presented a summons—now "suprannuated"—to the government at Providence. The dispute over the Narragansett country was coming to a head. In response to a petition from the local settlers, the assembly of Rhode Island had extended them protection and excluded intruders, a move Elisha Hutchinson, John Saffin, and Richard Wharton of Massachusetts protested in a letter to London.[20]

The council of Massachusetts, dominated by the land speculators, intervened. Andros had not yet arrived in America. Joseph Dudley, the president, along with Fitzjohn Winthrop and Wharton, went down to Kingston in the King's Province and on 23 June 1686 established their jurisdiction, commissioning their colleagues as justices of the peace and officers of the militia. Kingston, Westerly, and Greenwich under Rhode Island now became Rochester, Haversham, and Dedford.

The provincial regime at Providence now faced a double challenge. Seemingly it chose not to oppose that from Whitehall. On 29 June the General Assembly publicly declared it would not contest a suit at law at Westminster, so Governor Walter Clarke, acting for the corporation of Rhode Island, wrote the king. The Rhode Islanders were a loyal people, although despised by their neighbors in the adjacent provinces. They now begged for their former privileges in matters of religion, particularly in the taking of oaths, and that Newport be made a free port. They made another, vague request: that no person to be set over them who was not suited to their nature. The Quakers were opposed to an arrangement to include Rhode Island within a jurisdiction dominated by the regime at Boston, many of them having fled from persecution in the Bay colony. New York under Dongan seemed preferable to Massachusetts.[21]

In Whitehall Sunderland and the other ministers of the crown seized on this seeming acquiescence by the General Assembly. Since the provincial government had agreed not to stand suit over the charter, the lords of the Committee for Trade and Plantations recommended that Andros receive the surrender of the patent. He was to ensure the inhabitants of Rhode Island of the royal protection and countenance. Although the king in council in the spring of 1687 again ordered writs against the charters of Connecticut and Rhode Island, legal proceedings were never pressed. Presumably the corporate authorities at Hartford and Providence had voluntarily relinquished their patents. Considering the duty and affection so expressed by the Rhode Islanders, James II granted their petition for liberty of religious conscience. They would enjoy such other privileges as Andros might judge consistent with the royal service.[22]

As royal governor for New England Edmund Andros proved unreceptive to the pleas for particular privileges by the land speculators, men who hitherto had accepted the takeover in Massachusetts by the royal government. Faced with conflicting claims and evidence over the status of the Narragansett country, the ministers of the crown had left it to Andros, once he arrived in New England, to investigate the situation and then report back to London. When Andros proved unsympathetic to the claims of the speculators, he lost the only significant support enjoyed by royal government in the Bay colony.

As events in New Hampshire had demonstrated, disputes over land between proprietors and townsmen were difficult to resolve. The intervention of a royal governor on the Piscataqua had only heightened tension and exacerbated the situation, particularly since Edward Cranfield proved corrupt, vacillating, and cowardly. He had first supported, then opposed, and then supported again the claims of the putative proprietor, Robert Mason. Cranfield was accused of misrepresentation and misrule by William Vaughan and other provincial leaders who challenged Mason's claims to the proprietorship of New Hampshire. In 1685 Cranfield had withdrawn from the colony, leaving the administration of government to Walter Barefoote and the few other councilors at Portsmouth who had supported his generally unpopular regime.

In England Nathaniel Weare, sent over on behalf of the inhabitants to oppose Mason, apparently convinced the lords of the Committee for Trade and Plantations that Cranfield had violated his instructions in the judicial hearings involving Mason's suits against the townsmen. The Privy Council suspended the decison of the provincial court favoring Mason, allowed William Vaughan to appeal to the king, and ordered Mason to forebear instituting any suits for a time. This action by the crown was based on procedural faults rather than on substantive issues, however. Mason still held to his claim as confirmed by the opinion of the highest judicial authorities in England, the chief justices of the courts of King's Bench and Common Pleas: the Mason family was legally entitled to the soil of New Hampshire under patents issued by a corporation to whom James I in 1620 had bestowed the region.

In addition to repudiating the actions of Cranfield in the suits over land titles, James II had also pardoned Edward Gove, an assemblyman of New Hampshire who had led a comic opera revolt against the governor. Tried and convicted in New Hampshire of treason, he had been shipped off to London in chains and imprisoned in the Tower of London.

The behavior of Cranfield during the suits Mason had pressed in the New Hampshire courts did not in any way impair the substance of Mason's claim as stated by the judges in England a decade before. In December 1686 the king in council, on the recommendation of the Lords of Trade, dismissed the appeal of Vaughan and allowed the judgment of the provincial court in New Hampshire in behalf of Mason to stand. The contention of Richard Waldron and dozens of other townsmen that for fifty years they had been in peaceable possesion of lands now claimed by Mason counted for nothing.[23] The grant to his grandfather took precedence. The villagers would have to pay quitrents to Mason.

Pressing the advantage, early in 1687 Mason asked that the crown instruct Andros to have his title recorded in New England and to ensure that he as proprietor not be disturbed. Even before Andros had arrived in New England, the councilors in Massachusetts appointed by the crown had moved the public records from Portsmouth to Boston.

Mason returned to America, but did not live to capitalize on the decision rendered in his favor. He died in the fall of 1688. His claim then passed to Samuel Allen, a merchant of London with whom he had entered into partnership hoping to obtain a contract to supply the Royal Navy with great masts for the king's ships. But Allen received satisfaction neither from the Navy Board nor from the inhabitants of New Hampshire. The commissioners of the navy in London recommended against a contract with Allen on the ground that no dependence could be had for supplying masts from New England unless from merchants already established in the trade. They preferred dealing with Sir John Shorter and Sir William Warren, traders with connections among the merchants in the Bay colony and on the Piscataqua.[24] And in the towns of New Hampshire resistance to the claims of Samuel Allen was no less strong than that to the pretensions put forth by the Masons.

Between 1685 and the spring of 1688 royal authorities had annexed to Massachusetts Bay six disparate provincial regimes, each with diverse social composition and ethnic and religious elements, thus creating a dominion superficially strong, but a province with little cohesion and unity. New Yorkers appealing to the crown had wanted an independent colony enlarged so as to encompass the Jerseys and southern New England. Few had wanted incorporation into a government based in Massachusetts. The townsmen of New Jersey were limited in their outlook, concerned with local affairs and the confused status of the proprietary governments of East and West Jersey. In Connecticut and Rhode Island, officials had accepted only reluctantly, if at all, annexation to the administration at Boston as the lesser of evils. Only a few of the more ambitious leaders with particular economic interests, such as the Winthrops (members of the Atherton Associates) had cause to support the administration of Andros. While the townsmen of Plymouth, Congregationalists for the most part, welcomed unification with Massachusetts, they resented a fundamental defect in the government of the Dominion of New England—the lack of an assembly of representatives from the towns to vote taxes and enact laws.

The new Dominion of New England had never really taken hold. Control by the officials of the new administration was precarious; indeed, outside Boston and Manhattan, it was almost nonexistent. The inhabitants of New England, New York, and the Jerseys had little cause to accept the new arrangement when a challenge came to Edmund Andros in Boston; they had little reason to support the dominion.

CHAPTER 4

Massachusetts Bay, 1685–88:
From Commonwealth to Dominion

THE BURDENS imposed upon Edmund Andros when he went out to preside over New England would have tested the patience and wisdom of a Solomon. The king's ministers of state had great hopes for the new governor. Henry Hyde, second earl of Clarendon—as lord lieutenant of Ireland he himself would be sent to govern a population resenting English rule—was optimistic. Andros "understands the people, and knows how to manage them."[1]

Half a centry before, almost from the very inception of Massachusetts Bay, the colony had come under the control of self-discovered saints convinced that their task was to establish a biblical society governed by a godly elect. Except for a relatively few men wealthy enough to qualify for the right to vote by a tax-paying qualification, membership in the corporation as defined by the General Court derived from full membership in the established Congregational churches in the towns, churches enjoying an ecclesiastical monopoly. Full church membership came to the saints, those testifying to saving grace. After a half-century had passed, fewer than one-third of the adult men in the colony were freemen, entitled to vote for or to hold provincial office.

Direct and immediate supervision by officials appointed by the king of England had come to the Bay colony only after a protracted dispute lasting for a generation. Some merchants of Anglican persuasion had consistently complained of disenfranchisement under the Puritan government, but they were few. More numerous were the men who adhered to the Congregationalist faith, men eligible to hold elected office under the charter, but who perceived that sooner or later some concession would have to be made to the crown, liberty of conscience and political rights granted to peaceable Protestants, and freedom allowed the king's subjects to appeal from the local courts to England. To make no concession might jeopardize the entire Puritan system established under the charter. The moderates favoring concession had never been able to prevail over the commonwealthmen, those convinced that in the charter granted by Charles I in 1629 they possessed a heavenly endowed patent granting power to the elect of God to establish the rule of saints, a government independent of England. Outside the realm the monarch had but titular authority. As Samuel Nowell, one of the more outspoken of the commonwealthmen, had put it in 1683 to an agent sent to London to fend off attacks by the crown, "By our Pattent we have full & absolute power to rule & governe."[2] The authorities of Massachusetts Bay had sought to delay complying with royal demands, to procrastinate, by sending emissaries to the court at Whitehall not empowered to make concessions, hoping that the uncertainty of the English political scene or the intervention of God might once again save the Puritan state. Indeed, more than forty years before, the outbreak of civil war and the overthrow of the monarchy had saved the saints in Massachusetts.

But time had apparently run out on the saints. The Stuart monarchy survived the efforts of the opposition Whig politicians; Providence had not intervened, and after years of delay, the royal courts at Westminster had vacated the charter of Massachusetts Bay. Joseph Dudley, although a man of impeccable Puritan lineage, accepted the decision, and, with Edward Randolph, he drew up a list of men from among the moderate faction to sit with him on an interim council for Massachusetts. Some of the individuals appointed to serve under the presidency of Dudley were related by marriage, but almost all were involved in speculative land ventures in New England. Hitherto they had not succeeded in winning approval for their claims from the various provincial regimes. A royal council under their control might sanction their titles.[3] Four of the men named with Dudley in the commission, Simon Bradstreet, John Pynchon, William Stoughton, and Nathaniel Saltonstall, were elected officials of Massachusetts, eleven were residents of the colony. John Hincks came from New Hampshire, Francis Champernoun and Edward Tyng from Maine, and Fitzjohn Winthrop of Connecticut nominally represented the King's Province, the Narragansett country. With the exception of Edward Randolph and Robert Mason (and he died in 1688), all were either native to New England or had lived there for many years. The neat balance was upset when Simon Bradstreet and his son, Dudley, along with Saltonstall and Champernoun, later refused to serve.

Dudley with the other members of the council held authority as an interim government for Massachusetts, New Hampshire, Maine, Plymouth, and the Narragansett country. Would they give way to a conventional royal administration of governor, appointed council, and elected assembly? Immediately after the vacating of the charter at Westminster in November 1684, the crown officials, when considering the instructions and commission for a new governor, had in mind allowing him to call for an elected assembly, a project they dropped later that month.

Several months passed with no action. Charles II died early in February 1685, and James succeeded to the throne. Randolph, then working with Sunderland and the earl of Rochester, himself submitted proposals to the Committee for Foreign Plantations on a government for New England. He listed three dozen towns—twenty-two in Massachusetts, nine in Plymouth, and five in Maine—to have liberty to choose representatives for an assembly. When reporting to Sunderland, the lord president of the council, on 26 August the lords of the committee specifically asked that Sunderland obtain the king's views on a clause relating to an assembly to be called in Boston for passing laws and voting taxes. Both the attorney general and the solicitor general agreed that such a body was justified. Notwithstanding the forfeiture of the charter, the inhabitants retained the right to consent to laws and taxes. Evidently the lords of the Committee for Trade and Plantations and the law officers accepted the doctrine that the rights of Englishmen included the privilege of electing a representative assembly. But Sunderland did not. He was later reported to have boasted that it was by his advice that the king had struck out of the commission for the governor of Massachusetts the provision for a representative assembly. By the end of October 1685 the choice for governor had fallen on Andros, but his commission had yet to be drafted.[4]

Not until the end of 1685 did Randolph depart for America with copies of the legal order vacating the charter of the colony and the commission for Dudley and the other councilors. Until the royal agent arrived, the government of Massachusetts was unsettled by various, at times conflicting, rumors. Some local officials were neglecting their duties. On 18 March 1685 the General Court was forced to order selectmen, grand jurymen, constables, and tithingmen of the towns to enforce the laws against the inhabitants breaking the Sabbath, drinking, and "misspending their time in public houses of entertainment." The deputies and magistrates thought it necessary to renew "our couenant with God, which hath binn neglected too much in the most cheurches." The ministers and congregations must "use all possible wajes & means for the vpholding of church discipjne."

That summer thirty-one ministers of the province met in Boston, where they dined together at a tavern kept by George Monk. As William Hubbard of Ipswich announced, they concluded that the authorities under the charter must not give way until the General Court had seen and evaluated a commission from the king establishing another government. Three days later, with Governor Simon Bradstreet confined to his home with a severe cold, the two houses of General Court divided over the issue of whether or not to recognize any commission from the crown. John

Higginson, Richard Wharton's brother-in-law, argued that they ought to surrender in case a governor arrived with a royal warrant.

Later that year the spirits of the commonwealthmen soared. They were put in a "hurly burly" when "ye Whigg News" arrived of uprisings in the British Isles: the supporters of James II had been routed, and the Protestant duke of Monmouth proclaimed king. At this, the General Court voted a day of Thanksgiving, but canceled the celebration when a true account reached Boston. By the autumn men were openly drinking the health of the prospective royal governor. In the spring of 1686 Samuel Shrimpton, a long-time opponent of the Puritan regime, openly declared before the board of assistants that there was no Governor and Company of the Massachusetts Bay in being. He was ready to prove this if called to do so. Governor Simon Bradstreet acknowledged that the charter had indeed been vacated in England, but he insisted on a proclamation to that effect being sent him. The deputy governor, Thomas Danforth, a leader of the commonwealth faction, pleaded that the charter government must not be "tumbled down" until the king called for it.[5]

Finally, on 14 May 1686, Edward Randolph arrived with a copy of the judgment from the court at Westminster and the king's commission for Dudley to preside over a council to govern Massachusetts, Plymouth, and New Hampshire pending the arrival of a governor. Randolph immediately took coach for Roxbury, where Dudley lived. The two men then sent Major John Pynchon and William Stoughton to summon the provincial magistrates that they might learn of the king's commands. The next day, Saturday, Dudley sent for Major John Richards, Samuel Sewall, and Governor Thomas Hinckley of Plymouth to examine the exemplification of the order vacating the charter.

Not until the following Monday did the assistants and the deputies from the towns assemble as the General Court at the town house in Boston. The officials of the chapter government sat on one side of the room; Dudley, Pynchon, Captain Bartholomew Gedney, Robert Mason, Randolph, and Winthrop, all named in the commission for the royal council, took seats on the other. Spectators filled the room.

Taking the initiative, Dudley addressed the men who sat opposite him, not as the corporate government, but merely as principal gentlemen and chief inhabitants of the several towns. After Dudley had displayed the exemplification and his commission under the Great Seal of England, the deputy governor, Thomas Danforth, spoke up. He supposed Dudley and his colleagues did not expect an immediate answer. Dudley refused to discuss the issue; he left.

Several members of the General Court, the major general of the provincial militia, Daniel Gookin, John Richards, and Samuel Sewall, then addressed the group. Some favored issuing a protest; others opposed such a course. Some men favored calling in the elders to pray; others thought this pointless, Dudley and his colleagues having declared themselves to be the king's council. The foundations being destroyed, Sewall asked, what could the righteous do?

The next day a few of the righteous, the elders, sought to dissuade Dudley from accepting the royal commission, but in vain. At best the two Bradstreets, father and son, and Nathaniel Saltonstall refused to take office. The king's commission for a council abridged them of their liberty and was contrary to Magna Carta. The same could have been said by many men in Massachusetts of the government imposed by the Puritan saints.

The climax came on Friday, 21 May 1686, at another meeting of the General Court. Several influential officers of the militia, including Gedney and John Higginson, were prepared with their companies to support the new regime. The commonwealthmen adopted a letter signed by the provincial secretary, Edward Rawson, addressed to Dudley and those who accepted office from the king, warning that their commission made no certain provision for the administration of justice and was too arbitrary. As inhabitants of Massachusetts, "their liberty as Englishmen" as related to passing laws, to laying taxes, and indeed to the unquestioned privileges of the subject was transferred "upon yourselves." Hitherto these commonwealthmen had not concerned themselves with the liberties and privileges of those subjects in Massachusetts who were not freemen. Ironically, they were now raising the same objections the lords of the committee of James II's Privy Council and the crown law officers had raised the previous year.

The commonwealthmen advised Dudley and his colleagues to consider whether such a defective commission was sage, either for them or for the inhabitants of the colony. If they were satisfied, they might take on the government, but the deputies and magistrates of the old regime could not give their assent to such an arrogation. Yet the commonwealthmen promised to behave as true and loyal subjects of the king and to make their address for relief "unto God" and, in due time, to their "gracious prince." Danforth and his supporters made one last gesture: they *adjourned* the General Court until the second Wednesday in October. One of the fire-eaters, Samuel Nowell, prayed God would pardon each magistrate and deputy; he thanked the Lord for the fity-six years of mercy He had given them. A weeping marshal general then declared the General Court not dissolved, but adjourned. Many knew better; they shed tears as they left.[6]

The adjournment, rather than the dissolution, of the General Court, Dudley thought inconvenient, but he was confident of the ability of the royal council to deal with the commonwealthmen. He did not have long to wait for a challenge. Edward Rawson, to whom the records of the charter government had been entrusted, refused to turn them over to Benjamin Bullivant, the recent immigrant from England whom Dudley appointed provincial attorney general. Before Rawson would give up his trust, he demanded the arrears of his salary as well as a further monetary compensation for his trouble in sorting documents.[7]

Another recent arrival was Robert Ratcliffe, M.A., an Anglican priest sent out by the bishop of London and the lords of the Committee for Plantations. With Ratcliffe's arrival, latent animosities between Congregationalists and Anglicans surfaced. Before leaving for Massachusetts, Randolph had requested that the Lords of Trade order the provincial council to set aside one of the Congregational meeting houses for the use of communicants of the Church of England. Some members of the committee opposed such an order as unnecessary. If given liberty of conscience in religion, the Puritans would voluntarily submit to having one of the three meeting houses in Boston assigned for the use of the Anglicans.

Christian brotherhood did not extend that far in Puritan Boston. As Randolph reported, the ministers of the Congregationalist churches made "ill use" of the king's indulgence on religion, some of them employing treasonable words from the pulpit. He complained to Dudley, himself once a Congregational minister, but in vain. Of the eighteen members of the council appointed by James II, only Randolph and Robert Mason were Anglicans, and the putative proprietor soon left to press his land claims. The councilors would provide no funds for Ratcliffe. At best they assigned him a room in the town house where he could officiate. The communicants of the Church of England later held their thrice-weekly services at the exchange. The question of assigning one of the Congregational meeting houses surfaced later when the governor arrived. Randolph poured out his grievances to William Sancroft, archbishop of Canterbury. Dudley claimed the provincial government had done its best for Ratcliffe; there was nothing in the public treasurey for him. It was the practice in Massachusetts, the president explained, that ministers rely on "voluntary" contributions. Ratcliffe need only attract more "auditors" to increase his stipend.[8]

The financial base of Dudley's administration was weak. Fearing repercussions from the failure to allow an assembly, the councilors were content merely to continue excise and import duties. They had retained in office many of the justices of peace and militia officers, but did institute some changes in the legal and judicial system. No longer would jurors be elected, but selected by marshals from a panel consisting of freeholders and inhabitants. To offset opposition and garner support, Dudley and his colleagues had appointed to office some adherents of the old commonwealth faction.

Randolph had railed for years against these men. Isolated and ignored, he was now reduced to sending off bitter complaints to Whitehall and Lambeth Palace. The Congregational ministers were crying out "open mouth" against the Book of Common Prayer: "whoremongers and adulterers" would sooner go to heaven than those who worshipped according to the Church of England. The councilors appointed by the king seldom met, and when they did, they quarreled. They could agree on nothing but sharing the country among themselves and laying out large tracts of land. Randolph reported the inhabitants of the province dissatisfied for want of an assembly of deputies from the towns with power to raise money and to make laws. It was imperative that Sir Edmund Andros, the governor-designate, hasten over, for "we are in great confusion."[9]

In England Andros was preparing to depart for America. On the basis of the reports from Randolph in Boston, men in the Plantation Office were apprehensive. John Povey, assistant to William Blathwayt, was particularly struck by the warning the commonwealthmen had given Dudley and the councilors of the danger in accepting a royal commission to govern without an assembly. Povey hoped Andros would find "little occasion" for the small detachment of soldiers, the hundred or so troops he was then drawing out of the camp at Hounslow Heath outside London. Blathwayt himself was skeptical over the use of soldiers in New England. Except as a small honor guard for the governor, they would be to no purpose except as a charge against the crown, for if the inhabitants proved "refractory," the Royal Navy's interdicting their shipping would be "much more effectual" than a thousand soldiers who "cannot cost less than £20,000."[10]

Sir Robert Southwell, to whom Povey and Blathwayt had been confiding their fears, had drafted a commission for the governor. With the advice and consent of the council Andros would have power to continue such laws as were already in force and to impose additional rules as well as taxes. Until a revenue was settled in the colony Andros would receive one thousand pounds in England as an annual salary. Since the proposed commission did not provide for an assembly, Povey doubted Andros would have cause for satisfaction: a plantation government without an assembly "seems very mysterious." Andros himself was apprehensive over the arrangement by which he would need only the consent of the appointed council to levy taxes and promulgate new laws. By the instructions issued him on 19 October 1686, all revenue collected went for the immediate use, support, and security of New England.[11] That same day Andros sailed for America.

Surprisingly, Boston accorded the royal governor a friendly reception. In London Blathwayt viewed this as a triumph, so much so that he was moved to have it announced in the *Gazette*.[12] Andros had arrived on 20 December. Accompanied by Dudley and eight companies of provincial militia, Major John Richard's unit among them, he went promptly to the town house, where his commission was read and eight of the councilors sworn into office.

The first sign of trouble came over the Church of England. At the time Boston had three Congregational meeting houses, the First Church, the Second (or Old North) Church, and the Third (or Old South) Church, with James Allen, Increase Mather, and Samuel Willard as ministers. The governor lost no time inquiring about some accommodation in a meeting house for church services. The next day four men from each of the three congregations met at the home of James Allen of the First Church to consider what answer they would give. They agreed unanimously: in good conscience they could not consent to their meeting houses being used for worship according to the Book of Common Prayer. The next evening Increase Mather and Samuel Willard went to the home of Mrs. William Taylor—she had been born Rebecca Stoughton—where the governor was lodging, so to inform him. Andros did not *then* press the issue; he went to the town house to attend services.

Several weeks passed before Andros again raised the question. He sent Randolph to obtain the keys to the Third Church. Samuel Sewall and others of the congregation protested: the land and building belonged to the members, and they would not allow them to be used for Anglican services. Unconcerned, the governor prevailed on Goodman Needham, the sexton, to open the doors of the Old South Church.[13]

It was not all disharmony. From the outset of the new regime the Winthrop brothers were close to Andros. The very day the governor arrived in Boston, he had asked especially for Fitzjohn. Andros was a guest at the home of Wait Winthrop, where Samuel Sewall, a proprietor of the Narragansett lands, "thankfully acknowledged the protection and peace we enjoyed under his Excellencie's Government." Fitzjohn, another of the proprietors, hurried up to Boston to join the governor's council, and at the behest of Andros he wrote to John Allyn in Hartford urging the officials there to accept annexation to Massachusetts. The king greatly desired to promote the interest and prosperity of the people. He had granted an indulgence in matters of religion and would graciously protect them in all their civil enjoyments.

Fitzjohn found no material alteration in the judiciary; councilors would serve as judges for their former colonies. Andros had also appointed Dudley, William Stoughton, Thomas Hinckley of Plymouth, Wait Winthrop, Nathaniel Clark, and John Coggeshall as a standing committee to revise and to collate the laws. Those councilors who had formerly served in the legislatures had recommended continuing the tax of one penny in the pound, to be levied with the consent of the majority of the council, for the support of government. Ever pragmatic, Fitzjohn Winthrop assured his associates in Hartford that all matters would conduce to the growth and prosperity of the people and that the governor would readily allow such procedures in the courts as might be most for the ease and benefit of the populace in general.[14]

Security against foreign enemies was a matter of general welfare. With the fortifications and defenses of New England in poor condition, Andros needed to raise money. The merchants favored a tax on land, but Dudley, Stoughton, and others involved in large-scale land speculation hoped, so Randolph gleefully reported, to lay all "upon the trading party" and to have their lands assured them without confirmation from the governor. Quitrents they would not consider. Whatever the source of governmental revenue, the people thought it "hard" to have money raised without an assembly.

Before leaving London, Andros had reviewed the claims of the land speculators. Nothing they added after he arrived in Boston led him to support their titles. In the summer of 1687 he submitted an adverse report denying the title of the Atherton Associates to the Narragansett country and Richard Wharton's claim to a seignory in Maine. Nor did he accept the arguments of Stoughton, Dudley, and Wharton for a law confirming them in possession of other large tracts. As Andros saw the situation, all lands had reverted to the crown with the revocation of the charter. He required claimants to sue for new patents to confirm their titles and proposed to grant previously unpatented lands if the petitioners agreed to pay a quitrent of two shillings and sixpence per one hundred acres.[15]

By this course Andros lost the support of a critical element from the upper stratum of Massachusetts society.

The governor further alienated the local magnates who had hitherto cooperated with the royal regime by appointing outsiders, men who had come up from New York, such as John West and John Palmer, to offices in the dominion government. The vast expanse of the dominion also reduced the number of councilors who attended to public business at Boston. The members from Rhode Island and Plymouth disliked traveling at their own expense. Lack of remuneration and a growing disenchantment with Andros further caused attendance to decline.

Late in the summer of 1687 resistance to the regime flared up in a few outlying towns. Under the commission from the crown Andros with the advice and consent of the council had authority to levy taxes. The governor found the local county rates in Massachusetts unequal because of the disproportion of prices and values of livestock set in different communities in the colony. He proposed an alternative system: to have a specific sum of money, one thousand pounds, raised and to allow the council to assess quotas on the counties and the towns. On 23 August 1687 the town meeting of Ipswich in Essex County protested against the levying of a rate without the consent of an elected assembly. A week later Topsfield followed suit. Imposing taxes only by the authority of the governor and council infringed the liberties of the English subjects of the king and interfered with the laws of the land, enactments requiring that there were to be no taxes without the consent of the assembly.

John Wise and several others were brought to trial charged with contempt and high misdemeanors. One member of the council, John West, was alleged by Wise to have dismissed the claims of privileges under Magna Carta by contending that the colonists had no rights other than an exemption from being sold as slaves. By another version later put out, West had declared: "Mr. Wise[,] you have no more priviledges Left you yn not to be Sould for Slaves."[16]

That Wise and other saints in Massachusetts were claiming in 1687 the rights of Englishmen under Magna Carta was not without irony. For half a century, until but one year before, the statutes, laws, and taxes imposed in Massachusetts had been based on nothing more than the consent of the self-professed godly elect. Most of the adult men in the Puritan commonwealth had not enjoyed the rights of Englishmen. At the time, Andros himself made little of the episode in Essex County: several persons, chiefly in Ipswich, had raised disturbances about the payment of their rates, but had been tried, convicted, fined, and bound over to keep the peace. All was now quiet.[17]

After experiencing an initial sense of euphoria over the reception first given Andros in Boston, by the fall of 1687 officials in Whitehall were aware that all was not well with the royal regime in Massachusetts. Richard Wharton arrived in London to contest the report of Andros and West rejecting the claims of the land speculators to the Narragansett and Niantic countries. He also sought English capital and a patent from the crown for a speculating venture in mining and naval stores. By March Wharton had obtained the backing of Sir John Shorter, timber magnate and lord mayor of London, and of Daniel Coxe. Included in Wharton's new project were his brother-in-law Wait Winthrop, Nathaniel Higginson, John Pynchon, Elisha Hutchinson, and William Stoughton. The

Lords of Trade merely recommended that the crown come to no decision on a patent for mines without hearing from the governor and other concerned parties in New England. They further contended that any patents issued to the Atherton Associates for the Narragansett and Niantic lands ought not to prejudice the rights of other claimants. The speculators must also pay quitrents.[18]

Andros had formulated a comprehensive land policy for Massachusetts. He proposed to divide the land into ungranted and granted soil, with the former reverting from the defunct corporation to the crown and to be awarded to individuals by the new dominion government. Men able to present some evidence of ownership or of having been granted their lands under the previous charter administration would have to apply to the governor for confirmation of titles and pay an annual rent of two shillings and sixpence per hundred acres to be free of any further obligations. Quitrents had not previously been required in Massachusetts, although they had been imposed in royal colonies elsewhere. Andros and his predecessors as governors of New York had forced townsmen there holding titles from a New England colony to apply for confirmation. Prior success in New York might have encouraged Andros in Boston. To him, applying a system employed in the other royal colonies was a simple means of raising money, but to landowners of whatever religious or political persuasion, it imposed a new form of tax. Previously under the chartered government they had paid rates on real property.

In seeking to compel compliance, Andros ordered writs of intrusion against several prominent colonists, regardless of their political affiliation. Eventually about two hundred men acquiesced and applied for confirmatory patents from the provincial attorney general, James Graham, an Andros associate from New York. Samuel Shrimpton, a well-to-do Anglican merchant, determined to hold out, while Samuel Sewall, a Puritan, although he applied for a patent of confirmation, resolved to take the issue to London.[19] There the Reverend Increase Mather, the pastor of the North Church in Boston, later used the grievances of the landholders in a campaign undertaken against Andros with James II. But the emphasis Mather and his colleagues placed was on religion. The governor, so the complaints ran, was violating the Catholic king's declaration on freedom of religious conscience.

From the outset of his administration Andros had asked of the three Puritan congregations in Boston the use of one of their meeting houses for an hour or two each day so that Robert Ratcliffe might conduct Anglican services. Eventually the governor had his way. Over the protests of Sewall and others of the Third Church, the Anglicans met at their meeting house from eight to nine o'clock in the morning and for another hour in the afternoon. The arrangement seemed to have worked no hardship. On Sunday, 24 June 1688, the Anglican Communicants left the building at the prescribed hour, "so we have very convenient time," Sewall noted in his diary.[20] Nonetheless, the issue gave the opponents of the royal administration an additional grievance.

In opposing Andros, Increase Mather and Samuel Willard had hit upon the idea of charging him with violating the king's program for religious toleration: in supporting Anglicans and Quakers he was denying Congregationalism. They would take their complaints to the king. First the ministers in Boston and then the congregations approved a mission to London. Who would undertake the task? Mather, if his flock consented. As he himself related, "I sett my self with Fasting and prayer, to seek the Lord about it." On 10 December 1687: "I spent the day alone with God in my study, and prayed to him, that if Hee would not have me to go for England that then the brethren of the church might not consent, but that if God would have me to go, that then he would incline the Hearts of the Brethren accordingly, so should I know his mind." The propositon put so, how could Mather not go? Providence indeed must have sanctioned his mission, for the following day the members of the congregation of the North Church unanimously assented.[21]

The devil's disciple in the form of Edward Randolph, long the opponent of the orthodox Puritans, intervened. He sued Mather for slander, charging him with falsely accusing Randolph of putting Mather's name to a treasonous letter sent in 1683 to Dissenting English ministers in Amsterdam. But a jury in Boston returned a verdict in favor of Mather and ordered Randolph to pay the costs of the trial. He appealed to England, charging Mather, the Reverend Joshua Moody of Portsmouth, and Samuel Nowell with publicly affirming antimonarchial principles. Avoiding Randolph's informers, Mather on 7 April 1688 secretly took ship for England to present the case against Andros and his administration.[22]

Arriving in London late in May, Mather wasted no time. Within three weeks Blathwayt at the Plantation Office ruefully noted that Mather had already had "audiences of the Great ones" and was busily engaged in an effort to have the governor replaced. He hoped Andros "had taken such Root in His Ma[jes]tie's good opinion as to withstand some Shocks."[23] Such was not the case. What aided the campaign of the Puritan divine was the king's need for support for his policy of toleration. James II needed the Protestant Dissenters. Their leaders in London could make good use of the charges against the governor, whether substantiated or not. Samuel Nowell, the fire-eating Puritan divine, as well as two of the Narragansett proprietors, Elisha Hutchinson and Richard Wharton, were also then in England.

In London Mather had contacted Stephen Lobb, pastor of an independent congregation in Fetter Lane and a familiar figure in court once James II began wooing the Dissenters. Through Lobb, Mather met the king in the Long Gallery at Whitehall, where he presented the address subscribed by the leading Puritan ministers in New England thanking the monarch for his gracious declaration of indulgence. According to Mather's later account, on receiving this token James II assured Mather: "You shall have a Magna Carta" for freedom of religion. With the bishops strongly opposed to any abrogation of the privilges of the Anglicans under the test and penal laws, James II needed the support of both Protestant Dissenters and Roman Catholics. Even the Papists at court were courteous to Mather. Father Petrie, the king's confessor, supposedly was ready to concern himself on behalf of Mather, but the New Englander, suspicious of Catholics as "serpents," dared "not Trust him." Mather preferred to work through Protestants with influence at court—William Penn, Lobb, and the celebrated Presbyterian divine, Vincent Alsop.

Pressing the attack against the royal administration in Boston, Mather sought to link the king's policy on religion with the cause of the commonwealthmen in Massachusetts. On 1 June when he again saw James, he charged Andros with failing to comply with the king's declaration: some of the monarch's subjects, he claimed, had been fined and imprisoned because they had declined, out of scruple, to swear on the Book of Common Prayer. The governor had threatened, Mather alleged, to employ armed soldiers to prevent the ministers and their congregations from observing a day of thanksgiving to acknowledge God for his goodness in making James king. According to Mather, the monarch then declared himself ready to aid the New Englanders. Mather must submit his complaints in writing. The minister kissed the king's hand and took his leave.

A month later on 2 July in the royal closet Mather presented a petition and a memorial on behalf of New England. Lobb, who was also present, added a further argument in support of Mather's request: the king's showing kindness to New England would have a good influence on the Dissenters in England.[24]

That summer Mather, Samuel Nowell, and Elisha Hutchinson submitted additional petitions listing complaints against Andros and the Anglicans in Boston who had traduced the commonwealthmen as disloyal. Under the regime of the governor they had not been suffered to set aside days for prayer and thanksgiving, not even for the royal declaration for liberty of conscience. The service of the Church of England had been forced upon their meeting houses; punishment had been threatened upon anyone who gave money to maintain a Nonconformist minister; and lands belonging to Dissenters had been given to Anglicans. Whole towns lived in dread of having of their lands seized unless they gave money to have titles confirmed. The authorities in Massachusetts had told them they were no better than "slaves," with no title to property or right to English privileges. Some men had been imprisoned without cause, others forced to pay fines extorted by petty officials. Finally, the college built at Cambridge for the use of Congregationalists, it was commonly reported, would be taken from them and given to the Church of England.[25]

To save their fellows from these horrors, the three emissaries from New England on 10 August 1688 submitted to the Lords of Trade and Plantations a list of remedies. These called for the confirmation of titles to private land, with local agencies, town meetings, and courts to decide matters of common lands. Mather and his colleagues submitted further proposals relating to government, taxes, and religion. After a sum of five thousand pounds had been provided for the maintenance of government, no other impositions were to be laid or any law passed but by a general assembly, a body consisting of a governor, council, and elected deputies. As to religion, the men from Massachusetts proposed that liberty of conscience prevail, that no man be compelled to support a religion he did not profess, that each religion be left free to maintain itself, and that all meeting houses and the college remain with those who had established them. This petition the Lords of Trade referred to the crown attorney general, Thomas Powis, for report. But according to a marginal notation on the paper of proposals, the committee struck out those portions relating to the assembly and to churches.[26] This might have been the work of Robert Spencer, earl of Sunderland, the lord president of the council.[27]

In 1688 on the issue of religion in New England, the king himself intervened. He granted Mather another interview on 26 August. The Puritan divine reminded James of his prior assurance to confirm to his subjects in the colony their liberty and property according to the royal declaration. Mather asked that the matter be expedited: "If your Majesty shall be kind to New England," it would have "a good Influence on your affairs here." James enjoined Mather to trouble himself no further; he would take care that the matter be dealt with promptly.

Mather saw the Catholic monarch again on 16 October—as it turned out, for the last time. As Mather later recorded the meeting, the king "told me that property, liberty, and our Colledge" should "all be confirmed to us." According to a memorandum penned into the entry book for New England in the Plantation Office, the king was pleased to declare that he would grant the colonists full and free liberty of conscience and the exercise of religion. Harvard College was to be governed as formerly by a president and fellows. These terms he would confirm under the Great Seal. The day following the king's promise to Mather, the Lords of Trade and Plantations ordered the attorney general to examine the requests submitted by Mather and his colleagues and to compare them with the provisions of the commission and instructions James II had issued to Andros.[28]

All might yet be restored. In the face of rising discontent in England over the policy of religious toleration imposed by royal prerogative contrary to parliamentary statute, James II on 18 October was forced to issue a proclamation restoring to the municipal corporations in England the liberties held under their former charters. Although this proclamation did not mention the corporations in New England (the chartered provinces of Massachusetts Bay, Connecticut, and Rhode Island), Mather and his colleagues were eager so to interpret it.

The gentlemen from Boston had capitalized on James II's need to win the support of English Dissenters for his policy of religious toleration. But the king's concessions to the Nonconformists in England had not succeeded. Interpreted by Anglicans as an attack on the established Church of England and the mere forerunner for the introducton and eventual establishment of Roman Catholicism, James's actions by October 1688 had brought his crown into jeopardy.

A pervasive long-ingrained fear of Catholicism, coupled with the threat of war in Europe and in North America, created an explosive situation. In 1688 Governor Edmund Andros had traveled to Manhattan to annex New York and the two Jerseys to the Dominion of New England. On receiving disturbing news from the frontier, he left Captain Francis Nicholson, his deputy, and three councilors to administer affairs at Manhattan before hurrying north and east. The Indians, supported by the French from Canada, had opened hostilities. Across the Atlantic James II too faced the threat of foreign invasion. Angered by the policy of the Catholic monarch on religion, some among the king's subjects had issued an invitation to William of Orange to cross the North Sea and save England for Protestantism.

CHAPTER 5

The Revolution of 1688

EARLY IN HIS REIGN, James II, the Catholic king, had embarked on a program to emancipate his coreligionists, a dangerous course, for Cromwell and Charles II before him had failed to win fuller religious and political rights from parliaments dominated by zealots, either Puritan or Anglican.

When the Anglicans would not consent to the destruction of their political and ecclesiastical monopoly, James II had turned to the Dissenters. Expressing an aversion to persecution on religious grounds and his conviction of the need to allow his subjects liberty of conscience, the king had nonetheless pledged to maintain the clergy of the national church as by law established, but he had also declared that it was his will as the monarch that the execution of the penal laws in matters of religion be suspended and the religious test stipulated by Parliament no longer be required of men to hold office.

Although the reaction to the royal declaration of indulgence had been mixed, James pressed the campaign to secure repeal of the discriminatory laws. After a survey conducted by the king's agents revealed that prospective candidates for a new parliament generally would not vote for repeal, James inaugurated a systematic attack on the charters of boroughs to remodel the municipal corporations so as to insure that men favoring his views on toleration would be returned to Westminster. Late in April 1688 the king announced his intention of summoning a parliament, again issued his declaration of indulgence, and, the following month, ordered that it be read in all of the churches on two successive Sundays at the usual time of divine services. Few of the clergy complied. Seven bishops, among them William Sancroft, the primate of England, petitioned the king, protesting that the royal declaration to dispense with the laws had been founded on a power Parliament had declared illegal on three occasions in the past twenty-five years. For their pains the bishops were charged with seditious libel and committed to the Tower of London. Two days later, the queen, thought by many to be incapable of bearing children, was delivered of a son, a Catholic heir to the throne. Rumors went about that the infant was actually the son of a tiler, brought to the royal bed in a warming pan. On 29 June the bishops were tried, but acquitted; the judges in their summations to the jury had ruled that their petition was no libel.

That same day seven Anglican notables sent off an invitation to William of Orange, nephew of James II and husband to his older daughter Mary, to save England for the Protestant cause. Their allegiance to the Church of England was greater than their loyalty to the monarch who seemed to threaten the church. From the Netherlands William in October issued a declaration to justify the naval and military expedition he undertook across the North Sea on behalf of Protestantism. He favored such laws as Parliament might pass to bring together Anglicans and Protestant Dissenters and promised to protect all who lived peaceably from persecution because of religion. In the face of the projected invasion James II belatedly made concessions, ordering a restoration of the municipal charters forfeited earlier that year. Would the charters for the corporate colonies in America be included? The king's concessions were not enough. On 5 November William and the Dutch landed at Torbay. Many men flocked to his standard, among them Philip, Lord Wharton; Richard Coote, later earl of Bellomont; and the king's nephew, Edward Hyde, Lord Cornbury.

As James II procrastinated, support for him diminished; more and more men, fearing to end on the losing side, went to William's camp at Exeter. The king sent his queen and their infant son off to France. He himself stole away from London on the night of 11 December. Recognized and apprehended at the coast, he was brought back to London, but then saved William embarrassment by escaping to France, where he sought the protection of Louis XIV.

Who reigned in England and with what sanction? Following the flight of James II, on the advice of the peers, the prince of Orange summoned a convention Parliament to meet at Westminster. At the head of a provisional government he issued a proclamation authorizing all officials in the kingdom, except those who were communicants of the Church of Rome, to continue in office until further notice. After the convention Parliament had gathered, the Commons issued a declaration: the safety and welfare of the Protestant subjects were inconsistent with having a popish king on the throne. A majority in the House of Lords objected, however, to certain language employed by the lower house, that James in fleeing the country had "abdicated," thus creating a "vacancy" on the throne. By the terms of an agreement reached in conference, both houses of Parliament offered the crown to James's daughter Mary and a regency to William, her husband. The prince refused these terms. Parliament then offered the crown to William and Mary jointly, but accompanied the offer with a Declaration of Rights. By these conditions the new monarchs, proclaimed on 13 February 1689/9, must govern England and the dominions according to the laws of Parliament. What laws Parliament would propound for the national church and the Dissenters remained to be settled. Six bishops and four hundred priests of the Church of England would not go back on their oath to James Stuart, however, and refused to accept William and Mary as heads of the church. These nonjurors lost their ecclesiastical places.

The crisis over the church and the succession to the English throne became an element of a major international conflict when James with support from Louis XIV in March landed in Ireland. War with France broke out the next month. No small part of the decision of William to undertake the expedition to England had been to appropriate the financial, military, and naval resources of the kingdom for the benefit of a coalition he had formed against Bourbon France.

Two points critical to the reaction against James II both in England as well as in the American colonies proved difficult to resolve, the status of the corporate charters and the rights of Protestants dissenting from the national church. William had hoped to revise the laws so as to make almost all Protestants eligible for civil office. He and the ranking Whigs also desired an act for religious toleration to allow freedom of worship for Protestant Dissenters and an act of comprehension, a law to adapt the Anglican liturgy so as to encourage the great bulk of the Dissenters to enter the Church of England. The Act of Toleration passed in May 1689 was intended to apply to the relatively few Dissenters who would be left out of the national church once comprehension had been achieved. The law gave some relief to Nonconformists, but did not grant complete religious liberty or legal equality for their meeting places. It merely exempted them from some of the penalties of the Restoration ecclesiastical code and required those who desired to avail themselves of its privileges to take oaths of allegiance and to make a statutory declaration against Catholic doctrine. Nonconformity was still illegal; the law proscribing it remained, with only the exaction of penalties forbidden. Roman Catholics did not benefit even from this concession.

William and many men who had supported the Protestant revolution assumed that the great bulk of the Nonconformists would be comprehended in the Church of England once its liturgy was adapted to meet their objections. But when opposition within the Anglican Church doomed any bill for comprehension, the Dissenters remained as numerous as before and outside the national church.

The Test Act, passed in 1673, required any holder of civil office to repudiate the Catholic doctrine of transubstantiation and once a year to receive the sacrament according to the rites of the Church of England. Protestant Dissenters, if they wished to hold office under the crown, were forced to conform occasionally, that is, to take communion once a year at a parish church. This practice raised much resentment for many years.[1]

The restoration of civic liberties, the charters of the corporations "illegally" coerced by James II and his brother, also proved a vexing problem. On this issue the agents from Massachusetts actively lobbied with the new Parliament and monarchy.[2] Increase Mather was busily engaged at Whitehall and at Westminster with the Dissenter political interest. Early in January 1689 he contacted Sir Henry Ashurst, son of an influential London Nonconformist, son-in-law of the Presbyterian Lord Henry Paget, and brother-in-law of the Dissenter leader in the House of Commons, Paul Foley. Mather was also in touch with John Hampden and Gilbert Burnet, the latter a confidant of the prince of Orange. The elder statesman of English dissent was Philip, Fourth Baron Wharton.[3] Wharton himself conducted the Puritan divine from New England to an audience with William on 9 January 1688/9.

For weeks William, his advisers, and the politicians in Westminster heard only the arguments of Mather and his colleagues on the situation in New England. Nowell died in London, but the ranks of the Puritan lobby increased with the arrival of Samuel Sewall, the Boston merchant, and William Phips, an uneducated Maine fisherman whose good fortune in recovering a treasure trove from a sunken Spanish ship had won him a knighthood from James II.

The parliamentary road to secure the Puritan goal was slow and uncertain. When Sir Joseph Tredenham on 16 March 1688/9 moved in the House of Commons a resolution from the committee on grievances to bring in a bill restoring all corporations in England, Wales, and the dominions as they were at the restoration of the monarchy in May 1660, the Dissenters were able to add "and New England and other plantations." But the bill did not pass the House of Commons until the next session, and then it failed in the House of Lords. In committee the peers had agreed that the charters of the plantations should be considered separately from those of the corporations in England.[4]

An approach to the new court at Whitehall seemed the more certain way. Early in 1689 Mather had an interview with the prince, who at that time referred him to his private secretary and Lord Wharton's cousin, William Jephson. The connection proved most rewarding.

After assuming the government, the prince of Orange on 12 January 1688/9 had ordered a circular sent to all of the governors in the colonies informing them that the Lords and Commons of England and the aldermen and common council of London in convention had asked him to take the administration of public affairs into his care. All officials in the colonies, except Roman Catholics, were to continue in office pending orders from England. A copy of this notice was also drafted for Sir Edmund Andros, governor of the Dominion of New England, the official commissioned by James II to administer public affairs in the entire region in North America from Saint Croix to the Delaware. Andros never received this order continuing him in office. On the application of Mather and his protégé, Sir William Phips, the letter was stopped and ordered not sent. As Mather later expressed it: "This (if there had been nothing else) was worth my voyage for England."[5] Because of the intercession by Mather, Andros never received official notification of the change of government in England. Deprived of this critical information, Andros was vulnerable to specious charges made by his opponents in Massachusetts.

In London Mather now had to convince the ministers of state and the new king that Charles II and James II had illegally vacated the charter of Massachusetts Bay. From The Hague, Abraham Kick, an English minister with extensive connections in the international Puritan community, had already written to William to this effect.[6] On 16 February 1688/9 the king appointed a new committee of council for trade and plantations. It included the higher ranking ministers of state, among them the earl of Danby, the marquis of Halifax, and the two principal secretaries of state, the duke of Shrewsbury and the earl of Nottingham. The first order of business assigned to them was to prepare orders for proclaiming the king and queen in the colonies and for continuing all persons (except Catholics) in their offices. The committee was to meet on 18 February. The night before, Mather stopped in at Shrewsbury's office in Whitehall, where a clerk apprised him of the forthcoming meeting and advised him to attend with several "gentlemen," particularly Sir Henry Ashurst. The next day Phips and Mather presented a petition to the Plantation Board charging that the charters of the four corporations of New England, Massachusetts, Connecticut, Rhode Island, and Plymouth—in fact, the last had no charter—had been taken away illegally. They begged for the restoration of their ancient privileges and recognition of Simon Bradstreet, Thomas Hinckley, Robert Treat, and Walter Clarke as governors of the four New England corporations. The following day the council ordered the circular sent to the colonies for officials there to proclaim William and Mary. But the order to Andros was deferred until the matters of the New England charters could be reviewed.[7]

Because of the efforts of Mather, Phips, and Ashurst, Andros never received this order and consequently did not, before a coup overthrew him, proclaim William and Mary or take the oath to the new monarchs.

This failure served as an excuse for his opponents in Massachusetts to ovethrow him in the name of the Protestant cause.

Mather and Phips appeared before the Committee for Trade and Plantations again on 22 February to claim that the charters to the New England colonies had been illegally vacated. They now found themselves faced with a formidable opponent, Sir Robert Sawyer, the attorney general under Charles II who had prosecuted the writ against the charter of the Bay colony. Sawyer argued that the courts of King's Bench and Chancery had vacated the patent because the government at Boston had acted illegally, contrary to the terms of the charter. Yet without hearing any evidence from royal officials in New England in rebuttal to the charges of arbitrary administration by Andros, the Lords for Trade and Plantations made a major concession to Mather and Phips. They agreed to recall Andros and to recommend, a new establishment, a permanent arrangement to preserve the rights of the populace. In so reporting to the king, the committee made clear its central concerns: royal revenue in the colonies and the threat of invasion by the French.

The agents from Massachusetts lost on one significant point, however. Rather than restoring the old charter, the king in council on 26 February 1688/9 ordered a new charter drafted. For the immediate future it would appoint two commissioners to take over the administration of government in Boston. The Plantation Board planned to hear recommendations from merchants and New Englanders then resident in London as to men suitable to be named to the commission.[8]

Through the intervention of Lord Wharton, head of the Dissenter peers, Mather had an interview with the king on 14 March. He later recorded that although William professed that the New Englanders were "a good people," he feared that there had been "irregularities" in the government of the dominion. Despite a pledge by Wharton on behalf of the colonies to be "their Guarantee," the king would go no further than what had been decided the previous month, to recall Andros and to issue a new charter.[9]

Mather and the Dissenters in London did not have it all their own way. Men in London familiar with the events inducing the royal government to act against the independent-minded saints in New England were even then making their views known. Sir Robert Southwell twenty years before as clerk of the council had drafted reports on Massachusetts. He and his protégé, William Blathwayt, held office under the new monarchs. Southwell, now appointed to the Customs Board in London, was advising Nottingham, one of the principal secretaries of state. Late in March he warned against restoring to the New Englanders the "unsurped" privileges they had previously enjoyed. To reinstate the charters and to allow the proprietors, particularly those of East and West Jersey, their pretensions would confound the settlement of government in America. Those in London who supported the New Englanders with "such power and ardour," a clear reference to the Dissenter lobby, did not suspect the intention of the "republicans" who solicited them. Such was the influence of the Dissenters that no man dared open his mouth to the contrary for fear of being crushed. Blathwayt, who best knew the state of affairs in America, dared speak no more unless to the king himself, or to Danby or Nottingham. The ministers must discuss the matter fully before Parliament acted on the bill for restoring charters. The king ought to hear Blathwayt "nakedly expose the State of His Western Dominions" before the proceedings at Westminster "run too farr, and . . . the crown be irreparably damnify'd thereby."[10]

The bureaucratic veterans did not go unchallenged. On 18 April—it was a momentous day in Boston—the Privy Council directed Shrewsbury to solicit from those men then in London with the most considerable interest in the northern colonies the names of persons the king might appoint as governor and deputy governor.[11] William and the ministers of state evidently were contemplating retaining the dominion, but with an elected assembly. The New Englanders, Samuel Sewall and Increase Mather, continued to cultivate the Dissenter interest in Parliament and in London. They called on Lord Wharton; Sir Robert Harley, head of an old Dissenter family with long-standing interests in the overseas plantations; and Thomas Papillon, member of Parliament of Huguenot extraction with trading connections in Massachusetts. As Sewall put it to Papillon, in aiding the New England cause "you will be partner with God, Who is wont to be concerned in relieving the oppressed."[12]

To Danby, Halifax, and the other members of the Committee for Plantation Affairs, the critical issue was mundane, the military security of the northern colonies. On 26 April 1689 they concurred in the recall of Andros, but warned that the crown must quickly settle such a government in the region as would enable the English colonists by their united forces to oppose the French in Canada and in Nova Scotia and to carry out any further military ventures the king might require. Without such union the French might easily possess the dominion and trade of northern America. The need for an adequate arrangement for defense in the colonies transcended revolutionary politics. The Lords of Trade resolved to urge the king to move against the other provinces—Maryland, Pennsylvania, and Carolina—proprietaries who did not hold themselves subject to the king's immediate government or render to the crown any account of their proceedings. William III ought to take such measures as would better bind the proprietaries to the interests of the crown and place them in a better posture for defense. The new king seemed responsive.[13]

Events in America would outdistance decisions made in London; nor would the men in Whitehall be free to act without taking into account vested interests. On 6 May 1689 an order went out for persons in London, merchants, inhabitants of the colonies, and others concerned in the affairs of New England, New York, and East and West Jersey, to testify before the council on the proposal to send out a governor. Samuel Sewall traveled up to Hampton Court to attend the meeting, expecting to find Mather, but the New England divine was not there. He later pleaded a fever as his excuse, yet as Sewall noted, Mather had been that very day at the Exchange. Others spoke for the chartered colonies before the royal council. On behalf of the proprietors of New Jersey, Doctor Daniel Coxe asked for time, but Sir Robert Sawyer, the former attorney general who had prosecuted the writ against the Massachusetts charter, urged prompt action by the government. Instead, the council gave the spokesmen for the provincial corporations and proprietaries a week to show cause why the king should not appoint a governor general. In the interval they were to attend the crown law officers with copies of the grants and charters.

The colonial lobby in London received a setback with the sudden death of Richard Wharton, who had been zealously refuting the arguments of William Blathwayt. Undaunted, the New Englanders gathered the next day to plan their strategy, and on 18 May, by agreement, Increase Mather, Elisha Hutchinson, and Samuel Sewall along with two solicitors took coach for Hampton Court. But on arriving they found themselves dismissed "sine Die."[14] Sawyer, Blathwayt, and the old-line bureaucrats apparently had succeeded in having a decision delayed. They had presented a paper recapitulating the reasons for the writ against Massachusetts and the legal status of the other provinces brought into the dominion. Connecticut and Rhode Island presumably had surrendered their patents, while Plymouth had never received a charter from the crown of England. As to East and West Jersey, the power of government claimed by the proprietors was derived from the duke of York. Since James had not been sovereign at the time, his right to bestow such authority was doubtful. In the view of Lord Chief Justice Sir John Holt and others among the king's legal officers, the monarch now had the right to establish such government as he thought fit for the better protection of his subjects. As for the remaining proprietaries, it was for Parliament to consider whether or not to bring them to a closer dependence on the crown of England.[15]

The Protestant court at Whitehall, although opposed to provincial government without representative assemblies, seemed on the verge of continuing the program of closer control and unification undertaken during the reign of James II. Unknown to the ministers of state, dramatic events in Boston and the repercussions in New York and Saint Marys had already limited the alternatives open to them.

CHAPTER 6

Rebellion in New England

BOSTON IN THE SPRING OF 1689 was the key to the momentous events which determined the political configuration of English America for almost one hundred years. The causes, if not the circumstances, behind the overthrow of Sir Edmund Andros and the dissolution of the Dominion of New England were and remain not entirely clear, embellished in rhetoric and involving perhaps the deliberate destruction fo incriminating evidence. Was the fall of Andros the result of a mass, spontaneous uprising of a people united by a commitment to a common ideology and reacting to common fears, real or imagined, or was it the outcome of a carefully devised plan, conceived and executed by men disgruntled with their position in the dominion regime who appealed to the prejudices and apprehensions of an uninformed populace and unjustly charged those in authority with betraying Protestant society?[1]

Some evidence is lacking, apparently by design.[2] Much of what remains for an understanding of what occurred in Massachusetts in the spring of 1689 is partisan, ex parte accounts, one-sided propaganda put forth by those who assumed control and published to justify their charge that the governor was a Jacobite, perhaps even a Papist, ruling illegally and plotting with hostile Indians and the French against the Protestant inhabitants. Andros and his few supporters, for their part, seeking to clear themselves, charged that the coup was, not the result of a spontaneous, popular outpouring of sentiment, but rather a contrived effort by unscrupulous men seeking their own advantage.

The possible consequences of Puritan ideals or the charges the commonwealthmen leveled against the royal officials in New England essentially do not speak to the motives of the men who penned them, nor do they necessarily reflect what men believed as distinct from what they professed. Certain ideas—particularly in the later years of the seventeenth century, fear of Catholicism and dread of Papist plots—were familiar to almost all men in the English world, but were not professed, much less accepted by all within this community. Why did some men profess, others scoff at the charge of conspiracy by the royal officials? In

Massachusetts men were divided, not by different beliefs, but by the degree of proximity to the administration of Andros and in their mundane goals. Neither ideology, religious sentiment, nor abstract principles separated many of the men in Massachusetts who had found themselves on opposite sides during the quarter century following the restoration of monarchy.[3]

Royal government without the benefit of a representative assembly had come to Massachusetts in the spring of 1686. Initially it met no resistance. Some of the moderates who had held civil and militia commissions under the charter government took up appointive office under the crown. Others, Anglicans denied any political role under the commonwealth, had openly welcomed the royal commission. Men united by a common involvement in land speculation in New England—and some closely related by family—had dominated the council under Joseph Dudley. For the great bulk of the inhabitants the change in government had not altered their relations to the provincial regime. About two-thirds of the adult men in the Bay colony had had no voice in provincial affairs. Not having enough property or not having been admitted full members of the church, they were not eligible for freemanship in the corporation.

Once Andros arrived in Massachusetts at the end of 1686, he rigidly followed what he thought was the royal interest. By foolishly rewarding men he had known in New York with office in the dominion regime, he had alienated support. By insisting that the congregations in Boston make available one of their meeting houses for a few hours in the week for Anglican communicants, he had given the Congregational elders and the ministers an opportunity to claim that he was violating religious freedom. By insisting that men obtain confirmation of their titles to land and pay an annual quitrent or run the risk of having their lands given to others, he was threatening property and introducing a tax novel in New England, but not in America, and threatening all landholders, high and low, Puritans and those dissenting from Congregationalism. By enforcing the parliamentary navigation code he alienated those merchants who had hitherto accepted royal government. By rejecting the claims of the land speculators, no matter how correct his assessment of their pretensions, he further eroded his base of support. By 1688 there were relatively few prominent men with reason to support the governor in time of crisis.

To involve the rank and file, the ordinary townsmen in Boston and in the surrounding villages, the commonwealthmen needed more. They had to link Andros and his administration with a threat seemingly endangering all, one bringing into play deep-rooted emotions, the specter of Popery and invasion by the hated French and savage Indians.

Fear of Catholic plots was part of the cultural heritage of most

Englishmen in the later seventeenth century, but the tales of conspiracy circulating in Massachusetts during the early months of 1689 did not spring forth spontaneously as did Athena from the brow of Zeus or have a life of their own. Men must have propagated and disseminated these rumors.

Those leaders in the Bay colony dissatisfied with the royal regime early in 1689 were aware of several factors which served to undermine the governor. In Boston and elsewhere in New England it was appreciated that James II had promised Increase Mather that the crown would look into the charges of oppression made against Andros. Evidently a rumor was circulating that Sir Thomas Powis, the attorney general, had actually reported that the courts at Westminster had illegally vacated the charter. If so, the commission by which Andros governed was faulty. It was also known that James, in order to win support against the prince of Orange, then threatening to intervene in England, in October 1688 had issued a proclamation restoring the charters of the borough corporations. There was some talk in New England that this concession extended to the patents of the provincial corporations; if true, the governments in New England would revert to the status existing before the establishment of the council under Dudley and the formation of the Dominion of New England.[4]

In October 1688 James II had also sent word to his officers in America of the threatened invasion by the Dutch under William of Orange and had ordered them to resist any similar ingress into the colonies. On receiving these instructions, Andros, on 10 January 1688/9 had charged all officials within his jurisdiction to be vigilant. Because of Mather's work in London what Andros did not officially learn until it was much too late was that James had fled England, that William of Orange had assumed power at the behest of a convention Parliament, and that he and Mary had been proclaimed king and queen. Once before, in 1686, Bostonians had received word of the overthrow of James II and the crowning of a Protestant monarch, only to learn subsequently that the Whiggish news was false and that the supporters of the duke of Monmouth had paid with their lives for rebelling. Understandably, Andros would hesitate in 1689 to act merely on rumors.

Andros was under a heavy burden; he had to administer a vast expanse of territory. In 1688 he had traveled to Manhattan to incorporate New York and East and West Jersey into the dominion and later that year had hurried off to the eastern frontier on learning of the outbreak of hostilities with the Indians. On the way he had gathered up some eight hundred or so militia from Massachusetts to support the two hundred regulars stationed at Pemaquid on the far frontier. The rustic youths from the Massachusetts towns proved to have little stomach for a campaign; by March they were streaming back to their villages. Leaving Major Anthony Brockholes with orders to keep the two hundred troops in good order, Andros hurried by to Boston to gather support. He reached the dominion capital on 22 March. Vessels arriving from the West Indies had brought news of the landing of the prince of Orange at Torbay the previous November,[5] but because of the intervention of Increase Mather, Andros had not received orders from the prince to continue as governor or instructions to proclaim the Protestant monarchs. The failure to proclaim William and Mary allowed his opponents to charge that he intended to side with the deposed Catholic king and to betray New England to the barbarous Indians and the Catholic French from Canada.

As early as January several bizarre rumors were circulating. They did not come into being spontaneously or drift hither and yon as the leaves on the wind. Caleb Moody of Newberry testified that one Joseph Baylie of Newberry had given him a paper, one that Baylie claimed to have found on the road. Styled "New England alarmed to rise and be armed, let not Papist you charme," the mysterious document warned the people of the danger under an arbitrary government. A thousand men had been pressed out of Massachusetts and marched off to the east under pretense of destroying enemy Indians, although in truth not one hostile native had been killed. That same month Joseph Graves, his wife Mary, and John Rutter of Sudbury related a conversation they had had with Solomon Thomas, an Indian, who allegedly revealed the existence of a plot whereby the French, the Irish, and the Indians would come down in the spring to destroy Boston and other towns. Andros, so their tale went, had given the Indians a book, one better than the Bible, with a picture of the Savior, the Virgin Mary, and the twelve apostles. All men who did not turn to the governor's religion and accept this popish book would be destroyed. Purportedly, Andros had commanded the Indians, when they prayed, to call on the Virgin. When Graves and Rutter told their tale to Justice Bullivant—he was an Andros appointee—the magistrate concluded that a "parsell of felows had devised a parsell of lys and had fathered them on a pore Indean." Early in April Stephen Greenleaf and George Little recounted under oath before John Woodbridge, a justice of the peace, what they had heard from William Sargeant of Amesbury, who had lately been among the natives. The Indians were saying that the governor had agreed with several tribes, the Mohawks among them, to "come downe" upon the English. Andros had given them some money and clothing.[6]

On 4 April 1689 John Winslow arrived in Boston from the West Indies, bringing with him copies obtained in Nevis of the declaration issued by the prince of Orange when he had landed in England the previous fall. According to pamphlets later issued condemning the governor, Winslow refused to show the prince's declaration to Andros, fearing, he alleged, that Andros would suppress them. Andros had Winslow jailed, it was claimed, for bringing in treasonable libels, but not before copies of the declaration were circulated about the town. But for the intervention of Increase Mather in London, the ship carrying Winslow to Boston might have brought Andros official word of the change of government in England. More than two years before, erroneous information had arrived in Massachusetts of the overthrow of James II by the duke of Monmouth and the earl of Argyle—news joyously welcomed but later proved false. For Andros early in April 1689 to have commited himself merely on rumor might have proved fatal to him.

Force would now be employed against the royal governor. Several disgruntled seamen aboard the royal frigate *Rose* in Boston harbor, hearing the news of James II's flight to France, took the initiative. Led by Robert Small, the ship's carpenter, they deserted to the town, spreading the tale that John George, captain of the *Rose,* and Andros were plotting to set fire to Boston. Rumors of Papists setting fires had been commonplace in London for a generation.

With wild rumors circulating and men from the eastern frontier marching on Boston, the magistrates who had held office under the charter administration and some merchants assembled at the home of Cotton Mather. Thomas Danforth, the leading commonwealthman, later claimed this secret meeting was held, not to launch a revolution, but to forestall bloodshed, an appropriate statement for men seeking to avoid the charge of conspiring to overthrow the government. But given the speed and precision with which the principals involved in the events of 18 April acted, they had to have planned and coordinated matters.[7]

Shortly after sunrise on the morning of 18 April, rumors spread in the northern environs of Boston that men in the south end of the town were rising; residents in the south heard the same rumor of their fellows in the north. Captain John George of the *Rose* was quickly seized when he came ashore about eight o'clock. Responding to the beating of drums, about a thousand Bostonians rose in arms and formed themselves into companies. Hundreds of militiamen from the neighboring villages streamed into Boston "with suspicious alacrity." A group of armed men appeared before Wait Winthrop's house and "requested" that he take command. Protected only by a small detachment of fourteen soldiers— about two hundred regulars under Brockholes were off defending the frontier in eastern Maine—Andros and the other officials of the administration were hustled off to jail.

Fifteen men then set themselves up as a provisional council of safety. They represented almost all elements alienated by Andros during the thirty months of his regime. There was a nice balance; five of the council of safety, including Wait Winthrop, had served as councilors of the dominion; five had been magistrates under the charter; and five were merchants who had not held office. The revolutionary leadership chose the aged former governor Simon Bradstreet as president, with Wait Winthrop as commander of the militia.[8]

At noon on the day of the uprising the committee of safety at the town house issued *The Declaration of the Gentlemen, Merchants, and Inhabitants of Boston and the Country Adjacent.* A long, contentious document, replete with florid charges, it began with a reference calculated to stir the rank and file, the "horrid Popish Plot," wherein the bloody devotees of Rome had in their "Design and Prospect" nothing less than "the Extinction of the Protestant Religion." Then came an indictment in violent, exaggerated language of the regime under Andros. Toward the end there appeared a reference to the success of the "noble Undertaking of the Prince of Orange, to preserve the three Kingdoms [England, Ireland, and Scotland] from the horrible brinks of Popery and Slavery." Two weeks before, John Winslow had brought in news of the landing of William; the reference to the prince toward the end of the document might indicate that the body of the text was composed some time before Winslow arrived.[9]

When Simon Bradstreet sent off to William a brief account of the assumption of power by the council of safety, he maintained that the men of Massachusetts had merely followed the prince's own example in overthrowing tyranny and slavery. Proof of the charges against Andros would follow in good time, Bradstreet promised.[10]

In the ensuing weeks several anonymous pamphlets cataloging the charges against the dominion government appeared. For the most part they were based on *ex parte* affidavits gathered well after the alleged crimes occurred. When officials seized with Andros—Robert Ratcliffe, Edward Randolph, and John Palmer—were later shipped off to England, they issued denials, charging the insurgents with conspiring to seize power to gratify their personal ambitions.[11] Even while confined in jail in Boston, the dominion officials were able to send off lengthy justifications for their conduct to Whitehall.[12] But the men who had carried out the coup controlled public opinion in New England.

Of the twenty-four men imprisoned with Andros during the uprising, only four were New Englanders, the others military officers and officials appointed by the governor or the crown. Those responsible for their incarceration were united in opposition to the program followed by Andros, but not all wanted to return to government elected by the freemen under the old charter. The merchants Peter Sargeant and Samuel Shrimpton, men excluded from power under commonwealth rule, had seen the royal council under Joseph Dudley as a means for advancement, but they had not joined in the overthrow of the dominion to restore the charter regime. They now sought to eliminate an administration they could not control and one unsympathetic to their aims. To these men, a new charter was preferable.[13]

The last vestige of royal authority, limited as it was, soon disappeared when the revolutionary committee of safety sent a detachment of milita to Pemaquid to take possession of the fort held by Major Anthony Brockholes and Lieutenant James Weems. Short of supplies, the two officers could not hold the king's soldiers, "corrupted" as the troops were by the news brought in from Boston. The settlers in the region, menaced by several hundred Indians armed by the French, insisted that Weems remain in command of the fort, he being "no papist." Brockholes, a Roman Catholic, was carried off a prisoner to Boston. On 2 August, the Indians attacked the fort. The depleted garrison surrendered the next day.[14]

By the middle of July news of the coup had reached London. John Riggs, an emissary of Andros, had managed to slip away to Manhattan, where he took ship for England. Once in London, Riggs presented a long narrative of the events of April as well as copies of the declaration issued by the revolutionary junta explaining their actions and a petition to the crown from Andros. As the king's private secretary, William Jephson, related, the men in Whitehall, presented with differing accounts, were at a loss as to the status of government in New England. On 25 July, the king in council authorized an ambiguously addressed letter to be sent to those persons then preserving the peace and administering the laws in Massachusetts to continue in office and to send Andros and the other officials imprisoned with him by the first available ship to answer to the king for whatever charges had been made against them.[15]

Who preserved the peace and administered the laws in Massachusetts? The men who had overthrown Andros had acted from different motives. Under the old charter—vacated illegally, so the commonwealthmen held—8 May was the day set each year for elections. The commonwealth partisans on the committee of safety and Joshua Moody and James Allen of the First Church demanded that the council declare the charter of 1629 in effect and issue writs for an election. Only a minority of the adult men of the colony, those admitted to freemanship under the former patent (for the most part because of a religious qualification), would have been eligible to vote.

The demand to revive the old order split the revolutionary coalition of commonwealthmen, moderates, Congregationalists, merchants, and land speculators who had joined to sanction the overthrow of Andros. The more intransigent among the ministers publicly took the position that the charter came from God, not the king, that they were but nominal subjects of the monarch. This the commonwealthmen had enunciated even before the charter had been vacated. They had regarded Charles II as but their titular sovereign. Joshua Moody allegedly declared that the people need not wait until word came from London, where Increase Mather was appealing to William III to acknowlege the old patent. The charter was as valid now as it had been in 1660. Simon Bradstreet, the last governor elected under the old commonwealth era and a man willing to make some concession to monarchy, recommended to Allen and Moody that they exhort their congregations to obey the committee of safety. The two ministers took no notice. On a day set aside for public fasting, Allen took as his text the last three verses of Ezra, chapter 9: "Shall we break thy commandments again and intermarry with the people who practice these abominations?" Allen made clear his displeasure that some among the community of saints suffered their children to marry outside the pale. Moody, no less zealous, exhorted his congregation to stand to the liberty whereto God had called them, and he thanked the Lord for restoring their judges of old. No king, no power; no one in England had any authority over them more than the privileges of their charter would admit.[16] The secular leader of the commonwealth faction was Elisha Cooke, who had succeeded the former magistrate, Thomas Danforth, now sixty years of age and grown cautious. Cooke would prove no less zealous and rigid than Moody or Allen.

William Stoughton, also once a magistrate, but a moderate who had accepted office under Dudley in 1686, argued against having the former officials under the charter resume their stations. Massachusetts was a colony, and its inhabitants must await orders from the crown or run the risk of being accused of setting up a free state. In holding this view Stoughton and the other moderates among the Congregationalists agreed with certain recent arrivals, mostly Anglican merchants, such as Nicholas Page and John Nelson, who opposed a revival of the charter government and favored a royal administration, one that they might control. The two groups had similar economic interests, and their families, in some cases, had intermarried.

The issue of a successor government came to a head when sixty-six delegates elected from several towns met in Boston on 10 May. They agreed to request Bradstreet and Danforth, as well as the assistants and representatives elected in May 1686, to assume the government and to enforce the laws then existing. The council of safety rejected this resolution on the ground that many of the towns had not sent delegates to the convention. Another convention was called for 22 May. The elections for delegates were probably the most permissive ever held in Massachusetts to that time, for few of the villages restricted participation to members of the old provincial corporation, that is, the men who, for the most part, were full members of some Congregational church.

Returns ran strongly in favor of resuming the old charter government, but with one important qualification, one critical to the concept of the Puritan commonwealth: freemanship must not be limited to church membership. What had mattered in Puritan Massachusetts, what had distinguished the Zion in the wilderness, was not the formal institutional arrangement of the provincial government, the institutions set down in the charter for a joint-stock company by the crown of England but the religious test required of the great bulk of men to qualify for freemanship. The sentiment expressed in the open voting for the convention late in May constituted an emphatic rebuttal of the old standard.

A compromise of sorts between the majority in the convention and the members of the council of safety was effected on 24 May. The *form* of government as prescribed in the charter would prevail. The members of the council who had previously held office as magistrates agreed to serve again; those who had not would withdraw. The convention would then elect a sufficient number to bring the total on the governor's board of assistance up to twenty, the number specified in the charter. But aware of their vulnerable position, the members of the committee of safety declared that they did not intend to invoke the charter. They would call themselves the council of safety of the people and serve only until word came from London. They then sent off addresses to William and Mary congratulating them on their accession and begging them to sanction the take-over in Boston.[17]

From the debates held in Boston in the spring of 1689, it was evident the old political divisions still prevailed among the populace. The schism extending back over a generation reflected a division of opinion between men who regarded Massachusetts as virtually an independent commonwealth and those who for various reasons—expediency, the desire for political advancement, or economic gain—would acknowledge some degree of dependence on the crown of England. The strength of the former view was evident in the decision made by the convention to send Elisha Cooke and Thomas Oakes to London to join Increase Mather and Sir Henry Ashurst. A sharp disagreement between Mather and the emissaries of the convention over whether to insist on the crown's recognizing the old charter or to accept a new, but restrictive, patent further reflected this basic disagreement in Massachusetts.[18]

That the old mentality was still strong among the delegates from the rural towns in Massachusetts was evidenced in the resolution the convention adopted relating to Andros, Joseph Dudley, and Edward Randolph. To revolt was not the right of all men. Citing the Old Testament, the majority of the delegates resolved that, if any man conspired or attempted traitorously or perfidiously to alter and subvert fundamentally the form of government, he was to be put to death. Andros they declared guilty of receiving and executing an illegal commission and of exercising arbitrary and despotic powers contrary to the fundamental laws of England and Massachusetts. They also returned indictments against Randolph, Dudley, John Palmer, John West, and James Graham.[19] Held without bail in the common jail in Boston, Randolph referred sarcastically to the town as New Algiers, thus comparing Massachusetts justice, not with the fundamental laws of England, but with Moorish despotism.

Confined as he was, Randolph placed some hope in addresses from loyalists in New England sent to the king and queen. By these remonstrances the ministers of state in Whitehall would no longer be deluded by the "lies" put forth by the insurgents that the rebellion had been the act of the people. Rather, it had been the work of a clique: a few ministers, Charles Morton of Charleston, Moody, Allen, young Cotton Mather, the Anabaptist preacher William Milborne, some members of their congregations, and a number of former magistrates.[20]

Some men in New England mourned the loss of unity the dominion had offered against the French and Indians. New England, once united and thus formidable, had now fallen apart into several "little independent kingdoms." From Newport Francis Brinley complained of the lack of a proper, settled government. If the old regime returned, there would be no living in Rhode Island for "sober men." To be governed by officials locally elected would be near "anarchy." From Boston, Benjamin Davis reported all in confusion. He loved the Bay colony as much as any of the men who had overthrown Andros, but he hated rebellion. The overthrow of the royal governor had accomplished little good. Indeed, since the recall of the provincial militia by the insurgent government, the Indians had slaughtered many settlers and destroyed several villages in Maine and along the Piscataqua. Pemaquid had fallen, and the alarm sounded as far south as Marblehead. Few men had turned out in response to the call by the weak provisional government.

Seeking to justify the insurgent administration to the crown, Simon Bradstreet dismissed such complaints as coming from malcontents, "strangers" who had come to Massachusetts only after the imposition of the Andros regime and who were trying to create confusion by false reports. Yet Bradstreet too admitted the Indians, doubtless incited by the French, were carrying their depredations into Maine and New Hampshire and raiding beyond the Merrimack. Ever the Puritan, Bradstreet assured the Lords of Trade in Whitehall that it was for God to give the colonists success, although as yet He had not blessed their efforts. The entire expense of defending New England had been borne by a few private persons, there being no public treasury. So extensive were the Indian raids that some men feared that the English might abandon the entire region east of the Piscataqua.[21]

The unity of New England, artificially imposed under the dominion, had collapsed. In the provinces annexed to the royal colony, the former officeholders, once they learned of the incarceration of Andros, were inclined to take up their old positions. Even before the overthrow of Andros, there had been talk in Hartford that the provincial regimes would revert to their former status by reason of the proclamation issued by James II in October 1688 restoring the charters of the corporations in England. But the information supplied by Richard Wharton from London had been vague. Nor was the situation entirely clear once Andros fell, for the officials of the former corporations in Connecticut and Rhode Island were in a different position from their counterparts in Massachusetts. The royal courts at Westminster had vacated the patent of the Bay colony; they had taken no action on the writs sued out against the charters of Connecticut and Rhode Island. James II and his advisers had assumed on the basis of ambiguously worded letters from Providence and Hartford that the provincial officials had voluntarily accepted annexation to the royal Dominion of New England.

In the spring of 1689, when word came to Hartford of the jailing of Andros, Robert Treat and the majority of the justices of the counties appointed by the royal governor proposed to hold a court of election under the provisions of the charter of 1662. They met little resistance. The opposition offered by Gershom Bulkeley, although heated and pointed, was futile. The eldest son of a minister of Concord, Massachusetts, Bulkeley had graduated from Harvard College in 1655 and moved to Connecticut, where he had served as a minister for a time before devoting himself to medicine and then law. He was among the men Andros had appointed to the commission of peace. With a few others from the region about New London, such as William Rosewell and Edward Palmes, opponents of the Winthrops, he protested against the fact that Treat and the other former officials of the corporation resumed their offices and established the old charter government. Legally, they could not hold a court of election; they were not a body politic, no longer the Governor and Company of Connecticut. To hold an election they must first be restored to their former capacity by the crown. What Treat and his colleagues proposed in the spring of 1689, Bulkeley argued, was rebellion and treason. His arguments went for naught. Bulkeley had to content himself with sending his protest to Whitehall and later printing an attack against the new regime in Connecticut, *Will and Doom; or, The Miseries of Connecticut by and under an Usurped Arbitrary Power*.[22]

Late that spring Treat and his colleagues sent off an address to William III asking for confirmation of the charter. William Whiting, a former resident of the colony but now a merchant in London, to whom they dispatched the petition, thought it contained several objectionable passages. On the advice of counsel he refused to present the document and declined further to act as agent. He was too old to play the courtier; he could not follow business as closely as once he had. More important, perhaps, the colony still owed him money, about five or six pounds, which he had dispersed from his own funds in previously soliciting their affairs. Whiting had one piece of heartening news. In England there existed no record either of a surrender or a court judgment against the charter. This the former attorney general for the crown, Sir Robert Sawyer, and William Blathwayt, clerk for the Committee for Plantation Affairs, acknowledged. The patent issued in 1662 was therefore still valid, Whiting presumed. Although he would not act for the colony in any official capacity, he recommended Sir Henry Ashurst, already employed by Massachusetts, to act on its behalf.[23]

Rather than follow the advice of Whiting, officials in Hartford solicited another merchant of London, James Porter, to plead their cause. To cover expenses they sent him a bill of exchange for all of thirty-eight pounds. Porter declined the post. But Ashurst, Mather, and the two emissaries from the convention in Boston, Cooke and Oakes, intervened. A joint application by the New England colonies rather than separate solicitations seemed the more promising approach. As Whiting had reported, there was no record of a surrender of the charter or of a judgment against the patent. The men of Connecticut ought not to be too hasty with their money; it would go but a little way in Whitehall. The Bostonians hitherto had been at great expense supporting their agents in London to attend the court night and day, but with no success to date.[24]

The men of the Plymouth colony had followed much the same course as those of Connecticut. The former officials met following the overthrow of Andros, and, on 6 June 1689, the General Court adopted an address signed by Thomas Hinckley to the king and queen. As officials of the oldest province in New England, they asked for confirmation of their former rights and liberties.[25] What these were was impossible to say, for the various towns making up the confederation of Plymouth had never received a charter from the English crown to exercise the powers of government. At best they had a patent from an English corporation chartered by James I, but long since defunct, to hold land. This patent from the Council of Plymouth, Sir Henry Ashurst would later confuse with a patent from the crown.

Matters had not gone as smoothly in Rhode Island as in Plymouth and Connecticut. For some years the colony had been the scene of strife between various sectarians and townsmen contesting for lands. Within days of the jailing of Andros some leaders in Newport argued that since there was no government under the dominion and the charter of 1663 had not been legally rescinded, they might lawfully apply the patent issued by Charles II. Shortly thereafter a convention of forty men resolved that the former officials, including Walter Clarke, the governor, and John Coggeshall, his deputy, should take up their offices. But Clarke, a Quaker, would not act. His office would require him to prosecute the war against the French and Indians. It was Coggeshall who dispatched a petition to William III asking for confirmation of the colony's patent.

Consensus was lacking. Some men opposed reestablishing the corporate government; a few charged that the people in general were ignorant of the decision to impose the old order; others thought that most of the inhabitants were easily led into compliance or took the opportunity to advance their own interests by settling on disputed lands. The Narragansett country again became a bone of contention.

For some time government in Rhode Island was in disarray. Attendance by delegates from the towns to General Assembly declined; some towns refused to take part in the restoration of the chartered government. The collection of taxes fell off. A small but influential group of men actively sought the intervention of the crown. One of them was Francis Brinley, an Englishman who had come to America at an early age, settled in Newport, and won election to the board of assistants. Following the coup in Boston, he complained to Wait Winthrop, another of the Naragansett proprietors: "Unles some divine providence or human power releive us, nothing appears but ruine and confusion, property and priviledge (so much talkt of) will be destroyed, and all things else set up that may make a people miserable." Brinley would prefer a just and easy government, whatever form it took, but "an oppressive government is to be preferrd before . . . anarchy." He prayed Winthrop in Boston not to make these sentiments public, "for we, as in Bedlam, are Crazy braind."[26]

Edmund Andros, by unswervingly following what he deemed the interests of the crown in New England, had alienated almost all of the prominent elements in Massachusetts who might have supported the dominion and by his failure—understandable enough in the circumstances—to proclaim the Protestant monarchs had provided those opposed to the new regime a rationalization by which to arouse long-standing fears and deep-seated emotions among the rank and file. The coup carried out in April in Massachusetts led to the collapse of the dominion in New England, the overthrow of prerogative government by officials holding only the commissions of the monarch in London, and the revival of separate local jurisdictions in Boston, Providence, Hartford, and Plymouth.

But beyond this, it was still not clear who would govern and under what conditions. Those who had governed before Andros now had no mandate from either the Protestant monarchy or the populace of Rhode Island, Connecticut, Massachusetts, or New Plymouth. In New England some men feared the assumption of power by an unstable element and condemned authority held by intemperate extremists. There were reports of "Crazy brained" men elsewhere in America, and tales of inhabitants of New York who ran like "madmen" through the streets of Manhattan, where a "hot-brained" captain of militia and his followers had seized the reins of government.

CHAPTER 7

New York, 1689: Riot and Insurrection

IN SEVENTEENTH-CENTURY AMERICA social disruption and political up-heaval were latent, inherent in a situation of ethnic pluralism, social fluidity, fragmented political authority, and institutional immaturity. Their realization depended on events, often fortuitous, and the mistakes and weakness of men. The overthrow of the Andros administration in Boston in April 1689 touched off a sharp reaction in the Hudson River and Long Island communities and set the stage for a generation of bitter animosities.

With the proprietary provinces of East and West Jersey, New York had been annexed to the Dominion of New England less than a year before the uprising in Boston. The representative assembly—an institution coerced from the duke of York by men excluded from the higher proprietary offices—had ceased to exist. When Andros had left New York in the fall of 1688 to organize the defense of the eastern frontier, he had left Captain Francis Nicholson, the deputy governor of the dominion, and three councilors in charge at Manhattan. Nicholson, Nicholas Bayard, Frederick Philipse, and Stephanus Van Cortlandt were hardly adequate to preside over a province thinly populated, commercially underdeveloped, and rent by ethnic, class, and geographical divisions.

Military defense had long been a problem for New York. For years officials in Manhattan had called for outside support, for men and money from the neighboring Puritan colonies. Little aid had come from New England, but hitherto the numerous warriors of the Iroquois confederation, supplied and armed by the Dutch and English merchants at Albany, had provided a bulwark, raiding French lines of communication and attacking the northern and western tribes allied with the Canadians.

In the summer of 1685 a new governor had arrived at Quebec. Within two years Jacques Brisay, marquis de Denonville, had launched a well-organized campaign against the Seneca, the most populous of the Five Nations, had blocked the attempts of the merchants of Albany to penetrate the western trade, and had forced the Iroquois to accept a truce. Denonville was not content. Convinced that French Canada would never be safe from the menance posed by the Five Nations until the English who armed them were removed from Albany and Manhattan, he conceived a bold plan. If Louis XIV could not buy New York, the French must take it by force. In the fall of 1688 he sent Louis-Hector, chevalier de Callières to Versailles to present his plan for a campaign: an overland invasion through the Indian country by fifteen hundred troops to take Albany and a seaborne attack on Manhattan to capture New York City.

But the French court took no action until war broke out with England in the spring of 1689 and then only accepted a modified, reduced version of Denonville's proposal: to dispatch nine hundred men from Montreal first against Albany and then Manhattan, where two frigates of the French navy would join in the final assault. But Louis XIV's ships did not leave La Rochelle until 23 July 1689, and running into strong head-winds, they did not arrive at Quebec until 12 October, two months past due and too late for a campaign that year against the English.[1]

In the spring of 1689, well before the French force even left Europe for Canada, rumors circulated among the English and Dutch at Manhattan of a French invasion in conjunction with an Indian attack. Ironically, it was the French settlers about Montreal who felt the fury of savage war when some eighteen hundred Iroquois launched a surprise assault on Lachine.

Garbled versions of the secret plan Denonville entrusted to Callières might, however improbable, have been carried by Indians or traders from Montreal to Albany and then have been passed down to Manhattan. Here dissidents and opponents of the government linked these rumors of an invasion with an alleged conspiracy by English Catholics and officials of the dominion against the Protestant inhabitants.

By 1688 Englishmen on both sides of the Atlantic were familiar enough with tales of plots and conspiracies, some a century old and embellished with a common motif of fires, invasion by the forces of a Catholic monarch (whether Philip II of Spain or Louis XIV of France), and subversion by English Papists. Many men could remember the Great Fire of London less than a generation before, alleged to have been set by Catholics. As late as 1679, during the hysteria of the Popish Plot, rumor had it that the Papists had set fires in London. One Stubbs, when arrested, had implicated a priest named Guilford, who, he claimed, had told him the king would be killed so that a Catholic would succeed to the throne and England would be invaded by six thousand French soldiers.[2] The duke of York had converted to Catholicism in 1669, a fact well known. Tales of conspiracy by foreigners and Catholics were familiar to all, but were not accepted by all in America during the crisis in 1689. Some men rejected such tales as politically inspired by ambitious malcontents.

The rumors circulating in the spring of 1689 in America had a familiar ring to them. Those who passed them about had something to gain by branding their opponents as conspirators seeking to subvert the true religion and deliver the Protestant subjects into the hands of savage, brutal enemies. The ideology of anti-Catholicism and conspiracy in government served the interests of those who adopted it, but the rhetoric in turn may have captured some psychologically disposed who employed it. Such a man was Jacob Leisler. He, Abraham De Peyster, Johannes De Bruyn, Gabriel Minvielle, Charles Lodowyck, and Nicholas Stuyvesant commanded the militia companies making up the city regiment under Nicholas Bayard. Leisler was a man rigid in his judgments and inflexible in his behavior. He was often irrationally suspicious and distrustful, believing himself persecuted. He may have been suffering from paranoia. Leisler did not merely identify Catholics as conspirators, but in his outbursts would turn on men who had once supported him, but who had disagreed later with his actions. Such men too he called Papists.[3]

Among those Leisler resented were the proprietary and royal officials of New York. Only a few residents of the colony, protégés of the governor, had held high office. Some of the English placeholders had gone to Boston when New York was brought within the Dominion of New England. Nicholas Bayard, Frederick Philipse, and Stephanus Van Cortlandt, appointed to the council at Manhattan, were of the most prominent families, men who had risen and successfully made the transition from Dutch to English rule. In addition to serving on the provincial council, Van Cortlandt was mayor of New York; his brother-in-law, Peter Schuyler, was the leading official of Albany. For men of somewhat lesser rank and wealth the legislative assembly had offered a path for advancement, but by the commission given Andros this avenue had been lost.

Differing traditions, geography, and opposing economic interests also increased the potential for strife. The English in the towns on Long Island originally had settled under the jurisdiction of the Puritan colonies of southern New England. They had never completely accepted incorporation into New York, preferring government under Connecticut. They resented the commercial privileges the proprietary and royal officials afforded New York City in an attempt to stimulate and channel the export trade of the colony. Settlers across the bay in East Jersey also resented the efforts of the governors and merchants at Manhattan to restrict and channel their trade.

There was relatively little support for the regime established in Manhattan by Sir Edmund Andros when rumors of the dramatic developments in England and in Boston reached New York. The turbulent events of that spring and of the months following further widened the schism in

New York society. Both sides, proponents and opponents of the regime, charged the other with treason and violence.[4]

Nicholson and the councilors at Manhattan were under the same handicap as Andros in Boston; because of the machinations of Increase Mather in London, the officers of the dominion had not been on the list of officers receiving official news of the accession of the Protestant monarchs and orders from William III. What they did know for certain was that but a few years before when men had supported or acknowledged the duke of Monmouth and his pretensions as the Protestant claimant to the English throne, they had suffered the full penalty for treason. With the news of a projected landing in England by Dutch forces under William of Orange, James II had ordered all officials to be vigilant and to repel any invaders from the English dominions. On three previous occasions in the third quarter of the seventeenth century they had been at war with the Dutch.

In the spring of 1689 travelers arriving from the West Indies brought to the Delaware, Chesapeake, and Hudson settlements rumors of the landing of the Prince of Orange. As Van Cortlandt related the dilemma of the councilors at Manhattan, they dared not make the news public. On 26 April Nicholson and his colleagues learned that insurgents in Boston had seized Andros and overthrown the dominion. Next came word of war with France. The lieutenant governor and the councilors then agreed to summon the aldermen of the city and the officers of the local militia and to fortify the town. Bayard, colonel of the regiment, assigned some units of the militia of Manhattan to guard Fort James. The council then sent off letters to the justices of the peace and officers of the militia of the outlying counties and to Andrew Hamilton, the last deputy for the proprietors of East Jersey.[5]

These actions were hardly the measures of men preparing to betray the colony.

New Englanders from the towns in Suffolk County on Long Island provoked a crisis. On 3 May they issued a declaration similar in language to that put out by the insurrectionists at Boston complaining of heavy burdens imposed by an arbitrary power. Officers of the militia companies of Southampton, Easthampton, and Huntington demanded that the fort at Manhattan be placed in the care of men whom they could trust.[6] Armed men from Suffolk, Queens, and Kings counties who had served on the expedition sent by Andros to support Albany the previous year now gathered at Jamaica to demand pay. Through early May rumors circulated of an impending invasion by a thousand French soldiers accompanied by hordes of Indians. Nicholson was forced to send off a message to Albany denying as false the story that he had made an agreement with the French to cut off the Dutch and English inhabitants. Another rumor had it that one hundred Irishmen and other Catholics, hunted out of Boston, were now in the vicinity. According to still another tale bruited about, some among the small garrison at Fort James on Manhattan were Papists. News then arrived that there were Catholics gathered on Staten Island, threatening to cut the throats of the farmers and to burn New York. Bayard lent his boat to the more credulous so that they might cross over to see for themselves the absurdity of these rumors.[7]

By the middle of May the militia of Suffolk, Queens, and Westchester were massed at Jamaica, only fourteen miles from Manhattan. Fuel to fan the inflamed imaginations of the rustics came in the form of a rumor that Andros had joined forces with the French. With Nicholson and the councilors in need of money to fortify the city, several of the merchants began to dispute the imposition of customs duties as illegal. Such tactics had been employed successfully eight years before to force the proprietor to approve of an assembly. When Matthew Plowman, the Roman Catholic collector, would not submit his accounts, the councilors appointed a board of auditors. The officials of the dominion were losing control, however. On the arrival of John Riggs, the ensign who had served with Andros and was then on his way to London, Nicholson and the councilors gave him an account of the situation to carry to Whitehall.[8]

The crisis on Manhattan came to a head on the evening of 30 May in a dispute over control of the fort. Hendrick Cuyler, a lieutenant in the company of militia commanded by Abraham De Peyster, was in charge of the watch that evening. He ordered his corporal, Hendrick Jacobse, to post a sentry at the sally port. Nicholson, his authority challenged, then sent for Cuyler, who arrived at the deputy governor's room accompanied by the corporal. When asked what he was doing there, Jacobse answered that he was present to act as interpreter for the lieutenant. As the story was later told, Nicholson drove him out of the room. Cuyler subsequently alleged that Nicholson exclaimed: "There were so many rogues in ye Towne that he was not Sure his Life nor to walk ye Streets and that . . . Before it should longer be this manner he would sett ye towne on fyre."

Had Cuyler understood rightly? He had such a poor command of the English language that he had needed an interpreter to deal with Nicholson, and the interpreter was not then in the room. The insurgent militia officers made much of this alleged threat. It was incorporated into a manifesto and printed.[9] Cuyler and De Peyster quickly spread word of the threat they claimed Nicholson had made. Soon the air was filled with the noise of beating drums, and the town with milling men in arms. Some militia gathered at the home of Captain Jacob Leisler. Others under Sergeant William Churcher flocked to the house of William Merrit, where the city magistrates had gathered, demanding the keys to the fort. On the advice of the civil officials, Nicholson complied. Citing the threat purportedly made by the lieutenant governor, the militia captains, in the name of the inhabitants and the soldiers, took possession of the fort.

In effect, the officials of the dominion had capitulated. The populace of Manhattan was kept in a state of anxiety when two of the captains of the city militia, Lodowyck and Leisler, reported that four or five vessels had been seen within Sandy Hook. Believing the ships to be French vessels, some men were ready to fall on the councilors. Leisler and the militia officers controlling the town closely interrogated all men who entered Manhattan, intercepted all letters, and read all documents intended for Nicholson and the councilors.

One of the ships arriving on 3 June was a sloop from Barbados. Churcher and a file of musketeers boarded her and took off a passenger, one John Dischington, to the fort, where Leisler demanded he hand over the papers he carried. The hapless Dischington gave up several printed newsheets, among them a *Gazette* published in London containing the proclamation of William III. Two days passed before Leisler and Lodowyck allowed Dischington to deliver the papers to Nicholson.[10]

With the situation out of control—Van Cortlandt and Bayard to appease the more zealous were even forced to obtain a certificate from the consistory of the Reformed Church in the town that they were faithful communicants—Nicholson as early as 6 June decided he had best leave for England to give the administration an account of events. He departed New York City about 10 June, but did not take ship for England until 24 June.

The decision by Nicholson, a Protestant who held a royal commission as deputy governor of the dominion, to leave New York was a critical mistake. It allowed Leisler and the other insurgents to claim for themselves the de facto government. They threatened to clap Van Cortlandt, Bayard, and Philipse, the councilors under the commission for the dominion, into jail—Nicholson too, if they would lay hands on him. The lieutenant governor, "altho a pretended" Protestant, they charged, countenanced "the Popish party"; refused to evict Matthew Plowman from the local customs house and the king's soldiers, "being most Papists," from the fort; and secretly entertained several soldiers, "wholly strangers in the Towne, being some Irish."[11]

A struggle then ensued between the two sides for the mantle of legitimacy. Two emissaries from Connecticut, Nathan Gold (or Gould) and James Fitch, brought in printed orders from England to have the king and queen proclaimed. In a heated exchange, Leisler upbraided Van Cortlandt, calling him a traitor and a papist and the other officials of the dominion in New York "Popish Doggs & Divells." Some men threatened with physical assault fled the city. But on 24 June William Merrit delivered to Van Cortlandt a printed copy of the declaration of William and Mary dated 14 February confirming in office all Protestants who had held their positions on 1 December 1688. Acting on this order the councilors of the dominion regime discharged the Catholic Matthew Plowman as collector of customs.

Any authorization or sanction from the Protestant monarchs for Van Cortlandt, Bayard, and Philipse and the aldermen of the city directly threatened the pretensions of the insurgents. On 25 June Leisler and two officers of his militia company, Joost Stoll (a dramshop-keeper) and Jan Meyer, with about twenty armed men appeared at the customs house, where Leisler delivered a pronouncement: the provincial councilors and municipal officials had no authority. They were all "Roages, Rascalls, and Divells," and one of them, Nicholas Bayard, "Popishly affected." During the course of a long argument Leisler physically attacked Bayard, and Stoll laid violent hands on Robert Wenham. When Wenham demanded of Leisler by what authority he questioned the interim commissioners of the customs, Leisler allegedly replied his authority was by the choice of the people of his company of militia.

Menaced by men brandishing swords, daggers, and cudgels, Bayard ran to a neighboring house, but when the enraged militiamen began pounding on the door and threatening the occupants with fire and sword, Bayard escaped and then fled the city. The insurgents now set up a cry of treason; they had discovered a plot to kill the Protestant leaders. Throughout the town, drums beat out an alarm. Van Cortlandt would not leave his house for two days. When he finally ventured out to hold a mayor's court, Leisler sent Paulus Richards to warn him that "the people would hale the Magistrates by the leggs from the Town Hall." The municipal officials then confessed to Van Cortlandt that they would not risk being abused and beaten. To save face they resolved to adjourn their court for a month in the hope that the fury of the mob would have abated.[12]

To lay some claim to wider support, the insurgent leaders issued a call for the inhabitants of the other towns to send delegates to a convention to be held on 26 June. Significantly, the townsmen of Suffolk County on Long Island who had triggered the revolt against the officials of the dominion were little inclined to support the insurgents and the Dutch residents of New York City. They preferred the jurisdiction of Connecticut. Some villages refused to participate in the convention, and among those taking part in other towns, the selection of delegates was by a minority of the adult men. Most of the towns in Queens, Suffolk, Ulster,

Albany, and neighboring East Jersey refused to participate. Several of the eighteen delegates who did attend the convention at Manhattan soon withdrew, so that when the group turned itself into a committee of safety, it consisted of no more than thirteen men from New York, Westchester, Kings, Queens, Staten Island, and the two East Jersey hamlets of Hackensack and Elizabethtown.

The insurgent committee of safety hardly represented more than a portion of the populace of Manhattan and the immediate environs. The two delegates from Manhattan, Samuel Edsall and Peter Delanoy, dominated the body. On 28 June the committee began to assume the functions of government. It appointed Leisler commander of the fort, Abraham Gouverneur clerk, and Delanoy collector of customs. The following month it constituted itself a council of war and in August commissioned Leisler as commander in chief of the province.[13]

Initially this insurgent government represented at best only a few towns, and probably a minority of the inhabitants in ten communities at most. Because of extreme pressure exerted by the insurgent regime and the need for aid against expected French attacks, several other communities reluctantly recognized the authority of the revolutionary junta at Manhattan. Later that summer another firebrand joined the ranks of the rebel chieftains when Jacob Milborne returned from Holland. Brother of William Milborne, the noisy Anabaptist preacher and Fifth Monarchyman who had taken part in the revolt against Andros in Boston, Jacob Milborne had long held grievances against Andros dating back to the latter's administration in New York a decade before. Milborne soon became Leisler's deputy, son-in-law, and, as some thought, his evil genius.

New York City was the key to the success of the insurgents. In a community where bands of armed militia controlled the streets, Leisler had little difficulty in having his supporters elected to office. When Leisler attempted to imprison Stephanus Van Cortlandt, the councilor fled. The control of the rebels over Manhattan was assured, but their authority extended only to the region immediately about the town. Other communities remained aloof if not openly hostile. At Albany a convention called for the county later complained of the exercise of "an usurped Power . . . by a Private man without ye least Shadow of authority."[14]

The insurgent junta kept the residents of Manhattan in a state of tension and alarm. On the evening of 16 August four young students from Harvard passing through the province stopped off at the home of William Merrit. Someone reported to Leisler that the four youths had refused to answer the challenge of a sentry and had run into Merrit's home and there shut the windows and door. An alarm was sounded; a report spread that

Andros and Nicholson had come to capture the fort. Leisler dispatched an armed party to take the mysterious strangers into custody. Common sense finally prevailed the next morning, and the youths were released.

Other men were not so fortunate. Jacobus Van Cortlandt, Brand Schuyler, Philip French, and Edward Buckmaster, seized by the revolutionary government, remained in jail. Some individuals arriving in the city were apprehended by armed militia and interrogated, and their papers and letters were opened.

To justify these high-handed actions the revolutionary junta began to gather "evidence," ex parte and ex post facto. In a deposition sworn before Gerardus Beekman, Charles Lodowyck claimed to have heard Nicholson say that the inhabitants of New York were a conquered people, men who could not expect the same rights as Englishmen. The prince, that is James II, might lawfully govern them as he wished. Beekman also took depositions from Richard Shute, Barent Witt, and Thomas Mollenax. The latter related that an Indian sachem, Wisscanow, had boasted the year before that Andros had given the natives wampum and asked them to be ready to serve him by the next planting time. According to Shute, the Indians had related that Andros promised them wampum "utterly" to destroy the Christians. They were to have joined him in the spring when he would arrive with five hundred men to attack New York. Witt testified to having seen several canoes filled with Frenchmen on Frederick Philipse's estate. Vessels had been reported traveling between New York and Canada, but when Witt had reported to Philipse the rumors of a plot, the councilor had merely laughed. It was foolish to be afraid. So Witt testified.

Milborne added more fuel to the fire: James II had sold the country to Louis XIV and had recalled Dongan when the governor refused to hand over the province. Andros, Bayard, and the other councilors, however, had undertaken to surrender New York to the French. With so many wild tales being bruited about, the rumormongers scarcely spared anyone in authority. One Nicholas Browne testified before Beekman that, having been in the royal service in England, he had several times observed Francis Nicholson at mass, especially in the king's tent at the army encampment at Hounslow Heath.[15] (Evidently the Protestant monarchs were not sufficiently aware of Nicholson's popish inclinations. When he returned to London later that year, they gave him a commission as lieutenant governor of Virginia. But then, they may not have been as paranoid or, perhaps, as unscrupulous as some of their nominal supporters in America.)

By the middle of August, having collected evidence to support the charges of oppression and treason by the deputy governor and the councilors, the members of the committee of safety in New York were ready to send their case to England. Their emissary was Joost Stoll, the dramseller raised to the rank of ensign in the insurgent militia. In a one-sided summary of the events occurring that spring and summer, the rebels accused Bayard and Van Cortlandt of malicious designs, the particulars of which were too long to relate in a letter. No doubt Stoll would be able to supply the details.[16]

Unknown to the insurgent leaders, in London the issue had already been decided against them. Earlier that summer John Riggs had arrived with letters from Andros, Nicholson, Philipse, Bayard, and Van Cortlandt. By the end of July the ministers of state had agreed on a message to be sent to Nicholson, whom they presumed was still at his station. In view of the assurance the king and queen had received of the deputy governor's dutiful submission, William and Mary authorized him to continue in office and to call upon such freeholders as he thought fit to assist him.[17]

Uncertain of the situation in New York, the king and the lords of the Committee for Plantation Affairs had addressed this authorization to the deputy governor and, in his absence, to those who for the time being took care to preserve the peace and administer the laws of New York. They used the same formula as that contained in the orders sent to Massachusetts. John Riggs was to carry this authorization across the Atlantic.[18] But Francis Nicholson had already left America. He did not arrive in London until after the orders had gone out. The deputy governor brought with him a letter from the provincial councilors to the duke of Shrewsbury describing the deplorable state in New York: the fort was in the hands of the rabble, no person or estate was safe, and the colony was on the verge of ruin unless speedily relieved.

This account and the testimony of Nicholson proved decisive. On reviewing the situation on 31 August, the Committee for Plantation Affairs advised that a governor with two companies of royal troops be dispatched forthwith, the soldiers to remain in New York until the situation was settled. Two weeks later a royal warrant authorized the crown law officers to draft a commission for Colonel Henry Sloughter as governor of New York.[19]

Quick action was not forthcoming, unfortunately, as it turned out, for the peace of New York. Several weeks passed before Shrewsbury, one of the principal secretaries of state, notified the Committee for Plantations to prepare dispatches for the new governor. This task the Plantation Office did not take up until 28 October. There was little doubt how Sloughter viewed the situation in New York: the government was held by a rabble, and the province invaded by the French and hostile Indians. A strong military force was necessary as well as a renewal of the alliance with the Iroquois. To help defray the expense, the neighboring provinces of Connecticut, East and West Jersey, and Pennsylvania ought to be united with New York.[20] Sloughter had accepted the assessment of the officials of the dominion regime.

By the middle of November Joost Stoll had arrived in London and presented the case for the insurgent council of safety under Leisler. He asked that New York receive a charter similar to that granted Massachusetts in 1629; if a governor and deputy had already been selected, their qualifications ought to be reviewed and their views toward the inhabitants of the colony ascertained. Sloughter had already received backing from the traders in the London mercantile community, those with connections in New York. Twenty-one merchants, among them, Ralph and Thomas Lodowyck, sent in a petition thanking the king for appointing Sloughter and urging the monarch to send over a military and naval force.

From the list of names the governor-designate presented at the end of the year of the men to be named in his commission as councilors, it was clear whose version of the events in New York Whitehall had accepted. Philipse, Bayard, Van Cortlandt, Thomas Willett, and Gabriel Minvielle, were among the men he recommended.[21]

The insurgents who had seized power had not won approval.

Had the men who had carried out the revolt in the spring and summer of 1689, however mistaken, been genuinely seized by a fear of subversion? Had they been motivated solely by a suspicion of Catholicism? Why had other Protestants in New York not shared their fears? They were all heirs to a common cultural legacy of anti-Popery. Not all, perhaps only a minority, of the inhabitants of the colony professed to accept the charge that the officials of the dominion government were involved in a conspiracy. Those who made the charge or who accused doubters who would not accept this indictment as popishly affected benefited from so branding their opponents.

To analyze the revolt by concentrating on New York City and to view the uprising as a protest of the Dutch inhabitants against the domination of a minority of Englishmen and a handful of well-to-do Dutch families is to distort the situation. The English villagers on Long Island may have taken part in the initial protest against the dominion regime, but they did not thereafter freely support the revolutionary council of safety. Leisler enjoyed support from the Dutch residents in New York City and the immediate environs, but not elsewhere in the colony. The predominantly Dutch community of Albany strongly resisted him until military necessity forced the inhabitants to submit. Although Leisler with military force behind him called for an elected assembly, he did not have popular support outside Manhattan and the area immediately around the capital. He used the assembly to wrest control from the faction he unjustifiably branded as Jacobite and Papist and to raise a force against the Canadians. Once the assembly had served his narrow purpose and once delegates began to consider the plight of those men Leisler had arbitrarily imprisoned, he prorogued it.

Under James II the administration of New York was very narrowly based. The confusion and uncertainty created by the events of the spring of 1689 presented certain men with an opportunity. The opposition to the entrenched officials also had a personal aspect. Jacob Leisler and Jacob Milborne in their behavior gave signs of mental instability. John Blackwell, passing through New York on his way from Philadelphia to Boston, thought Leisler to be mad. Some though the insurgent chieftain a figurehead manipulated by shrewder men. Of humble origins, Leisler had married Elsje Tymens, the widow of a wealthy merchant. The union brought him into the foremost families of the province, but he had become embroiled in a bitter legal action and alienated from his relations by marriage, the Van Cortlandts and the Van Rensselaers. The case was still pending in the local courts and the breach still open in 1689. At best, Leisler had been on the periphery, not at the center, of power, where his social and economic position might have entitled him to be. His violent temper and unstable personality had involved him in open quarrels both with his relations and with Andros during the latter's term as proprietary governor.

Milborne, the man who became Leisler's chief lieutenant in the insurgent government following his return to New York in the summer of 1689, had also clashed with Andros and carried a grudge against English officials. He had been an indentured servant in Connecticut and the West Indies before entering trade. While in London in 1680 he had prosecuted a suit against Andros. He had then described himself as a merchant.[22] In 1690 he married Leisler's daughter Mary.

Milborne's first wife was the daughter of Samuel Edsall, a member of the original insurgent council of safety. Born in Reading, England, Edsall had migrated to New Amsterdam, where he married Jannetje Wessels. Their four daughters married Milborne, Benjamin Blagge, Peter Delanoy, and William Lawrence. All four of Edsall's sons-in-law belonged to or supported the insurgent junta. The inner circle of the insurgent leaders consisted of a small group of men related by marriage and holding common grievances. They were men of some wealth and social status, who aspired to higher offices. Under the dominion such places had been few. They had gone to others.

Once before, in 1681, ambitious men, including newly arrived English merchants and factors, had challenged the entrenched officeholders in New York. They had forced the proprietor, if he hoped to pass on the cost of maintaining the government, to grant a legislative assembly, a body offering recognition and a path for further advancement.

For the men who had seized power in 1689 the question was, not self-government as against autocratic royal authority, but who would hold office in New York under the aegis of the Protestant monarchy of England.[23]

This was exactly the issue when John Riggs after a long voyage on 8 December 1689 reached New York with the letter from William III and the Privy Council addressed to Francis Nicholson, the deputy governor in the dominion regime, or, in his absence, to such men who for the time being took care to preserve the peace and administer the laws of the colony. Nicholson had long since departed, but Van Cortlandt, Philipse, and Bayard—the men named in the royal commission of 1688—were in New York. On learning of the arrival of the messenger from England, Philipse and Van Cortlandt hurried to the fort to meet Riggs. There they found Leisler. By a literal interpretation of the superscription on the document Riggs brought, Leisler claimed that he was the man to whom the royal authority was directed. He took the packet out of Riggs's hands. The messenger attempted to deny his claim, but Leisler launched into a long harangue against Philipse, Van Cortlandt, and Nicholson. When Stoll arrived in London with the evidence gathered by the insurgent junta, he boasted, Nicholson would be hanged. Actually, Nicholson had already received the king's commission as deputy governor of Virginia.

Two days after commandeering the letter Riggs had brought from England, Leisler took for himself the title of lieutenant governor and commander in chief of the province of New York.[24]

The ambiguity of the language employed by the court at Whitehall in the document for maintaining the government in New York had created a pretext for Leisler and the insurgents to claim the sanction of the Protestant monarchy. The issue might have been quickly resolved had Sloughter, the governor commissioned by William III, arrived promptly. But some fourteen months passed before Sloughter made his appearance with a force sufficient to restore order. In the weeks following Leisler's assumption of the title of lieutenant governor, he had over forty men who held civil commissions under the dominion imprisoned. Thomas Dongan, Stephanus Van Cortlandt, and Robert Livingston managed to escape; Nicholas Bayard and William Nicolls were kept in close confinement without bail in Fort James, now renamed Fort Williams. During their incarceration, their homes were pillaged.

The indiscriminate charges, the threats and the violence committed on men and their property made for Leisler implacable enemies. When Sloughter arrived, they would take their vengeance. The actions of the Leislerians and the reactions of their opponents fueled the fires of hatred for a generation to come.

The Leislerian regime at Manhattan received little support among the townsmen in East and West Jersey. With the overthrow of the dominion administration, there was no central authority to govern the six thousand or so inhabitants. In the eastern province Andrew Hamilton had last served as deputy for the proprietors, but in 1688 those shareholders resident in England had apparently negotiated with the crown to relinquish political jurisdiction. Not for several years was their authority again recognized. In the interval local officials in the individual towns and hamlets administered justice. Much the same situation prevailed in West Jersey. Following the collapse of the dominion, George Hutcheson and William Biddle, on behalf of the resident proprietors, the West Jersey Council, raised the issue of proprietary right in the province with Daniel Coxe in England, but the question remained unsettled for some years to come.[25]

New York was perhaps the most diverse of the English provinces in America, a society lacking in social, ethnic, and economic cohesion, one suffering from institutional defects in government and seemingly under attack by external enemies. As elsewhere in America, here too were ambitious men and long-standing resentments. Unstable personalities and ambitious figures had fanned long-held fears to arouse the populace. But cohesion among the various groups was lacking. Little united those who toppled the government in 1689 and those who simply refused to support the dominion authorities. By failing to act decisively, Nicholson and the councilors had allowed a small coterie to prejudice their authority and to seize control. The outbreak of war shortly thereafter forced other communities in the colony, hitherto skeptical about the insurgents— indeed, hostile in some instances—to accept the revolt as an accomplished fact. The dilatory reaction of the ministry in London, the failure promptly to clarify the legal situation and to dispatch officials to Manhattan, prolonged the rule of the insurgents and allowed them to extend their control.

CHAPTER 8

Beyond the Delaware:
Quakers, Catholics, and Protestant
Associators, 1689

ALTHOUGH NEVER INCLUDED in the Dominion of New England and never deprived of representative assemblies, English colonists living in the provinces west and south of the Delaware were also concerned with the momentous developments in London during the winter of 1688–89. Nor were they immune from the dramatic events occurring in Boston and Manhattan the ensuing spring. Tensions within each of the proprietary provinces—only Virginia was a royal colony—once word arrived of the seizure of power in Boston and New York were such that proprietary authority had virtually ceased to exist by the end of the year. South and west of the Delaware ethnic pluralism, social fluidity, and fragmented political authority too threatened to disrupt communities.

In Pennsylvania and the lower counties on the Delaware, government on the provincial level had not functioned smoothly for some time, when rumors reached the inhabitants of French and Indian incursions: aroused by "ye Papists" in Maryland, marauding warriors were threatening "ye Ruine of the Protestants in these parts." A few of the justices and sheriffs in the lower counties had called on the planters to take up arms, and some men at Newcastle expressed dissatisfaction that King William had not been proclaimed. But old Puritan Governor John Blackwell, appointed the previous summer by the proprietor, a friend of the deposed monarch, had not received any orders to do so.[1] William Penn, the Quaker who had supported James II in his attempt to relieve Dissenters and Catholics of the restrictive laws against them, was in no position to supervise the affairs of his province. Rumored to be a secret Catholic, a Jesuit even, Penn was suspect to the new administration at Whitehall. He was later thought to be involved in a Jacobite conspiracy.

Even before the revolution in England, the proprietor had experienced great difficulty with his contentious fellow Quakers in Pennsylvania, particularly with the more prosperous landowners and merchants led by Thomas Lloyd, who contested with him for control of the machinery of government. Revenue due the proprietor was also a sore point.

116

Penn had waived quitrents on land until 1685, but even then the Quakers would not pay. The proprietor had appointed an old Puritan and Commonwealth official then living in Boston as his deputy. Penn had appreciated that an overhaul of the structure of government was necessary and that he needed someone in Philadelphia to take firm control. Animosities had too long prevailed there. John Blackwell's task was to suppress them. He must not allow the assemblymen any latitude or initiative to debate or amend bills. They were merely to accept or reject proposals put before them. This procedure conformed to the charter issued to him by the crown, Penn claimed. He threatened, should the assemblymen and elected councilors attempt to alter it, to turn to the English government.

Yet Penn was inconsistent in his actions, for he had promised Thomas Lloyd, Samuel Carpenter, and other councilors in Philadelphia that if the Puritan governor did not please them, the proprietor would dismiss him.[2] Thus Penn had undermined Blackwell, had given the Quaker leaders an incentive to oppose the new governor.

The personalities of the principals involved told against harmony. Blackwell was cantankerous and obdurate; Thomas Lloyd, childish and petty, but effective in opposition, as was his Welsh kinsman, David Lloyd. For these strong-willed men there would be no compromise.

Both Thomas and David Lloyd snubbed the new governor, Thomas refusing to recognize his commission from the proprietor until it had passed the provincial seal, an instrument Lloyd held. As keeper of the seal and master of the rolls, he could obstruct Blackwell's efforts to function as proprietary deputy and provincial executive. David Lloyd, principal clerk of the provincial court, and the Quaker justices were to argue that they were independent of both the council and the governor.

Within a few weeks of Blackwell's arrival, he and Thomas Lloyd clashed over the commission for justices of the peace for the county of Philadelphia. With the support of some councilors Lloyd contended that he held the great seal immediately from Penn; Blackwell with authority of a lesser seal could not order him about. Outraged, the proprietary deputy appealed against "such Cabals" to Penn. "For you are our Oracle upon all accounts; and by your words we stand or fall." Government in Pennsylvania was in a state of confusion and many of the Quakers confirmed in their coolness, if not outright hostility, by Penn's weakness, "by the Honey of your concessions, having tasted too much of it; more indeed than their stomacks can beare."[3]

Unknown to Blackwell, Penn had already made the most serious concession of all, a promise to remove the governor if the Quaker leaders would not accept him. On 25 February 1688/9 at a meeting of the council,

Samuel Carpenter refused to accept Blackwell as governor, the proprietor not having power to commission one. David Lloyd also challenged Blackwell's authority. The governor ejected him from his offices and refused to admit Thomas Lloyd when the voters from Bucks returned him to the council. Blackwell also disallowed John Eckley his seat, on the grounds of an unfair election. The Quaker magnates then charged Blackwell with depriving them of their liberty and invading their rights under the charter, as they called the legislative enactment Penn had accepted in 1683. Griffin Jones, one of the few key men to support the governor, claimed the Quakers aimed at rebellion.[4]

Again Blackwell turned to Penn. In April he offered to resign. The proprietor chose to accept the version of events offered by Carpenter, Joseph Growdon, John Simcock, and the other opponents of the governor. Less than a year before, Penn had urged his deputy to rule with firmness. He now reversed himself, chiding Blackwell for quarreling and commanding him to withdraw his indictment of Thomas Lloyd. He then offered to select his deputies from several names submitted by the councilors, but "whatsoever you do[,] avoide factions & partys, whisperings & reportings, & all animositys," he implored. To Blackwell he offered the lesser positions of supervisor of his estate and agent for the proprietary revenue. Blackwell contemptuously spurned the gesture. When he left Philadelphia the following winter, he sent off to the proprietor a sharp letter recounting Penn's promises and shortcomings. He had had enough of the proprietary and the Quakers of Pennsylvania, a people with whom neither God nor man could prevail. Government could not be supported with such a people and under a jurisdictional arrangement such as Penn had permitted.[5]

Proprietary government had also collapsed in Carolina. In Charles Town the dispute centered around the frame of government, the Fundamental Constitutions, originally promulgated in 1669 and subsequently amended by the proprietary board in England. At issue were the disposition of land, control of the trade with the Indians, and the traffic in Indian slaves, as well as political power.

The Anglican settlers from the West Indies—the Goose Creek faction—and their allies had dominated the settlement since its founding despite the attempts by the proprietors to establish a counterweight by encouraging the migration of English Dissenters, Scottish Presbyterians, and French Huguenots. In opposing the administration of Governor James Colleton, the West Indians claimed the proprietors were abrogating or unilaterally altering the Fundamental Constitutions. By the close of

1689 provincial government was nearly at a standstill, and the laws were expiring, since the legislature had not met for some time. At this juncture Seth Sothell arrived in Charles Town. As a proprietor he enjoyed precedence over Colleton and offered legitimacy to the opposition. He adopted the cause of the West Indians.[6]

A proprietor suitable to the opposition leaders in one section of Carolina had been totally unacceptable to their counterparts in the settlements about Albemarle Sound. Earlier that year they had banished Sothell from the remote, northern region. Little was known of the circumstances of the principal inhabitants overthrowing Sothell. The uprising—it probably occurred after May—may have had no relation to events in England or elsewhere in America.

The authority exercised by the distant proprietary board in London over this nearly isolated region had been nominal at best. Following a rebellion against proprietary and royal customs officials in 1677, the proprietors had received a warning from the crown to exercise proper control. But they had had difficulty in finding a man to govern, one who was competent and not involved with the contending factions in Albemarle. Finally, they had sent out one of their own members, Seth Sothell. Following capture and enslavement by Algerine pirates, Sothell had finally reached Carolina. He soon ran afoul of George Durant, one of the leaders of the earlier uprising. Attempting to have Durant imprisoned, the governor found himself accused of taking bribes and arbitrarily seizing property. Tried by the local assembly, he was found guilty and banished from the region for twelve months. He journeyed south to Charles Town, where the opposition faction then embroiled in a dispute with Governor James Colleton welcomed him.[7]

The other proprietors in London, the earls of Craven and Bath, Peter Colleton, and John Archdale (the last acted for his son, a minor) evidently did not share this faith in Sothell. They hoped the allegations of injustice on his part were false, but having learned that the inhabitants of Albemarle had risen against him they suspended Sothell until the matter was fairly determined. In the interval they appointed Colonel Philip Ludwell as their governor for Carolina.[8]

Philip Ludwell was no stranger to political turmoil and rebellion. He had been one of the councilors against whom Nathaniel Bacon and his followers in 1676 had complained and one of the staunchest supporters of Governor Sir William Berkeley during the civil uprising in Virginia. Subsequently Ludwell had fallen out with commissioners sent out by the crown to investigate the cause of the conflict. With Robert Beverley he had gone over into active opposition.

In Virginia in 1689 the events of 1676 seemed to be repeating them-

selves. In the spring William Byrd had complained over the crop of tobacco, the colony's staple: "Never so much rotten as it is at this time that
ever I saw, and I fear most concerned will find it sufficiently bad."[9]
Among the planters some had complaints against the governor, Francis,
Baron Howard of Effingham. On behalf of the burgesses Ludwell had
taken ship to England to present their grievances. The governor was
oppressing them by exacting illegal fees, by turning men out of office, and
imprisoning them without trial. He had abused his power of erecting
courts and appointing officials and had failed to provide the assembly
with accounts of revenue, arms, and ammunition available in the colony.[10]

The governor, suffering from a severe and protracted illness, had
secured permission to leave Virginia for England. In his absence during
the winter of 1688–89, the senior councilor, Nathaniel Bacon (the elder)
was presiding over the government when rumors reached Virginia of
dramatic events in England, the landing of William of Orange and the
flight of James II. More disturbing stories circulated on the northern
Chesapeake, on the frontiers of Virginia and Maryland, tales of a conspiracy by Catholics to raise thousands of Seneca Indians to strike the Protestants. Adherents of the Ludwell-Beverley faction, George Mason and
John Waugh, the latter a parson in Strafford County, were spreading
these rumors. Less than ten years before in Maryland, opponents of the
proprietary regime had sought to stir up the populace with similar tales.
Parson Waugh was already in disfavor with authorities in Virginia for
marrying couples runaway from neighboring Maryland. He had also become embroiled with one of the local magnates, William Fitzhugh, in
legal actions over title to lands. Fitzhugh, a planter, merchant, and lawyer,
with his friends had usually prevailed in the elections in Stafford County
to select burgesses. His law partner, George Brent, was a Catholic. News
of the Protestant Revolution in England and rumors of a Papist plot on
the Chesapeake gave Waugh an opportunity. From his pulpit he directed
a stream of invective agaist Brent and other Catholics.

Bands of armed men assembled in Stafford and neighboring Rappahannock. Fortunately for the authorities at Jamestown—unlike the
officials of the dominion regime in Boston and Manhattan—they had
received official word of the change in government in England. On 27
April 1689, Bacon and his colleagues on the council proclaimed William
and Mary. Recalling perhaps how Sir William Berkeley had vacillated
thirteen years before when challenged by insurgents, the councilors acted
decisively to check any insurrection in the northern frontier counties,
apprehending the "unruly and unordered spirits" who, under the "pretext of Religion," had taken to arms.

The councilors also moved promptly to quash the absurd rumors then circulating. An Indian, so it was said, had brought in information that the Catholics living in Maryland had raised thousands of hostile warriors in the north. This information had been "improved" by some men who desired to "fish in disturbed waters." Nicholas Spencer, the provincial secretary, was convinced that certain opportunists had fabricated this tale, particularly when after the councilors attempted to have the Indian questioned, they were told that he had been discovered murdered in the forests. Spencer persisted and had the warrior apprehended. When asked why he had not come forth but had hidden in the woods, the Indian pleaded that his white friends, so he called them, had warned him that he would be hanged if he did. Spencer concluded the entire tale had been fabricated by a rabble in the northern counties to justify their taking up arms, plundering, and robbing.

Several men, Parson Waugh among them, were taken into custody in Stafford County, charged with instigating rumors of the spurious plot. Two hundred armed followers vainly attempted to rescue them from the local sheriff. Councilors resident in the Northern Neck, Richard Lee, Spencer, and Isaac Allerton, stood firm and with the aid of other prominent settlers, and the militia of the northern counties quashed the tumult despite threats by the "Rabble" of murder and plunder in reprisal. By acting decisively and quieting the fears of the inhabitants, the provincial authorities never allowed the situation to deteriorate as predecessors there had allowed in 1676.[11]

Nicholas Spencer died that fall, but Nathaniel Bacon, Allerton, Richard Lee, William Byrd and the other councilors had the situation well in hand. The countryside was quiet. By this time the court at Whitehall had decided to appoint Captain Francis Nicholson, recently arrived from Manhattan, to administer the government of Virginia as deputy to Lord Howard of Effingham. Because of ill health and perhaps the animus he had stirred in Virginia, the governor remained in England. The councilors who had so effectively put down "Parson Waugh's Tumult" were confirmed in office. In the instructions issued to the lieutenant governor the crown continued a policy initiated under Charles II of shifting the burden of taxes, holding fewer and consequently less expensive meetings of the assembly, and imposing no financially burdensome projects on the local populace.[12] Grievances of this nature, so officials at Whitehall had concluded, had contributed to the rebellion thirteen years before. Their amelioration had been one factor in limiting the scope of the disturbances in 1689 to Stafford and Rappahannock. Two other factors had been critical. The councilors at Jamestown had acted promptly and vigorously, and they had received orders from London in April to proclaim the Protestant succession.

The authorities in neighboring Maryland were not as fortunate.

Rumors propagated by Parson John Waugh and other opportunists in northern Virginia were carried across the Potomac and Chesapeake and circulated in Charles and Calvert counties in southwestern Maryland. In the proprietary colony conditions were unsettled, and a tradition of open revolt against the Catholic overlord was well established. As recently as 1681 John Coode and a few dissidents had attempted to capitalize on similar tales of Catholic duplicity and Indian incursions to stir up the planters against the proprietary regime.

Maryland appeared ripe for upheaval. For almost twenty years the economy of the colony had been depressed as tobacco prices had remained low, the result of overproduction on the Chesapeake. Political opportunity was linked to the holding of property. Before 1670 all freemen could vote, but that year the proprietor restricted the franchise to men holding fifty acres of land or property worth forty pounds. Yet these economic and political factors, developments in Maryland affecting a great many men, may not have been instrumental in bringing about a political crisis in the summer of 1689. Had they been relevant, the reaction against the Calvert proprietary would have been widespread, extending throughout the colony among the rank and file. But in 1689 conditions remained stable at the local level; government in the counties ran smoothly despite an upheaval at the provinical capital at Saint Marys. Broadening the franchise was not an issue in 1689, and the men who rose against the Calverts did not initiate any basic changes. As evidenced by the situation in Charles County, the imposition of a property qualification in 1670 had not deprived many freeholders of the vote. The great majority of them had enough land to qualify for the franchise. Probably all freeholders and men with long-term leases could vote.[13]

The uprising carried out in Maryland in 1689 was confined to a few counties, the work of only certain discontented elements within Maryland society. The counties on the eastern shore of the Chesapeake, Somerset, Dorchester, Talbot, and Cecil, as well as Anne Arundel and Baltimore in the northwestern shore, were relatively quiet. The three counties in the southwest, Calvert, Charles, and Saint Marys, were home to the men who led the uprising against the Calverts. The planters who opposed the proprietary regime were either men affiliated with the Church of England or men closely related by family ties with personal grievances against the Calverts, were individuals who had risen to prominence but were denied further advancement because of the enmity of the proprietor or the domination of the key provincial offices by a small clique of Catholic gentry and Calvert relatives.

Among the inhabitants of Maryland, the Protestant planters were a majority, but most were not adherents of the Church of England. This distinction the leaders of the revolt, those who formed the so-called Protestant Association, did not make when they accused the Calverts and the Catholics of plotting to destroy Protestants.[14] That they believed that such a plot existed is open to serious question. Having claimed to have proof of such a conspiracy and having promised to send the evidence to England to justify their revolt, they failed to do so.

According to the insurgents, the Catholic councilors had contrived to betray the Protestants in Maryland to the French and northern Indians; the proprietary council and the Catholic governor, William Joseph, had deliberately prorogued the assembly to prevent their design from being discovered; they had deliberately denied the succession of the Protestant monarchs in England. Proof of these charges, the insurgents claimed, they could present to William and Mary. Yet as was later noted at the Plantation Office in Whitehall, the evidence was never in any way presented.[15]

Because of a set of bizarre circumstances, the proprietary government in Maryland in the spring of 1689 did not proclaim the accession of William and Mary. A week after the succession of the Protestant monarchs had been published in London, on 20 February 1688/9, Lord Baltimore attended the Lords of Trade and Plantations. At that time he received orders to dispatch a copy of the proclamation to Maryland. The proprietor then sent if off to Governor William Joseph by a messenger, one Broom. While waiting in Plymouth for passage to the Chesapeake, Broom died.[16] Had Baltimore followed the situation closely, he might have had a duplicate of the proclamation sent in time to prevent an outbreak on the Chesapeake that summer. He did not. His carelessness jeopardized his proprietorship.

In Maryland proprietary officials were left to their own devices when rumors spread from Stafford County across the Potomac in Virginia of an Indian uprising and a Catholic conspiracy. Authorities in Jamestown, having received official word by 27 April of the transfer of power in London, had been able to quiet the tumult in Virginia. Joseph and the proprietary councilors were not that fortunate.

When Charles, Baron Baltimore, had left Maryland to defend his boundary against the claim of William Penn, he had commissioned a group of councilors as deputies for his minor son, Leonard. A trimumvirate of Henry Darnall, Baltimore's Catholic cousin, Nicholas Sewall, and William Digges controlled the administration. Following complaints made in England against their rule, Baltimore, unable to return to America, had commissioned a new governor, William Joseph. The choice was impolitic, for Joseph was Catholic and an outspoken advocate of divine right and proprietary privilege, sentiments he made clear in his opening address to the provincial assembly in October 1688.

A crisis for the proprietary regime developed early in Joseph's administration.

In the spring of 1689 Henry Jowles, a Protestant planter located on the Patuxent, warned William Digges, a member of the provincial council, that some of the inhabitants were in an uproar over a rumored Indian-Catholic conspiracy, a plot allegedly contrived by Henry Darnall, a relative of Baltimore whom the proprietor had appointed provincial chancellor. The Protestants, Jowles affirmed, looked to Digges to lead them. Reacting to the threat, Governor Joseph, Darnall, and Clement Hill of the council agreed to send the chancellor out to clear his name of these baseless charges.

Darnall and Hill carried out an investigation in Calvert and Charles counties. The rumors were false; so Jowles, Digges, Kenelm Cheseldyne, John Addison, Ninian Beal, and eleven others testified on 27 March in a signed declaration. Yet within four months many of these same men would lead a revolt against the government and seek to justify their assumption of power by charging that the proprietary officials were indeed engaged in this plot. Throughout the spring of 1689 men continued to promote the hoax that the Catholics of Maryland were collaborating with the French and northern Indians to cut off the Protestants or, at least, "reduce them to ye See of Rome." Provincial officials, they charged, had concealed the orders coming from England to proclaim the Protestant king and queen.[17]

Other rumors were about, indicating a plot of quite a different nature, one concerted by John Coode and his relatives, including Gerard Slye, then living in London. For over a generation Coode's relations had opposed the proprietary family. He later boasted he had overturned the provincial government to take out his revenge on the Calverts.[18] By the middle of July Coode was raising men along the Maryland side of the Potomac. With him were John Campbell of Saint Marys; Henry Jowles of Charles; Nehemiah Blakiston, a royal collector of customs who had been involved in a bitter dispute with Baltimore; and Kenelm Cheseldyne, another relative of Coode, who had served as speaker of the assembly and provincial attorney general until dismissed by the proprietor.

While Coode and his cohort were gathering a force, Governor Joseph, Chancellor Darnall, and the councilors at Mattaponi remained inactive. Finally, Sewall and Darnall traveled up the Patuxent to raise the loyalists, but before they could return, Coode and the insurgents on 27 July invested Saint Marys. Digges surrendered the capital after his men refused to fight. A week later Joseph, Darnall, Nicholas Sewall, Edward Pye, and Clement Hill also capitulated. Shortly before seizing power the insurgents had issued "The Declaration of the Reasons and Motives for the Present Appearing in Arms of Their Majesties Subjects. . . ." The document listed seventeen charges against the proprietary regime. It was larded throughout with anti-Catholic sentiments and heavily veneered with exaggerations, half-truths, and outright falsehoods. The proprietor and his advisers were accused of discriminating in favor of the Catholic Church, nullifying and suspending laws, imposing harsh sentences, charging excessive fees, and illegally employing force against innocent Protestants.[19]

The men who overthrew the proprietary regime represented only a segment of Maryland society; they came from a specific region of the colony, the lower western shore. A small group of men, most of the leaders were related to or neighbors of John Coode. Blakiston, Cheseldyne, Jowles, Ninian Beal, John Campbell, Humphrey Warren, and William Purley—the younger sons of English gentry—had migrated to the colony in the two decades following the restoration of the Stuart monarchy in 1660. The dominance of the clique upon whom the proprietor had conferred provincial posts had blocked the road to higher office and status.

Other Anglican planters, also recent immigrants, waited in the background. To consolidate their position, the insurgents needed wider support. On 3 August they sent off an address to William and Mary announcing that they had rescued Maryland from the hands of enemies of the Protestant monarchs.[20] A call then went out for four delegates from each county to convene in the capital on 22 August.

From the response to this summons it was evident that the rebel movement represented only a fraction of the populace of the colony. In Calvert County in the southern portion of the western shore Michael Taney (the sheriff), Richard Smith, and sixty-six other men on 20 August signed a protest, one questioning the professed motives of the insurgents. They refused to select delegates until required to do so by a lawful authority in England.[21] In Anne Arundel County, a Puritan stronghold, Richard Hill and others also protested on the grounds that such an assembly was too expensive. In other counties reaction was mixed, and the planters were hesitant. Apparently, relatively few men took part in the elections, polls conducted under armed surveillance. The choice presented them in most instances was a mixed slate, a combination of candidates supporting the coup and moderates.

Thirty-five men gathered at Saint Marys late in August. Three delegates elected did not attend; four arrived later. There were few veteran officeholders among them. For most of these Protestant Associators the acquisition of an important political office was a relatively recent, if not a completely new experience. Those who previously had held high office, with few exceptions, had suffered a political decline. In some cases they had been dismissed. All were above average in wealth, and most, like Coode, Jowles, and the other insurgent leaders, were the younger sons of English gentry, immigrants who had arrived in the years since 1660 and afterwards had married well. They were largely strangers to the proprietary political circle; four had held commissions as sheriffs and eight as officers in the militia, but twenty-three, two-thirds of them, had served as justices in the counties.[22]

Seven men—Cheseldyne, Coode, Blakiston, Jowles, John Addison, John Courts, and Gilbert Clarke—dominated the early proceedings of the Protestant Association. They provided the membership of the committee instructed to investigate and report on the Papist plot. Addison, Jowles, and Clarke had been involved first in spreading and then in denying the rumor of a Catholic conspiracy.

What motivated them? A sincere, if misguided, fear of Catholicism or political ambition? After only a very few days the committee reported on 4 September. If found that the Catholic officials appointed by Baltimore had indeed conspired to betray the Protestants to the French and northern Indians. A grave danger still existed because of the malicious endeavors of Joseph, Darnall, and Nicholas Sewall. Of this they had evidence, proof they would send to the king and queen. They never did.[23]

Late that summer the insurgent leaders moved to solidify the control of the Protestant Association over the province. In an ordinance passed on 4 September they named militia officers and justices of the peace for the various counties and for the city of Saint Marys. Men opposing the take-over were now proscribed, but Captain Richard Hill, Richard Smith, and Michael Taney continued active. Through Henry Darnall they managed to get out their version of the revolt. The account Charles Carroll sent from Saint Marys to Baltimore in London was most damaging. Coode, Blakiston, Cheseldyne, and their cohort had engaged in "wild fancys" and had evicted not only Roman Catholics from office contrary to the provincial act of toleration but also Protestants who would not accede to their rule. They had threatened to hang anyone who presumed to justify the right of the proprietor and had employed armed men to overawe the voters in the county elections for their illegal assembly.[24]

The loyalists as well as the Associators could employ the rhetoric of liberty. Taken prisoner by the revolutionary junta, Richard Smith announced himself to be a "free born Subject of England." As such he demanded to know what law of England or of Maryland he had violated to be so incarcerated. By a law of the English Parliament abolishing the arbitrary Court of Star Chamber, a grievous institution contrary to Magna Carta, the privileges of Englishmen had been set forth, among them the provision that a man should be imprisoned only by original writ or matter of record and be heard before justices lawfully commissioned. Judgment must come by the common course of law. All men were satisfied, Smith remonstrated, that the Lord Baltimore had a bona fide right to the proprietaryship of Maryland. It had not in any way been taken from him, as John Coode had alleged.[25]

The insurgent chieftains when in their cups apparently reveled in the tradition of revolt, taking for themselves the names of past rebel chieftains. Ninian Beal became "Argyle" after the Scottish noble who had led a revolt against James II in 1685, while Coode in a gesture of disdain called himself "Masaniello" after Thomaso Aniello, the fishmonger who in 1647 had led a revolt against Spanish rule in Naples. Coode boasted that his reign in Maryland would survive longer than that of the Neopolitan.[26]

The people of Maryland were badly divided. A score of Protestants had been imprisoned; several proprietary men had gone into hiding; and some officeholders in the counties feared to serve under commissions issued by the insurgent regime. Both sides circulated conflicting petitions to be signed and then sent to London. Remonstrances from Kent, Calvert, Talbot, Cecil, and Baltimore counties condemned the charges against the proprietary government as fictitous and scandalous, protested the denial of the rights of Englishmen, and asked for the restoration of the proprietaryship. Remonstrances favoring the coup d'etat received support in Charles, Somerset, Kent, Talbot, Calvert, and Saint Marys.[27]

In transmitting the addresses favorable to the "Protestant" cause to the Lords of Trade in Whitehall, John Coode sought to place the revolutionary government in Maryland within a broader context. The insurgents had received word of an attack on the northern frontiers of English America by the French. Although Maryland was somewhat shielded by the Protestant regimes in Massachusetts and New York, the province would remain in an unsettled state until the king's will was known,[28] that is, until William III gave his sanction to the insurgent regime.

Faced with the need to wage a major struggle in Europe, to resist French-aided Jacobite attempts to restore James II, and to fight a war overseas, how would the Protestant monarchy react to the assumption of power in the colonies by the insurgents?

CHAPTER 9

The Contest for a Massachusetts Charter, 1689–91

As the most populous and the strongest province in New England, Massachusetts Bay was critical to the decisions made at Westminster and Whitehall for English America. Even before the fall of the dominion, in London, Increase Mather sought to convince royal authorities that Sir Edmund Andros was governing illegally. With the succession of the Protestant monarchs he broadened the scope of his attack: the revocation of the patent to the Governor and Company of the Massachusetts Bay was void, and the charter of 1629 still valid. This contention, Sir Robert Sawyer, the former attorney general, had refuted at a hearing in February 1689. At that time William III's Privy Council had also rejected the interpretation of the New England divine, but the Committee for Trade and Plantations did recommend the issuance of a new charter to preserve the rights and privileges of the colonists, but with one restriction. Any new patent must reserve a dependence on the crown.[1]

As between these two goals, where to draw the line? Opposed to the bureaucrats, Blathwayt and Sir Robert Southwell, in the contest to win over the king and the higher ministers of state—Thomas Osborne, earl of Danby (now created marquess of Carmarthen), the earl of Nottingham, and the duke of Shrewsbury—was a coalition of Dissenters. From New England it included Increase Mather, Samuel Sewall, Samuel Appleton, Elisha Hutchinson, and Sir William Phips; from England, Sir Henry Ashurst, London merchant and politician; William Whiting, a London trader with connections in New England; and Philip, fourth Baron Wharton. The Dissenting peer was liaison with the royal court.

On 14 March, a few weeks after the decision taken at the council to issue a new charter for the Bay colony, Wharton introduced Mather to the king. William, perhaps on the evidence presented at the council board the previous month, observed that there had been some irregularities in New England (as Massachusetts was often called), although he expressed confidence that the inhabitants there were a good people. According to Mather's later account, Wharton spoke up, pledging that he would be "their Guarantee"; he and Mather would stand bond for the future good behavior of the New Englanders. At this time William agreed only to recall Andros to give an account of his administration.

In the weeks following, Mather, Sewall, and Ashurst continued to meet. How could they get around the testimony of Sir Robert Sawyer on the vacating of the charter some five years before the various misdemeanors?[2] These appeared in a summary of the reasons cited in the writ of scire facias for annulling the patent presented at the Plantation Office late in May. An attached memorandum summed up the condition of the neighboring colonies. In the opinion of Lord Chief Justice John Holt and other judges, better to govern and protect the king's subjects the crown might now constitute such government as the king thought fit.[3]

To circumvent the arguments of Sawyer and other bureaucrats, Ashurst had included the chartered colonies in America in a bill the Whigs were promoting in Parliament for restoring the charters of the English boroughs vacated or surrendered during the reigns of Charles II and James II. Yet as Mather noted, matters did not go smoothly in Parliament. The bill "sticks in the Birth." He had Ashurst continue to exploit the avenue open for them at court. Accompanied by Lord Wharton, Mather once more saw the king in the summer of 1689. By this time he could bring William III the glad tidings of the revolution carried out in Boston in the name of the Protestant monarchy. With the help of the Dissenters of New England, Mather hinted, William could become emperor of the American continent. The colonists asked only that they might enjoy their ancient, that is, former, rights and privileges. William was gracious in his reply, but would not commit himself.[4]

Another obstacle arose in the form of the accounts of the events in Massachusetts delivered by John Riggs, the envoy sent by Andros from Boston. At the end of July the king and council decided to require the insurgent committee in the Bay colony to send the governor and other officials incarcerated home to answer charges against them. On 12 August Shrewsbury gave Mather a royal letter addressed to those persons in Massachusetts who for the time being took care to preserve the peace and administer the laws, authorizing them to continue in government until they received further orders. Mather and his colleagues from the Bay then prepared to leave England, but Mather was detained at Deal, where his son was taken ill. Both Mathers returned to London 3 October.[5]

Evidence damaging to the cause of the Massachusetts charter was accumulating. By the fall of 1689 letters from Edward Randolph complaining of continued violations of the acts of trade and navigation and of illegal arrests had arrived in London. Seizing on these, Sir Robert Southwell and his colleagues in the Customs House entered a protest against the insurgent regime. On 30 October the Committee for Plantation Af-

fairs took up the exemplification of the judgment given against the charter of the Bay colony with its long, detailed list of charges against the
Puritan government, complaints Randolph had compiled some years before.[6]

That same day at Westminster, the House of Commons appointed a
committee to prepare a bill for restoring the corporations whose charters
had been vacated or altered under Charles II and James II. Through the
efforts of Ashurst and Mather, the plantations in America, the chartered
colonies, were included. The bill passed the House of Commons and then
went up to the Lords, where it had its first reading on 11 January 1689/90.
The court then intervened. Halifax, the lord privy seal, conferred with the
king and explained the situation. Apparently William had not fully appreciated the consequences of restoring the charters. Ironically, it had
been Halifax in the fall of 1684 who had protested against the decision to
establish a government in the Bay colony without an elected assembly
once the charter of 1629 had been vacated. The influence of the ministers
of state probably induced the Lords after extended debate to agree on 23
January 1689/90 to consider the patents of the colonies separately from
the charters of the municipal corporations in England. Whatever the case,
the entire bill fell with the prorogation of Parliament four days later.[7]

Increase Mather continued to press for the restoration of colonial
rights, arguing that the charters of four New England colonies, Massachusetts, Rhode Island, Connecticut, and Plymouth—in reality, the
latter had never received a patent from the crown—had been deprived
illegally. He prayed the king to restore the privileges of the New Englanders. In May 1690 when the House of Commons again ordered a bill
brought in for the restoration of charters, Mather applied to several
members to so word the measure as to include the New England patents.
But on 23 May Parliament was adjourned. Mather did not think it would
meet again until the winter.[8]

Whitehall rather than Westminster was the critical arena where the
protagonists waged their struggle over a charter for Massachusetts, one
lasting over a year, well into 1691.

On a winter's day in February 1690 the bark *Mehitable,* Gilbert Bant
master, had left Boston harbor for England. She carried Sir Edmund
Andros, Edward Randolph, Joseph Dudley, and the other officials of the
dominion to London to answer charges made against them by the insurgent regime of Massachusetts. Two members of the revolutionary convention, Elisha Cooke and Thomas Oakes, adherents of the Puritan
faction who had so strenuously resisted any efforts to alter the biblical
commonwealth, had already left for London to prosecute the case and to

assist the agents, Mather and Ashurst. With them went Ichabod Wiswall, an emissary for Plymouth.

Both groups, the spokesmen for the provisional governments and the royal officials, arrived in London within a day or two of each other. On Monday, 7 April, Cooke, Oakes, and Ashurst hurried to Whitehall to meet with Shrewsbury, and the next day, accompanied by the secretary of state, they went to Kensington, where Ashurst read their address to the king. Later that day at the Royal Exchange they received notice to attend a meeting of the Lords of Trade set for 10 April.

Andros and the other officials of the dominion had moved to have the charges against them dismissed. Did the agents have anything to lay before the committee? Did Cooke, Oakes, and Mather have an credentials? Yes, but not with them. The agents had brought "testimonials" relating to the officials of the dominion, affirmations they hoped would sufficiently vindicate the proceedings of the provisional government at Boston. They asked for time to prepare their case to be presented by their counsel, Robert Humphreys. He was the solicitor employed six years before by the corporation of Massachusetts to contest the suit brought against the charter. Lord President Carmarthen thought the request for time reasonable.

The day set for the hearing was 17 April. Counsel for each side would argue the matter. The agents must leave their case against Andros in writing with the secretary for the Committee for Plantation Affairs, William Blathwayt, by 14 April, the Monday before the hearing, to allow Andros time to read the charges and to prepare an answer. On the designated day Humphreys presented the written case against the governor. It contained three main points: Andros had governed illegally and arbitrarily; he had attempted to suppress news of the Protestant revolution in England; and he had aided the hostile Indians against the English colonists. Whatever the merits—if any—of the charges contained in this paper, the document was unsigned. After much discussion among the agents, Humphreys, according to Cooke, had advised them that there was no need for anyone to sign the charges. At the hearing on 17 April presided over by Carmarthen and Nottingham, no one could be found to sign or to take responsibility for the accusations.[9]

Both sides that day had the benefit of eminent counsel: for the agents from Massachusetts, Sir John Somers, a prominent Whig politician, and Edward Ward; for Andros, Sir George Treby and Sir Robert Sawyer, the former attorney general who had prosecuted the writ of scire facias against the charter.

Taking the lead, Sawyer launched an attack on the misdeeds of the

Puritan colony, but Carmarthen cut him short. The committee then took up the charges against the officials of the dominion. These complaints, counsel for the agents claimed they were ready to prove: the men who had overthrown Andros had suffered from the oppression of an arbitrary government. In rising against Andros they were no more to blame than the lords of the committee now conducting the hearing when they had acted against James II. At this point Joseph Dudley moved the committee to have the agents produce their credentials and to have them sign the charges made against the king's officers. The complaints in question, the agents replied, came from the populace of Massachusetts, from the "whole body of the People." From "the Rabble," Sawyer retorted. Increase Mather later claimed to have urged Cooke and Oakes earlier to sign the indictment, but they had begged off. They were not free to sign; only Ashurst and Mather could formally act as agents for the regime in Boston. But Ashurst and Mather also declined to sign, not having seen what proofs Cooke and Oakes allegedly had brought with them. As Mather put it: "Wee had bin children had we done it upon their saying they could prove what was asserted." The New Englanders, as a consequence of their hemming and hawing—their performance was reported in newsletters—faced ridicule in the city and in the country. What may have been decisive was the threat of legal action against them by Andros for damages had they taken responsibility for the charges.

The lords of the Committee for Plantation Affairs released the dominion officials from custody and dismissed the paper of complaints against them. Shortly afterwards Nottingham, one of the two principal secretaries of state, escorted them to the court at Kensington where the king, after a warm reception, pledged to provide for them. William III later appointed Andros to the governorship of Virginia and Dudley to the council of New York. In a mere formality the Privy Council on 24 April accepted the conclusion of the Lords of Trade.[10]

Although the agents had suffered a setback, they persisted in what Cooke called their "great business," the settlement of the government of Massachusetts. Their friends among the English Dissenting community judged they could best achieve this through a new charter. The time was not propitious. William III was then occupied with preparations for a campaign in Ireland, where James II, backed by French money and men, had landed. Shrewsbury was ill—he was to resign shortly—and thus there was left only one principal secretary of state to conduct affairs.

Nor did the adherents of the old commonwealth regime have it all their own way. Charles Lidget and other merchants in London who traded to New England had already presented to the Plantation Office an address from Boston signed by over forty men requesting the appointment of a governor and council to join with an elected assembly to replace the provisional government. For better defense and mutual security they wanted the separate provinces to have one governor. Various accounts arriving at the Plantation Office from hard-pressed inhabitants in Maine, from residents in Charleston, and from Anglican communicants in Boston recounted their distress under the prevailing government.[11] On 27 May Andros himself submitted a detailed account of the situation in northern America. He ended on a somber note: the French and Indians would probably invade the heart of New England unless the king took speedy action.[12] To obtain additional information the Plantation Office sent out a summons to the Royal Exchange for merchants with correspondents in New England and men knowledgeable about the situation in America to attend the board. Preparations for the king's departure for Ireland precluded taking immediate action, however.

For much of the summer of 1690 the agents were occupied answering complaints by Edward Randolph and Sir Robert Southwell and his colleagues at the Customs House. The news arriving from America was mixed. Although the fort at Casco Bay was lost to the French, Blathwayt could take some solace. From Boston, "freebooters" under Phips had had "a little Revenge" by plundering Port Royal.[13]

The summer of 1690 brought good news for the officials of the two provinces of southern New England. At the behest of William Whiting, the London merchant acting for Connecticut, Sir Henry Ashurst had obtained an opinion from Edward Ward that the "voluntary" surrender by the corporation of Connecticut of the charter in 1687 did not invalidate its patent. The corporation had not given up the charter under its public seal, and no legal record of the surrender existed in England. The public officials in the colony might lawfully execute the powers granted in the charter, notwithstanding the annexation of the Connecticut towns to the government under Andros. In this opinion, Sir John Somers and George Treby, the crown law officers, concurred.[14] The same reasoning applied to Rhode Island.

The status of Massachusetts, Plymouth, and New Hampshire, also part of the dominion, remained unclear. The majority of the settlers in the Piscataqua towns, resenting the claims of the proprietors, wanted to continue under the Bay, but the officials of Plymouth, through Ichabod Wiswall and Increase Mather, sought to obtain royal sanction as a separate colony.

The status of Massachusetts was the central issue. Despite the apparent urgency of the situation in New England, events in the British Isles took precedence. William III, occupied with the Continent, had not appointed a successor to Shrewsbury as secretary of state. Nottingham found the Queen would "not dispose of any thing w[it]hout the King's directions." Anxious for a solution, Mather approached the queen through the countess of Sunderland—"Southerland," he called her—a very pious and prudent lady. Mary allegedly assured the countess not to trouble herself. The New Englanders would have what they desired. She had spoken to the king, who had promised her they would have their privileges restored, so Mather recorded.[15]

What privileges the inhabitants of Massachusetts would have, had yet to be resolved, to be determined in a protracted negotiation lasting many months. Not until the first of the year did Ashurst and Mather set down proposals for a new charter. These covered several critical points. The province would include not only Massachusetts but the Narragansett county—that portion of Rhode Island claimed by Connecticut—as well as Maine, purchased by the provincial government at Boston in 1679 from the proprietary Gorges family, and New Hampshire, then claimed by the London merchant, Samuel Allen, through purchase from the Mason family. In 1677 judicial authorities in England had confirmed the right of the Masons only to the soil of New Hampshire.

By the proposals Mather presented, the government of Massachusetts would include a general assembly of representatives elected by the *freemen,* not the freeholders or the inhabitants. Under the old charter the General Court had admitted to freemanship men who were full members of the established Congregational churches in the towns. In response to extreme pressure from the crown, in 1664 it had admitted others who could meet a high tax-paying qualification. In 1691 Mather, Oakes, and Cooke, adherents of the old commonwealth party, hoped to have the corporation of Massachusetts consist of all men who had formerly enjoyed freemanship and those who would be admitted by the General Assembly. Unless the legislature drastically changed the qualifications, this would confirm political power to a minority of the adult men, the members in full communion of the Congregational churches. The Puritan spokesmen apparently did not ask for any guarantee for religious liberty to limit the authority of the dominant Congregationalist government.[16]

The territorial ambitions of the Massachusetts agents soon came into question. Samuel Allen entered a protest, supporting the claim to New Hampshire he had purchased by the opinion of two chief justices of England delivered in 1677 confirming the title of the Mason family.[17] A more serious challenge now arose. Mather's son, "the young pope," some called Cotton Mather, had been drumming up support in Boston for his father. In opposition to the "charter-mongers," a group of Anglicans and merchants in Boston and Charleston sent over to Sir Purbeck Temple in London an address protesting the proposed restoration of those who had controlled Massachusetts under the old charter. Formerly the crown had had no voice in the choice of officials or making of laws. Those controlling the corporation had admitted only such persons as they wished, depriving all others of the privileges of Englishmen.[18] Mather, Oakes, and Cooke dismissed the signers as opportunists, ill-informed men, or persons of little or no estate. This was hardly the case, according to information supplied to the Plantation Office when the Lords of Trade called for further testimony.[19]

William III was still absent from London. On 9 April 1691, the same day the Committee for Plantation Affairs received the protest from Boston against the charter party, Increase Mather had a long interview with the queen. The New Englanders had suffered cruelly at the hands of invading French and Indians, he informed Mary, merely for declaring in favor of the Protestant monarchs. If restored to their former privileges, they would serve the king and queen. Would Mary speak with William?[20]

In the spring of 1691 there seemed to be much uncertainty in Whitehall over the government of Massachusetts. Two weeks after Mather asked the queen to intercede, the Lords of Trade commissioned Henry, Viscount Sydney—he had succeeded Shrewsbury as secretary of state—to sound out Mather. Would the agents accept a new charter, one with privileges as great as any enjoyed in the dominions of the crown, leaving it to the king to commission the governor and council and the representatives of the inhabitants to pass laws, as did the Commons of England? Carmarthen was to broach the matter with the king. Would the monarch have his own appointee in Massachusetts to assent to all acts of the government as in other colonies, or would he leave the power of making laws solely to the people and the officials elected by them? Mather again had an opportunity to plead his case. Through the intercession of William Cavendish, earl of Devonshire, he had an interview with the king. The inhabitants of the Bay colony were a loyal people who had ventured their lives to enlarge the king's dominions by an expedition against Canada; if restored to their privileges, they would do so again. But what were the objections to a governor appointed by the crown? The men of Massachusetts were different in one respect from those of the other provinces, Mather replied. They were "congregational men" and Presbyterians; "such a Governor will not suit with the people of New England as may be very proper for the other English plantations."[21] William apparently made one concession: the agents could nominate a person as governor who might in his religious convictions be acceptable to the colonists. But the king would commission the governor.[22]

The king was off again to Ireland, leaving the Committee for Trade and Plantations to complete the business. On 14 May the lords instructed the attorney general, George Treby, to prepare a draft charter for their inspection. Over the next few weeks Treby, Somers (the solicitor general), and officials at the Plantation Office undertook a thorough review of the past relations between the crown and Puritan Massachusetts, inquiring into the charges of misgovernment at Boston, repeated failure to enforce the navigation code, unjust impositions of capital punishment by biblical injunction, and enacting laws repugnant to the statutes of England. The review made it clear that, by the proposals set forth by Mather and his colleagues, they wanted to perpetuate the old system and to restrict the franchise.[23]

In sharp contrast were the provisions for a charter submitted by royal officials. The inhabitants of Massachusetts must have their immediate dependence on the crown of England by a governor appointed by the king. He would participate in the legislative process with power to call assemblies of the inhabitatns and with them enact such statutes as might be agreeable to the laws of England, statutes to be transmitted to England for approval. The governor would have power to establish courts and appoint all officers necessary for administering justice and executing laws. All of the Christian inhabitants of the colony ought at all times to enjoy freedom of conscience and religious worship.

As Treby and other officials at Whitehall emphasized, the election of a general assembly must be by freeholders, rather than by freemen (the great bulk of whom under the old regime in Massachusetts had qualified as members in full communion of some Congregational church).[24]

Seeking to preserve some power for the godly elect, Mather and Cooke entered a series of counter proposals. They asked that freemen, those admitted to the corporation by the assembly (presumably the full church members admitted under the old charter) as well as freeholders—men with property of a certain value—exercise the vote and be eligible to hold office. The General Court, not the governor, ought to appoint judges and erect courts, including admiralty tribunals.[25]

Opposition arose within the Plantation Office to several of the proposals made by the agents and to a draft charter submitted on 8 June by Treby. Given the past behavior of the Bay colonists, there was no reason to grant them any more privileges than those enjoyed by the inhabitants of any other royal colony. To give the vote to others than freeholders and to allow an elected council would ensure the domination of the old church party. Finally, the General Assembly ought not to control judicial functions and appointments. The Plantation Office also saw defects in Treby's draft. It failed to allow the governor a veto in making laws and in dissolving the assembly. Above all, the General Assembly too strongly resembled the General Court under the old charter. The commonwealthmen who had for so long resisted the crown would thus be continued in power.[26]

Although the Lords of Trade did make some concessions to the spokesmen of the commonwealth faction, they adopted the substance of these criticisms. They conceded to the legislature a role in choosing some judicial and law-enforcing officials, but the governor appointed by the king would have a veto over all laws and other acts of the assembly. Laws passed in the Bay colony had to be transmitted to England for confirmation by the king. Roman Catholics were excluded from the freedom granted all other Christians for liberty of religious conscience. The Lords of Trade further struck at the power of the commonwealth faction when it ordered the attorney general to amend the draft he had submitted so that freeholders had the vote in electing representatives to the assembly. The agents in England could name some freemen, not exceeding one hundred, who, although not freeholders, might also vote.

Mather, Cooke, Oakes, and Ashurst persisted in their demands, but by the end of July they had made a critical concession on the franchise. The vote for provincial office in Massachusetts would be based, not on a religious, but on a property qualification: income of forty shillings a year from land, or fifty pounds in personal property. But the agents still hoped further to restrict liberty of conscience, to limit the powers of the governor in the selection of officers and in vetoing bills, and to deny to the crown an indefinite period for confirming legislation.

The Lords of Trade then referred the matter to the king. Nottingham sent over the amended draft of the charter to Sydney, the other principal secretary of state, then with William in the Netherlands.[27]

As Nottingham pointed out to William III, two points were critical: the selection of judicial officials and the election of councilors by the assembly without the approval of the governor nor ultimately of the king. If William gave up the first, he relinquished entirely the administration of justice. By relinquishing the second he would admit the elected assemblymen to a virtual partnership in government. If he lost both, little would remain of the dependence the colonists owed to the crown, for the power to reward and to punish—patronage—would be in the hands of the local assemblymen. The Committee on Plantation Affairs had already made all the "condescensions" to the colonists which could possibly consist with the king's sovereignty over them; they had already granted more than to any of the other provincials. Further concessions might encourage others—perhaps at home—to make bold demands if they could be so easily obtained merely by the asking. Differences of opinion on this matter, the Tory secretary of state assured William, were not a party matter, unless between men who would support the king's legal, just authority and those who would, little by little, leave him none.[28]

When the king stood on the matter did not remain long in doubt. He would by no means accept the objections of the provincial agents. [29] At best he would allow them to nominate the initial board of assistants, their names to be listed in the charter. These councilors would continue in office until the last Wednesday in May 1693.

The territorial extent of Massachusetts Bay had yet to be determined. Late in August Ashurst submitted a petition from Mather asking that the patent for the colony include Nova Scotia, Maine, and New Hampshire and contain a clause providing that the charter not deprive any person of rights or privileges. This petition the Lords of Trade took up on 2 September. They agreed that all former grants of land made by the governor and council and all property legally vested in the inhabitants should be protected.[30]

By 6 September Treby, the attorney general, had submitted a second draft of the charter. At this point Plymouth, but not New Hampshire, was included within the boundaries of Massachusetts. The survey undertaken in the course of drafting the new charter had confirmed that the government of the Piscataqua towns had reverted to the crown some years before and that the towns of Plymouth had never had a patent from the king to establish a separate government. The Committee for Plantation Affairs now resolved to incorporate within Massachusetts the region east of the Piscataqua River and to require that the council include residents from Plymouth, Maine, and Nova Scotia. By implication the decision rejected the claim of the Gorges family. Maine, sold by the Gorges family to Massachusetts in 1678, remained part of the Bay colony.

New Hampshire continued a colony apart. Samuel Allen petitioned the crown to appoint him as governor and John Usher, a merchant of Boston and former treasurer of the Dominion of New England, as his deputy. Inasmuch as Usher offered to bear the expense of maintaining a separate administration, the Lords of Trade accepted the offer.[31]

By the terms of the draft charter completed late in the summer of 1691, the government of Massachusetts consisted of a governor appointed by the king, an assembly elected by the freeholders in the towns, and a council chosen annually by the assembly subject to the approval of the governor. The initial board of assistants was named in the charter. Four of the eighteen councilors were from Plymouth. The governor enjoyed a veto over all bills and could adjourn, prorogue, and dissolve the assembly and exercise martial and admiralty authority. With the advice and consent of the council he appointed all commissions of oyer and terminer, sheriffs, marshalls, justices of the peace, and officers of the courts of justice. To be eligible to vote in provincial elections, a freeholder had to have land valued at forty pounds or a personal estate of fifty pounds. Inhabitants of Massachusetts would enjoy all of the liberties and immunities of freeborn and natural subjects as if they resided in England. Except for Roman Catholics, all Christians had liberty of conscience in the worship of God.

The assembly had power to constitute courts and with the consent of the governor to make reasonable laws, provided these were not repugnant or contrary to the laws of England. The monarch retained a negative on all laws, elections, and acts of government. Laws passed in Massachusetts must be sent to England by the first opportunity to be approved or disallowed. If not rejected within three years, they remained in force until repealed by the assembly.[32]

On 17 September the draft was read before Mary and the council, who ordered Nottingham to prepare a warrant for the queen's signature for passing the charter under the Great Seal. The following day Ashurst and Mather asked that the names of the first governor (Sir William Phips), his deputy (William Stoughton), and the councilors be inserted in the charter. Among those from Massachusetts, Mather nominated Simon Bradstreet, John Richards, Nathaniel Saltonstall, Wait Winthrop, Samuel Sewall, and Bartholomew Gedney; from Plymouth, Thomas Hinckley, William Bradford, John Walley, and Barbaras Lothrop.[33]

In these nominations Mather had a clear purpose. By selecting Hinckley, the former governor, and other influential men from Plymouth, he hoped to mollify resentment over the failure to secure a separate charter. Hinckley and his colleagues had sent Ichabod Wiswall to London to obtain a patent, but had failed to support him adequately. He had then recommended that they employ Ashurst and Cooke to manage their affairs at court. The Plymouth officials had chosen Ashurst as having the greater political influence. Wiswall blamed the decision to annex Plymouth to Massachusetts on Mather.[34]

The nomination of Phips and the remaining councilors reflected a division in the ranks of the agents, one mirroring a schism among the men who had overthrown the Dominion of New England. The names of Cooke and Oakes did not appear on the list Mather submitted to the Plantation Office. The two emissaries from the provincial convention had come to London for the express purpose of restoring the old charter. This had proved impossible, so Mather had decided. Not Cooke and Oakes; they refused to accept any compromise. To Cooke it seemed Mather had failed to promote the express goal of the agency; he had been duped into acquiescing in unnecessary concessions. He had blatantly attempted to increase his own influence by having his parishioners appointed to the governorship and the council.[35]

Cooke would return to Boston to rally his supporters, the unreconciled commonwealthmen, in opposition to Phips and the new regime.

On one critical point, the adherents of the old Puritan faction, the men who believed that only those giving strong evidence of God's redeeming grace should determine the destiny of the Biblical society, had already been repudiated in Massachusetts. Following the overthrow of Andros in perhaps the most permissive elections ever held in the colony, with few towns restricting participation to freemen, the returns were overwhelmingly in favor of resumption of the charter of 1629, but with a *qualification*: the substitution of a small property requirement for voting.[36] On this issue, the ministers of state in Whitehall who had insisted that religious standing not determine voting rights may have been closer to the sentiment of most men in Massachusetts than Elisha Cooke.

Mather had been more realistic in his assessment of the situation in London than Cooke and Oakes. As he himself later admitted, he had not obtained all he had wanted. Yet despite the objections of Blathwayt and Sir Robert Southwell, he had succeeded in packing the government with men favorable to the revolution and in putting a New Englander in the governor's chair. The people of Massachusetts would enjoy English liberties under a charter with privileges greater than those colonists in other royal provinces enjoyed. The inhabitants of the Bay would conduct themselves with appropriate loyalty and affection, Mather prior to his departure for Boston late in October 1691 assured the king. Phips had earlier enlarged the monarch's dominions by capturing Nova Scotia from the French. His appointment as governor would further obligate the king's subjects in New England.[37]

Later that year the new governor received his commission. Better to provide for the defense and security of the provinces of northern America, Phips was made commander in chief of all the forces of New Hampshire, Rhode Island, the Narragansett country, as well as Massachusetts Bay.[38]

William III and the higher ministers of state had also compromised, had accepted the Protestant Revolution in New England. Initially, before learning of the overthrow of the Dominion of New England, in the face of an apparent threat from the French they had looked with favor on political union for the northern colonies under closer direction from England. But from the outset, the Protestant monarchy had determined that the colonists would enjoy a representative assembly. After April 1689 it had been forced to accept the existence of separate, discrete political jurisdictions. William III, Nottingham, Carmarthen, and Shrewsbury, like

Charles II, James II, and Sunderland, mistakenly placed faith in the ability of governors to control the political situation in America while financially dependent for their salaries and, more important, for military expenditures on revenue locally sanctioned in America.

To gain the support of Massachusetts, the most populous and wealthy of the northern provinces, a colony without whose cooperation little could be achieved against the French and hostile tribesmen, the crown had accepted the promises of Increase Mather and named William Phips as governor. Lowborn, uneducated, he yet had some military ability and had the support of Mather, presumably one of the most influential of the New Englanders. The ministers of state had gratified the agent, allowing him to name the "king's" governor. Phips was hardly this—as the men at Whitehall would appreciate, but only some years later.[39]

At first all seemed to go well, as an anxious Nottingham assured an apparently skeptical Blathwayt. After Mather had returned to Boston, he wrote the Tory secretary of state that the people of the Bay were well pleased with their new charter. He had exhorted the assemblymen elected under the terms of the patent to vote an address of thanks to the king and queen. The new governor too seemed optimistic over the chances of raising volunteers for a campaign against Canada. But Phips sounded one sour note. A few men in Massachusetts too much "idolized" the old charter and even sought to prejudice the governor.[40]

Elisha Cooke had refused to accept compromise. He had returned to Boston to lead the attack on Phips and Mather waged by the unreconciled Puritans, the remnants of the commonwealth faction, the men who had been threatened by the abolition of the religious test for voting and office holding. The struggle for power, continued parochialism, and the ever-present, pervasive factionalism in Massachusetts and elsewhere made difficult the task of governing for men armed merely with the king's commission.

CHAPTER 10

London and America, 1689–95:
The Aftermath of Revolution

IN THE HALF DOZEN YEARS following the revolution in London and in the American colonies, the new royal administration faced several critical problems in seeking to establish its authority over the dominions across the Atlantic. Political instability in England resulting from rivalry between Whigs and Tories, administrative shortcomings, and the need to settle a religious establishment and to reconcile the Protestant Dissenters—a problem of more than passing interest to those in American who had assumed power—plagued the new government. In addition to appeasing religious sensibilities, any formula for settling Anglo-colonial political relations had also to take into account commercial interests and the financial concerns of the state—the pattern of overseas commerce and the protection of the trades in tobacco and naval stores vital to the New England and the Chesapeake colonies as well as to the revenue of the crown. Above all loomed a condition of chronic war with France and, later, also Bourbon Spain.

International and intercolonial conflicts threatened particularly the northern colonies, but also mandated that something be done with the proprietary Carolinas, Maryland, the Jerseys, and Pennsylvania. As proprietaries they did not hold themselves subject to the king's immediate government; that is, their governors were not appointed by or immediately subject to control by the king and his ministers. Inasmuch as they had been granted in absolute proprietary, they claimed a right of government limiting the monarchy.

In 1689 royal and proprietary control over North America had virtually colapsed. The ministers at Whitehall hardly knew who governed there. That year they had addressed orders in America to those who for the time being preserved the peace and administered the laws. The situation hardly had improved by the summer. William Jephson, personal secretary to the king, admitted that the administration did not know in what condition the government in New England stood.[1]

Over the next few years several factors limited the ability of the government to carry out a concerted program. The threat of a French-backed Jacobite invasion of the British Isles and a major war in Europe occupied much attention. Until 1696 no single official or board devoted full attention to the colonies. At home, political divisions, disputes over the religious settlement, and economic dislocations affected decisions made for the colonies across the Atlantic.

Political instability and disputes between parties over offices weakened the ability of the administration to act. Whigs and Tories were not as tightly disciplined as they were later to be. They did not always vote consistently. In the early years of the reign the parties consisted of loosely connected groups whose leaders might agree on some, but not all, questions. Not all issues were party matters. Party labels defined attitudes toward the revolution and certain fundamentals (the religious question, for example), but not on all matters, including colonial affairs. No group, Whig, Tory, country, or court faction, constituted a majority in Parliament; consequently, ministries consisted of shifting coalitions with the king free generally to choose his own ministers.

To carry out the royal policy William III preferred to rely as little as possible on Whig or Tory partisans, particularly members of the Whig junta, men like Sir John Somers, Edward Russell, and Charles Montagu, who hungered for office. The king was inclined toward moderates, the marquis of Halifax, the earl of Danby (now marquis of Carmarthen), the Tory earl of Nottingham, and the Whig duke of Shrewsbury, or a man of business like Sidney Godolphin, less attached to party and more inclined to administration.

The appointments made by William during his first year on the throne, rather than producing balance, accentuated divisions and stimulated animosities to the point that the work of government was impaired. The Whigs had turned their attack on men who in serving the previous two monarchs had strengthened the royal authority by allegedly illegal methods. To get at these opponents the Whigs had promoted a bill to restore the corporations, a device to establish for their supporters a monopoly of local office and thus to create the basis for a permanent majority in the House of Commons.

Disillusioned with the Whigs, William reshuffled his administration, turning to Nottingham and the Tories. But when the Tories in turn overplayed their hand in 1694, the king accepted, but reluctantly, the Whigs, bringing in Somers as lord keeper, Sir John Trenchard as a principal secretary of state, and Charles Montagu as chancellor of the Exchequer. It was not an impressive administration. As one observer complained: "We have a weak ministry at Present. Poor Duke Shrewsbury will be quite blind, & Sir J[ohn] Trenchard stone dead very shortly."[2]

The need for political support often overrode a reputation for laziness or lack of application to business when appointing men to office.[3]

The tendency of dispensing with the large, unwieldy Privy Council and relying on the advice of a few councilors sitting as a committee continued under William III. One standing committee dealt with trade and foreign plantations (including the Channel Islands). No matter relating to the colonies was ever decided upon until first examined and reported upon by this body. Serving as Lords of Trade and Plantations were the higher ministers of state, including the lord president, the lord privy seal, and the two principal secretaries of state. Two clerks of the council, one William Blathwayt, a veteran in this capacity, attended them.[4] Blathwayt was well versed in colonial affairs, having served at the Plantation Office since 1675. By purchase he had also acquired another administrative post, secretary at war.

William's personal preferences, the death of the queen, and the idiosyncracies of the principal ministers all worked to weaken the higher level of administration, including the conduct of colonial affairs. Shrewsbury, a neurotic bachelor, disliked routine. He had resigned as a principal secretary of state in 1690 and only reluctantly returned to office four years later. During his second term he left most of the work to the other secretary, first Trenchard and then Sir William Trumbull, or to his undersecretary, James Vernon.

The office of principal secretary of state had become central for the administration of the overseas colonies, for this was the office through which decisions were translated into action and all letters, orders, and petitions to the monarch passed.[5]

Dutch-oriented and head of a Protestant coalition in Europe opposing Louis XIV, the king was determined to keep control of foreign relations in his hands. He appointed Nottingham and Shrewsbury as secretaries because he needed men of rank and political influence to offset the contending parties. At times he was content to have men of lesser stature fill the secretariat or to leave one of the posts vacant for an extended time. During such intervals the burden fell on Blathwayt or James Vernon, Shrewbury's assistant. The conduct of colonial affairs suffered.

To limit the influence of the principal secretaries in foreign affairs, William when campaigning on the continent or on his annual trip to the Netherlands took along with him Blathwayt, the secretary at war. Hardworking and with a good command of languages, Blathwayt acted as a third secretary of state, but only for the duration of the king's stay on the continent.[6] Blathwayt had influence, but less than Vernon, and like Vernon he needed a political figure of the first rank to further his ideas or to advance the candidacy of his nominee for office.[7]

Competition to place colleagues was keen. When John Tucker, an undersecretary, learned of the death of a provincial official in Maryland—his post was worth 300 pounds a year—he urged John Ellis, Ormond's secretary, to have the duke solicit the king. "Apply tonight otherwise Blathwayt may probably be too nimble for us both."[8]

Despite the appearance of structure and order, the administration of plantation affairs at Whitehall left much to be desired. John Sheffield, earl of Mulgrave, was dissatisfied with the Lords for Trade and Plantations. They should meet on a regular schedule, rather than at the humor of the lord president, and be obliged to "look after their business." In 1694 Blathwayt confided to a colleague that several of the clerks and underclerks "were so blind that they could scarce read, therefore ye Councilboard was but ill served at present."[9]

Complex, at times intractable, problems relating to religion, commerce, procurement of stores for the Royal Navy, and military affairs, as well as obstreperous men, also frustrated the orderly transaction of colonial matters. Convictions and prejudices on religion had been central during the short reign of James II and the revolution which had cost him his crown. Men in America were eager to learn what course the Protestant monarchy would follow. In 1687, when William Penn had sought to win approval from the prince of Orange for the abolition of the Test Act, William had refused to support the Quaker, viewing the statute excluding Catholics from office as a bulwark for Protestants. This very argument was used against the king during the first political test of his reign in England over the nature of the established national church and the degree of toleration allowed Dissenters.

The earl of Nottingham, a spokesman for the Anglican Church faction, but also an advocate of reconciliation with the Dissenting Protestants, in conjunction with some members of the episcopal bench and leading clergymen in London played a key role in advancing proposals both for toleration and comprehension of Dissenters within the Church of England. On 27 February 1688/9 Nottingham introduced into the House of Lords two related bills: one to define Anglican doctrine so as to allow Dissenters to accept the Church, the other to tolerate under carefully limited conditions Dissenters—relatively few, it was expected—who could not accept comprehension, who would not return to the established national church.

Without consulting the Tory ministers of state, William III proposed additionally to eliminate the Test Act, which required all prospective officeholders to receive the sacrament according to the Anglican service. He favored making all Protestants eligible for office. In the House of Commons a coalition of Tories, moderates, and Whigs opposed this measure to strip the Anglicans of their monopoly of political office. The Act of Toleration—intended for the relatively few Dissenters who would elect to remain outside the national church—passed. It contained only modest concessions. Dissenters who took the oath of allegiance could workship in their own meeting houses, places of worship registered with a bishop or local magistrate with doors unlocked.

It was expected the bulk of the Dissenters would accept the national church, but in the elections for the convocation held at Westminster in November, the parish clergy selected some of the most intransigent of their brethren to represent them. Despite the support of Archibishop Sancroft and Bishop Compton of London, the moderates failed to win significant changes in the liturgy and doctrine of the established national church. The great bulk of the Protestant Dissenters remained outside the Church of England with this failure of comprehension; they enjoyed but a limited, ambiguous toleration. Only those men willing to take the sacrament according to the Church of England were eligible for office.[10]

The Protestant Revolution had brought but few changes in the religious code enacted by the Cavalier Parliament under Charles II; nor did it bring innovations in the basic navigation code enacted by the same Parliament for the overseas trade and commerce of England and the colonies. By these statutes granting English and English colonial shipping a monopoly of the carrying trade with the plantations, the government aimed to build up the potential for naval power; by channeling certain products of the colonies through English ports before they were carried to other markets, it raised a lucrative revenue. Since duties imposed on West Indian sugar and Chesapeake tobacco and taxes levied on European goods carried via English ports to the colonies brought in a considerable sum of money to the crown, royal officials reacted sharply to potential threats to this source of revenue posed by smuggling in England or violations of the navigation code in America and by disruption of transatlantic trade by war.

Also of concern was the welfare of the commerce of England as it related to the trade with the overseas colonies. Henry, Viscount Sydney, as lord lieutenant of Ireland, was under instructions to encourage the export of foodstuffs to the plantations and to advance the trade of Ireland, but only as far as might be consistent with the laws providing for the welfare and commerce of England.[11]

But in what did the economic welfare of England consist? To which of several conflicting interest groups must the government respond?

During time of war this dilemma was especially acute in procuring stores for the Royal Navy and in allocating men and ships for the overseas trades.

At the outset of the conflict with France in 1689, both the fighting ships of the Royal Navy and the cargo carriers of the English merchant fleet were largely dependent on foreign sources for stores. Although American merchants, factors and correspondents of London contractors, had for some time supplied the Navy Board with masts for the great ships of war as well as bowsprits and yards from the forests of New England, England was still dependent for many masts and much hemp, tar, rosin, planks, and spars on the Baltic lands. American supplies were not competitive in price. Proximity and lower labor costs gave the Baltic suppliers an advantage. Yet there were difficulties in trading to the Eastland; enemy fleets might interdict the narrow passage from the Baltic, and supplies were subject to control by the Tar Company of Stockholm, a series of chartered monopolies originating in 1648. The last chartered company, the Tjärunhandelssocieteten, organized the 1689 and protected by high-ranking officials of the Swedish crown, refused to allow the export of pitch and tar except at prices fixed by the company.[12]

Faced with immediate and potential obstructions, English officials and merchants looked across the Atlantic. But adequate development of naval stores and mines—much iron and copper went into ships—required governmental encouragement and support, both imperial and provincial.

The prospects attracted several competing gangs, including some Anglo-colonial consortia. Richard Wharton, the Massachusetts speculator and promoter, had already laid the foundations for an ambitious project to exploit the timber and mining potential in New England. Frustrated by the opposition of Governor Edmund Andros, he had come to London, where he and Sir John Shorter had organized a group of investors to raise one hundred thousand pounds to promote a New England venture. They had petitioned the crown for a charter incorporating them as a joint-stock company, when the death of Wharton and the overthrow of James II put a halt to their activities. Sir Matthew Dudley then assumed leadership. Not until 1691 did they renew their application for a charter. Others entered the contest, some English, some American, some mixed Anglo-colonial (the New Jersey Company and the Pennsylvania Company).

Sir Stephen Evance, a London financier, and Thomas Lake, a London merchant—both born in New England—formed one consortium. They joined Sir William Phips of Massachusetts, John Smith, and Thomas Doctor in a London-Massachusetts lobby. Sir Henry Ashurst, a prominent Dissenter and politician, and Samuel Allen, another Londoner who had purchased the proprietary claim of the Mason family to New Hampshire, later joined the group.[13] Another New Englander involved in the timber trade was Gabriel Bernon, a factor in Boston and partner of the contractor, Captain John Taylor.[14]

Other interests joined in the competition, the governor of New York on behalf of merchants of Manhattan, and Gerard Slye, the stepson of John Coode, on behalf of Maryland traders.

Presented with various projects, the Lords of Trade and Plantations threw open the competition; they ordered notice to be posted at the Royal Exchange that due consideration would be given to all proposals for importing naval stores from North America. In the ensuing contest for contracts, three factors were decisive: quality, price, and the political influence the bidders were able to muster. Competition was particularly sharp between two Anglo–New England syndicates, Dudley and his associates, and the Phips-Ashurst-Evance-Allen consortium.[15] The various groups opposed to the venture initiated by Richard Wharton argued that a patent issued to a joint-stock company would infringe on the charters of the New England provinces. Moreover, speculators—jobbers—in stocks might manipulate the venture. Despite the opinion of Attorney General Edward Ward that the proposed charter would not impinge on the patents of the New England colonies and the promise given by the members of the Dudley group that they would not sell their shares for at least three years, the venture did not progress. Other obstacles remained. The commissioners of the Admiralty could see no reason why anyone should be excluded from the trade in naval stores. At a loss as to what course to take, the Lords of Trade and Plantations in March 1694 called in representatives from the various competing interests. Ashurst and Evance argued at this meeting that Massachusetts would "inevitably" be ruined should any group receive a patent to engross the mines and trade of New England.

Over the protests of Dudley and John Taylor, the Lords for Plantation Affairs accepted a trial offer by Ashurst and Evance to bring over within a year a shipload of stores for testing. Months passed, and the ship did not arrive. The enterprising Taylor did not wait. In March 1696 he secured a license to search the woods of Maine and to fell as many trees as would be necessary to supply the navy with masts, yards, and bowsprits for the next five years.[16] Ironically, the next month a small vessel belonging to Evance and Ashurst came up the Thames. She was but half-loaded. When tested by officers at the royal dockyard at Deptford, the timber and treenails she delivered proved too "infirm," too weak to be of service, and the planks and knees very "tender." Worm holes testified to decay. The New England contractors had been incompetent. The knees—they took the greatest stress and required the greatest strength—had been cut cross-grained. A slight strain would cause them to break. The rafters for oars and the pitch might be serviceable, but the tar was of too "hot" a "temper" for the ropemakers. Many of the samples were defective, and the financial terms submitted by the contractors inadequate.

Chagrined, Evance and Ashurst pleaded that the trees had been chosen by unskilled persons and cut during the wrong season. Over the objections of Dudley and others, the Lords of Trade gave them another chance. Ashurst and Constantine Phips, an agent for Massachusetts, were allowed to nominate two men, the Navy Board another two, to conduct a survey in New England.[17] Years passed before the surveyors reported. Sir Matthew Dudley and the other subscribers for working mines and producing naval stores in New England waited in vain for a royal charter.

Other economic and commercial interests, also varied and often conflicting, were involved in the decisions affecting England's overseas shipping and commerce during the war. All merchants and traders wanted protection for their vessels and cargoes, but the government also had a direct financial interest from the customs revenue derived from overseas trade. The revenue from the cargoes brought in by the tobacco and sugar fleets from the Chesapeake and the West Indies amounted to a considerable sum of money. In the summer of 1691, when French privateers were threatening the sea approaches used by returning merchantmen, the marquess of Carmarthen complained to the king over the failure to provide adequate protection at Torbay. Two of the largest Virginia merchantmen were taken in the Soundings. They would have paid twelve thousand to fourteen thousand pounds in customs. It was with some relief that Nottingham the next month noted the safe arrival at Kinsale of the Barbados fleet and merchantmen from the Chesapeake. They would bring in at least three hundred thousand pounds in revenue.[18]

To safeguard revenue accruing from imports, the administration had dispatched orders to the governors in the colonies to enforce the statutes on navigation and the surveyors in England to call for troops to assist in destroying tobacco grown contrary to parliamentary statute in Gloucester, Worcester, Warwick, and Hereford. Spokesmen for the court in the House of Commons resisted attempts made on behalf of the planters and merchants involved in the tobacco trade to reduce the duties added in the first year of the reign of James II. But the Commissioners of the Customs did support the position of the merchants in the tobacco trade that the provincial assemblies ought to outlaw the export of tobacco in bulk, a method of shipment facilitating smuggling.[19]

The allocation of merchant vessels for the fleets sent out each year posed another problem. Because of the bulk of the cargoes and the value of the customs they paid, the West Indian and Chesapeake trades ranked high in the annual competition among the various overseas trades for ships and crewmen. With a limited number of seamen available, the merchant trades had to compete among themselves and with the Royal Navy. Dozens of merchants engaged in the tobacco trade alone, and tradesmen in rival ports competed with Londoners. The problem for the Chesapeake traffic was particularly vexing, for it involved bulk cargoes and long stays in American waters before the vessels returned to England.

Late in the summer of 1690 the Committee for Trade and Plantations called in representatives of the various trades: Hudson's Bay Company, African Company, Canary Islands, Spain, Mediterranean, Chesapeake, and the West Indies. The tobacco merchants asked for an allotment of twelve hundred sailors to man sixty vessels; they expected to bring back cargoes paying two hundred thousand pounds in customs. Twenty-five merchants, including William Whiting, formerly of New Haven in Connecticut, spoke for the New England trade. They needed relatively few ships for the direct trade between England and the northern provinces, but these colonies were necessary in supplying the West Indian plantations with essential provisions.

The formula decided upon by the committee on 21 September 1690 allotted the West Indian and Chesapeake fleets each twelve hundred men with the distribution of the mariners among the ships of the individual merchants to be left to the Commissioners of Customs. Carmarthen, the lord president, suggested that the number be proportional to the amount in customs each merchant expected to pay.[20]

A somewhat different procedure prevailed the next year for the Chesapeake trade. Thirty-three of the principal merchants of London selected Micajah Perry and Peter Paggen to allocate the ships and crewmen assigned them. But the Londoners had cause to complain over the number of sailors employed by the merchants of the outposts. Enjoying a geographical advantage, vessels from Bristol and the ports in the west and north of England that winter arrived earlier on the Chesapeake than did their rivals form London. Their masters were able to scoop the market by falsely reporting that there would be no fleet from London.[21] Following complaints from the merchants in the metropolis, the government also restricted the merchants of the outports in the number of ships and seamen they employed in the tobacco trade.

In 1693 the system was set. Thirty-one hundred and twenty seamen were allowed to vessels engaged in the plantation traffic, with 1,188 assigned to ships for the Chesapeake. The Commissioners of Customs determined the distribution of ships and sailors for each of the trades and regions and the proportion between London and the outports.

Competition was also keen for the limited resources of the Royal Navy, for the convoys, the vessels escorting the merchantmen through enemy infested waters. In February 1693 the merchants trading to Bilbao and San Sebastián asked for additional frigates to be assigned to protect their ships. These were hardly adequate later that year when disaster struck the eleven English and five Dutch convoys escorting the Smyrna fleet. Off Lagos they met the Toulon squadron, more than seventy French ships of the line. Over eighty English merchantmen were lost.

Along the wide arc covering the approaches to the British Isles, protection was needed, as French privateers awaited the return of the merchantmen, including the heavily laden, clumsy bulk carriers from the Chesapeake. Not even the northern passage between Ireland and Scotland was safe. To meet the threat of the hostile raiders, the Commissioners of Revenue in Dublin called for more convoys and cruisers.[22] The clamor for naval protection continued. Traders wanted not merely cruisers to patrol the approaches to the British Isles but convoys to escort the merchantmen to and from America.[23]

Military as well as naval protection in North America was imperative. In 1689 the English and Dutch nations had became enbroiled in what proved to be an extended conflict with Bourbon France. For almost a generation, with but one brief interlude, hostilities raged in Europe and in the colonies. William III and his ministers adopted a "continental" strategy, committing the great bulk of English resources to a major effort in Europe and leaving the American colonies to their own resources. Occupied elsewhere, but depending on the provincials to resist the French in North America, the royal administration was hardly in a position to compel the colonists to accept a more dependent role, one subservient to the crown. It needed the cooperation of the provincial regimes to further the interests of the monarchy against the French in the Western Hemisphere.

The king and his councilors did see the need for union in America and supervision of the proprietary and chartered colonies as helpful for the defense of the English dominions in the Western Hemisphere, as had the men who had served James II. Following the declaration of war against France, a committee of the council recommended quickly settling a government for the northern colonies to allow these provinces by their united forces to oppose the French and to carry out whatever ventures might be required in the Western Hemisphere. Without such union the French might easily possess the dominion and trade of northern America.

The potential for coordinating the military resources of the English colonies which had previously existed under the Dominion of New England had been lost with the overthrow of Sir Edmund Andros and the resurrection of the separate provincial regimes. With the incarceration of Andros in Boston and the flight of his deputy, Francis Nicholson, from New York, there was no royal official at large in America with the requisite military experience and training. Nicholson, before being forced to abandon his duties at Manhattan, had sent word to London of the Indian attacks on the northern frontiers.

Intelligence from Boston seconded the urgency of the situation. The English in the north, but recently united and formidable, were again divided into several jurisdictions. Simon Bradstreet, nominal head of the provisional government at Boston, confirmed the extent of Indian raids into Maine, New Hampshire, and across the Merrimack. Efforts by the revolutionary regime to defend against the French and Indians had been unsuccessful. John Usher, a merchant who had served on Andros's council, predicted openly that unless the crown sent over a governor with a standing force and united the petty governments, the country was in danger of being overrun. Edward Randolph from his confinement in Boston recalled for the Lords of Trade the resolution of the late Charles II to prevent the ill consequences of too many petty governments by setting up a unified administration. A thousand or more good soldiers would regain lost territory and return the inhabitants of the Bay colony to a firm dependence on the crown. Otherwise the French would overrun the English provinces.[24] Randolph was ever prone to exaggeration.

The initial response in England was far short of what Randolph and the other royal adherents in America hoped. After John Riggs, the ensign who had delivered the messages from Andros and Nicholson, testified, the Lords of Trade in August 1689 recommended only that a governor be dispatched to New York with two companies of foot soldiers to supplement the two companies already stationed on the northern frontier. Later that year Nicholson himself arrived in London, but he was clearly unacceptable to those who had taken over government in Boston and Manhattan. The crown sent him back to America, but to Virginia as lieutenant governor. Once there, he found little hope for cooperation among the colonies, given the disorders prevailing both in the northern colonies and in the southern proprietaries.[25]

Timely, adequate aid did not come from England. Not until early March did Colonel Henry Sloughter arrive in New York with two companies of royal soldiers to take up his post as governor. He found the task of defending the colony against the French and their Indian allies compromised by the political animosities prevailing in New York and the unsettled conditions in the neighboring provinces. Sloughter died within a few months, and once more Van Cortlandt and Bayard put out an urgent plea for an experienced military officer to serve as governor and for the crown to join the neighboring colonies, Connecticut, East and West Jersey, and Pennsylvania to New York, at least for the duration of the war.[26]

Support for union, but for union more limited in scope, came from the Puritan element in New Hampshire. Through William Wallis, a timber merchant, and William Whiting, the London trader who acted at times as agent for Connecticut, two of the principal inhabitants on the Piscataqua, William Vaughan and Richard Waldron, sent off addresses to the king and queen relating the deplorable condition of the region and asking that the towns of New Hampshire be joined to the Bay colony. Without the support of Massachusetts the New Hampshiremen must abandon their villages.

Political and military considerations as well as the claims of the proprietors impinged on the decisions made at Whitehall and Hampton Court whether or not to consolidate. The request from the Piscataqua towns to be joined to Massachusetts arrived too late to do any good, if indeed it had any chance. Samuel Allen, the London timber merchant who had purchased the proprietary title to New Hampshire from the Mason family, had received the sanction of the crown as governor.[27]

The proprietors of Pennsylvania and Maryland were not as fortunate, or, perhaps, as influential. The Quaker William Penn, thought by some a secret Jesuit, was outlawed as a suspected Jacobite and was thus ineligible to govern Pennsylvania. The Catholic Lord Baltimore was considered to have been too remiss in not notifying the provincial regime in Maryland of the accession of the Protestant monarchs and in not providing for the defense of the inhabitants to be allowed to hold the government of Maryland.

A trio of experienced military officers received commissions as governors, Colonel Benjamin Fletcher for New York, Colonel Lionel Copley for Maryland, and Colonel Edmund Andros for Virginia. While attempting to stiffen colonial resistance to invasion and to provide more competent military direction, the crown did not do away with the colonies as separate political entities as had been done under James II. It allowed the existing divisions to prevail (with one exception, Plymouth), at the same time providing experienced officers as governors in the most critical provinces and granting them command of the militia of the neighboring colonies. The provinces remained distinct from each other, each with its own civil officials and representative assemblies, but royal governors now were empowered to call out quotas of their militia for the defense of New York and New England.

The choice of officers as governors reflected, in part, political influence, as in the case of Copley, but also the particular concern of the king, as in the selection of Fletcher. William III had insisted that the governor of New York, a weak and exposed colony, be "a person of experience," one "bred up a soldier." The king had singled out Fletcher for the post. His performance during the campaign in Ireland against James II had brought him to the attention of the Protestant monarch.[28]

The command of the militia of New England initially went to Sir William Phips, the rough Maine seaman who led an expedition of New Englanders against the French in 1690. At the behest of Increase Mather, agent for the Massachusetts provisional government, Phips had received an appointment as governor of Massachusetts. As Blathwayt, the secretary to the Plantation Board explained it, the appointment of Phips was to be the means "by which His Maj[es]ties authority is to be reset[t]led in those parts."[29] Evidently Mather had implied that the appointment of Phips would ensure competent leadership and the active support of the New Englanders in the struggle against the French.

The Protestant monarchy had accepted the dissolution of the Dominion of New England. For a time in the spring of 1689, before word came of the overthrow of Andros, William and his council, while preserving political unity in the north, responded to the plea of Increase Mather to recall the governor.[30] Once the court appreciated that the Dominion had been overthrown, it was forced to accept Massachusetts, Rhode Island, New York, and the other provinces as separate provinces. Rather than appointing a governor general, the crown named individual executives for Maryland, New York, and Massachusetts with authority to draw upon the militia of the neighboring corporate provinces. With the exception of Plymouth—it had never received a charter and was now merged with Massachusetts—the various provincial regimes were allowed to maintain their civil jurisdictions, each with an elected assembly.

William III and his ministers of state, Whig and Tory, while accepting the overthrow of the Dominion and the resurrection of the former separate colonies, would not allow the unsettled state of affairs created as a result of the Protestant insurrections to continue in Boston, Saint Marys, and Manhattan. From information reaching Whitehall, the Committee for Plantation Affairs had concluded that New York was under "no Legall or settled governm[en]t[,] being in the hands of one Leister [sic]," a "Walloon who had sett himself at the head of the Rable."[31]

The legal status of the governments of the chartered colonies varied. The patent of Massachusetts had been vacated in the royal courts at Westminster, but the proprietors of East and West Jersey and the authorities of Connecticut and Rhode Island allegedly had voluntarily surrendered their political authority. That the proprietors of the Jerseys had ever received a valid patent from the crown was doubtful.

Some among the old-line bureaucrats familiar with the problems encountered with the Bay colony and the other provinces over the years, Sir Robert Southwell and William Blathwayt, had counseled against allowing the proprietary and chartered governments to resume their "usurped" privileges. To do so would confound the resolution of problems in the northern portions of America and lessen the dependence of the colonists on the crown of England.[32]

William Penn and Lord Baltimore for the time being had lost the power to appoint governors. It remained to be seen whether royal officials, Phips in Boston, Fletcher in New York and Philadelphia, Andros in Virginia, and Copley in Maryland could mobilize the English in America, restore stability, and render the colonists more dependent on the crown of England.

CHAPTER 11

The Aftermath of Revolution: Proprietary Carolina and Royal Virginia, 1690–96

THE MEN WHO HAD FORCED James II to flee England and who served the Protestant monarchy in Whitehall would not restore to America consolidated government solely by appointed officials. But the provinces north of the Delaware, if not unified to provide greater protection against the French, must yet coordinate their military efforts. As for Pennsylvania, Maryland, and the Carolinas, these proprietary provinces were not immediately under the crown; ordinarily, the king did not appoint the governors or the councilors. Under Charles II and his brother change had been imposed through the royal courts at Westminster or, at least, through the threat of judicial writ. Conscious of the objections raised to the exercise of the royal prerogative, the men who served William III eschewed this approach. The lords of the Committee for Plantation Affairs advised that it was for Parliament to consider bringing the American proprietaries to a closer dependence on the crown. In the spring of 1689 they suggested that those of the king's privy councilors who sat in the House of Commons move that Parliament take the problem under consideration.[1]

During the next decade the administration made no such move; it adopted no consistent policy; it imposed no unified posture for defense for the individual colonies. The proprietaries, for the most part, continued as before. Political influence, private interest, and parochial concerns continued to dominate in governmental circles.

Unwilling or unable to go to Parliament and hesitant to adopt judicial or prerogative action, the ministers at Whitehall seized on a temporary expedient, a formula given judicial approval: in case of extraordinary circumstances, emergencies arising through default or neglect by proprietors or those appointed by them, the crown might, for a time, name a governor for a colony. This rationalization they applied only in two instances and, in the case of Pennsylvania, for a very limited time.

As the experience with Virginia, a royal colony, demonstrated, simply appointing a governor and councilors did not allow ministers at Whitehall control over men and events three thousand miles across the

Atlantic and several weeks, or even months, removed in time. It was even more difficult in provinces where ethnic and religious tensions strained the social fabric and endemic factionalism weakened governmental institutions. Parochial interests, the ambitions of local men, and social and political divisions sharply limited the ability to achieve stability and cohesion, to enforce the acts of trade and navigation, and to coordinate English military operations in North America.

South of New York, a frontier colony of about fourteen thousand inhabitants exposed to hostile incursions, an immense territory extended for hundreds of miles to the Savannah River and Spanish Florida. It included eight separate or nearly autonomous jurisdictions, only one directly under the crown. Only at Jamestown ordinarily did a governor and council appointed by the king preside.

Of the more than two hundred thousand inhabitants in the English colonies in America, about half lived in the region south of New York. Of these, three-fourths lived in the Chesapeake provinces, with Virginia, the oldest of the English plantations, boasting about fifty thousand souls. Farther to the south lay Carolina, divided into two widely separated communities, each with its own government. About eight thousand people inhabited four districts around Albemarle and Pimlico sounds beyond the Virginia line. South Carolina with a population of about four thousand settlers had yet to experience the great growth triggered later by the production of naval stores and the cultivation of rice.

The two Carolinas, not yet distinguished nominally, might easily have qualified for a take-over by the crown. In the region south of Cape Fear ethnic and religious animosities sharply divided society, and factional conflict paralyzed government. The English in the West Indies had already suffered heavily from French depredations, and in the near future the subjects of Louis XIV would plant the fleur-de-lis on the Gulf coast and on the lower Mississippi River. But in 1690 the threat from the French and the Spanish in Florida was only potential, not immediate.

The board of eight proprietors to whom Charles II a generation before had granted a charter, despite the titles possessed by a few of its members, had never exercised effective control over the settlements. By 1690 the number and political weight of the proprietors had diminished. The first earl of Shaftesbury, the first duke of Albemarle, John and William Berkeley, and Sir George Carteret had died; their shares had been absorbed and passed on to minors or lesser men, Thomas Amy, Seth Sothell, and John Archdale. When Sir Peter Colleton died in 1694, his share went to his infant son, to be administered by an executor, William Thornburgh. John Archdale, a convert to Quakerism, managed another share, purchased for his minor son. Not until 1694 did the English courts declare John earl of Bath, the heir to the share held by Albemarle. The portion initially held by Shaftesbury had gone to his grandson, Maurice Ashley, a man in his early twenties.

Only one of the proprietors was on the scene in America during the turbulent months of 1689. Seth Sothell had been sent out by his colleagues following a warning by the crown to establish some order. Although Sothell had some supporters in the Albemarle settlements,[2] he fell afoul of George Durant and the leading planters. They charged him with bribery, corruption, and extortion and would have packed him off to England had he not begged to submit the issue to the local legislature. The assembly gave judgment against him, ruling the proprietor must leave Albemarle and abjure the government. Learning that the settlers alleging injustice had risen against Sothell, the proprietors in London appointed Philip Ludwell, a long-time resident of Virginia, as governor with authority to inquire into the causes of the rebellion, the second in Albemarle within a dozen years. Sothell's capitulation and the behavior of the leading planters, the proprietors condemned as prejudicial to the honor of the crown and their own dignity.[3]

Philip Ludwell was no stranger to rebellion. One of two brothers who had emigrated from England to the Chesapeake, he had staunchly supported Governor Sir William Berkeley during the revolt led by Nathaniel Bacon in 1676. He later married the governor's widow. Appointed to investigate the situation in Carolina, Ludwell found himself challenged in Albemarle.

Following the enforced departure of Sothell, one John Gibbs, a distant relative of the duke of Albemarle, as the self-proclaimed heir to a proprietary share, put forth a claim to the governorship. In June 1690 he issued a declaration denouncing Ludwell as an impostor and led a party of armed men to break up a court session at Pasquotank. Ludwell, absent from Albemarle, had commissioned a member of the council, Thomas Jarvis, as his deputy. In London the proprietors repudiated the claim of Gibbs under the Fundamental Constitutions, and when the English courts awarded the Albemarle proprietary share to the earl of Bath, Gibbs lost all legal standing. Ludwell, resident in Charles Town, was confirmed as governor, with Jarvis as his deputy in the northern settlements. The proprietary board then allowed the elected assembly to meet separately from the council and to initiate legislation and amend bills.

Order was restored, in part because of the tact employed by John Archdale when sent out by the proprietary board in 1694. Thomas Harvey, who had taken over on the death of Jarvis, and the proprietary deputies and other members of the council professed themselves satisfied with the Quaker proprietor.[4] For a while, the Albemarle precincts were quiet, but only for a time. Within a generation revolt again disrupted the government.

Confused institutional arrangements and weak proprietary government also made for instability in the southern portion of Carolina. When Sothell fled to Charles Town, he quickly fell in with the Anglican planters and merchants from the West Indies, who for two decades had sought to control the government, the distribution of land, and the trade in animal skins and Indian slaves. In the summer of 1690 government was at a virtual standstill as a result of the extreme positons taken by opponents and proponents of Governor James Colleton. At this time the men opposed to the proprietary regime might have considered the feasibility of the crown's assuming the administration with a governor amenable to them. For the moment Seth Sothell served their purpose; as a proprietor he was the highest ranking official in the colony. The situation was serious if not critical. In the West Indies the French had captured Saint Christopher and were rumored about to strike at Carolina. Word had come of the overthrow of three English governments in the north. In Charles Town the provincial laws were about to expire because the legislature had not met for some time and quitrents on land were falling due.

Ethnic and religious divisions further set men against each other. For the English Dissenters and the alien Scots and French Huguenots, proprietary government had served to protect them against the domineering Anglicans from the West Indies. John Stewart had expressed their resentment when he referred contemptuously to Maurice Matthews and James Moore, leaders of the Barbadian Goose Creek faction, as "Mine Heer Mauritius" and the "heating Moor."[5]

Although several of the Goose Creek men thought compromise possible, some of the supporters of Colleton refused to consider it. Landgrave Thomas Smith, with the assistance of Paul Grimball, Stephen Bull, and Charles Colleton, drew up and circulated a petition asking the governor to declare martial law. On 26 February 1690 James Colleton complied and the following month forbade trading with the Indians except under regulation and ordered landowners to begin paying quitrents to the proprietors.

That summer Sothell arrived from Albemarle. He offered to the opponents of the governor the opportunity to seize power with some pretense of legitimacy. Hitherto they had objected to the frame of government imposed by the overlords in London; but under the Fundamental Constitutions, as a proprietor, Sothell had precedence over Colleton. Matthews and Moore collected five hundred signatures on a petition asking Sothell to assume control. Colleton and his council, contesting Sothell's authority, issued a call to the militia, but finding themselves outnumbered, they gave way.

A purge of proprietary supporters, including those with commissions from the board in England, followed. Sothell then subjected Colleton to the same treatment he had received in Albemarle. On 22 December 1690, the provincial legislature, firmly under the control of the Goose Creek men—many of the planters in the outlying precincts had difficulty coming to Charles Town to vote—passed a bill barring James Colleton from office and banishing him from the colony. Also proscribed were Stephen Bull, Thomas Smith, and Paul Grimball for their role in proclaiming martial law. To win support the assemblymen passed another bill granting denizenship to French and Swiss Protestants, provided they registered within six months. This concession was only temporary, however.

The London-based proprietors reacted sharply to the news of the coup. Repudiating the actions of Sothell, they recalled him to England to answer charges. Tumultuous petitions, they warned the Barbadians, were a dangerous example, punishable by death. Disallowing the legislation enacted under Sothell, they threatened to surrender their power of government to the crown: they would not permit themselves to be imposed upon or the populace to be oppressed.[6] To make the assembly more representative and to lessen the domination of the West Indian faction, they authorized Philip Ludwell to call an assembly of twenty representatives, seven each from Berkeley and Colleton counties, and six from Craven, the last inhabited for the most part by French Huguenots. The earl of Craven and the other proprietors were concerned by the challenge from two sources, royal as well as Barbadian. Ludwell was to appoint none to office but such as were well affected to the crown and its officers.[7] Notwithstanding proprietary instructions and the departure from the colony of several of the extremists, James Colleton, Sothell, Maurice Matthews, Robert Quary, and Andrew Percivall, Carolina society remained badly divided. Paul Grimball and the planters who had supported James Colleton and had been proscribed from office during Sothell's regime were not inclined to make peace with their enemies. For them the rule was to do unto others as they had done unto them. Some men, like Joseph Blake, Stephen Bull, and Ralph Izard, were more moderate, but the two houses of the legislature could agree on little.

Confident of success, the proprietors now paid little heed to the possibility that the crown might take over the administration. They insisted on prosecuting men who refused to pay quitrents, and they would accept no alteration in the system of government or part with any of their powers until the people were more "orderly."[8] Philip Ludwell found it impossible to serve under these conditions. He threw up his post and returned to Virginia. For a time Thomas Smith, a deputy for Thomas Amy who held a patent of provincial nobility as a landgrave, with the consent of the council assumed the government, but he too found the conditions imposed by the proprietors and the discontent of the planters, particularly over the terms for taking up land and paying rents, made his task impossible. In the fall of 1693 he notified the proprietors that he and others intended to leave Carolina and settle elsewhere. A previous governor, Joseph West, equally frustrated by the unsettled conditions in Charles Town a decade before, had taken the same course. Smith resigned after warning that it was impossible to manage Carolina unless a proprietor came out with full power to settle grievances.[9]

This bleak assessment finally moved the proprietors to action. After several meetings at Thornburgh's home they decided to send out John Archdale. He had specific authority to submit provisions of the Fundamental Constitutions to the assemblymen for approval, but in selling land he was to reserve a *just* annual rent. Some months passed before Archdale left for America, but even while on his voyage, he entertained doubts over his mission. From Madeira he wrote back to London suggesting that the proprietors defer the matter of quitrents. Craven, Ashley, Bath, and Thornburgh refused. Nothing would secure their interests in Carolina as well as a steady income. They did not expect the payment to discourage persons from buying land or settling in the colony. To the contrary, Carolina, they expected, would become a refuge for those oppressed by arbitrary government elsewhere.[10]

For the French settlers in Carolina, however, the threat of arbitrary rule came from the Anglicans who dominated in the assembly at Charles Town and opposed the proprietors. Hitherto the Huguenots had enjoyed full privileges under the terms of the charter from Charles II to the proprietors; they had freedom of religious conscience, held commissions as justices, and voted for members of the privincial assembly. In recent months some men in Charles Town challenged the right of these "strangers" to sit in the assembly, to hold office, or to take up lands. The arrival of Archdale in the fall of 1695, according to one observer, "has a little suspended their fury." Ironically, resentment against the Huguenots— they numbered some four hundred to five hundred settlers out of a population of about four thousand—now seemed stronger in the old proprietary faction led by the English and Scottish Dissenters. Supporters of the former governor, James Colleton, they could not forgive the Huguenots for previously backing Seth Sothell.[11]

The Quaker Archdale initially took the side of the Huguenots, but he soon appreciated that he could not achieve what his colleagues in England

expected of him if he insisted on full political rights for the French inhabitants. Consequently, when he issued writs calling for the election of a
new assembly of twenty members, he stipulated that they be returned
from Berkeley and Colleton counties, but not from Craven. Contrary to
orders, he compromised with the anti-French element in the legislature
on the dispute over land and rents. Despite the advice he sent back to
England, his colleagues from an Olympian position—William Thornburgh's house on Tower Hill in London—would not acquiesce. Archdale
must not grant lands to any person but for a valuable quitrent. Even to
abate any of the arrears in rent might be an ill precendent, lessen the
authority of the proprietors, and render them liable to contempt.

Caught between the intractable proprietors in London and the stubborn opposition in Charles Town, Archdale chose the course best suited
to meet the immediate problem, "for ye humor of our People will not be
drove butt are to bee ledd even to [t]hat w$^{ch:}$ is to their own Interests to
doe." Past experience with the Fundamental Constitutions had so taught,
he argued with his colleagues in London.[12] Taking the initiative, early in
1696 Archdale worked out a compromise with the leaders in the local
legislature on paying rents and financing the provincial government. The
agreement would not be altered without the consent of the assembly. By
the terms of the settlement, landowners could pay quitrents in commodities suitable for the local rather than the English market, and the
proprietors would remit all arrears in past rents if the assembly would
provide for the construction of a new fort and pay seventeen hundred
pounds in back salary owed by the proprietors to former governors in lieu
of the debts due to the proprietary board. As part of the arrangement the
legislature passed a stringent law for repossessing lands if rent was in
default for thirty days or more. All revenues derived from rents would
remain in Carolina to pay the salaries of proprietary officials.

The compromise came at the expense of the French settlers. This the
proprietors in London initially refused to accept. For a time they remained adamant in support of the Huguenots, reproaching Archdale for
the "expedient" of not issuing a summons to the inhabitants of Craven
County to elect representatives to the assembly as formerly. Recognizing
the problem caused by the disparity in population between the counties,
they recommended increasing the number of delegates from Berkeley by
five, from Colleton by two.

The financial advantages of the arrangement worked out by
Archdale proved too tempting. Craven, Bath, and the other proprietors
finally abandoned the French. Although they never assented to the laws
enacted in early 1696, they allowed them to remain in force. When
Archdale left the colony that year, he selected as governor Joseph Blake,

the son and heir of Benjamin Blake, one of the leading Dissenters who had come to the colony a decade before. Archdale also arranged for Blake to purchase a proprietary share.[13]

Stability in government under proprietary rule seemed to have come to South Carolina. Despite a somewhat wider geographical representation among the political leaders in the colony, the men from Berkeley County dominated the legislature if only by their advantage in living close to the seat of government, in being able to attend more readily than the representatives from the outlying districts. Yet within a few years signs pointed to a breakdown in the compromise Archdale had effected on land and rents. Stability was only short-lived. Tension was inherent in a society characterized by mobility at the higher levels and ethnic and religious pluralism and governed by a proprietary board commanding little respect, evoking little fear, and demonstrating but timidity and inconsistency. The next generation of ambitious men easily toppled the proprietary regime in Charles Town.

In contrast to South Carolina, Virginia possessed a government depending directly on the crown; that is, the king rather than proprietors commissioned the governor and his council. Such an arrangement, the ministers of state at Whitehall ever since the day of Charles II expected, would promote greater political stability and induce closer adherence to parliamentary statutes regulating the foreign commerce of the overseas plantations. Events on the Chesapeake, when viewed clearly, did not confirm such an assumption.

Even with experienced officials such as Francis Nicholson and Edmund Andros presiding over the administration of Virginia, problems— some profound, some petty and personal—involving matters of privilege and authority frustrated royal officials. Certain issues were common throughout America. How best to award office to gratify the socially ambitious and yet build support for a governor and the policies of the crown? How best to raise revenue to finance local government and support the larger English cause in the Western Hemisphere? How best to meet the economic needs of the populace within the restrictions imposed by the parliamentary navigation code, a particularly trying problem during time of war when English shipping was short and the temptation strong to resort to alien merchantmen, a practice proscribed by the acts of trade? Other problems were peculiar to the Chesapeake and the Old Dominion: marketing the colony's staple, the orderly export of the annual tobacco crop from designated ports or locations, and the drain on revenue available to the local government from the rights to quitrents and escheats in the Northern Neck, the region between the Potomac and the Rappahannock held by the heirs of the Culpeper family in England.

Virginia seemed quiet enough in 1690 when Francis Nicholson, cleared of the fanciful charges leveled against him by the insurgents in New York, arrived at Jamestown with a commission from the crown as lieutenant governor. The councilors who had predominated in political life since the Restoration had kept a firm grip, easily putting down the malcontents in Stafford County who had sought to capitalize on the confusion resulting from the Protestant Revolution in England.

New men were coming to the fore by 1690 as death and retirement thinned the ranks of the sons and nephews of the country gentry and merchants of England who had migrated to the Old Dominion roughly a generation before. More and more natives of Virginia began to take their places on the county commissions, in the House of Burgesses, and on the governor's council. They aspired to the places their fathers held. The local magnates resented outsiders winning posts, the "inconvenience" of places going to men who did not reside in the colony but who named a deputy, drew a large profit, and did nothing themselves.

Some English officials too were prejudiced against any but the well-to-do holding high office. Nicholson "heartyly wish[ed] . . . yt no Plebians" be countenanced for fear of the precedent it would set in America. The absentee governor, Lord Howard of Effingham, objected to Charles Scarborough's sitting on the council. He had but a "small estate," and his bills of exchange were generally protested in England. It helped to have influence in England, either at Whitehall or in the London mercantile community. William Byrd and Christopher Robinson could rely on the influence of the great tobacco merchants, Micajah Perry and Jeffrey Jeffreys.[14]

James Blair, a contentious Scottish cleric with extensive connections on the episcopal bench in England, became almost a power to himself in Virginia. He married into one of the established families in the colony, one in a clan dominating higher offices during the last decade of the seventeenth century. Such was his position in the province and in the metropolis that at times he could frustrate official policy and undermine royal authority in Virginia.

Through the influence of Gilbert Burnet, later bishop of Salisbury, Blair in 1683 became a clerk to the master of the rolls in Chancery Lane. Here he met John Tillotson, later archbishop of Canterbury, and Henry Compton, bishop of London. It was Compton who sent Blair out to Virginia as his commissary. Although the authority of the see of London over the Anglican church in America and the status of the bishop of

London's commissary there were debatable, the contentious and ambitious Blair was not deterred.

Attempting to establish an ecclesiastical court, Blair came directly into conflict with the planters in the counties who controlled the vestries of the parish churches. As commissary he called for the Anglican clergy of the colony to convene in July 1690. Once assembled, the clerics adopted a plan to reform alleged abuses in the church by establishing ecclesiastical courts to try both clerical and lay offenders against church law. Not one to keep his opinions to himself, Blair publicly proclaimed that he was putting into execution ecclesiastical laws against "Swearers," blasphemers, and "all whoremongers[,] fornicators and Adulterers, all drunkards[,] ranters and profaners of the Lords day." When two of the clergymen authorized by Blair attempted to bring county officials before their courts, the lieutenant governor intervened. The House of Burgesses supported Nicholson.[15]

Two other projects were dear to Blair's heart: putting clerical salaries on a secure basis and establishing a college to educate and train the youth of the colony for the ministry of the Church of England. On this last issue Blair had the support of Nicholson and the assembly. They sent him to London in the spring of 1691 to solicit the crown for aid. On the advice of Burnet and other bishops, Blair did not broach the matter with the Committee for Plantation Affairs, but planned to have the bishop of London, the Queen, and Tillotson, the primate of England, raise the issue directly with the king. But William was occupied with other matters that winter, and Archbishop Tillotson was confined to Lambeth Palace by the severe weather. Another obstacle soon appeared when, after the unexpected resignation of Lord Howard of Effingham, his successor as governor of Virginia, Edmund Andros, came out in opposition to Blair's proposals to divert revenue from the quitrents in Virginia for the projected college. Another potential drain on the revenue available for the provincial government lay in the proposal to divert money paid in quitrents and the plantation duty imposed by Parliament in 1673 to cover the salaries of Blair and the other clerics.[16]

The sources of revenue to meet the financial needs of the provincial government at Jamestown were limited. The plantation duty of 1673 was a tax of one penny on every pound of tobacco carried from the colony by ships not having given bond to land tobacco in some English port. The provincial legislature had imposed an additional tax on tobacco, two shillings on every hogshead exported. Two shillings was also due the crown for every hundred acres of land as quitrent under the terms of an early Virginia charter. For some years the income from the rent collected in the southern portion of the colony had gone to two of Charles II's courtiers, but in 1684 was pledged by the crown for the use of the provincial administration. As of June 1691 there was only a limited sum, £1,985, at hand from quitrents.

Neither the Commissioners of the Customs nor the Treasury Board raised serious objections to Blair's projects. And Tillotson had finally brought them to the attention of Mary. Consequently, on 1 September 1692 the queen in council ordered that two-thousand pounds from the rents and other sources be set aside for the college with any surplus money to go for the maintenance of Blair and the parish clergy. That winter, Andros, the governor-designate, received orders to promote appropriate enabling legislation in the House of Burgesses. To complete Blair's triumph, the Scot received an appointment to the governor's council.[17]

Andros did not take kindly to the diversion of critical funds for the support of the civil and defense establishments to maintain the clergy and finance a college. Relations between the governor and the commissary worsened when the income for the college failed to come up to expectations. As revenue dwindled, the burgesses showed little inclination to aid. Blair blamed Andros. An open break between the two men came at a meeting of the council in April 1695 when the more senior members challenged the right of the Scot to sit on the board. Andros suspended him. But Blair used his superior influence at Lambeth, Fulham, and Whitehall to win reinstatement.

The basic problem of revenue remained. There were simply too many demands on the limited financial resources of the colony. In the summer of 1696 Blair and fifteen other clergymen delivered a protest to the governor after he had sent an address to the House of Burgesses strongly implying that the clerics were not in dire circumstances. The parish clergy denied the implication of avarice thus imputed to them.[18]

Revenue to pay for the support of the civil government, for the clergy, the college, and military efforts was limited. The interdiction of merchant vessels from England cut down the amount of tobacco exported and consequently reduced the revenue from the duty of two shillings per hogshead imposed by the local government. In addition, rents from lands in the Northern Neck went, not to the provincial administration at Jamestown, but to absentee proprietors: Margaret, the widow of, and Catherine, the daughter of Thomas, Lord Culpeper. In 1690 Catherine married Thomas, fifth Lord Fairfax. Despite the largesse of James II in confirming the grant of the Northern Neck, Culpeper had supported the Protestant prince of Orange. He had served on the commission acting for William and Mary before they arrived in London, and Fairfax had helped to hold the north of England for the revolutionary cause. The provincial administration in Virginia had pleaded vainly to have the Northern Neck returned to the Old Dominion.

The Culpeper-Fairfax interest attempted to set up a land office for the region between the Rappahannock and the Potomac and through local agents, their relatives Nicholas Spencer and Philip Ludwell, to collect rents. Personal rivalries were involved in the dispute over the Northern Neck and the operations of the proprietary agents as well as resentment that revenue went to the proprietors in England rather than to the provincial administration. This was particularly serious at a time when money was needed for arms and ammunition to aid in the defense of the colony.

William Blathwayt—one of his posts was auditor general of the plantation revenue—was anxious that the proprietary be restored to the crown, that is, to the royal government in Virginia, but he appreciated that the executors of Culpeper's estate could not be brought to accept reasonable compensation, given the exaggerated account of the income Philip Ludwell had given them.

Following a report by the crown attorney general in January 1693 holding that the patents for the Northern Neck were valid in law, the proprietors returned to the attack and had their agents, now George Brent and William Fitzhugh, open a land office.[19]

Brent and Fitzhugh encountered strong opposition from planters who claimed their lands under provincial headrights. One of the magnates in the region, the young Robert Carter, launched a calculated attack in the House of Burgesses. He may have wanted the agency for himself. Brent and Fitzhugh especially resented what were acknowledged as unfair accusations by Carter against them. Despite the support of officials in Whitehall, for some time Fairfax could not overcome local opposition to the collection of rents from the Northern Neck. The denouement did not come until several years later, early in the eighteenth century, when (according to Robert Beverley) Colonel Richard Lee, one of the largest of the landholders and a member of the provincial council, made a private composition for his own lands, thus acknowledging the claims of the proprietors. "This broke the ice," according to Beverley; other planters then followed suit.[20]

As before, quitrents from The Northern Neck went to the Culpepers and to Fairfax rather than to meet the needs of the provincial government. The impact of war further reduced income, the duties paid on the export of tobacco, as fewer ships arrived to carry off the annual crop. During the second summer of the war with France, William Byrd, the provincial auditor, complained to the London tobacco house of Perry and Lane: "I was never so put to it for frieght in my life, having about 200

Hogsheads still by me." A considerable amount of tobacco remained on the Chesapeake that year for want of shipping. This would much "prejudice" the revenue of the crown at home as well as lessen it in Virginia, Byrd predicted to Blathwayt. The next year merchantmen again were in short supply. In 1692, the London fleet's failure to arrive "will keep that branch of the revenue behind hand," Byrd predicted. Early in 1693 he reported that "tobacco is worth very little here being no Ships to carry itt away." Three years later the provincial auditor in returning to his superior in London his accounts explained that again revenue had been much reduced, "occasioned chiefly by our having no fleet from London this year." About thirty sail had arrived from Bristol and other outports, but the majority of them, "being small vessels have little advanced the revenue."[21]

The shortage of merchantmen and the fierce competition for freighters to carry off tobacco jeopardized the regulations for loading and shipping tobacco.[22] The scarcity of vessels qualified under the parliamentary navigation acts to carry tobacco to England and to import English and European manufactured goods was an open invitation for Virginians and foreigners, particularly Scots, to breach the navigation code of the mother country. Violations of the shipping statutes were not restricted to foreigners and colonials, as the controversy over the shipment of bulk rather than packaged tobacco to England illustrated. Importation of bulk tobacco was favored by the merchants of the outports, where it was easier to avoid payment of customs by smuggling to the disadvantage of the "fair" trader, who by paying duties was undercut in price. Inasmuch as eliminating importation of bulk or loose tobacco would facilitate collecting duties, the Board of Customs took the side of the Londoners against the merchants in the outports and the provincial planters. The crown ordered the governors on the Chesapeake to secure from the colonial legislatures an act prohibiting the export of tobacco in bulk.[23]

Enforcement of the navigation and customs regulations on the rivers of the Chesapeake Bay by collectors and naval officers fell almost entirely to local men appointed nominally by the crown but on the recommendation of the governor and his councilors. In Virginia the latter arrogated these potentially lucrative posts to themselves. In the spring of 1692 Edward Randolph conducted a survey of the customs establishment on the Chesapeake. He found members of the council or their close relatives occupying key positions. They were too busy, too indifferent, too far situated from the scene, in some cases, too unscrupulous or corrupt, he charged, to check the Scots and other interlopers who traded in violation of the navigation code.

That same year merchants in the metropolis also complained of the damage to their trade resulting from vessels trading directly to the Chesapeake and Delaware from Scotland. Such traffic unfairly punished legal traders who, in observing the carrying code and returning cargo to England, there had to pay a heavy duty on landing their tobacco. In answer to these complaints the ministers of state in Whitehall were prepared only to authorize the governors on the Chesapeake to hire two or three frigates to patrol local waters. This effort was hardly adequate. Complaints continued to come in charging a pervasive pattern of illegal trading and trafficking with pirates.[24]

One immediate consequence in Virginia of the shortage of English shipping and the rise in illegal trading was a further diminution of the revenue available to the provincial government.[25]

As the oldest and one of the most populous of the English colonies, Virginia was expected to contribute to the defense of other provinces, those to the north immediately exposed to incursions by the French and their Indian allies. Lieutenant Governor Francis Nicholson, having served in the Dominion of New England as deputy governor at New York, was particularly concerned at the chaotic, poorly prepared state of the English colonies. Shortly after he took up his post at Jamestown, he conducted a survey of Virginia and dispatched Cuthbert Potter to report on the situation in the northern provinces. The results were not encouraging. Virginia was poorly prepared and inadequately fortified, and because of the poverty of many men, its militia were poorly armed. The efforts of English arms against Canada had come to little because of faulty communications and the failure of the several governments to cooperate. If the Five Nations were lost to the English cause, the war would be brought down the Delaware and Susquehanna rivers to Virginia. The Quaker colonies could not be expected to offer much, if any resistance. When the lieutenant governor placed before his council the situation in the north, the board asked Nicholson to inform the home government of the shortage of ammunition in the colony, inadequate fortifications, the reduced revenue, and the disorder prevailing in the provinces to the north. Unstable conditions in the northern colonies rendered the Chesapeake region all the more vulnerable. Nicholson and the councilors of Virginia suggested the crown place these provinces under a more settled government.[26]

In 1692 Nicholson gave way to Sir Edmund Andros, formerly governor of the Dominion of New England. Before leaving for his new post Andros asked permission to dispose of one thousand pounds from the quitrents to meet any threat posed by the French and Indians. On arriving in Virginia he found the revenue to be in arrears and the militia indifferently armed, few men being able to provide themselves with weapons and ammunition. The colony had neither powder nor cannon shot. Nonetheless, Andros managed to scrape up six hundred pounds for New York after the French had invaded, burned the castles of the Mohawks, and threatened Albany. But by 1694 he could offer no further aid to New York. The back country of the Chesapeake lay open to attack by hostile Indians, and the income available to the administration was insufficient to meet the necessary charges of his government.

When called upon by the crown in 1695 to raise money for the assistance of New York, the burgesses in Virginia refused, initially pleading their poverty and the cost of defending the frontiers of their own colony. Protecting New York would not aid Virginia. Andros at length prevailed on them to vote five hundred pounds out of an impost on liquors, a sum he thought inadequate. The income remaining to the provincial government to meet contingent charges was insufficient. Later that year the crown ordered stores from the royal ordinance sent to Virginia.[27]

Matters were but little improved the following year. Andros received orders to send a quota of men from Virginia for the relief of the northern frontier, but on learning that the other provinces were not sending their militia units—contributing money instead to recruit men in New York—he did not order a contingent from the Old Dominion but instead sent off a sum equal to one thousand pounds in New York currency. Again the provincial administration was not able to meet current expenses. The London fleet had failed to arrive; the last crop of tobacco had been slim, and the next was not likely to be better. The burgesses met in April, but, apprehensive over an epidemic of smallpox, they prayed for a recess. Unable to prevail on them to attend to business, Andros prorogued the assembly.[28]

The tenure of Andros as governor in Virginia was short-lived, a victim of the political ambitions of his colleague Nicholson, anxious to move from neighboring Maryland to the more lucrative and prestigious post in Virginia, and the animosity of James Blair, commissary of the bishop of London. Appealing to the prejudices of the primate of England and the bishops, Blair and Nicholson undermined Andros. Receiving no support from Whitehall and in ill health, Andros begged to be allowed to return to England. The victory of Blair and his relations on the Virginia council was but another example of private, parochial concerns influencing political decisions in administrative circles.

CHAPTER 12

Protestantism Triumphant:
Maryland Under the Crown, 1690–96

As DEVELOPMENTS in Maryland following the overthrow of the proprietary government of the Catholic Lord Baltimore illustrated, a provincial
regime depending immediately upon the crown was hardly a guarantee
that the policies of the court at Whitehall would be carried out. Moreover,
despite the appointment of a governor and council by the king and the
sanction of the crown for the Protestant politicians who had assumed
power at Saint Marys, Maryland continued to be wracked by factional
strife, petty animosities, and an unseemly scramble for profit and place.

The small group of men headed by John Coode, Kenelm Cheseldyne, and Nehemiah Blakiston who had seized power in the name of a
Protestant Association, despite claiming to have positive proof, were
never able to substantiate the charges of conspiracy they claimed justified, even compelled, their assumption of power. Indeed, many Protestant inhabitants did not credit the accusations or accept the coup d'etat.
Consequently, support for the insurgent regime was initially limited, and
the revolutionary government for the remaining months of 1689 made
little effort to coerce the skeptical for fear of antagonizing the populace.

A chance encounter early in January 1690 gave Coode and his colleagues an opportunity to embellish on the theme of a brutal Catholic
conspiracy. Following the take-over by the Associators, William Digges,
a Protestant councilor, and Nicholas Sewall, a stepson of the proprietor,
had fled to Virginia. On the night of 3 January 1690, Sewall with a few
men in a small yacht returned to the Patuxent to pick up supplies at his
home. Sewall was on shore when John Payne, an official who held a royal
commission as collector of customs and a warrant from the insurgent
regime, challenged the crew of the yacht, demanding to come on board.
An exchange of shots followed. One crewman was wounded, Payne
killed.[1]

Coode and the Associators seized on the killing of Payne to consolidate support and reorganize the government through a convention and an
executive council, or committee of safety. Power was now concentrated in
a tightly knit core of original rebel leaders and their initial supporters,

with Coode as governor, Blakiston as president of the committee, and Henry Jowles and Kenelm Cheseldyne as ranking assistants.

The coup had not constituted a united uprising of Protestants against Catholics despite the name "Protestant Association" assumed by the insurgents. Nor was it a revolt of one economic class against another, or a "democratic" movement carried out in the name of the populace, as the participants claimed. Men of the same religious persuasion and of comparable financial position as the Associators, planters who lived under the same allegedly unjust proprietary regime, did not participate in the overthrow of Lord Baltimore's government and refused to accept the revolutionary administration. A large proportion of those signing petitions against the Protestant Association were practicing Anglicans. One, Thomas Smith of Talbot County, appealed to the bishop of London to intercede with the crown against Coode and his allies.[2] The only distinct Dissenter group identified as receptive to the revolution was the community of Presbyterians concentrated on the lower eastern shore. They dominated Somerset County, the only district outside the three home counties, strongly supporting the coup. Widespread maladministration of justice, corruption within the legal system, costly and inefficient government, and monopolization of office would have prejudiced all groups and classes in Maryland, except the extended proprietary family, against the government of Baltimore, but not all men participated in and supported the revolution. The very poor settlers—perhaps the least informed, the most susceptible to propaganda, and those most likely to benefit immediately and directly from the closing of the courts and the ensuing stay on tax and debt collection in the initial confusion—were passive. Merchants and attorneys, men seeking to enhance their position, became increasingly important among the insurgents. The leaders were the men with personal or familial grievances or grudges against those exercising authority under Baltimore. Seizing the initiative, they consolidate their power. Ironically, Coode and his allies imposed on the inhabitants much the same injustices they had charged the proprietor and his officials with perpetrating.[3]

If the leaders of the Association were to maintain their control, they must also convince the authorities in Whitehall. In corresponding with the secretaries of state Coode sought to create a certain impression: the revolutionary government was concerned with the larger Protestant cause in America, particulary with the fate of Leisler's regime, an administration faced with invasion by hostile Indians and the popish French. It feared the consequences of Papist lies and misrepresentation. The ministers of the king must not heed allegations by Henry Darnall of Protestants plundering Catholic subjects. Coode and his colleagues were in a position, so they claimed, to prove all of the charges they had set forth in their declaration, and a good deal more.[4]

Leaving Nehemiah Blakiston to preside over the committee of safety, Coode and Cheseldyne in the summer of 1690 took ship for England to lay their case against the proprietary regime and Baltimore before the Protestant court.

The men at Whitehall needed little convincing. Twice in the past decade the crown had contemplated legal proceedings against Baltimore's charter; once before, in 1684, a royal customs collector had suffered violent death in Maryland; once before Baltimore had been so presumptuous as to claim that merchantmen on the Potomac River must enter and clear with proprietary officials and not with officers stationed on the Virginia shore, thus denying needed revenue to the royal government in the Old Dominion. In addition, he had failed to act after the messenger he had dispatched to Maryland in February 1689 with orders to proclaim the Protestant monarchs had died before he could take ship for America.[5]

Early in January 1690 the lords of the Committee for Trade and Plantations took up the reports received from Maryland. To find some arrangement conducive to the royal service in the colony, they consulted the attorney general over the powers held by the proprietor under his charter.

Lord Baltimore was not inactive. He pleaded that the committee secure the testimony of residents of Maryland then in London and traders familiar with his administration on the charges made in the declaration sent by Coode. Among those persons he named to be consulted were Anglican priests and Barbara Smith, the wife of a loyalist imprisoned in Maryland.[6] Baltimore also seemed ready to make some concessions: to reform the government of the colony and to issue a commission to Henry Coursey, a member of the Calvert entourage, but an Anglican, as proprietary deputy governor. He would also appoint to the council other men, such professing Protestants and persons of good repute as the merchants trading to Maryland would designate. They could examine fully into the truth of the allegations the Associators made.

This procedure the crown ignored. On 30 January 1690 the king in council ordered a letter sent to Maryland addressed to those who for the time being took care to preserve the peace and administer justice. They were to continue in office pending a full investigation. Several weeks later the court received a petition from William Payne, a doctor of divinity and brother to John Payne, charging that his brother had been murdered while performing his duties as a royal official by Papists confederated with Nicholas Sewall. The alleged murderer he described as a popish governor who refused the collector's orders to submit to the authority of William III. In April 1690, the king in council apparently accepted this version of the altercation on the Patuxent River earlier that year.[7]

By the late spring the ministers of state had resolved to take over the administration of Maryland and to send out a governor to provide for the security of the people and the defense of the province. The man selected was a colonel in the army, a protégé of Carmarthen, lord president of the council. Colonel Lionel Copley in the fall of 1688 had secured the port of Hull for the prince of Orange when William had invaded England. This hardly qualified him for the delicate political task in America. Lazy, petty-minded, and concerned with his immediate profit, Copley proved a poor choice as governor of Maryland. From the outset he insisted on powers and perquisites as full as those enjoyed by the governors in the royal colonies and half of the income from the duty on exported tobacco and the quitrents. The revenues of the proprietor of Maryland were then disputed in America between Baltimore's agent, James Heath, and the insurgent government.[8]

The charter to the Calvert family had never been legally rescinded. Could the crown then appoint a governor? Carmarthen consulted the lord chief justice of the Court of King's Bench. Sir John Holt ruled that Baltimore must be found by an inquisition to have forfeited his rights, but in case of necessity the king could lawfully commission a governor, although he must be accountable to the proprietor for the profits accruing from the colony. Apparently enough doubt remained. The attorney general in the summer of 1690 received orders to proceed by writ of scire facias against the patent. But had the proprietor done anything to warrant this legal action? Apparently not, for the administration abandoned this tack in favor of the less drastic course suggested by the lord justice. The attorney general, George Treby, in commenting on the draft of the commission for Copley used the rationalization provided by Holt: the assumption of the government of Maryland by the crown was the only means of preserving the colony. It was necessary to take the administrtion out of the hands of men who had neglected and endangered the province, but, as far as possible, the laws, customs, and property of the inhabitants of Maryland must be preserved.[9]

This rationalization, weak as it was, was placed in jeopardy that fall. In October 1690 John Coode and Kenelm Cheseldyne, two of the ringleaders in the disturbances, so Baltimore called the insurrection, arrived in Plymouth. They were freely spending the embezzled money due him, the proprietor charged. The Lords of Trade set a date for a hearing. On Thursday, 20 November, Coode, Cheseldyne, and Baltimore appeared at the Plantation Office, but as the emissaries of the insurgent government were not prepared to answer charges against them, the hearing was postponed for two days. On 22 November Baltimore introduced evidence undermining the rationalization employed by the crown to justify appointing a governor. Moreover, the Lords of Trade had received a letter from Nathaniel Bacon, president of the council of Virginia, a document contradicting the version offered by the Associators of the circumstances of the death of John Payne. In the petition Baltimore presented, Henry Coursey, Richard Hill, and the other "ancient Protestant" inhabitants remonstrated that they had long enjoyed peaceful government under the proprietor and his father, a tranquility upset by Coode and his accomplices, who now seized records, plundered estates, lawlessly maintained themselves by force, and branded those who did not accept them as traitors.[10]

Coode and Cheseldyne could only offer the declaration of the reasons for taking up arms adopted by the rebels of Anne Arundel County in July of the previous year, not the proofs of a conspiracy the council of safety later claimed to have gathered. At a subsequent meeting at the Plantation Office, Coode and Cheseldyne sought to discredit those who supported the proprietor. Coursey, Hill, and the others had no authority to speak for any but themselves. The agents then submitted dozens of articles against Baltimore, his deputies, and the judges in Maryland.[11]

Baltimore and Richard Hill got in one damaging blow against the self-professed champion of Protestantism in Maryland in the form of depositions made before the mayor of Plymouth by Edward Burford and Simon Amberly after the *Edward and Mary*, the vessel carrying Coode and Chesldyne, had arrived in England. Why, Burford and Amberly had asked Coode, had he taken to himself the government of Maryland? As they told it, Coode had answered: "God Damn me what I did was in prejudice or revenge to the Lord Baltimore." Burford had also testified that Coode had boasted that if they went to Ireland or France, he could do better than Burford, for he, Coode, could make a popish Mass.[12]

The case for the Protestant Associators hardly seemed convincing. It was openly bruited about London that the several articles against Baltimore, on examination, "have been found to be vain and frivolous." Indeed, the crown dismissed the charges made by Coode against Henry Darnall of opposing the prince of Orange. After hearing witnesses for both sides, on 1 January 1691, the Lords for Plantation Affairs recommended that the matter in dispute between the revolutionary convention in Maryland and the proprietor be referred to the governor to be sent out by the king. The emergency justified the crown's naming an executive for the proprietary province.[13]

Baltimore resisted the decision. He would not sign the commission drawn up by Attorney General Treby for a governor. In his view it contained clauses prejudicial to the privileges granted the proprietor by the charter. He insisted on his rights by patent to appoint a deputy, although he was willing himself to commission a Protestant and to entrust the militia and military stores to Protestants. He asked that no commission be made out until he was heard by counsel, a request the ministers after some hesitation refused. Lord Sydney ordered the commission for Copley prepared. One-half of the revenue from the duty in Maryland on exported tobacco and the ship duties were to be applied toward the cost of government. Officials appointed by the Treasury and Customs boards in London were to collect the money.[14]

Who would reap the fruits of the royal harvest? Whose names would appear in the commission to Copley as councilors in Maryland? Months passed before the issue was resolved by a compromise, but one generally favorable to the Associators in Maryland. Slates of candidates were submitted by Copley—probably after consultation with Coode and Cheseldyne—and Baltimore as well as by Captain John Hammond, a merchant of Maryland and a Quaker turned Anglican who had recently arrived in London. To aid in choosing the various candidates, the Plantation Office referred the slates to Micajah Perry, who then consulted with his fellow traders to the Chesapeake. The Lords of Trade wanted a council consisting of Protestants, men of substance and integrity, and persons acceptable to as many people in Maryland as possible. Consequently, Coode and Cheseldyne, the men most offensive to the supporters of Baltimore, did not receive serious consideration. The depositions given against them before the mayor of Plymouth may also have told.

Others reaped the benefit of their labor in overthrowing the proprietary. Seven men named in the commission to Copley had received the endorsement of Copley and the London merchants, two others of the governor alone, but all nine had sat as delegates to the Associators' assembly and seven on the grand committee. Before the Privy Council confirmed the list, three more names were added. Sir Thomas Lawrence—he had attended the Middle Temple with William Blathwayt—having been named provincial secretary, was appointed to the council as a matter of form. The names of James Frisby and Thomas Brooke had headed the lists submitted by Baltimore and the merchants. They were the only men nominated by the proprietor the crown accepted.

On the council of Maryland as appointed by the crown, the Associators predominated, but the most offensive of them had been excluded. The new council was geographically more representative than its proprietary predecessor. All but one of the men named were nominal Anglicans, one, a Presbyterian, and two others either former Quakers or men with Quaker wives. Almost all of them were first-generation settlers, men economically well off who had not previously advanced far in provincial government. For most of them, the highest post they had held was that of justice of the peace. Two of the councilors, Nehemiah Blakiston and George Plater, also received commissions from the crown as receivers of the revenue.[15]

Some details of the financial establishment for the new regime had yet to be settled. These later caused considerable controversy. One-half of the revenue in Maryland was to go to the proprietor, but Baltimore's agent, Henry Darnall, had been prevented from collecting what was due the proprietor. Copley was under orders to see that in the future Baltimore's receivers suffered no hindrance. Sir Thomas Lawrence also had claims, the perquisites pertaining to the office of the provincial secretary. In Maryland the offices of clerks of the counties were at the disposal of the secretary, not the governor. Inasmuch as the secretary had to give security for the good behavior of the clerks, he was allowed a tenth of their annual income as a fee. Copley apparently acquiesced in this arrangement. He promised not to encroach on Lawrence's interests or to infringe on the provincial laws. His word proved to be worth little. Lawrence also came to an arrangement with Baltimore. In lieu of a portion of the naval officers' fees for entering and clearing ships, which the proprietor took for himself, Lawrence received the gratuities for licensing ordinaries and public houses.[16]

Unfortunately for Lawrence, Governor Copley arrived in Maryland well before the provincial secretary. He quickly secured an act from the assembly setting aside for himself the income from licensing ordinaries. Lionel Copley proved a most unhappy choice if the ministers at Whitehall had hoped for a governor to end the bitterness and strife in Maryland. Under Copley, factional struggle continued, fueled by the governor's greed.

In the ensuing scramble for office, power, and money, the coalition which had succeeded the proprietary regime disintegrated. When Copley arrived at Saint Marys in the spring of 1692 and called his first assembly, the Associators held a majority of the forty-two seats in the lower house. About one-third of the members were indifferent, perhaps even unsympathetic to those who had overthrown the proprietary regime. A small core of the delegates had resisted the take-over. The new governor, employing his influence on behalf of the Associators, formed an alliance with Nehemiah Blakiston, who had presided as provisional executive. Copley and Blakiston struck quickly to eliminate any potential opposition. They refused to allow James Frisby, Baltimore's nominee, to take his place on the council and charged Frisby, Peregrine Browne, and John Browne with engaging in sedition, actively disrupting the government, vilifying the king's officers, and setting the people against them. To ensure control of the assembly, the Associators dismissed seven representatives, five on technical grounds. By law, ministers, keepers of ordinaries, and sheriffs could not serve. This prohibition in the past had not always been observed.[17]

The assembly—now purged—passed a bill to establish the Anglican Church in Maryland. By this act parishes and elected vestries had authority to draw upon the sheriffs for the tobacco due from the general tax placed on all tithables. But this and supplemental statutes passed in 1694 and 1695 failed to win approval from the Privy Council in England.[18]

Ironically, the first significant attack on Copley's administration came from an ardent Anglican, the busybody customs officer, Edward Randolph. While on a tour of inspection of the Chesapeake and Delaware, Randolph had received an appointment as deputy auditor of the revenue in Maryland. Almost as soon as Copley arrived, Randolph made known his presence, informing Copley that as governor he was bound under penalty of one thousand pounds to swear to enforce the acts of trade and navigation. Copley would no doubt comply so as not to give his enemies a handle against him.

Randolph followed up this heavy-handed hint with a visit to Saint Marys. He found the governor "grown very fat, he drinks much and pleases himself in amusing easy hearers with large & fulsome discourses of his Conduct in obtaining this Gov[ernmen]t." Copley had already suffered a stroke and seemed most ill.

Never one to see good in people, Randolph contemptuously dismissed the council, comparing it to a tailor's cushion, composed of bits and pieces—Scots, English, Irish, many openly abetting illicit trade. Nehemiah Blakiston he found to be a "starched formall fellow[,] as great a knave but not as cunning" as Joseph Dudley of Massachusetts. He had been but a poor lawyer before obtaining the post of collector of customs for the Potomac. Now the chief supporter of the governor, he carried "a great streak amongst those silly animals," the other councilors. George Plater, the collector for the Patuxent district, was Copley's second "jackall." His chief task now was to search out wine for the governor among the incoming ships, having already presented Copley with a horse and put a "young wife at his Excell[s] service." In a less scurrilous vein Randolph dismissed the provincial attorney general as a "Dull Welsh" lawyer. As "Master of Ceremonies" he directed the councilors and assemblymen "how they are to behave themselves" toward the governor.

Randolph was contemptuous of most of the officials of Maryland as socially inferior. Colonel David Browne had been a Scottish "peddler,"

Nicholas Greenberry, a "Highway man" in England, and Charles Hutchins a "broken London carpenter." He had seen better men rejected in the House of Burgesses in neighboring Virginia than most who sat on the council in Maryland. He found "tolerable" only Colonel George Robotham, "a half faced Quaker"; Thomas Tench, an Irish merchant; and Henry Jowles, a surgeon.

Little love was lost between Randolph and his chief in Whitehall, Blathwayt, on the one hand and Copley and the councilors in Maryland on the other. Copley, when in his cups, Randolph reported, claimed Blathwayt was a Jacobite and a great enemy to the Protestant monarchs. John Coode on his return to the Chesapeake added fuel to the dispute between the royal officials. Disappointed at his failure in England, he primed Copley with tales: Blathwayt and Baltimore were working surreptitiously to have Francis Nicholson appointed governor. If true, Copley charged, Blathwayt had in manner "robbed me and family of our bread." Blathwayt hastened to assure Copley: Coode's information "is little to be depended on if you consider the person and his morals." Yet he expressed surprise at Copley's refusal to admit Blathwayt's patent as auditor of the plantation revenue. Even the New Englanders had received it "without the least scruple."[19]

Relations among the crown officials continued acrimonious. Randolph condemned the governor, councilors, and attorney general and accused the collectors of the customs, Blakiston and Plater, of conniving to conceal widespread violations of the acts of navigation and of extorting bribes from illegal traders. In turn, the accused treated Randolph as an open enemy. Both sides abused the other. Copley charged the deputy auditor of the plantation revenue with malicious representations, of casting base aspersions, and of carrying himself with scurrilous haughtiness under the pretext of zeal for the royal service. But worst of all: Randolph's only associates were Papists or men professedly disaffected to the government. And even they could hardly afford a good word for him behind his back. They befriended him only to disrupt Copley's administration.

In fact, others supported Randolph's charges. Merchants in England trading to the Chesapeake and the Delaware complained of direct traffic between Scotland and Maryland, Virginia, and the Delaware ports. As legal traders adhering to the navigation code they could not compete against those who avoided paying customs duties.[20]

Controversy over revenue—a portion to be applied to the colony's defense—and perquisites of office continued to plague the government of Maryland. From the outset of the royal administration, Copley, the councilors, and the assemblymen contested with the proprietor for certain revenues: the duty on exported tobacco, the powder, or port, duty on incoming vessels, and various fines and amercements. In London the English solicitor general, Thomas Trevor, worked out a compromise: Baltimore gave up his rights to the two shillings per hogshead on exported tobacco but retained the fourteen pennies per ton on shipping. To Trevor it was plain the provincial law supported the claim of the proprietor. It would be a dangerous precedent to upset it by mere verbal testimony as to the presumed intent behind the statute when initially passed.[21]

A more formidable antagonist entered the contest against Copley and his allies in Maryland, one with influential friends in London. Before Copley had left for the Chesapeake, the governor-designate had come to an understanding with Sir Thomas Lawrence over the fees and perquisites of the secretary's office: income from licenses for taverns and a portion of the salaries of the clerks in the counties. When Lawrence arrived in Maryland, he found that Copley had approved two bills passed by the assembly diverting the greater part of the fees of the secretary's office to the governor and the remaining portion to another official. Refusing to accept the situation, Lawrence placed his own nominees as clerks in several of the counties. One of the men he so "corrupted"—the word Copley used—to accept a clerkship under the aegis of the secretary was Colonel Henry Jowles, a member of the council unhappy with the role assigned him. The governor had been awarding clerkships to his own favorites and supporters, William Taillard, Blakiston, and John Llewellin.[22]

The governor moved quickly to quash the challenge. With the support of his allies on the council, Blakiston, Greensberry, David Browne, and Tench, he dismissed Jowles and Lawrence and had the secretary jailed, accused of a dozen crimes, including consorting with and countenancing none but Papists and avowed enemies of the government and alleging false and scandalous reflections on the administration. In the opposition of the provincial secretary, Copley professed to see a conspiracy involving Lawrence, Randolph, and Baltimore and Blathwayt in London to replace him with Nicholson. Faced with the wrath of the governor, Randolph fled to Virginia and the protection of Edmund Andros. Copley came down on those men, Jowles and Charles Carroll among them, who had expressed any sympathy for Lawrence.

During the first months of 1693 the councilors loyal to the governor busied themselves investigating alleged treasonous speeches and unrest. To prevent the opposition, including adherents of the proprietor (men charged with being Jacobites), from uniting, the governor twice prorogued the assembly.[23] But Copley's health and his position deteriorated.

His wife died in March, and for much of the spring and summer he was bedridden.

Not until the late summer of that year did the Committee for Plantation Affairs in London take up the dispute in Maryland. The Lords of Trade found no grounds for the proceedings against Lawrence. Even if the accusations against him should prove true, the actions taken against the secretary had been illegal and arbitrary. Copley must furnish Lawrence with a copy of the charges against him so that the secretary might have an opportunity to answer them. In the meantime Lawrence could resume his office and gather any evidence he needed for his defense.[24] When this rebuke was delivered, Copley was no longer concerned. He had died on 8 September 1693.

Rivalry for control of the provincial administration following the death of Copley threw the government of Maryland into further disarray. The lieutenant governor, Francis Nicholson, was in London at the time of Copley's death. Dissatisfied with the inferior role in Virginia after the arrival of Andros, he had returned to London, where Blathwayt and James Blair sought something better for him. Nicholson already had a reputation for a short temper, but as a firm churchman he also had the support of Nottingham. It was the secretary of state's view that Nicholson "should stay on this side of the water" until "some good thing" came up for his "preferment or satisfaction."[25]

Copley's death opened the way for Nicholson. But until he arrived at Saint Marys, who would govern? By the peculiar wording of Copley's commission, in the event of the *death* of the lieutenant governor (Nicholson) and in the *absence* of the governor (Copley), Andros of Virginia was to assume command. But it was Copley who was dead and Nicholson who was absent. Was the commission to be taken literally?

Power, influence, and the perquisites of office were at stake. Strident factional conflict intensified, precipitating a struggle for control of the council between Blakiston, Greenberry, and Tench on the one hand and Lawrence and Henry Jowles on the other. The intervention of Andros on two occasions did not alleviate the situation. Since there existed no certain copy of the charges against Lawrence and he had never been given the opportunity to answer the accusations, Andros ordered the provincial secretary restored to his offices. He also named Greenberry president of the council, but with the advice of the other members of the board he suspended Blakiston. The collector of customs died a week later. As Edward Randolph had predicted, Blakiston's accounts were in a state of disarray. He died owing the crown some fourteen hundred pounds. Greenberry and some others wanted to have George Plater, the collector for the Patuxent, take over the vacant Potomac district, but Randolph, the surveyor general, without consulting the provincial council, named Philip Clark, a local planter. After Plater complained, Andros overrode Randolph.[26]

As Andros appreciated and so informed Whitehall, a strong resident governor was needed at Saint Marys. The task fell to Nicholson. Appointed early in 1694, the new governor intended to start his administration with a clear slate. He proposed to the Lords of Trade that a pardon be sent to America for all men for offenses they committed before Copley took office.[27]

Nicholson arrived at Saint Marys in July 1694 to begin what turned out to be a tenure of almost five years as governor. He found a colony rent by factionalism with no cohesive political or social institutions. In the past the assembly had not played an important role, while local county boards had often been staffed by incompetents or dominated by neighborhood magnates as their personal domain. A relatively young man of thirty-nine years with both military and civil experience, Nicholson was intent on proving himself. But he was also a man with a violent temper and strong prejudices; government would be served by employing men of substance, not plebians. The new governor was also a staunch Anglican, and his commitment to the Church of England played a large role in his administration of Maryland.

Little had been done to implement the act passed by the local assembly in 1692 establishing the Church of England when Nicholson took office. There were only a few Anglican clergymen precariously supported by voluntary contributions or living from the income of the plantations of their wives. Quakers and Roman Catholics in Maryland had joined in opposition. Nicholson appreciated that to attract the best men in the colony, the "able, rich and honest," he would have to appoint to office others in addition to Anglicans. Several of the most competent men for ability and estates were Quakers, Catholics, and "disaffected" Protestants. Although the governor did not discriminate on religious grounds when making appointments, he did push vigorously for the Church of England, particularly the collection of the tax of forty pounds of tobacco per poll for the support of the Anglican clergy as required under the law passed during Copley's administration.[28] In addition Nicholson approved two supplementary acts passed by the provincial legislature, one in 1694 and the other the following year for erecting free schools. But the latter statute did not reserve a power to the crown to appoint visitors.

The Privy Council in England disallowed the measure as well as the Act Concerning Religion passed in 1692 establishing the Church of England. Dissenting Protestants openly and Catholics covertly had objected to the last law inasmuch as the measure declared the laws of England, including the ecclesiastical code, to be in force in Maryland. The act also contained a clause requiring that the Great Charter of England be observed in the colony, a provision authorities in London found to be at variance with the title of the act. According to Sir Thomas Lawrence—he was then in the metropolis—the ministers of state feared that the clause referring to Magna Carta would touch on the king's prerogative. Appeals from the colony might go to the courts at Westminster rather than to the king in council.

Nicholson used his influence with the assemblymen to pass a new law, but found it impossible to carry it through, so he informed Archbishop Tenison, without some clause about "liberty & property, w[hich]h yo[u]r Grace very well knows, English men are fond of." Quakers, other Dissenters, and Catholics continued to balk at paying the tithe to support Anglican clergymen.[29] The Anglican church was a sensitive issue in Maryland, and despite Nicholson's sympathies, he moved discreetly, perhaps overly so. Fearing the reaction of the assembly dominated by Associators, he did not dare initially to reveal the reason for the royal disallowance.

Nicholson had first to build a political base. He set out to recruit able men for office, discharging offenders and incompetents and encouraging and fostering the careers of young, educated men, of whom, unfortunately, there were too few in the colony. Appointments to the commissions of peace in the counties gave him the greatest opportunity. In reorganizing the provincial appellate court he sought to appoint as judges men from the various counties and those with legal experience as well as adherents of the various political factions.

Relations with the assembly continued frustrating. Although the expenses incurred in calling frequent sessions caused resentment, Nicholson persisted in summoning delegates from the counties to the provincial capital, six times in two years. The governor summoned, but the assemblymen procrastinated, accomplishing little. John Coode, rebellious as ever and smarting from a public humiliation he received from Nicholson, along with Philip Clark, an ambitious planter, was ready to seize the lead in organizing fresh opposition. And in London, Coode's stepson, Gerard Slye, awaited an opportunity to campaign against the governor.

For a time, to Nicholson things seemed quiet. As the spring of 1696 approached, he wrote to the Plantation Office: the colony, although very poor, was peaceable.[30]

Following the Protestant uprising, it had not been enough for the crown to follow the simple formula of appointing a governor to take turbulent Maryland under the immediate care of the crown, as the respective careers of Copley and Nicholson demonstrated. To still rampant discord and dampen factionalism required forcefulness, intelligence, and purpose, qualities all too rare in the political society of the late seventeenth century. Whatever else Nicholson accomplished, occupied with problems in Maryland, he had been able to provide little aid—only token support—to the English efforts in the north against the French.

Nicholson's political horizon was not limited to the Chesapeake; his purview took in more distant boundaries. For some time, he and his emissary in London, Sir Thomas Lawrence, had concerned themselves with the security of the other English colonies and the reception given alien ships, pirates, and privateers in New England, the Delaware colonies, and Carolina. The situation in Pennsylvania and the counties on the lower Delaware particularly distressed Nicholson. The Society of Friends was now rent into contending sects, and the control exercised by the proprietor and his deputies over the government was as weak and lax as ever. Like Copley before him, Nicholson condemned the ineptness of proprietary government and the gross violations of the acts of trade and navigation in the ports along the Delaware. He exhorted the crown to strip William Penn of authority and to assume control.[31]

Although little if any evidence had substantiated the claims of the leaders of the Protestant coup—ambitious men of substance denied high office in proprietary Maryland—of misrule and conspiracy by the proprietary and Catholic faction in Maryland, the ministers of state had seized on the unstable situation caused by the uprising in Saint Marys to place government in Maryland directly under the crown. Yet the strength of royal government in the province and the ability of officials to end factional strife and social discord depended less on the institutional arrangement thus imposed than on the strength of personality and the integrity of the men appointed to preside over the government, as the careers of Nicholson, Copley, and their successors demonstrated. After five years Nicholson left Maryland to take up his post across the Potomac in Virginia. Maryland under his successor was again the scene of partisan strife.

CHAPTER 13

Quakers and Proprietary Government, 1690–96

DESPITE the seemingly unequivocal recommendation of the Committee for Foreign Plantations in the days immediately following the declaration of war against Louis XIV to seek parliamentary sanction for the crown to take over the proprietary governments in America, the men at Whitehall neither moved with dispatch nor consistency to carry out this goal. They had acted against Baron Baltimore, but not against the proprietors of Carolina or East and West Jersey, and equivocated in their relations with William Penn, although the formula they employed to justify the assumption of government in Maryland might well have been utilized against the overlords of the other proprietaries. As the inconsistent behavior of the ministers of state, especially their relations with William Penn, demonstrated, in the world of Whitehall, personal influence often outweighed rational administration.

Early in 1690 the situation in Philadelphia strongly resembled that in Charles Town. The provincial government was at a virtual standstill; its authority over the three lower counties on the Delaware, almost nonexistent. A sharp break had developed between the absentee proprietor and his few supporters and the vigorous, self-confident Quakers led by Thomas Lloyd. From England Penn had attempted one expedient after another, consistently giving way before the strong-minded Quaker leaders in Philadelphia. He never appreciated that pious platitudes could never be the ultimate sanction of government. Penn's failure consistently to support those he entrusted with authority contributed to the weakness of government. Men in opposition understood that if they persevered, sooner or later Penn would give way. More often, it was sooner. John Blackwell, the old Cromwellian from New England whom Penn had once employed, fully realized the weakness of the proprietor, accusing him of inconsistency—indeed, of duplicity.

By 1690 Blackwell had had quite enough of the Quakers and of Pennsylvania. On leaving Philadelphia following his last meeting with the council, he sent the proprietor a blistering letter condemning once more the "insupportableness of Governm[en]t under your Constitution &

people, men who despise all Dominion & dignity that is not in themselves." Neither man nor God could prevail with them. The "wild beasts"
of the forests could better govern the witless zealots who made "a
monkey-house" of the sessions of the assembly. Doubtless Blackwell was
rigid, uncompromising, and militant, but given the circumstances of the
government and the contentiousness of his opponents, could anyone have
done better?[1]

The proprietor's position in England further clouded the situation in
America. His friendship with James II and his open support for the
Catholic monarch's policy on religious toleration led the more unscrupulous and the more gullible to conclude that he was a Roman Catholic,
indeed, as some said, a secret Jesuit. Penn had corresponded with the
deposed king at his court at Saint-Germain. The letters were carried over
to France by Richard Graham, Viscount Preston, who with Matthew
Crone was engaged in a Jacobite conspiracy. In June 1690 the Privy
Council issued a warrant to apprehend Penn and others alleged to be
engaged in a plot to restore James. Penn sought the intercession of his
friend, Henry, Viscount Sydney (later earl of Romney), now a principal
secretary of state, but Nottingham and the solicitor general urged that he
be prosecuted. Evidently Penn was saved when Crone withdrew his testimony against him, leaving only the word of Preston.[2] Until the close of
1691 Penn was in no position to deal with affairs in Pennsylvania.

Officials in Philadelphia acting in the name of the proprietor generally ignored Penn, who by terms of the royal charter was required to
submit the laws of the colony to the crown for review. In June 1691 Penn
complained that he had received no copies of the laws. Later that summer
he wrote to the contentious Quaker magnates in Philadelphia, "all my
loving friends," to put aside their private interests and resentments for the
public good. One faction had complained of a surreptitious meeting of the
council, another of an incompetent election. "Cannot you bear a little for
ye Good of ye whole at least till it please God to bring me among you?"
the proprietor implored.[3]

Among the divisions existing in Penn's territories in America was
one between the men who predominated in the upper counties, the province of Pennsylvania, and those residing in the lower counties on the
Delaware, a region outside the confines of the charter granted Penn in
1681 and populated for the most part by people other than Quakers. In
the province where the Friends predominated, Thomas Lloyd and his
adherents—Arthur Cooke, John Simcock, and Joseph Growdon—
following the departure of Blackwell, had consolidated their power,
stripping their opponents, Griffith Jones, William Markham, and James

Claypoole, men who had dared to support the proprietary deputy, of their offices.

When assemblymen representing the upper and the lower counties met at Newcastle in March 1691, they clashed over the nature of the executive authority. With few exceptions the Quakers wanted a single executive; the majority from the lower counties, fearing domination from the province, preferred to have the councilors jointly exercise administrative authority. Several councilors from the Delaware withdrew rather than submit to Lloyd. By the winter of 1692 he remained as Penn's deputy in the province only; William Markham, a cousin of the proprietor, presided over the lower counties. To the merchants and planters on the lower reaches of the Delaware, an administration controlled by Quakers offered no relief to the chronic threat of French privateering raids against the long, exposed shoreline.

Quaker society in Pennsylvania now experienced two shocks, one secular, the other doctrinal, which threatened the community of Friends.

In 1692 the council of Pennsylvania proposed a general tax on real and personal property. Although not prohibitive, the tax was presumably intended for the use of the financially embarrassed deputy governor, Thomas Lloyd. The measure provided several diverse groups alienated from the ruling clique, non-Quakers, unseated officeholders, and remnants of the proprietary faction, a common issue. Two hundred and sixty-one freemen of the county of Philadelphia—they included almost all of the lesser merchants, shopkeepers, and artisans of Philadelphia—claiming the tax threatened them with "Bondage and Slavery," protested to the assembly.

Many of the men whose names appeared on the petition against the general tax were supporters of George Keith, a temperamental Scottish Quaker. In contrast to the majority of Friends who still adhered to the simple faith of the inner light, the ability of each person to formulate his own creed, Keith saw the need for ordered, external tenets. The logic of his ideas and the reception afforded him in the Quaker communities was eventually to lead him to Anglicanism, but before that his preaching divided the society of Friends in Pennsylvania. The Quaker magistrates and the public, or traveling, ministers saw in his arguments a threat not only to religious unity but to civil authority. In a community already rent by secular strife, the traveling ministers professed to see in Keith and his doctrine a threat to the last sanctuary for peace, the Quaker meetings.

The doctrinal controversy had its political and social dimensions. Leading the orthodox Friends were Thomas Lloyd and his active supporters. Of the several hundred Quakers who publicly opposed Keith, none was known as a political opponent of the deputy governor. Among Keith's adherents were men who led the oppositon to Lloyd, as well as displaced officeholders, lesser traders, and shopkeepers in Philadelphia. The Keithian heresy sharply divided the Quaker community for two years before the dominant elders in Philadelphia prevailed.[4]

Viewed from the perspective of Whitehall, where the ministers of state were attempting to coordinate the military efforts of the northern colonies against the French, the situation prevailing in Penn's territories constituted decided maladministration of government. William III had personally chosen an experienced military officer who had served with him in Ireland, Colonel Benjamin Fletcher, to govern New York and to command the militia of the neighboring provinces. With New York a vulnerable, exposed colony, a province critical to the English position, the neighboring corporate and proprietary colonies were expected to contribute men and money to support her in the common effort against the French.

Neither Penn nor his officials had committed any offense to warrant legal proceedings against the charter in the royal courts at Westminster, but the crown employed the same rationale against Penn it had used against the proprietor of Maryland. Because of "great miscarriages" in the administration of government and the absence of the proprietor, Pennsylvania had fallen into disorder, confusion leading to the breakdown of the public peace. As a consequence the province was left unguarded against the enemy. For the better security of the subjects of the crown, the king and queen took the administration of government into their own hands. By a commission issued to the governor of New York, they empowered Fletcher to administer the government of Penn's territories.[5]

William Penn did not accept the decision. He sought to preserve his position as proprietor and to undermine the royal governor. He openly warned Fletcher: "I am an Englishmen...." The country, that is, the soil and the government, were inseparably the property of the proprietor; no writ had been brought, no trial conducted, no legal judgment given against him. The lords of the Committee for Plantation Affairs who had recommended stripping him of his political authority must have acted on the basis of faulty information, he conjectured publicly, or from an excess of care for the English territories. Consequently Fletcher must "tread softly" and with caution. Penn also dispatched a message to the principal Quakers in America, urging them to insist on "your patent [that is, *his* charter] with wisdome & moderačon but steddy integrity."

Penn also outlined the arguments the Friends must use. Doubtless the royal takeover was the result of faulty recommendations by envious neighbors and an "excess of care in the Lords [of Trade] to preserve the Colonyes from the French." Set forth the "falshood of it," he urged the Quaker leaders. They could send their views to the lobby of Friends in London and Bristol, who would present them at court.

By this time William Penn was in desperate financial straits as a result of the fraudulent dealings of his steward in Ireland, Philip Ford, and of his own carelessness or naïveté. Having contracted to give Ford three hundred thousand acres of land in Pennsylvania if unable to pay his debt to him, Penn was forced to ask one hundred of the wealthier inhabitants of the colony each to lend him one hundred pounds interest-free for three years.[6]

Fletcher arrived in Philadelphia in the spring of 1693 to inaugurate his administration and to raise money for the defense of New York. By the terms of his commission the elected assemblymen could initiate legislation, but the laws they enacted must be sent to Whitehall within three months of passage for approval by the Privy Council. Officholders must take an oath or declare their loyalty to the crown. Fletcher offered Thomas Lloyd the first place on the council, but when the aged Quaker leader spurned the advance, Fletcher applied the same tonic Lloyd had previously administered to supporters of John Blackwell. He appointed nine of Lloyd's opponents, five of them non-Quakers, to the board. He completed the takeover by naming Markham as his deputy and appointing new slates of magistrates in the counties.

The expedient of the crown's appointing a governor proved to be of little value, particularly as Fletcher's primary responsibility lay, not on the Delaware, but on the Hudson. Having heard that the French were on the march, he departed for Albany to confirm an alliance with the Iroquois. After two weeks of maneuvering with the Quaker-dominated assembly he had little to show: a modest money bill, but no appropriation for the defense of New York. Fletcher was skeptical that Pennsylvania would ever contribute while the Friends controlled the assembly. Six of the Quaker leaders—Thomas Lloyd, his kinsman David Lloyd, Thomas Dockett, John Symcock, Griffith Owen, and John Bristow—were making plans for a restoration of government to Penn. They seemed bound for England.[7]

Fletcher's reports to Whitehall appeared decisive. The Lords of Trade and the Privy Council acted swiftly. On 8 February 1694 the committee ordered the attorney general to review the charter issued Penn in 1681. It specifically cited the denial by Pennsylvania of assistance for the defense of New York and Penn's letter to the inhabitants bidding them to protest against Fletcher's commission. But Penn had friends in high places, among them Rochester, Sydney, and Sir John Trenchard, then a principal secretary of state. Moreover, the crown law officers, Edward Ward and Thomas Trevor, equivocated in their assessment of the circumstances under which the crown might assume the government of Pennsylvania. As long as the exigencies described in the commission to Fletcher—extraordinary emergency arising through default or neglect by the proprietor or the officials appointed by him—prevailed, the king could commission a governor.[8]

Ward and Trevor had given the king and council a way out. Should they decide that the conditions previously justifying the crown appointing a governor no longer existed, they might restore the authority of the proprietor. Penn had to pay a price to win back the right of government, his only resource, since his arrangement with Ford clouded his title to the soil of Pennsylvania. As a condition for the crown restoring the proprietary, in the summer of 1694 he agreed immediately to repair to the colony to take charge of the government, there to secure obedience to all requests for quotas of men and money for the defense of New York and to continue Markham as deputy. If royal orders were not obeyed, he must turn back administration of government to Fletcher, who still had the right to claim a quota of eighty men and other assistance for the defense of the northern frontier. On 9 August the queen in council approved this arrangement and eleven days later modified Fletcher's commission accordingly to strip him of governmental authority over Pennsylvania.

To obviate the charge of neglecting the government, Penn had promised to go to America "at once." According to report, he intended to leave in about a month.[9] Late in November Penn sent out an ambiguously worded letter to the Friends and brethren in Philadelphia by which they could understand that "by the good providence of God" he was restored to the administration of government. He hinted only vaguely of the conditions attached. "A word to the wise is enough." It was hoped his return to the colony would put an end to their various troubles. Until he arrived he prayed them to be careful that the charter be strictly observed.[10] Five years would pass before Penn left for America.

The proprietor had urged the Friends in Philadelphia strictly to observe the charter—but what charter? The patent issued him by Charles II in 1681 by which Penn was legally responsible to the crown, or the second "frame of government" passed by the assembly of Pennsylvania in 1683, a provincial law commonly called in the colony a charter? The ambiguity of Penn's injunction did not allow his deputy, William Markham, and the two assistants appointed by the proprietor, Samuel Jennings and John Goodson, to proceed with any certain authority. Thomas Lloyd died in 1694, but his kinsman, David Lloyd, a Welsh lawyer, assumed the lead in opposing the proprietary officials. To the younger Lloyd and his followers it was clear from experience that both the proprietor and the crown might manipulate the membership of the council. The assembly seemed less susceptible to their influence. During Fletcher's brief tenure, the assembly of Pennsylvania, like assemblies elsewhere in royal colonies, had the right to initiate bills.

David Lloyd now launched a campaign to secure a new frame of government, one to shift power from the council to the assembly. He seized the opportunity presented in October 1696 when Markham called the assembly into session to fulfill the demand from the crown that the colony meet its obligation for the defense of New York. There would be no vote for supplies unless the former frame of government was restored. Markham gave in. He even submitted a basic ordinance. The assembly then passed both the money bill and the bill establishing his frame of government. Under this statute voters elected both houses of the legislature, but the assembly had the right to initiate bills. The measure also lowered the requirements for voting in the counties from ownership of one hundred to ownership of fifty acres of land and shifted the franchise in Philadelphia from men who paid scot and lot—a widespread parish assessment—to those who held fifty pounds in property. These alterations were designed to strengthen the position of the Quakers by basing the assembly on a rural and urban middle class.[11]

From New York, Fletcher made much of the controversy between Markham and the Quaker politicians: the Lords of Trade could see that Friends in Pennsylvania had as little regard for the proprietor as they did for the king's service. They sought by their own authority to erect a new model government of their own invention. The Philadelphians were growing rich and thriving by trade while the New Yorkers suffered under the burdens of war.[12] Fletcher had joined the ranks of officials complaining of the chartered proprietaries and urging their abolition.

Penn arrived in his province in 1699. He remained for only a short time before hurrying back to England to face a challenge to proprietary government raised by a newly established Commission for Trade and Plantations. In his need he was forced again to make concessions to the dominant faction controlling the local government, an administration which from the vantage of London seemed culpable in that it failed to adhere to the parliamentary navigation code and adopted laws inimical to the statutes of England.

The proprietors of East and West Jersey were most vulnerable to a royal takeover, for it was doubtful whether they had every legally possessed the power of government, not having received a charter from the king. When the crown had pressed to consolidate the administration of the northern colonies in 1688, the proprietors resident in the British Isles had seemed prepared to surrender their claim in exchange for recognition of their rights to the soil. East and West Jersey then passed into the Dominion of New England. But with the incarceration of Governor Andros in Boston and the flight of Francis Nicholson from Manhattan, the two Jerseys were left with nothing more than local (town) administrations. Uncertainty surrounded the surrender of the British proprietors in 1688.

Edward Byllynge in 1685 had appointed the last deputy governor in West Jersey. When the proprietor died two years later, his heirs sold his holdings to Doctor Daniel Coxe, a court physician and commercial speculator with extensive holdings in America, including both East and West Jersey. In 1690 Coxe approached Joseph Dudley, then in England preparing to embark with an English expedition to New York, with an offer, subject to the approval of the crown, to take on the management of both East and West Jersey, or at least to establish some order in the provinces until a better arrangement could be made. Dudley rejected the proposal.[13]

When the war in America intensified, when French raids on the exposed northern frontier mounted, and when the financial and human resources of New York proved inadequate, the ministers of state in Whitehall came to a decision. The neglect demonstrated by the proprietors of East and West Jersey and Pennsylvania justified placing these provinces under the jurisdiction of the governor of New York. On 11 February 1692 the Privy Council ordered a commission for Fletcher implementing this decision drafted. But Daniel Coxe and William Dockwra, the London-based secretary for the East Jersey proprietors, prevailed on the ministers to reconsider the matter.

Coxe was then in the process of liquidating his holdings. In March he sold the bulk of his shares, including two of the twenty-four portions in East Jersey and twenty-two of the one hundred shares of West Jersey, to a syndicate of forty-eight London merchants and investors for the sum of nine thousand pounds. For the ministers of state the critical issue was support for the defense of New York and the northern frontiers. In March 1692 the Privy Council, with the queen presiding, confirmed the decision to place Fletcher in charge of Pennsylvania, but not the Jerseys. Apparently spokesmen for the proprietors had made extravagant promises to support New York. The governor at Manhattan would be empowered to draw seven hundred men—far more than required from any of the other colonies—from the Jerseys for the defense of the northern borders.

The sale of proprietary shares by Coxe and the subsequent dealings of the syndicate to whom he had alienated his holdings complicated matters. The West Jersey Society, so the organization of London investors was called, was initially headed by Sir Thomas Lane, alderman and later lord mayor of London. It issued sixteen hundred shares of stock at ten pounds each. This turn of events disturbed officials at the Plantation Office. On 18 April the Lords of Trade recommended that the lord president, Carmarthen, press for a writ of scire facias against the proprietors of East and West Jersey, the power of government having been assigned in several "parcels."[14]

The threat, if it was that, seemed effective. That spring the English proprietors of both divisions placed the militia under the command of Fletcher. They so instructed officials in Perth Amboy and in Burlington.[15] These promises of military support came to nothing. Still the Lords of Trade did not pursue the threat of legal action; the crown did not assume the government of the Jerseys. But the West Jersey Society and the Board of Proprietors of East Jersey received no positive acknowledgment from the crown of the right to exercise governmental authority. They simply assumed this was to be treated as a piece of property, to be bought and sold, transferred without consulting the crown.[16] William III and his ministers failed to disabuse them of this notion.

Acting on the assumption that they were legally entitled to govern, the British-based proprietors of both divisions selected Andrew Hamilton, a Scottish merchant then resident in East Jersey, as governor. Since Hamilton expected to reside in Perth Amboy, he named Edward Hunlocke, a merchant of Burlington, as his deputy in West Jersey. Jeremiah Basse, an erstwhile Baptist preacher, became land agent and general factor for the West Jersey Society.

Hamilton did not have an easy time. The Quakers settled on the left bank of the Delaware saw in the London syndicate a threat to their domination, while the proprietors resident in the colony ignored by their counterparts in England organized to resist any control emanating from outside the community. In East Jersey opposition to proprietary authority was strongest in the towns of Elizabeth, Woodbridge, Piscataway, Newark, Middletown, and Shrewsbury in Essex and Monmouth counties. Here the earliest settlers had received patents for land from the first English governor at Manhattan before he had received word that the duke of York had disposed of the region. Many townsmen refused to pay quitrents to the proprietors, but for young, ambitious men like Lewis Morris, support for the proprietors and their governor initially marked the path to higher political preferment.

Three issues dominated political affairs in East Jersey: support for the defense of New York; titles and rents on land from grants made in the first year of settlement by the first English governor at Manhattan, Richard Nicolls; and the right of the proprietors of East Jersey to conduct trade and establish a port free from the payment of customs at New York. For officials at Manhattan, goods entering a duty-free port established under the aegis of the proprietors of East Jersey drained revenue needed for the support of New York. The proprietary regime of East Jersey also needed funds, as was well appreciated by the provincial assembly when it granted Governor Hamilton only a minimal sum of money. It refused to pass any other bills in order to demonstrate displeasure at the decision of Lewis Morris and the other provincial judges in suits of ejectment brought on behalf of the proprietors against landholders in Elizabeth.[17]

The assemblymen at Perth Amboy also struck out against Manhattan, where royal customs officials were under orders from London not to allow any trade prejudicial to New York. The auditor general of the plantation revenue, William Blathwayt, had instructed the collector at Manhattan, Chidley Brooke, to insist that Jerseymen pay duties at New York on any goods they imported, East Jersey being a dependency of New York. In retaliation the assembly at Perth Amboy passed an act cutting off shipments of timber to New York. To require duties at Manhattan, but none at Perth Amboy, Brooke complained, would seriously damage the trade of New York and greatly reduce the revenue available for the defense of the colony. The many divided interests among the chartered governments, he predicted to Blathwayt, would lead to ruin, for a divided people would encourage the enemy to invade. Each of the petty governmental jurisdictions following its own interests aimed at independence with no regard for the needs of the crown, the course of all privileges. Such "is the short sighted policy of this American World."[18]

The failure of the assemblies of both divisions to contribute for the defense of the northern frontiers proved embarrassing to Governor Andrew Hamilton. He could only call for volunteers. Had he asserted a power to draft men, they would have fled to another colony. He professed himself both ashamed and aggrieved that the New Jerseymen were so awkward about military service. They complained of the exemptions given other provinces and of the failure of other colonies to comply with quotas assigned them. This situation must prevail, Hamilton predicted, until the burden of supporting the frontiers extended to "all North America." Debauched by their neighbors, the "stiff and obstinate" Jerseymen shut their minds to all reason. The English would ever be frustrated by the French until the crown sent out a force to root out the enemy or compel every colony to furnish and pay for its quota of troops. While it rested with the assemblymen to support or ignore the common military effort, while the people could choose either to march out against the enemy or to stay at home, there was no doubt of the outcome.[19]

The assessment of Andrew Hamilton, a man not bred or inclined to a military tradition, reached receptive minds at the Plantation Office. His views, coupled with similar sentiments expressed by other officials in the colonies, led men in Whitehall to conclude that the future well-being of the English dominions in America required a more rational coordination of defense efforts and an end to privileged chartered governments, administrations immune from direct control from the crown.

By the end of the decade the British proprietors of the two Jerseys had fully recognized the weakness of their position against the settlers and waived their claim to exercise governmental authority in exchange for a confirmation of their rights to the soil by the crown. This seemed but the first step in a program to have the crown assume direct control of all of the chartered governments in America.

The English communities in the Delaware Valley had shown little social cohesion and common purpose, rent as they were by religious and ethnic animosities and divided by economic interest as well was the clash of strong-willed men seeking political advantage. Efforts by the royal authorities to impose some control and to force the Quaker-dominated communities to contribute to the common defense had been marred. As the relations of William Penn and Daniel Coxe to the monarchy demonstrated, personal influence and private interest often outweighed rational, purposeful administration.

CHAPTER 14

New York, 1690–96:
Legacy of Hate

NEW YORK, its northern frontier open to French and Indian raids, its people divided by bitter hatred born in the reaction to the overthrow of the Dominion of New England, played a key role in the plans of English officials in London during the first of the extended conflicts fought over the course of several decades with the forces of the French monarchy. To coordinate the military efforts of the English, to hold the support of the Iroquois, and to end internecine strife were tasks difficult to achieve.

In 1689 William III and the coalition of Whigs and Tories who made up his first administration had accepted the demise of the Dominion of New England and had sanctioned for New York an elected assembly patterned after those sitting in the other English colonies. But the king and his ministers had bungled badly by applying to New York the formula they employed for Massachusetts, where they had allowed the men who had seized power to continue, even temporarily, to administer the government. For whatever their assessment of Simon Bradstreet and Wait Winthrop in Boston, officials in London had determined that Leisler " at the head of the Rable" had taken over at Manhattan.[1]

Had the Protestant king and the Lords of Trade not applied to New York the verbal formula used for Massachusetts, but made clear that they meant to have Nicholas Bayard, Frederick Philipse, and Stephanus Van Cortlandt, the councilors commissioned to serve under Lieutenant Governor Francis Nicholson, continue in office, matters might well have turned out differently. A generation of hate and civil strife might have been avoided. Seizing on the royal letter as sanction from the Protestant monarchy for his administration, Jacob Leisler for a time was able to prevail on men who would not otherwise accept his administration. As it was, support for Leisler in the province was limited. Distance, ethnic loyalties, and economic interests had divided the colony and weakened support for the former administration. But it was one thing for the New Englanders on Long Island, for example, not to support a government which denied them a representative assembly and demanded quitrents; it was another, once the Dominion of New England had collapsed, to support the revolutionary junta at Manhattan, despite its claim to stand for the Protestant succession in England.

Capitalizing on the ignorance of simple folk, charging their opponents in office with complicity in a Catholic-fomented conspiracy, and employing armed force, the insurgents had seized Manhattan. Jacob Leisler, Jacob Milborne, and Samuel Edsall with his relatives made up the core of the rebel leadership. Taking advantage of the confused state of affairs prevailing in 1689, these frustrated and resentful opportunists, men of middle rank, had displaced the officials of the dominion administration. Nicholas Bayard, James Graham, and Stephanus Van Cortlandt, men ousted from office who suffered from Leislerian rule, confused the position of the insurgent leaders by referring to them as rabble. Leisler, Edsall, William Lawrence, Samuel Staats, and Peter Delanoy were hardly of the lower order; nor did they desire the rank and file to participate in government. Leisler had to call an assembly to raise funds for his revolutionary regime in the conflict against the French and Indians.

The themes of religion and conspiracy served the insurgents well. Perhaps they did deceive themselves into believing the charges they hurled against their opponents, for a strong element of paranoia was evident in the rigid mentality of Leisler. Anyone who disagreed with him—former allies, even such staunch supporters of the Protestant succession as Fitzjohn Winthrop and the officials of Connecticut—he labeled Papists and conspirators.

Except for certain elements in Manhattan—the lower-class Dutch, for example—and its immediate environs, elsewhere in the province support for the insurgent regime was very limited. The majority of Albany, a Dutch community, resisted Leisler's authority, bowing only when compelled by force of arms and the need for support to resist the French and hostile Indians. Once the dominion regime collapsed, the English villagers on Long Island generally remained aloof. Even within New York City, the Leislerian movement was not entirely a class or ethnic phenomenon, an uprising of Dutch inhabitants displaced under alien English rule and deprived of economic opportunities by aggressive English and Huguenot minorities.[2]

Events in New York for a period of almost two years following the take-over by the insurgents laid the ground for future strife and hatred in the colony. More than any other factor, the violence of Leisler's rule, his extreme language, his imprisoning those who questioned his authority, his seizing property, his threatening the lives of the skeptical, divided society and earned for Leisler the hatred of men who suffered from his arbitrary rule. And this hatred brought to Leisler and his son-in-law and deputy, Jacob Milborne, the penalty of death. Once victorious, their opponents demanded their blood.

Leisler's tenure in power—and, perhaps, the ensuing generation of civil strife—was unnecessarily extended by the failure of the English administration promptly to take control in Manhattan.

William III and the Lords for Trade and Foreign Plantations did not consider Leisler and the insurgents fit to govern. Yet they allowed the revolutionary regime to continue for months. Henry Sloughter, the governor-designate, ought to have departed from England for his post early in 1690, even sooner. Problems in outfitting the two companies of soldiers and in readying a vessel to transport him delayed the governor for six months. When the *Archangel* finally left for America, she went by way of Bermuda, where on the night of 10 January 1691 she ran aground. Additional weeks passed before Sloughter reached Manhattan.

In the interval, during 1690, the insurgents consolidated their position. On 9 December 1689 letters from the court arrived in Manhattan. Leisler promptly seized the documents despite the claim of Philipse, Van Cortlandt, and Bayard that the letters authorized them, the councilors, to continue in office. Leisler, Staats, Delanoy and the others of the junta now declared themselves to the king's council, settled a panel of magistrates, and appointed officers to command the militia, all in the name of the Protestant monarchy. Bayard, William Nicolls, and others, they clapped into jail. To avoid a similar fate, Van Cortlandt and his wife fled the city.

To the north in Ulster County and at Albany, Peter Schuyler and Robert Livingston prevailed on the Dutch inhabitants to repudiate "an Usurped Power" by "a Private man without ye least Shadow of authority." But on the night of 9 February, French and Indian raiders left over sixty dead at nearby Schenectady. The inhabitants of Albany, unable to stand alone, were forced to accept the authority of Leisler when he sent Jacob Milborne with an armed band to demand that they acknowledge the insurgent regime. Robert Livingston fled, first to Boston and then to Hartford. When the commissioners appointed by Connecticut failed to satisfy the Leislerians over the status of the forces at Albany, the revolutionary council at Manhattan formally condemned the governor and magistrates at Hartford as abettors of rebels. Unless they placed their militia under the command of Leisler, they would be deemed enemies and treated accordingly.[3]

To Livingston, Bayard, and William Nicolls, Leisler seemed to have assumed the role of a despot, a Masaniello, threatening to seize persons and their property if they did not submit to his will. He mocked legal process, Livingston charged: the sword, not the law, settled the right.

Captain John Blackwell was perhaps kinder in his assessment. On his way from Philadelphia to Boston he had observed Leisler at Manhattan. He thought him a "madman." To undermine the credibility of those who dared question or oppose the insurgent regime, reports were circulated that they were Papists or supporters of the Catholic James II.

To enable the insurgent government to raise money, Leisler sent out warrants to return an assembly. Suffolk did not respond, while in the other counties the turnout was light. In April this "assembly" convened at the home of Robert Walters, Leisler's son-in-law and one of the representatives returned from New York City. The group passed one measure to raise threepence in the pound on all property and another allowing every town liberty to bolt and export flour, but when several delegates submitted a petition asking the release of the men held prisoners and a redress of various grievances against the rebel regime, Leisler prorogued the assembly. Insurgent militiamen then began breaking into homes and confiscating provisions and weapons.[4]

In May 1690 Joost Stoll, Leisler's emissary to London, returned with news that the crown had appointed, not Leisler, but Henry Sloughter as governor and that the Protestant monarch had commissioned Francis Nicholson deputy governor of Virginia. This was hardly an appropriate reward for a man, who according to the insurgents, was a Papist and a Jacobite who had conspired against the Protestant cause. Did sane, rational men in Manhattan wonder?

That same month came the first challenge in New York City to Leisler's authority. On 19 May thirty-six men, calling themselves merchants, traders, and principal inhabitants—they included several ministers of the Dutch churches as well as Charles Lodowyck, a merchant who had once sided with the insurgents—signed an address to William and Mary protesting the arbitrary power exercised by the Leislerians. Despite the royal proclamation for continuing all justices of the peace, the New Yorkers found themselves ruled by the sword and imprisoned and their property seized, all without legal warrant. Early in June the council of safety agreed to release those jailed if they would give bond for their good behavior and acknowledge the authority of Leisler as lieutenant governor.

Emotions ran high in Manhattan over the jailing of dissidents. At one point Leisler was caught in an angry crowd and jostled, perhaps even struck on the shoulder with a cane or an adze. Frightened, he called to his guards, who struck out with naked swords and musket butts. He then had the drums sound an alarm and cannon fired. For hours insurgent militiamen with drawn swords in their hands "ran like madmen through the streets" of the town, seizing those who happened to be out of doors and hurrying them off to jail. Leisler declared the persons opposing him were intending treason; he branded several men rebels. Over a score were jailed. Within two weeks twelve were released, but only after they had given bond and paid a fine. The riotous behavior of the armed militiamen and Leisler's indiscriminate charges apparently alienated some of his followers, but there was no organized resistance.

The council of safety controlled Manhattan and the environs by armed force. Later that year Major Thomas Willett with 150 men from Long Island marched on Manhattan, but when challenged by Milborne with a superior force, the Long Islanders scattered. They managed to get out a letter to England praying for deliverance from a situation "worse than Egyptian bondage."[5]

On a wider scale Leisler and Milborne in conjunction with the revolutionary government at Boston attempted the reduction of French Canada by force. Their plan provided for five hundred militia and fifteen hundred warriors of the Five Nations under Milborne to march from New York against Montreal. The expedition hardly had left Albany, when it foundered. Inadequate preparations and discord between the Leislerians and the commanders appointed by Connecticut halted the "army." The Bay colonists did somewhat better. Thiry-two vessels outfitted by private subscription sailed up the Saint Lawrence and landed twelve hundred men several miles below Quebec. But short of ammunition and with the French gathering against them, the New Englanders hastily abandoned the field. By the time the ships returned to Boston, many men had died of smallpox. By the new year the northern frontiers were again open to enemy incursions.

The insurgent regime at Manhattan faced a more immediate problem. On 23 January, Major Richard Ingoldsby, with two companies of English troops and several of the officials and councilors named by William III in the commission to Governor Henry Sloughter, arrived in New York. The governor, delayed in Bermuda, did not appear until 19 March. The delay was critical, vital in the case of Milborne and Leisler.

Ingoldsby, an experienced officer who had served with William III against the Jacobites in Ireland, carried a warrant from the Protestant king to command the detachment of royal troops, but not a commission as lieutenant governor of the colony. Leisler knew that Ingoldsby held a military commission, yet he proclaimed that Ingoldsby was a Jacobite leading an invasion.[6] He refused to hand over the fort. Leisler may no longer have been capable of recognizing reality. Peter Delanoy, Samuel Staats, and the others of the revolutionary council, for their part, might have hoped that Sloughter had been lost at sea or that by prolonging the issue they might salvage something of their authority. On news of the arrival of the English force, Leisler's opponents—some had been his victims—began assembling in New York City. The insurgent leaders branded them as persons disaffected to the interest of William III and Papists encouraged by the arrival of Ingoldsby. When Leisler had four of the redcoats arrested, Ingoldsby, supported by the officers from Long Island and officials from Connecticut, called out the provincial militia.

The crisis came in mid-March. On the sixteenth Leisler issued a manifesto: Ingoldsby, the evil men commissioned as Sloughter's council, and their confederates, as long as they persisted in claiming authority, were enemies of God, of William and Mary, and of the peace and welfare of the people of New York. Leisler and his followers must deny Ingoldsby the fort to secure themselves and their posterity from all power, authority, and force derived from the late king James II. Some among the insurgent militia had not lost their senses. Peter DeMill and Abraham Brazier refused to obey Leisler's command to fire on the redcoats. On 18 March Leisler ordered Ingoldsby to disband his troops, demanding a reply within two hours. None was forthcoming. Leisler's men then opened fire, in the ensuing exchange six men were killed, two wounded.

From this clash came the charge that the insurgent leaders were guilty of treason, waging war against the king.

Governor Henry Sloughter finally arrived on 19 March, a day too late, if indeed his arrival would have made any difference in the behavior of Leisler and Milborne. Leisler still refused to turn over the fort, but instead sent Peter Delanoy and Milborne to negotiate. Sloughter clapped them in jail. This broke the back of the insurgent movement, for Leisler may well have been but a figurehead. Many of the Leislerian militia were deserting, and the arrival of the trained bands from the neighboring counties strengthened Sloughter's hand.[7]

The treatment accorded the rebel chieftains proved critical to the future political and social stability of New York. On the advice of the royal council, Sloughter named a special court to inquire into the recent disturbances. A grand jury sworn by Joseph Dudley returned indictments of murder and treason stemming from the shots fired on the royal troops. Ten men were charged with riot and allowed bail on the grounds that they were ignorant persons led astray by the ringleaders.

The jurymen hearing the trials included both English and Dutch inhabitants. Throughout the proceedings Leisler and Milborne refused to plead, thus challenging the jurisdiction of the court: inasmuch as the Leislerians had received the sanction of the crown, the court appointed by Sloughter had no authority. Both the assembly convened by Sloughter and the jury condemned them. When brought before the court on 15 April for sentencing, the two men affirmed that they would not answer the charges until the crown determined the authority by which they had acted. The court then pronounced sentence: death by hanging.

The trial of the other insurgents followed. By early May eight of the thirty-two men arraigned had been convicted and sentenced to death. Some the governor pardoned. Among the "loyalists," as Sloughter termed them, several were particularly bitter with James Graham and William Nicolls, complaining that the failure to indict Samuel Edsall and Petter Delanoy was due to the favorable charge given by the instructing judge, Joseph Dudley. Ironically, the Leislerians later held Dudley responsible for the execution of the two leaders.

Governor Sloughter was inclined to leniency on the grounds that many who had followed Leisler had done so from ignorance. It would be sufficient to make an example of the ringleaders. The loyalists on the council, perhaps spurred by the humiliation and suffering they had experienced at the hands of Leisler and Milborne, pressed for the sentences against them to be carried out. Unless the administration punished the culprits, it would lose support. Sloughter reprieved all the prisoners but Leisler and Milborne, pending receipt of word from England. Bayard, Van Cortlandt, Phillipse, Nicolls, and Gabriel Minvielle—unlike Dudley, they had suffered at the hands of the rebel junta—demanded the death penalty: the peace and quiet of the province required it, and the assembly and the populace demanded it to prevent future disorders.

The stubbornness of the two condemned men in refusing to plead, their high-handed conduct over the eighteen months when they were in power, and the vengefulness of the men they had grossly accused and mistreated now all told against them. Sloughter gave in, and the assembly concurred. On 16 May the sentences against Leisler and Milborne were carried out.[8]

The Leislerians now had their martyrs. Almost immediately they initiated a campaign in London to reverse the attainders and to destroy, politically at least, their opponents. The executions did not quiet matters in New York, but Sloughter did not have to contend with the factious politicians. He died unexpectedly on 23 July.

In addition to the lives of six convicted Leislerians and a substantial estate, future political power was at stake. Jacob Leisler the younger traveled to London, where early in January 1692 he presented a petition to the Privy Council complaining that the executed leaders had been unjustly condemned. He begged for the release of the six men still under sentence whose estates the governor had confiscated and for a reversal of the convictions and the attainders passed by the assembly.[9] While the queen in council, in accepting a recommendation of the Lords of Trade, concluded on 17 March that Leisler and Milborne had been condemned according to law, as an act of mercy it restored their estates to their families. Three weeks later Mary announced her intention to pardon Abraham Gouverneur, Gerardus Beekman, Mindert Courteen, Thomas Williams, Johannes Vermillie, and Abraham Brazier when they applied to the crown. On 13 May 1692 the queen in council ordered the recognizances, bonds, and other court proceedings against the six discharged. That summer Mary issued a general pardon to all political offenders in New York and ordered an end to prosecutions.[10]

The fate of the Leislerians in New York was not divorced from partisan politics in London. Three years later, with the Whigs more strongly in the ascendancy, the younger Leisler turned to Parliament to reverse the attainder imposed in New York by a regime he labelled as "Tory."

In 1692 two more immediate questions remained to be settled. Who in New York would enjoy the fruits of political power under the administration of Colonel Benjamin Fletcher, the veteran army officer personally selected by William III to replace Sloughter? How could the crown coordinate military operations for the defense of the northern frontier? Initially Fletcher's authority extended over the governments of Pennsylvania and the Jerseys, but two years later the crown amended his commission. The neighboring colonies remained politically distinct, with the governor of New York empowered to draw of the militia of the Jerseys and Connecticut. It remained to officials and assemblies of each province, however, to determine whether they would fulfill the quota given them for any military campaign.

Local political considerations often determined the response to both questions, with the situation in New York being no exception, as the Leislerians and "loyalists," so Sloughter had called them, waged a protracted struggle. The dissidents condemned Joseph Dudley, Philipse, Van Cortlandt, Bayard, Willett, Richard Townley, William Nicolls, and Gabriel Minvielle either as Jacobites or men of little standing. In contrast they claimed for themselves the support of the populace and the mantle of the Protestant Revolution. In commissioning a council, the crown came down on the side of Bayard, Van Cortlandt, and Philipse, but perhaps in an effort to put an end to inflammatory rhetoric instructed Fletcher to allow no printing press in the colony without license.[11]

The political scene in New York was confused. Neither faction, Leislerian or loyalist (Tory, the opposition called it in an effort to appeal to the prejudices of the Whig ministry in London), controlled the assembly during the first portion of the new governor's administration. Neither side presented a united front, as each was rent by personal rivalries and sectional and economic interests, such as the right of a community to bolt and export flour. The loyalists might unite in opposition to their enemies, but once in power would fall out among themselves.[12]

Fletcher arrived in New York on 28 August 1692 to begin his administration. Within two weeks he found that he was among "a Devided contentious impoverished People." The provincial revenue was in arrears, with the government, subsisting on the personal credit of the councilors at interest of 10 percent. Revenue from taxes came in but slowly; trade had declined; and the inhabitants were discouraged by the burden of supporting the defense of Albany, the trading center essential to hold the loyalty of the Five Nations and the northern frontier, a burden left entirely to the province of New York by the neighboring colonies. The political situation was not promising. "Neither Party will be satisfied with Less then the necks of Theire Adversaries." While Fletcher did not entirely despair of bringing them to a "better understanding," he appreciated that it "must bee the work of some tyme."

Time the Leislerians did not allow him. Abraham Gouverneur was one of the six Leislerians convicted in April 1691 of murder but provisionally set at liberty pending final disposition of their cases by the crown. No sooner was Gouverneur free than he set off for England to undermine the loyalist faction in New York. Shipwrecked off Nantucket, he found himself stranded in Boston with but two shirts and a cravat, all that remained of his baggage. He still had pen and tongue, however. He soon filled the ear of Sir William Phips with grossly distorted accounts of the situation in Manhattan. A crude, outspoken man with a violent temper and poor judgment, Phips took the bait. He condemned "old King James's Council" at New York and labelled Fletcher a "poor Beggar," a man who sought not the good of the country but its money. When an account of Phips's outburst penned by Gouverneur fell into Fletcher's hands, the governor waxed indignant against the Leislerians and Phips. He now defended the loyalists, those on the council Phips had slandered as Jacobites attached to King James, as men zealous for the service of William and Mary and as the ablest people in ability and estates in the colony, always ready to advance money for the public good.[13]

If Benjamin Fletcher had intended at the outset of his administration to deal evenhandedly with the warring factions in New York, circumstances now inclined him to side with the loyalists, the councilors who financially supported the government. The Leislerians had openly attacked him. Four of the six released from prison but still under sentence of death pending formal pardon from the crown—Gerardus Beekmen, Mindert Courteen, Thomas Williams, and Johannes Vermillie—won election from the city to the assembly, but Fletcher and the councilors rejected their election—felons under sentence were ineligible to sit in the assembly—and ordered new polls. The Leislerians would not admit guilt, however; they would own to no crime. Not all of the Leislerians remained obdurate. Charles Lodowyck and Abraham De Peyster had once sided with the insurgents. Fletcher now welcomed their support as two of the "fittest" men in the province, considerable merchants, well affected, and ready to advance their estates to support the government.[14]

Fletcher became more dependent on the private credit of the members of the council to finance his administration as the defense of the northern frontier became more critical and the assemblymen more suspicious of the administration's disbursing of money. The appropriation and management of public funds was one of only two issues uniting the factions in the assembly. One of the few representatives who could understand a financial report, Peter Delanoy, chaired the assembly's committee on public finances.

To support the crown's government with one's personal credit could be an uncertain business, as Robert Livingston learned. For a generation English governors in New York had depended on the credit of private men to finance their administrations.[15] Governor Thomas Dongan, no exception, had drawn heavily on Livingston and others to supply the English garrison at Albany. A Scottish-born merchant who had married the widow Alida Van Cortlandt Schuyler, Livingston, through his London correspondent, Jacob Harwood, sought reimbursement and interest when Dongan finally returned to the British Isles in 1692 to have his accounts settled. To finance the war against the Canadians, Dongan had mortgaged his lands, slaves, and chattels in New York as security for the money disbursed by Livingston. But Harwood had used the treasury vouchers issued to him for Livingston's account to pay off his own creditor, Richard Meriwether, another London merchant. Livingston then decided to cross the Atlantic to confer with officials at the Plantation Office, William Blathwayt and John Povey, on the money due him and on Dongan's accounts. He took ship for England late in 1694. Caught in a violent storm and shipwrecked on the coast of Portugal, he was not able to reach London until the following summer.[16] Once there, he quickly made important connections. His advice helped shape critical decisions made by the administration and the politicians for the American scene.

Robert Livingston was not the only New Yorker to brave the Atlantic that year. Abraham Gouverneur also crossed the ocean to join forces with Jacob Leisler in behalf of William Lawrence, Gerardus Beekman, Peter Delanoy, and Samuel Edsall and to win a reversal of the attainder against the elder Leisler. The administration, now predominantly Whig, proved not adverse to the arguments presented in their brief.[17] In March 1695 Gouverneur and Leisler took their case to the House of Lords, seeking to clear the old insurgent regime of New York of any wrongdoing and to cast blame for the trial and execution of Leisler and Milborne on Joseph Dudley, who had presided over the judicial proceedings. Dudley had long since left New York for his native Massachusetts and was now living in England, where he enjoyed the favor and patronage of John, Lord Cutts, a high-ranking officer in the king's army.

A majority of the Lords Spiritual and Temporal were willing to accede to the petition by Gouverneur and Leisler to pass a bill reversing the attainder of the two Protestant "martyrs" of New York, but they omitted the words "arbitrarily, illegally and unjustly" before the phrase "convicted and attainted" at the end of the preamble of the proposed statute. The deletion thus cleared Governor Henry Sloughter, Dudley, and the loyalists of any charge of illegal action. The measure then passed the Lords and Commons despite the testimony given by Dudley and others as to the defiance of the insurgent leaders in 1691. Sir Henry Ashurst presided over the hearings of the committee considering the bill, and he supervised its passage. It received the royal assent on 3 May 1695.[18]

Both Ashurst and Constantine Phips, agents for the provincial government of Massachusetts, had supported the bill and joined in the attack against the loyalists on the New York council in an effort, some men thought, to discredit Dudley's candidacy for the governorship of the Bay colony.[19] While the two men may well have held a strong animus against Dudley (Ashurst particularly, for he was a man of very poor, at times irrational judgment, one governed by partisan passions), Dudley's pretensions at this time were hardly enough to allow him to compete against the Irish peer, Richard Coote, earl of Bellomont, whom the Whigs at court were then promoting for the post at Boston, made vacant by the death of Phips.

It was not Dudley who had to be discredited, but Benjamin Fletcher. To that end the Leislerians introduced fresh grievances against the governor at Manhattan, accusations of graft and corruption. In the spring of 1695 Peter Delanoy charged Fletcher with squeezing money out of the public and private purses, of encouraging pirates operating in the Red Sea, of subverting elections by making freemen of sailors and soldiers to give them votes, and of threatening those inhabitants inclined to support incumbent assemblymen. Further, Delanoy supplied William Penn, who was also eager to be rid of Fletcher, with more ammunition. How the colonists were to be free of the governor, by gentle recall or by disgrace, did not matter to Delanoy. What was needed, he argued, was a governor general with command of the militia of the northern colonies; the assemblies, the courts, and laws of each province might be left separate and distinct from those of the other colonies.[20]

On the need for a unified military command for the defense of northern America, Fletcher and previous governors of New York had agreed. Despite the promises of proprietors of the Quaker colonies, Fletcher's efforts to obtain support from Pennsylvania and the Jerseys had come to little. For some time the governor had been contending with officials in New England over the deployment of their militia, but with no success. Others before him had advocated drastic action, including annexation of the Jerseys and Connecticut. If united, the English colonies would be strong; if disjointed, they would remain weak and unable to defend themselves.[21]

The Protestant monarchy had not followed the path taken by James II, encroaching on the political prerogatives of the chartered governments. At best it had given Fletcher at Manhattan and Phips at Boston command of the militia of Connecticut and Rhode Island. In neither colony was there much support for this expedient. Fletcher could rely only on the few Anglicans who objected to paying rates for the support of the Congregational churches and a small clique associated with Gershom Bulkeley.

Officials in Hartford had reacted swiftly to the demands thus imposed on their militia. They sent Major General Fitzjohn Winthrop to London to seek confirmation of the authority of the provincial government as established by charter. Fletcher too sought to use the patent. The threat of a writ against the charter, or at least a sharply worded letter from the monarch, he suggested, would reduce the obdurate Yankees. The wisest and richest among the inhabitants, he alleged, sought to be under the king's immediate government. The English in America were torn apart by these petty little governments, these little commonwealths. Connecticut and Rhode Island railed against arbitrary power, yet exerted it themselves to the height of "Turkish Tyranny."[22]

Fitzjohn Winthrop pressed the case for Connecticut: under the guise of claiming only a quota of men for the defense of New York, Fletcher was intervening in the civil government. Winthrop and Christopher Almy, agent for Rhode Island, were prepared to agree to whatever quotas William Blathwayt, the secretary at War, might set for the two colonies, but insisted that the remainder of the militia continue under the jurisdiction of the civil governments of their respective provinces. Winthrop's arguments led to a review of the procedures for coordinating the military efforts of the northern colonies and of the charters of the New England corporations. After reviewing the patents and hearing evidence from the agents and their counsel, the crown law officers, Edward Ward and Thomas Trevor, concluded that the ordinary power over the militia did indeed rest with the governments of the corporations, but that in time of emergency the crown could designate a captain general to command. In time of peace, his power reverted to the governors of the respective colonies.

Connecticut and Rhode Island retained their separate political status, and under a plan worked out for the common defense, each of the colonies was expected to contribute a quota to Fletcher's command: Rhode Island 48, Massachusetts 350, Maryland 160, Virginia 240, Pennsylvania 80, and the Jerseys no more than 700.

The procedure proved unworkable, as Pennsylvania, the Jerseys, and Connecticut failed to comply, the latter on the ground that Fletcher had not called on the other provinces for their allotments.[23]

Fletcher would not have to concern himself much longer with the problem, so it seemed in the summer of 1695. From London Fitzjohn Winthrop had good news for his brother in Boston. The new governor of the Bay colony would be Richard Coote, earl of Bellomont, a "very good man," according to Winthrop. The scope of his commission was then uncertain, but, the crown having promised to continue the rights and privileges of the smaller colonies of New England, the agent hoped the new appointment would have no adverse effect on Connecticut.[24]

Richard Coote was a presumptuous Irish peer, short on money but long on a sense of his own worth. An early convert to the cause of the prince of Orange, he had been proscribed by James II but ennobled by William III. He was fortunate in his friendship with several ranking Whig politicans, particularly Shrewsbury, who in 1694 had written on his behalf to the king, "His condition . . . is necessitous to a great degree;" there were several persons, "members of Parliament, who lay great weight, and think his friends obliged to see him taken care of." Bellomont was indiscreet, the duke admitted, but loyal. The death of the governor of Massachusetts allowed Bellomont's Whig friends an opportunity to provide for "that poor gentleman."

Bellomont was unhappy with the salary of the governor of Bay colony, since it was voted by the assembly annually in contrast to that set by the crown for the executive of New York. With the king absent from England, the Whig magnates who dominated among the Lords Justices in council, a board of regents, hit upon a rationalization to make the position of Bellomont more palatable. No reliance could be placed on the provincial assembly in Boston annually to provide an adequate salary for the governor; for the crown to pay him out of the royal exchequer could set an ill precedent. The solution was to appoint Bellomont governor of two colonies, Massachusetts and New York. Fletcher would have to go. He had served at Manhattan for four years—actually three—and was by many men disliked. There was one obvious difficulty: Fletcher was a particular friend of William Blathwayt, then in Flanders as secretary to the king.

Shrewsbury undertook the delicate mission of writing directly to William. The king might be pleased to suspect Blathwayt, the duke gently hinted, of "some partiality" in supporting Fletcher, "no fault towards a friend."[25]

William III was unconvinced, so Blathwayt reported. It is doubtful whether the secretary at war would have misrepresented or distorted the king's sentiments in an open letter, one subject to later inspection and verification. William had agreed with the Lords Justices on the need to so arrange the salaries of the governors in the plantations as to have these officers depend solely on the crown, but the solution proposed by the Whig lords raised serious problems, communications between Boston and Manhattan being one. New York and Massachusetts had different political arrangements, one depending entirely on the king's commission, the other, very much less subordinate, on a royal charter. As a practical matter the financial solution proposed by Bellomont's friends—allowing Bellomont the additional salary of six hundred pounds a year as governor of New York—would be of little help, since money would still be needed to pay for a deputy, a trained and competent officer. That had been the situation under the dominion when Andros served in Boston and Nicholson in Manhattan.

The proximity of the French threat demanded a competent officer in New York. The king was unwilling to remove Fletcher while hostilities continued, for the governor was familiar with affairs there, the fortifications, and the neighboring Indians. William, familiar with Fletcher's record against the Jacobites in Ireland personally had selected him as an officer most fit to manage the war in New York.

The king agreed it was necessary that Bellomont have sufficient financial support as governor of Massachusetts without relying on the assembly, but he left it to the Lords Justices to arrange for an adequate salary, at least until it could be determined whether the inhabitants would do their duty to the king by settling an appropriate salary for the maintenance of the governor.[26]

Given the king's objections, if the Whig lords at Whitehall were to procure for Bellomont an additional salary, they must blacken Fletcher in the eyes of William III. The means to do so were already at hand.

During the exchange over Bellomont's salary in the summer of 1695, two New Yorkers had arrived in London. One was Robert Livingston, the other, a merchant seaman. Captain William Kidd had come with a letter of introduction to William Blathwayt from James Graham, speaker of the New York assembly, friend of Livingston, and father-in-law of Lewis Morris of East Jersey. Kidd, according to Graham, was a "gentleman" who had done the king signal service, aiding in the capture of Saint Christopher from the French and assisting Governor Henry Sloughter in quieting disorders in New York. He was zealous for the royal government. Having hitherto concerned himself in private business, he had sailed his brigantine to London hoping to find employment with the crown. Would Blathwayt use his influence in procuring him command of one of the king's ships?[27]

It was Robert Livingston who found employment for the peripatetic seaman, the command of a privateering expedition sent out to track down buccaneers preying on shipping in the Red Sea and Indian Ocean and to break up piratical trade between Madagascar and Massachusetts, Rhode Island and New York. Livingston became the intermediary between Kidd and Bellomont,[28] the latter acting as agent for a small group of Whig ministers, including the earl of Romney, Lord John Somers, Sir Edward Russell (earl of Orford), and Shrewsbury. Little did Bellomont and the Whig magnates appreciate how embarrassing their involvement with Kidd would prove.

In the summer of 1695 Robert Livingston was of more immediate use to Bellomont in the campaign to undermine Fletcher and to unite the governorships of New York and Massachusetts. For some time Fletcher had been under attack by the agent for Connecticut, by Doctor Daniel Coxe, and by the emissaries of the Leislerian opposition in New York. Livingston had journeyed to England seeking reimbursement from the Treasury for loans made Thomas Dongan, the former governor of New York. He arrived in London on 25 July. Three days later Fitzjohn Winthrop came to see him. The two went for a long walk. On 30 July Livingston delivered his papers at the Plantation Office, but, according to John Povey, Blathwayt's assistant, was not seen there for another month. On 10 August the New Yorker had a long conference with Bellomont, and that evening he dined with Daniel Coxe.[29] Two weeks later Livingston supplied witnesses to testify before the Lords of Trade that Governor Fletcher had sought to subvert elections in New York.

By early September rumor in London had it that, complaints having been made at the Plantation Office against Fletcher, the crown would join New York to Massachusetts with Bellomont presiding as governor. On 13 September the Lords of Trade again heard complaints against Fletcher. Three of the six members of the committee attending that day were either friends of Bellomont or connected in the venture with Kidd. The evidence presented during this hearing hardly proved that the governor had attempted to manipulate elections. Kidd testified that John Tuthall, the sheriff of New York, had told him to get those seamen from his vessel who were inhabitants of the province to vote for such candidates as Fletcher wanted returned. Yet Kidd could not say that Tuthall had acted by order of the governor. Although Kidd related that soldiers from the garrison at Fort William had come to the polling place, they had not carried arms and had not voted. Benjamin Bladenburg confirmed this. Another merchant captain, Giles Shelly, and Thomas Jeffreys also testified that Fletcher was not involved in the call for seamen to vote and that the soldiers had not interfered with or intimidated the voters.[30]

Fletcher's opponents had not proved their case against him. His supporters then took the initiative. In February, Gilbert Heathcote, an influential London alderman whose brother served on the New York council, submitted a memorial asking that the charges against the governor be dismissed before Livingston returned to America or that the governor be provided with a copy of the accusations so that he might better defend himself. The Lords of Trade had already agreed that Livingston should be paid the money he claimed, but it was to come from the revenue of the crown in New York.[31]

From friends in London Fletcher had already learned of the part Livingston had played against him. The governor marshaled the loyalists on the council, including Stephanus Van Cortlandt, Livingston's brother-in-law, against his detractors. Van Cortlandt, Caleb Heathcote, Minvielle, William Pinhorn, John Lawrence, William Smith—all supported Fletcher in his denials. They sent their own emissaries, Chidley Brooke and William Nicolls, across the Atlantic to state the case for the governor and council.[32]

The Leislerians kept up their attack. After Nicolls and Brooke on their voyage fell victim to a French privateer and were carried off to France, it was bruited about London that while captive at Saint-Mal they had drunk to the success of King James and confusion to his enemies and had been in communication with the Jacobite court at Saint-Germain. Indeed the two New Yorkers had been privy to a plot to assassinate William III.[33] Until Nicolls and Brooke could be exchanged or ransomed, Abraham Gouverneur and Jacob Leisler, ensconced in Crown Court in Board Street, had a clear field. They raked up the old charges against Fletcher. Peter Delanoy introduced a new transgression: the governor allegedly accepted bribes from pirates, Red Sea men, to overlook the booty they brought into New York.[34]

During the prolonged and far-flung conflict with France, letters of marque issued by the governors of New York and other American colonies to attack enemy vessels were used by masters and owners to cover an illicit trade with pirates at Madagascar raiding shipping in the Red Sea and Indian Ocean. Frederic Philipse and Stephen Delancey were said to be involved in such traffic. Fletcher defended himself from these charges. If reputable sea captains, mariners who had served other governors against the French, abused the commissions Fletcher gave them and turned pirate, it was a circumstance he could not foresee and could not prevent,[35] the very argument the earl of Bellomont would use when the depredations of Captain William Kidd, the privateer sponsored by Bellomont and the Whig colleagues, came to light.

Until the Whig magnates could undermine Fletcher's standing with the king, until they found an adequate salary for the governor-designate of Massachusetts, and until Bellomont stirred himself to leave for America, Fletcher remained in New York. Bellomont did not take ship until September 1697, two years after his appointment! In the interval the Whigs pushed the expedition by Kidd. Attempting to keep the project secret from Blathwayt, the ministerial partners now offered the king a share in their enterprise. Some of the governors in the colonies, friends of Blathwayt were, they charged, "suspected to have made considerable advantage by conniving at these pirates."[36] But according to information reaching officials of the East India Company, most of the vessels trafficking at Madagascar with the pirates operated, not from New York, but from Pennsylvania, Carolina, Massachusetts, and Rhode Island.[37]

Time had not brought any respite from the bitter strife in New York. The violence of the Leislerian rule had divided the community as the tenure of the insurgent regime had been unnecessarily prolonged by the failure of the ministry in London to act quickly. Despite subsequent efforts by the administration to reconcile the contending factions, the governors sent out to New York allowed themselves to become embroiled first with one side and then the other. Fletcher remained in New York until 1698, and in the remaining months of his administration he grew more partisan. Bellomont, who was to divide his time between Boston and Manhattan, was no less so, favoring the Leislerians. Partisanship in the provincial world had become enmeshed with party strife in the imperial capital.

CHAPTER 15

New England, 1690–96:
The Fruits of Revolution

Royal authority had been little in evidence in New England following the overthrow of Edmund Andros and the dominion regime in the spring of 1689. Conditions in Massachusetts, New Hampshire, Rhode Island, and Connecticut remained unsettled for months, and in some areas for years, as social animosities, political rivalries, and disputes between provinces disrupted the English community. The sources of dissension varied from colony to colony, but one was common to all: Who among the contending groups would govern? Compounding the issue was the excessively legalistic approach officials in Whitehall adopted toward the problem of defense and the authority of civil government as defined under the charters granted by Charles II to Connecticut and Rhode Island.

In both Hartford and Providence doubts existed over the legal status of government once men learned of the overthrow of the regime of Andros at Boston. Could officials who had governed before the "voluntary" surrender of the charters again exercise authority? Gershom Bulkeley, leader of a small Royalist clique in Connecticut, thought not. The eldest son of a minister of Massachusetts and a graduate of Harvard College, Bulkeley had broken with the orthodox-minded and had accepted office under Andros as a justice of the peace. He and others, Edward Palmes and William Rosewell, men with personal, family, and financial grievances against the Winthrops and other members of the established ruling order, welcomed the intervention of Governor Benjamin Fletcher of New York or any other outside authority into the affairs of Connecticut.[1]

At the other end of the political spectrum stood the son of another Congregationalist minister, the ambitious James Fitch of Norwich. A facile speaker, Fitch appealed over the heads of the more timid magistrates directly to the townsmen to reestablish government as it had existed under the charter. By seeking broader, even popular support, Fitch constituted a threat both to the old established families who for two generations had filled the highest offices and to the Royalists. He was a particular opponent of the Winthrops, who contested his purchase from a local Mohegan chief of an extensive tract of land in eastern Connecticut.

In 1689 the old magistrates assumed the government, but hesitantly, petitioning the crown for confirmation of the charter. To gain support and perhaps to undermine the potential following for Fitch, they secured a new suffrage law with more liberal requirements for admitting inhabitants as freemen: twenty-one years of age, a freehold estate of only forty shillings, and a certificate signed by the majority of the selectmen from the town. Months passed without official word from England on the status of the provincial regime until agents in London, appreciating that the royal courts at Westminster had never vacated the charter as they had the patent of Massachusetts, secured a written opinion from the crown law officers that the charter was still valid.[2] Despite this sanction, resistance to the provincial regime continued in several of the towns in Connecticut. Local officials at Wethersfield, Greenwich, Stamford, Norwalk, Simsbury, and Windsor refused to return their lists of rates. In October 1691 the General Assembly gave sheriffs authority to distrain estates and jail men delinquent in paying taxes. From Wethersfield, Gershom Bulkeley branded the arrests and seizures as destructive of liberty and property, contrary to the rights of the people, and contemptuous of the crown. Through the royal governor at Manhattan he sent an appeal to the king and queen. Fletcher supported the dissidents. He charged the provincial regime with maintaining a commonwealth, failing to support the common defense, and, along with the government of Rhode Island, violating the acts of trade and navigation. Encouraging him, Bulkeley continued to question the legitimacy of the provincial government.[3]

In the face of these attacks Governor Robert Treat and the assistants decided to send Fitzjohn Winthrop to England as agent for the colony. Winthrop's father more than thirty years before had undertaken a similar mission and had secured the patent from Charles II. Ostensibly, the provincial officials seemed merely to be seeking protection against Fletcher's claim to command the militia, but some among them may have had something more in mind. The refusal of some townsmen to pay rates for the support of the Congregationalist ministers and the appeal of James Fitch to the populace had made some magistrates anxious. As they saw it, confirmation of the charter would consolidate the authority of the ruling officials. So Samuel Wyllys, a member of one of the established families, privately informed Winthrop before the agent set out for London. In granting the charter, Charles II had required that the inhabitants of the colony be governed peaceably and religiously. To that end William and Mary ought now to declare that an able, learned, and pious ministry be maintained in all the churches of the colony. For subsistence, they ought not to depend on the arbitrary "humors of the vulgar sort of people." Wyllys looked to the crown to support the provincial establishment against the rank and file. To ensure that they enjoyed all the privileges of freeborn subjects, the king should declare that those men in Connecticut who desired the benefit of the common law and statutes of England would possess them without any infringement. It was a perversion of the charter to argue, as did some in the colony, that the patent prevented any appeal to the courts and laws of England. The wiser sort would never bear to have themselves enslaved to the arbitrary whims of their fellow colonists, to be deprived of the benefits of English law. In a veiled reference to the tactics employed by James Fitch and his allies, Wyllys urged Winthrop to secure a declaration from the crown that "persons of mean & low degree" not be employed in high offices, only men of "good parintage, education, abilitye, and integrity."[4]

The more immediate threat to the standing order in Connecticut came from Fletcher's claim to command the militia. In the ensuing contest in London between the governor of New York and Winthrop, the Connecticut agent prevailed, despite the plea of Gershom Bulkeley, Samuel Wolcott, and more than thirty other inhabitants of Hartford that they could never enjoy security for their lives, liberty, and property while a corporation held a monopoly of the administration of justice. Winthrop charged that Fletcher was meddling in the civil government.[5] After reviewing the charter the crown law officers confirmed the provincial officials at Hartford in their authority. Fletcher would have to be content with 120 militiamen from Connecticut, the quota assigned the colony for the defense of New York.

The proposed appointment of the earl of Bellomont as governor of Massachusetts in the summer of 1695 initially caused Winthrop some concern. He found the governor-designate well disposed to the people of the Bay colony, but his commission from the king gave him extended power over military affairs in New England. It might impinge on the government of Connecticut—"the ocean naturally swallows up the rivolets." It was hoped the settlement William III had made for the militia and his written confirmation of the rights of the provincial government would secure the officials at Hartford from the claims of royal governors. But with Bellomont procrastinating in the British Isles and the agents of the provincial regime of New York pursuing the issue in London, Fitzjohn Winthrop remained in England to look after the interests of Connecticut.[6] In London a larger threat, one posed against all of the charter governments, loomed in the near future.

Despite Winthrop's success against Fletcher and the council of New York, Samuel Wyllys was unhappy. Hardly any "gentlemen" had received a "graine of justice" since Winthrop departed for England. James Fitch had become "the principle Minister of State" during the agent's absence; most of the gentlemen had been excluded from the legislature, one replaced by "an eminent syder-drinker," another by a "person risen out of obscurity." The deputy governor, a Cromwellian in his "decreped old age," had been continued in office. Capable for some years only of drinking "flipp & takinge tobačo," he was allowed twenty pounds a year for these "needful comodytys." Oppression had continued, and even increased, Wyllys contended. Men in commerce, the traders and artisans, all had liberty to oppress the "husbandmen."[7]

While Fitzjohn served in London, his brother, Waitstill Winthrop, and certain of their associates from Massachusetts, the so-called Narragansett proprietors, had taken the opportunity to revive their claims before the king in council to the region of Rhode Island lying west of Narragansett Bay. Several of the putative proprietors—Richard Smith and John Fones, for example—were residents of Rhode Island, members of a Royalist faction unhappy with the turn of events in the colony following the collapse of the Dominion of New England. Relatively few in number, the Royalists in Rhode Island included several distinct elements: Narragansett proprietors whose claims the provinical regime had rejected, former officeholders under the dominion, new arrivals in the commercial centers, and Congregationalists (such as the Sanfords and Hutchinsons) and Anglicans (such as Francis Brinley and Jahleel Brenton) unhappy with the prospect of Quakers and Baptists ruling Rhode Island.

During the months following the incarceration of Andros in Boston, uncertainty prevailed over the government in Rhode Island. Was the charter of 1663 still valid? Some men would not accept office, fearing they would be held liable if the crown restored the dominion. Late in January 1690 John Coggeshall, the deputy governor, and six assistants signed an address to the king asking for confirmation of the patent. It was difficult to prevail on men to take the chief post. Walter Clarke refused to serve. The aged Quaker Henry Bull held office for a time, but then resigned, as did Coggeshall. Some towns refused to take part in a provincial administration, and attendance fell off at the general assembly. Taxes proved difficult to collect; wills went unprobated; and titles to land remained unrecorded.[8]

Disorganized and with an inchoate government, Rhode Islanders faced several problems: French privateers raiding shipping, Royalists disputing the authority of the charter regime, a neighboring governor demanding command of the militia, and two adjacent colonies claiming virtually all of the mainland territory of the province.

Late in 1692 the assembly sent Christopher Almy to London to seek the protection of the royal government. Inasmuch as Almy was not knowledgeable in the ways of Whitehall, his brother-in-law, John Greene, wrote to the veteran bureaucrat, William Blathwayt, asking assistance in obtaining confirmation of the royal patent with the privileges and boundaries of the colony as specified therein. Blathwayt may have appeared all things to all men, for, ironically, the Royalist, Francis Brinley, had also written the secretary to the Committee for Plantation Affairs asking for the king to appoint a governor for the colony.[9]

By virtue of a commission from the crown, Sir William Phips, governor of Massachusetts, had command of the militia of the neighboring colony, Increase Mather having promised William III he would be emperor of all America if he granted the Bay colony a new charter and appointed Phips governor. Through Almy in London, the Rhode Island authorities made known their objection to this commission and their unhappiness with discontented persons subverting their government. The Bostonians had an "untipothy" toward the regime at Providence because of differences in religion and the attachment the Rhode Islanders showed the crown.[10]

On one point—and it was critical—the regime at Providence won. Notwithstanding the authority given Phips over the militia, the charter to Rhode Island granted by Charles II in 1663 was still in force.

The disputes over boundaries with Massachusetts—the successor to the defunct colony of Plymouth—and with Connecticut over the Narragansett country were not as easily resolved. Although the crown appointed a commission consisting of the councilors of New York to survey the boundary with the Bay colony, the dispute over the region west of Narragansett Bay remained unsettled. In 1696 the attorney general, Thomas Trevor, concluded that the area fell within Connecticut, because its charter preceded that of Rhode Island.[11] What Trevor did not appreciate was that the agent for Connecticut who had obtained the patent in 1662 on behalf of the government at Hartford, the following year had conceded the disputed region in an agreement concluded with his counterpart from Rhode Island.

Uncertainty over government and conflicting claims over land also disrupted the towns in frontier New Hampshire. Following a decision by the chief justices of the courts at King's Bench and Common Pleas, in 1679 the crown had confirmed the rights of the proprietary Mason family to the soil but had taken over from Massachusetts governmental authority. The collapse of the Dominion of New England created a vacuum.

Opinion among the townsmen was divided, some favoring calling a convention to establish a provincial government, others wanting to join the Bay colony. Responding to a petition drafted by merchants of Portsmouth, John Pickering, William Vaughan, and Richard Waldron called upon the Bay colony to take over the Piscataqua settlements. In opposition a group of Newcastle inhabitants—numbering among them John and Robert Mason (sons of the recently deceased proprietor) and former officeholders under Edward Cranfield (the last royal governor of New Hampshire), Nathaniel Fryer, Robert Elliott, and John Hinckes— signed an address to the crown for another royal government. When Pickering and Vaughan took their case to Boston, the revolutionary council issued a warrant to the settlers of the Piscataqua towns to elect local officials. In March 1690 the Massachusetts regime accepted the election returns from Dover, Portsmouth, Oyster River, Exeter, and Hampton, despite protests by Nathaniel Weare that it could not exercise authority until empowered by the crown. In Hampton, where many residents feared the domination of Portsmouth in a regime controlled by Massachusetts, the townsmen rejected merger with the Bay. Such was the disorder that Nathaniel Weare feared the crown would intervene.[12] As expected, the opponents of Massachusetts took the issue to England. Hinckes, Fryer, Elliott, and a dozen other men of Great Island complained of the inadequate protection afforded by the "self-styled" government of Massachusetts and asked the king to appoint a general governor.[13]

In London another figure entered the contest. The heirs of Robert Tufton Mason, for £1,250, had sold to Samuel Allen, a London timber merchant and would-be naval contractor, the claims to the proprietary. In petitioning the crown to support his title, Allen cited the opinions handed down by the royal judges, Sir Richard Rainsford and Sir Francis North. He also asked for commissions for himself as governor of the separate colony of New Hampshire and for John Usher, his son-in-law, a Boston bookseller, as deputy.[14] For almost a year the proprietor engaged in a protracted contest with agents for the Bay colony in London, Henry Ashurst, Increase Mather, Elisha Cooke, and Thomas Oakes, who sought to have the authority of the Bay colony continued.

The agents faced another challenge. In the summer of 1691 the Gorges family revived its claim to Maine. In 1678 it had sold its title to Massachusetts; the Bay colony had become the proprietor of Maine. The Gorges clan now insisted that Massachusetts had forfeited its title with the revocation of its charter in 1684 and that the territory had reverted to the Gorges family. They asked for a new charter. Samuel Allen feared that if they succeeded, New Hampshire would be united with Maine and that, in a contest between Gorges and the Bay colony, Massachusetts would win out. He pleaded that New Hampshire be continued as a separate province and offered to assume the cost of maintaining a governor at Portsmouth.[15]

Early in 1692 the Lords for Plantation Affairs at Whitehall accepted a compromise, of sorts. The Gorges family received nothing. Massachusetts retained Maine, but New Hampshire remained a separate province with Allen as governor and John Usher his resident deputy. Two factors may have accounted for Allen's victory: the intercession of William Blathwayt on his behalf and the decision to place the militia of the colony under the command of the governor of Massachusetts. For all of Blathwayt's preaching about the need for system and order in governing the overseas colonies and his railing about private lobbying, he too stooped to use personal influence in behalf of private interest.[16]

The compromise—such as it was—reached at Whitehall proved unworkable. Allen remained in London entrusting the administration of the government to his son-in-law and deputy. Usher soon learned that he could get little support from the chief inhabitants he was forced to accept on the council or from the assemblymen. After conferring with the governor at Boston, Richard Waldron and William Vaughan asked for annexation to Massachusetts. Usher was soon involved in a jurisdictional dispute with Phips over shipping on the Piscataqua and with the assembly over the authority of the local courts dealing with suits over titles to land. Dominated by the opponents of the proprietor, the assembly refused to pass any bill unless Usher agreed to an act limiting suits to twenty pounds, thus preventing the proprietor from taking his claims to the provincial court. Unless Usher gave in, there would be no money appropriated for defense or the civil establishment. In these tactics Usher professed to see an antipathy toward royal government and an attempt to compel the crown to accept the merger of the Piscataqua towns with Massachusetts. To the Lords of Trade he suggested sending out at least two hundred soldiers under a general governor to preside over all of New England from Connecticut to Nova Scotia.[17]

For three years Usher engaged in a running battle with Phips in Boston and the proprietary opponents in New Hampshire, all the while directing a stream of letters to Whitehall pleading the need for a governor general and a large detachment of troops. The assembly remained obstinate. From time to time Usher retired to Boston, rushing back to Portsmouth when business became pressing. In the fall of 1694 after paying out over four hundred pound of his own funds, he laid before the assembly the need to raise an additional fifteen hundred pounds to support the government. The provincial representatives voted to raise only seven hundred pounds for one year. This would pay off the provincial debt, they concluded, and maintain a garrison of sixty men for six months. More, the colony was too improverished to do. In disgust Usher again retired to Boston.[18]

In 1695 agents for the Bay colony once more pressed in London for annexation of New Hampshire to Massachusetts as requested by the assembly and council. At a hearing held at the Plantation Office, Samuel Allen protested: annexation would cost him the whole of his rights and profits. He sought to shift the blame for failure to combat Indian raids to Massachusetts. Confronted by conflicting testimony, the Lords of Trade simply avoided coming to a decision by laying the evidence before the lords justices in council.[19] William III was again absent on the continent.

From New England, Usher seemed ready to throw up his post. He would no longer remain in New Hampshire—he was not safe there—but would retire to Boston. In a moment of weakness he pleaded to be relieved of his burden. He quickly reversed himself, but it was too late. Allen accepted his resignation and petitioned the crown to appoint a Piscataqua shipbuilder, William Partridge, as deputy governor.[20]

In New England John Usher seemed to have lost all sense of proportion, if not reality. Although the separate colonies ought to have their own governors, the king ought to send to New England a viceroy with five hundred or eight hundred soldiers. This was not the sentiment of a statist, a militarist bred in some royal court of Europe, but of a Boston bookseller frustrated after years of contending with obstreperous Yankee politicians. Massachusetts ought to be joined to New Hampshire rather than the Piscataque towns to the Bay colony, he recommended, for in this manner the government would more firmly depend on the crown of England. Certain elements in Boston, Usher warned, hated living under a governor appointed by the king. They sought the restoration of the old charter. "That is their onions and garlic."[21] They were as ungrateful as the biblical Jews looking back to Egypt.

Usher was correct in one sense. A strong element in Massachusetts had never accepted what it considered the failure of Increase Mather to secure the old charter, a patent under which for practical purposes Massachusetts had functioned as a Puritan commonwealth with the members of the Congregationalist churches in full communion predominating among the freemen, the members of the corporation.

Since the restoration of the monarchy in 1660, the inhabitants of Massachusetts had been divided on the question of relations between the province and the government in London. A small group of merchants, Anglicans in the main, denied political status commensurate with their social and economic position, had been openly Royalist, appealing to the crown to intervene and abolish religious qualifications for political participation, to enforce toleration for Protestants, and to allow appeals from the provincial courts to the crown in England. A more numerous group drawn from various segments of provincial society, moderate in view, had seen the necessity of coming to some accommodation with the English government. But the more rigid among the commonwealthmen had prevailed, certain that God would save His people as he apparently had done a generation before.

The intransigence of the Puritans had cost them the charter granted in 1629. James II had then imposed a regime without benefit of an elected assembly. Some among the moderates, William Stoughton and the Winthrops, had accepted office in the dominion, but had become disillusioned and in 1689 had joined the old commonwealthmen to overthrow Andros.

For some months in Boston and Plymouth doubt existed as to the status of government. Among the towns of New Plymouth, officials encountered opposition when attempting to exert control over the militia and collect rates. The General Court was reluctant to impose taxes without some mandate; it ceased to function as an effective government. Thomas Hinckley, although he had assumed his former office of governor, and some of the assistants seemed convinced that only the authority of the Bay colony would save orthodox religion and learning.[22]

In Boston a provisional administration, nominally headed by Simon Bradstreet, the last governor elected under the old charter, carried on. Its members had not dared to declare the old patent to be in force despite the demands of the Reverend James Allen and the Reverend Joshua Moody. Some men who had not formerly qualified under a religious test had participated in elections held in the towns for delegates to a convention. Early in December 1689 Samuel Sewall and Elisha Hutchinson had returned from London with a letter from the king to Bradstreet, The document fell far short of what the ruling coalition wanted: it merely empowered those administering the laws to continue until the crown came to a final decision. With the aged Bradstreet ill, the commonwealthmen took control. In February 1690 Elisha Cooke and Thomas Oakes left for England to join Increase Mather in an attempt to win reinstatement of the charter.

For two years Thomas Danforth and the exponents of the old orthodoxy controlled the provincial government. The church members in full communion still constituted a majority among the voters despite an extension of the franchise. In response to pressure from the towns, the General Court allowed any inhabitants in good standing who paid four shillings besides the yearly poll tax in a single county rate or who possessed real property to the annual value of six pounds to be admitted a freeman. Almost four hundred men were admitted in the next few months.[23] There was some resistance in Salem, Boston, and Charleston to paying rates and to opening the local courts. Timothy and John Cutler, John Nelson, Charles Lidget, Francis Foxcroft, and three dozen others petitioned the king asking for the appointment of a royal governor and council as well as for an elected assembly to govern what they described as a distracted community.

The failure of a military expedition against the French had further weakened the provisional government. In March Nelson laid before the council his plans for an attack on Port Royal, but the deputies rejected him as commander in chief—he was a merchant and thus not to be trusted—and selected instead Sir William Phips. Nelson scorned to serve under the crude, uneducated Maine fisherman.[24] Success did not come to Protestant arms in the campaign against the Catholic French and heathen Indians. According to the Anglican chaplain, Samuel Myles, Cotton Mather gave out that the cause of the calamities was allowing Anglicans the use of one of the meeting houses in Boston. The windows of the church had been broken and the enemies of the country—so the Anglican communications were called—threatened: a worse fate would befall them when Increase Mather returned with the old charter.

Rumors were rampant. One circulating in Boston in the fall of 1690 had it that Sir Edmund Andros was returning as governor. The "Tories are flush'd, and 'tis said were drinking Sir Edmund's health," recorded Samuel Sewall. Charged by the "charter-mongers" with being enemies to the country, the Royalists feared the consequences of the restoration of the old patent with unlimited power in the hands of the freemen. They would have authority to admit only such men as they wished to the corporation in which was vested absolute power, all others being debarred from the privileges of Englishmen.[25]

Not until late January 1692 did news come of the appointment of Phips as governor. On 8 February Captain Benjamin Gillam arrived from England with a copy of the new patent. On two points the "charter-mongers"—so the Royalists called the commonwealthmen—had lost. The king now appointed the governor, and freeholders rather than freemen had the vote. Despite the efforts of Increase Mather, the ministers of state had insisted on eliminating the religious test for the franchise. But in appointing Phips and the initial slate of councilors, William III and the Lords of Trade had accepted the recommendation of Mather on the assumption that he had great influence in the colony. By so doing they would secure the support of the Bay colonists for the English cause against the French in North America.[26]

The agents for Massachusetts in London had been divided in sentiment. While Elisha Cooke may have been more in touch with the political situation in Boston, Mather had better appreciated the reality in Whitehall, recognizing that the restoration of the old charter was impossible. He had not included Cooke or Oakes in the list of twenty men appointed to the initial council. Eleven of his nominees were Bostonians, six of them members of Mather's church. Six of the assistants under Bradstreet who had held out for the old charter were dropped, but Wait Winthrop and two other members of the original council of safety were selected. The balance on the council thus shifted away from the commonwealth faction led by Cooke and Danforth to the moderates. Massachusetts Bay remained divided, as did Boston. The north end was Mather's camp; the south, Cooke's stronghold.

Cooke and the unreconciled Puritan faction would not forgive Mather for compromising with the royal ministers in Whitehall. Elisha Cooke proved an able and resourceful protagonist in opposing Mather and his protégé, Phips. As tax commissioner in Boston, Cooke assessed the value of men's property, the basis for determining their eligibility to vote, and during his term of office, the number of voters in the town doubled. Not surprisingly, the south end, Cooke's base, predominated in the political life of the provincial capitol.[27]

On Saturday, 14 May 1692, Sir William Phips, accompanied by Increase Mather, arrived in Boston on the frigate *Nonsuch* to begin what proved to be a disastrous administration. He inaugurated the new regime with a bow toward Puritan sensibilities. He would not abridge the ancient laws and customs or infringe on the Lord's day by having his commission read on Sunday. Following the convening of the General Assembly at Boston, Mather reported back to Nottingham in London that the charter had been most favorably received. But later that year Phips added a significant qualification: some persons who too much idolized the old charter and envied the governor sought to prejudice his administration. In Whitehall Blathwayt had been doubtful of Mather's alleged influence in the Bay colony and critical of the decision by the ministry to follow his recommendations. On receiving word from Boston of the reception accorded the new administration, Nottingham—perhaps with a sense of relief—hastened to assure the skeptical secretary: "Mr. Mather writes me ... from Boston yt the people are well pleasd wth their new charter & there is come from the assembly an address of thanks for it."[28]

Several problems, some chronic, others new, disrupted the political and social scene in Massachusetts. Despite the promises made by Mather and the commission granted to Phips for command of the militia of the region, the military effort of the New Englanders continued ineffective.

The old animosities among the irreconcilables, the Royalists ("Jaco-bites," the old charter-mongers called them), and the moderates per-sisted. Factional animosities also fed on personal rivalries as strong-willed men clashed. A coarse, uneducated man, Phips was possessed of a brutal temper. One visitor on complaining after the governor heaped abuse on him was told by a councilor: "You must pardon him his dog-days; he cannot help it."[29] There were many such days.

Phips and Mather had returned to a people gripped by fear over the accusations of witchcraft in Salem. Acting quickly, the newly arrived governor appointed a special commission of oyer and terminer to hear cases: Wait Winthrop and Bartholomew Gedney (moderates); Samuel Sewall, John Richards, and Nathaniel Saltonstall (irreconcilables); and Peter Sargeant (a recently arrived merchant). Another of the moderates, William Stoughton, presided. Phips then departed for Maine to lead the struggle against the Indians and French while the special court opened proceedings early in June at Salem. When the governor returned later that summer, twenty men and women had been condemned and executed as wizards and witches; over one hundred more were in jail, with the community openly divided over whether or not to try them. The division over witchcraft did not follow the previously defined political rift. Sal-tonstall had resigned in disgust over the proceedings; Increase Mather argued against continuing the deliberations; Stoughton, the presiding officer, was for continuing the work of the court.

Phips, unhappy with the procedures employed, put a stop to the executions. During the trials afflicted persons, as soon as the suspected witches had gazed upon them, had fallen to the floor writhing in apparent agony. They swore that shapes or specters had emanated from the bodies of the accused at the bar and had tormented them, the accusers. Phips rejected such "evidence." The devil often disguised himself in the shape of innocent persons; to the governor's own knowledge, some of the ac-cused had led faultless lives. Mather and others among the divines in the colony supported Phips. In their judgment too, Satan might assume the form of an innocent man or woman; the look or touch of a suspected person was not sufficient proof. Phips ordered the accused released on bail.

William Stoughton, the deputy governor who had presided over the earlier hearings, insisted that trials be resumed. Following a reorganiza-tion of the provincial judicial system as required by the charter, Phips appointed a commission of five judges with orders not to use "spectoral" evidence. Fifty persons were then tried, and all but three were acquitted. Stoughton signed a warrant for executing the condemned, but Phips re-preived them and five others previously sentenced until the king's pleasure be known. Enraged, Stoughton refused to take his place on the Superior Court.[30] He was now an implacable enemy to Phips.

The deputy governor, despite his Puritan background, hitherto had been a moderate on the question of relations between Massachusetts and the crown. Through the influence of Mather he had become lieutenant governor. Following his public humiliation in the witchcraft episode, Stoughton joined the ranks of the governor's opponents, enlisting in a campaign with William Blathwayt to remove Phips and to replace him with Joseph Dudley. The latter's "great abilities are much wanted here," Stoughton confided to the secretary at the Plantation Office. Dudley had abandoned his career in New York and after a brief stay in his native Massachusetts had taken ship for England, where he served as fiscal and electoral agent for John, Lord Cutts, governor of the Isle of Wight.[31] Stoughton's support was not enough. Another decade would pass before Increase Mather was reconciled to Dudley, before he could overcome the "old prejudices" aroused by Dudley's presiding over the royal council for Massachusetts. Joining Stoughton in opposition to Phips was the provincial secretary, Isaac Addington, a near relation to Cooke. Increase Mather, when he nominated Addington, had not thought him so "bigotted" to the old charter government as he now found him. More was to come.

Mather suffered repudiation with the elections held in May 1693. The House of Representatives returned only eight of the men he had nominated to the council. Elisha Cooke, spurned by Mather in London, won election to the board, but the governor refused to accept him. Thomas Danforth attempted to bring the two Puritan leaders together, but with no success.[32] Cooke won a seat the following year.

In the fall of 1693 the opposition opened a series of attacks in the assembly where the partisans of the governor only narrowly carried an address that Phips not be removed. Since several of the governor's adversaries, although residents of Boston, sat for outlying towns—by electing Bostonians, the voters saved expenses—Phips's supporters secured an act with a residency requirement for representatives. Proclaiming this qualification invalid, six of the Bostonians, including Nathaniel Byfield, the speaker, attempted to take their places. On the morning of 30 May 1694 the representatives gathered in the town hall at Boston. After waiting for two hours, they sent a message to the governor asking to be sworn. Later in the day Phips sent word that he would not accept the representatives rendered ineligible to sit by the residency requirement. When Byfield attempted to remonstrate with the governor, Phips commanded him to hold his tongue. Byfield then wrote to Dudley in England to have the residency law disallowed. If the refusal to swear duly elected members stood, the governor could pack the assembly. Moreover, the law was contrary to the charter, Byfield concluded. In passing the measure the majority in the house had impinged on the privileges of the colony simply to revenge themselves on particular individuals. Byfield too wanted Dudley in the governor's chair in Boston. The sooner the better, for the danger to New England was then greater than ever, and, without a governor general, he predicted, the English should all be ruined.[33]

Phips's downfall came, not because of his relations with the dissident assemblymen, but because of his brutal treatment of two officials of the king. Richard Short, Captain of the royal frigate *Nonsuch*, had had a falling out with the governor over the captain's refusal to allow his crewmen to serve on a privateering venture sponsored by the governor. Despite the fact that Short was crippled in his right hand, the result of a wound, the hot-tempered Phips physically attacked him, stripped him of his command, and had him imprisoned for nine months. He broke into Short's chest, carried off his goods, and, sitting as an admiralty judge, condemned a French prize without reserving a portion for the crown or the crewmen who had taken the French vessel. He thus expropriated the king's share.[34]

The royal collector of customs, Jahleel Brenton, also fell afoul of the governor, over the enforcement of the parliamentary acts of trade and navigation and the local laws on shipping. In 1692 the provincial government had passed a bill establishing naval officers at seven designated ports in the colony. Phips and the council then published an order that shipmasters need clear their vessels with no other officials than the provincial naval officers. Brenton saw this as an effort to circumvent him. When he seized several ships for violating the navigation code, the local courts, supported by the governor, ruled against him. Indeed, Phips himself, according to Brenton, was engaged in illegal trade. When the collector attempted to seize the sloop *Good Luck* for illicit trading, Phips with about fifty men came down to the wharf, took hold of the unlucky Brenton, and, striking him with his fist and cane, threatened to break his bones and to imprison him if he did not give up the ship and her cargo.

Undaunted, Brenton appealed to the Customs House in London. The Privy Council then ordered an investigation into Brenton's charges. After consulting with certain persons of "credit and reputation" in London, men they did not name, the Commissioners of Customs recommended a panel of inquiry, one loaded against Phips.[35] The governor had an agent in London, Benjamin Jackson, a Cheshire man whom he had employed as his secretary. Jackson's task proved all the more difficult when the charge made by Captain Richard Short of embezzling the crown's share of prize money arrived. He claimed Phips could prove it false if given time.

The governor would have his opportunity. A letter from the king went out to Phips summoning him to London. Lieutenant Governor William Stoughton must give all men concerned in the complaints against Phips full freedom to collect authenticated copies of records and depositions. In this business Phips must not meddle except to gather only such evidence as he himself might require.[36] Stoughton, perhaps relishing the task, wasted no time in posting the call for information once the summons reached Boston. Phips, for his part, begged Secretary of State John Trenchard to pay no heed to the "malicious accusations" of his enemies until he was heard. The governor then marshaled support. On 31 October 1694 majorities in the council and the assembly adopted an address to the king and queen describing the deplorable conditions on the northern frontier and asking that they not allow complaints of a personal nature against Phips to deprive the colonists of his services as governor. This remonstrance notwithstanding, an eight-page printed pamphlet, *A Letter From New England*, found its way to London. It contained a bitter attack on Phips who "(they say) learned to write since he was married and cannot yet read a letter." The tract related Phips's conduct as a judge in the vice-admiralty court and in Chancery, his mistreatment of Short and Brenton, and his quarrels with the assemblymen. His relations with the eastern Indians, it alleged, were fraudulent, a means of monopolizing the traffic in beaver skins for himself.[37]

On 15 November Stoughton sent off to Whitehall affidavits of testimony to support the accusations against Phips, including a further damaging charge by Brenton: Phips had done his utmost to hinder the presentation of evidence, even threatening witnesses with cutting off their ears. Inasmuch as Brenton in his complaint against the governor had linked the councilors to Phips, they declared themselves parties to the cause, refused to allow many of Brenton's witnesses to be sworn, and endeavored to entrap and hobble them.[38]

Two weeks later Phips himself left for England on the *Diego*. He landed at Falmouth after a voyage of five weeks and hurried on to London, where he handed in a petition at the Plantation Office asking for a time to be set for a hearing on the charges against him. But before any action could be taken, Phips died. So ended the short, sordid tenure of the first governor of Massachusetts under the charter of 1691, a governor appointed to bring the Bay colony to a closer dependence on the crown of England and to enlarge the empire of William III.

Who would replace Phips? Joseph Dudley was not at this time

thought to be a serious contender for the post, notwithstanding the efforts of the Massachusetts agents and Abraham Gouverneur and Jacob Leisler to discredit him during the campaign to have Parliament reverse the attainder of the executed martyrs of New York. Given the domination of the Whigs in the ministry, Dudley stood little chance against the earl of Bellomont. With the impecunious Irish earl anxious for the governorship of both Massachusetts and New York, it was not Dudley who had to be discredited, but Benjamin Fletcher at Manhattan.

By the summer of 1695 the Whig magnates in the administration had determined on Bellomont—a very good man, thought Fitzjohn Winthrop—for the post at Boston. With the commission for the new governor then in preparation, Bellomont confided to the agent from Connecticut that he hoped to be ready to depart by the end of August. But if Bellomont was to have a salary ample and secure enough, Fletcher must go.[39] The Lords Justices in council during the absence of the king from England agreed that it was to the interest of the royal service that governors not depend on the beneficence of the assemblies. It would "make their Authority Precarious and Engage them in complyances that may be prejudicial" to the royal service in America.[40]

It fell to Shrewsbury to convince William III, for the monarch had personally selected Fletcher for duty in New York. The king raised serious objections to the proposed arrangement. He agreed that the salaries ought to be so settled as to have the governors dependent on the crown rather than on the assemblies, but New York and Massachusetts were not, under the current state of settlement, contiguous; they had different governments, one depending directly on the king's commission, the other, by charter, much less subordinate. Moreover there was little to be gained financially, for a deputy governor, an experienced, trained soldier, requiring a salary, must still be stationed at New York as a deputy governor, given the threat from the French and their native allies. William was unwilling to remove Fletcher, familiar as he was with the situation in New York, the fortifications there, and the neighboring Indian tribes.

The king commanded the Lords Justices to provide a competent salary for Bellomont as governor of Massachusetts, at least until the administration could determine whether the provincial assembly would settle a permanent appropriation. On 12 August the Lords Justices ordered the Treasury to provide Bellomont with one thousand pounds a year and two weeks later arranged with the Admiralty for a fourth-rate frigate to carry Bellomont to New England.[41]

Commitment to larger public needs and dispatch was not a quality often distinguishing administration for the overseas plantations. Well over a year after Bellomont's appointment, late in 1696, the earl wrote from Dublin to Secretary James Vernon that he still had New England in mind. Provided the king would allow him fitting appointments, he intended to depart in February. He declared himself resigned in the matter of salary if Shrewsbury and Lord Somers insisted, but could not Vernon sound them out to determine whether New York could not now be added to his jurisdiction? Fletcher had been there five years. When Bellomont had served that long, he should be very well pleased to give way to another. In an indirect attack on Fletcher, Bellomont proposed sending over five hundred soldiers under an experienced colonel and good officers to instruct the colonists in martial discipline and to teach them the use of weapons. But the colonel must be a quiet, brave officer, one not given to swearing, in order not to give offense to the people who were said to profess great sobriety, whatever they did in private. Thus Bellomont hoped to meet at least one of the objections to removing Fletcher.

The governor-designate now faced another potential rival: a faction in the assembly and council in Boston had addressed the king to appoint William Stoughton as governor. This was Blathwayt's doing, Bellomont conjectured, having been assured before leaving London for Ireland—possibly by Sir Henry Ashurst—that the secretary at war had procured the address. There was still another rival. With Bellomont procrastinating and letters from New England arriving with accounts of the distress of the inhabitants on the frontiers, Lord Cutts was advancing the candidacy of Joseph Dudley.[42]

Reports reaching London in 1696 indicated a deteriorating military situation in northern America, leading commissioners to a newly established Council for Trade and Plantation to represent the need for a governor for Massachusetts competent in military affairs, a governor with overall command of the forces throughout New England, better to provide for the security of the region. Stoughton and the council at Boston had complained that the Bay colony had borne the burden of the war. Connecticut had contributed little, Rhode Island and New Hampshire nothing at all. One New Englander, Stephen Sewall of Salem, had proposed a more drastic solution: sending over a viceroy and combining the several provinces into a larger administrative unit. The king's deputy must be a great nobleman and soldier. Should the crown carry out this proposal, the English in America would make up one body and one purse; they would then quickly send the French and their Indians "a-grasing."[43]

After a hiatus of some months, Bellomont set out for America, bearing commissions as governor of New York, Massachusetts, and New Hampshire with authority also to command contingents of militia from the neighboring provinces. The appointment of a "captain-general" resulted from the political pressure applied by the Whig junta and the need to provide direction in military affairs once the scheme for centralized government in North America had collapsed in 1689 and New England had become again a congeries of distinct political jurisdictions. Parochialism had prevailed among the northern colonies as Rhode Island and Connecticut resorted to their charters to buttress claims to privileges and exemptions from the authority of governors in the neighboring provinces. Even when chartered government had been brought under closer royal control, as in the case of Massachusetts, the results had been disappointing, despite the promises held out by Increase Mather for the administration of Sir William Phips. The Puritan commonwealthmen had proved irreconcilable, and factional animosities had fed on personal rivalries and the governor's idiosyncracies. Phips had not been a happy choice; he had been the king's governor in name only. After too long an interval Bellomont succeeded him, but forced to divide his time and attention between Boston and Manhattan with occasional trips to the Piscataqua towns, Bellomont achieved little before he died in 1701.

During the last years of the seventeenth centry, the hazardous military situation in America was but one of several problems facing officials in Whitehall, men also burdened with a crisis in English overseas trade brought on by the extended conflict with France, the erosion of the royal finances, and the debasement of the coin of the realm.

CHAPTER 16

The Board of Trade:
Origins, Personnel, and Problems, 1696–1700

From America repeated complaints over the deteriorating situation on the northern frontiers and violations of the acts of trade and navigation, especially in the chartered provinces, arrived in London at a critical time: for ministers of state, members of Parliament, and the English mercantile community were then deeply concerned over the depressed state of English overseas trade. Years of war had greatly strained the as yet rudimentary machinery employed by the crown to raise money. The debasement of the coinage of the realm by widespread clipping over the years further aggravated the financial problem. Additing to the government's difficulties was the bitter resentment of the gentry throughout the country over high taxes imposed on landed property and the interest paid to financiers and speculators to carry the mounting national debt. The members of the overseas trading community for their part complained vociferously over the losses they had sustained at the hands of French corsairs and the threat posed by Scottish and Irish interlopers, particularly in the traffic to the colonies.

War with France had given Irish and Scottish shippers excluded by the navigation code from direct trade with America an opportunity. In increasing numbers they sailed directly to the Chesapeake and Delaware, where they presented forged papers proclaiming them to be English.[1] Indeed, local officials in the colonies were conniving with these interlopers, according to Edward Randolph and London dealers in tobacco. By avoiding customs due on tobacco landed in England, the Scots could undersell the "fair" traders. This traffic in enumerated commodities such as tobacco and sugar deprived the crown of customs revenue. As early as 1693 some ministers at Whitehall gave thought to the need for legal action, especially against the chartered colonies, provinces alleged to be particularly lax in enforcing the navigation code. But the Commissioners of Customs would go no further than to recommend that the governors maintain small vessels to patrol local waters and to inspect arriving ships.[2]

English merchants were still unhappy, especially those in the outports who seemed prepared to go to Parliament with their complaints

231

against the administration. By 1695 a crisis seemed imminent, with English seaborne trade under attack, the ability of the administration to raise money strained, credit collapsing, and the coinage of the country debased. At this point the Scots undertook an ambitious venture in trade and colonization in the Western Hemisphere. There was no coordinated response in English governmental circles, as the king's ministers, the Lords, and the Commons addressed themselves to separate issues. Cooperation was difficult to achieve, for sentiment in the Commons was strongly against the administration, and the English commercial community divided, with merchants of the outports resenting the traders of London. The merchants of Bristol were particularly concerned over the intrusion of the Scots and the Irish and the failure of the government adequately to protect their ships. Through John Cary and their members in Parliament, Sir Thomas Day and Robert Yate, they sought a bill to secure the plantation trade.[3]

Reacting to legislation by the Scottish Parliament to encourage commerce, late in December 1695 the English House of Lords began considering the state of nation's trade and the condition of its coinage. The peers heard testimony from, among others, Sir Robert Southwell and his colleagues at the Customs House. Edward Randolph, the surveyor general of the customs in America, had already submitted several reports on widespread violations of the navigation code. Officials in the proprietary colonies were so hampered as to be unable to cope with local juries and courts. The Commissioners of Customs were even then preparing a bill for remedying defects in the statutes on shipping and trade.[4] The next month the House of Commons took the initiative. On 23 January the members ordered William Blathwayt, the secretary to the Committee for Trade and Plantations, and James Chadwick of the Customs Board to bring in a bill for preventing frauds and regulating abuses in the plantation trade. Four days later, Chadwick, a member for Dover, brought in a proposal reiterating the principal elements of the navigation code, but containing new provisions for their enforcement.

On this last point, the administration had also been concerned, for the Lords of Trade, sitting as a committee of the whole council, had referred to the attorney general a proposal to erect courts of exchequer, tribunals for the royal revenue, in America. They had also considered a proposal to place the proprietary colonies under the immediate authority of the crown, that is, to have the king appoint the governors, but in the opinion of the attorney general, the charters granted to the proprietors full power of government. The Lords of Trade then settled for a more limited course of action, merely to instruct governors to obey orders from the Customs Board for enforcing the acts of trade.[5]

At Westminster the Act to Prevent Frauds and to Regulate Abuses in the Plantation Trade quickly passed both houses of Parliament. It received the royal assent on 10 April.[6] This law, 7 and 8 Will. 3 c. 22, contained little new in substance; it repeated the provisions of previous acts restricting the carrying trade with the colonies to English and English colonial ships and required certain products of the colonies to be transported to some English port before being carried to market elsewhere. The act did contain new procedures for enforcing the navigation code. It required governors in the colonies to take an oath—one administered by officials named by the Customs Board—to carry out the laws. Governors in the chartered colonies, although not appointed by the crown, had to secure the approval of the king. Henceforth the Customs Board in London would directly supervise the entire customs establishment in America.

On one point the wording of the act proved ambiguous, even contradictory. To overcome obstructions by the common law courts and juries in the colonies, Randolph had pressed for the establishment of rival courts of exchequer, but the House of Lords in March 1696 had approved an amendment to provide that suits could be brought against a ship or goods in a court of vice admiralty, a tribunal usually dealing with maritime matters and suits between merchants and giving judgment without jury. Yet section 11 of the act as passed stated that "there shall not be any jury, but of such as are natives of England" (and presumably of the English colonies), thus implying that trials could take place before juries in common law as well as vice-admiralty courts.[7] The contradiction, apparently unnoticed at the time the act was passed, later caused much confusion.

Considered concurrently with the bill for preventing frauds was a proposal to create a commission for trade and plantations under the authority of Parliament. The establishment of a commission resulted from a complicated political situation in Parliament and the crisis in trade as a result of the war. Faced with a slump in commerce and the debasement in the coinage, in the fall of 1695 the principal ministers of state had sought the views of various individuals considered knowledgeable on economic and financial matters. Several among them had suggested some sort of council on trade, but only as an incidental component to solving the problem of the debased coinage.[8]

A council or board dominated by courtiers appointed by the administration or by the merchants of London ran contrary to the sentiments of many members of the House of Commons and the trading communities in the outports. As a result of recent elections the strength of the administration had declined. Most members, although anti-Jacobite and in favor of the revolutionary settlement, were opposed to the extension of royal power and probably disliked William III. They embraced the opposition program of the country Whigs. In the fall of 1695 during the debates over the state of trade, sentiment among the Tories and country Whigs favored establishing a parliamentary council of trade, an idea the king viewed as limiting the royal prerogative. The Bristol mercantile community was also apprehensive; the trading cities must be represented on any council by able persons acquainted with their particular interests, not by "Courtiers inexperienced in trade" or Londoners who would manipulate matters in favor of the metropolis without regard for the outports. The Bristol men urged their members, Sir Thomas Day and Major Robert Yate, to arouse the representatives from the western ports against London.

The debate over a council of trade reflected not only economic but political differences, for as Yate and Day reported, the issue was pushed in the Commons by some "warm men more in opposition to ye king . . . than for the good of the nation."[9]

The issue was closely contested at Westminster. On 9 January 1696 the Commons sitting as a committee of the whole house, divided and by a margin of one vote, adopted the proposal for a council of trade nominated by Parliament. Those voting with the court took this as an abridgment of the king's prerogative. Both sides posed the dispute in constitutional terms. Ironically, positions on party principles were reversed: the court Whigs, enjoying office under the king, argued for the prerogative; the Tories seemed "zealous for public liberty."[10] On 31 January the committee ordered a bill brought in for a council, but that was as far as the Commons got on the matter.[11]

Within a few days came the discovery of a Jacobite plot to assassinate William III. With the opposition in the House of Commons split, Shrewsbury and the court Whigs consolidated their position and set up an executive council with the higher officers of state as ex officio, and with John Egerton, earl of Bridgewater; Forde Grey, earl of Tankerville; Sir Philip Meadows; William Blathwayt; John Pollexfen; John Locke; Abraham Hill; and John Methuen as salaried members of this commission for trade and plantations.

Thus came into existence the commission commonly called the Board of Trade. For William and the ministers of state, it was the un- wanted child of political expediency, forced on the administration by the need to head off the attempt by the Tories and country Whigs to impose on the crown a council responsible to Parliament. As members of a junior board, the commissioners of trade carried little weight in administrative circles, and as servants of the prerogative they would be received with skepticism in Parliament. Repeated efforts in the coming years by the board to convince the Lords and Commons of the need to vacate the charters of the proprietary and corporate colonies in America met with no success.

The newly created Board of Trade was short of men with extensive knowledge of the colonies. Plantation affairs, not trade, would most occupy their attention. Only Blathwayt, and he was frequently absent with the king, and, to a lesser extent, Bridgewater were qualified on this subject. Locke had served briefly as secretary to an advisory board, but more than twenty years before. Nor was he as liberal on colonial affairs as some later thought. "The flourishing of the plantations *under their due & just regulations* [is] that w[hi]ch I doe & shall always aim at whilst I have the honour to sit at the board," he informed a Virginia correspondent.[12] Pollexfen and Hill were writers on economic affairs with little experience; Meadows and Methuen, diplomats. Bridgewater, while a capable presiding officer who stood high in the favor of the king, was overburdened with other duties. Tankerville was a courtier who owed his appointment to his connection with the second earl of Sunderland. Tankerville's appointment served to blunt the edge of his patron's opposition to a council of trade under the king.

The commission also lost scarce expertise on colonial affairs when John Povey, Blathwayt's protégé at the Plantation Office, failed to secure the secretaryship of the new board. Without him, some on the new commission thought, they "should be in ye dark," but Somers, the lord keeper, disclosed the appointment of William Popple, a broken-down merchant, a friend of William Penn and John Locke, and formerly a dealer in wine at Bordeaux "till ye World frownd upon him." His marriage to a woman with a portion of two-thousand pounds had revived his fortunes.[13]

Born as a reaction to resentment in Parliament over the administration's failures during the crisis over English trade and finances, conceived in political bickering, the Board of Trade seemed to have little prospect for success. Its mandate was purely advisory. A great deal would depend on the ability of the commissioners to compete with other administrative boards, the discretion allowed it by the higher officers of state, and the willingness of the Lords and Commons to accept its recommendations. As a most junior commission, it did not rank high in the pecking order. Indeed, a quick demise was expected. As one placeman reported to Blathwayt, "tis said, this 40 to 1 . . . it [the commission] will be againe controverted in ye next sessions of Parliament of w[hi]ch they may [make] a jest on the Exchange." Unable to control the appointment of the council, the Commons and the Lords insisted on annual reports from the commissioners as to what they had been doing to further overseas commerce. Following one such report, the outspoken Tory, John ("Jack")

Grubham Howe, derisively dismissed Blathwayt and his colleagues as commissioners "not of America but of Chimericall Affairs."[14]

Appreciating the inferior status of the board, some commissioners looked elsewhere for preferment. With the war winding down in Europe, some members of the diplomatic corps—George Stepney, Matthew Prior, and John Methuen—began seeking some "solid settlement at home." Methuen, the English envoy at Lisbon, saw the Council of Trade as a backwater, of little consequence. He doubted it would long survive. The lord chancellorship of Ireland seemed preferable.[15] As a result of the reorganization of the administration following the cessation of hostilities and the scramble for posts by the diplomats, Methuen and Matthew Prior found places in the Irish establishment. Stepney, although he had little knowledge of trade and colonial matters, was given a vacancy on the Board of Trade, an employment he acknowledged "more than satisfyes my Avarice & ambition for ye Salary is 1,000£ a year and ye company with w[hi]ch I am joyned is more hon[ora]able than w[ha]t i cou'd have hoped to keep." But in time Stepney came to view his duties at the Council of Trade as drudgery. He hoped to go to Berlin or Copenhagen as the king's envoy while continuing to draw his stipend as commissioner of trade.[16]

The new addition did not strengthen the board. Stepney was often absent, attending to other duties, as was Blathwayt, acknowledged by some as the only person at court sufficiently acquainted with American affairs. Because of chronic absences it was difficult to collect five commissioners to conduct affairs. In 1697 the number necessary to constitute a quorum was reduced to four.[17] Poor attendance remained a problem.

In colonial matters the duties of the commissioners were generally advisory. The members depended on the higher ministers of state to accept their recommendations. The king's choices of principal secretaries of state and political instability further weakened the ability to deal systematically with plantation affairs. Shrewsbury could not control the Whig junta and the court Whigs could not lead effectively in the House of Commons, where the country gentry vented their anger at the heavy taxes on land and the profiteering by court favorites and financiers. William III found the behavior of the Whig peers distasteful; they resented his lack of confidence in them. For a while James Vernon, a man of decidedly inferior rank and weight, presided over both the northern and southern departments of the secretariat, aided only by a small clerical staff. For some time the status of both posts remained unresolved. In 1698 there were two candidates from the diplomatic corps, Robert Sutton, Lord Lexington, and Edward Villars, Lord Jersey. The latter, according to Stepney, who knew him well, was of fair enough character, but was not a "very exact or laborious correspondent." Jersey was uncomfortable at Whitehall: "the noise of the place stun's one, and the continual going to Kensington [Palace, the king's residence] is not to be indured, I wish myself anywhere [else]," he had complained.[18]

Nonetheless, when Shrewsbury, ill and dispirited, at last received leave to resign, Jersey received the seals, much to the disappointment of Lexington, who had to content himself with the Board of Trade. He thought Ireland preferable to plantation affairs. Lexington was not even the first commissioner of trade; this honor went to Thomas Grey, earl of Stamford. He too had aimed higher, but had to be satisfied with the junior board. Their two noble predecessors had been promoted, one to the Admiralty, the other to the Treasury. It was hoped Tankerville would not forget his old colleagues. With the addition of Lexington and Stamford, Stepney thought the foundation of the Board of Trade "no less firm than the Church of St. Peter." But this was from the vantage point of Berlin, where Stepney now served. Lexington might aid the cause of the Commissioners of Trade with William III, Blathwayt speculated, but that which set them firm with the king did not always do so with Parliament "who will be glad of any occasion to undervalue us." It might just as well eliminate so expensive a commission. In 1699 Blathwayt himself would not earn his salary as commissioner, for he spent much of the year abroad with the king. That spring and summer the board was hard put to present a quorum for business, with Blathwayt, Stepney, and Hill on the continent, and Lexington at times absent from London.[19]

William III again reshuffled the ministry in the spring of 1699 following the parliamentary session in an effort to bolster the administration. The court Whigs had lost considerable strength when the voters returned an obstructionist House of Commons, one more country than any other since the revolution and dominated by the Tories and Robert Harley's country Whigs, now Whig in name only.

The Parliamentary opposition received fresh ammunition to use against the Whig junta by the affair of Captain William Kidd, the merchantman employed by Somers and the other Whig magnates in an expedition they financed against pirates. Much to the chagrin of Bellomont, word arriving in London reported Kidd himself as having turned pirate. In December 1699 when the House of Commons went into committee to discuss the state of trade, the Tories began snapping at the Whig lords. Evidently Charles Lodowyck, once a merchant in New York, supplied Robert Harley with the details of the private articles of agreement signed by Bellomont and the members of the Whig junta.[20]

To save themselves, the Whig chieftains threw Kidd to the wolves. He later died on the scaffold, but for Somers, who had fixed the great seal to Kidd's commission, and the others of the junta, their days in office were numbered. In 1700 the king dismissed Somers and named Jersey lord chamberlain. Sir Charles Hedges, judge of the Court of Admiralty, took over the southern department of the secretariat, James Vernon preferring the junior office. With the departure of Somers, John Locke, often ill and absent from meetings of the Board of Trade, resigned. Matthew Prior, who had served at the English legation at Paris, replaced him. Prior and Stepney had been boyhood friends at Westminister School. Neither regarded the Commission of Trade as important.

The balance on the Board of Trade had shifted to Blathwayt and his friends and the peers with whom he was comfortable. But with the king off again for the Netherlands, Blathwayt was gone from London. The board was shorthanded that summer. Prior was off to Europe, Stamford to Leicestershire, Lexington to Nottingham, and Pollexfen to the west country, leaving only Meadows, Hill, and Stepney to "keep up the face of business." Vernon, by direction of the king, was pressing them to report on dispatches from America. What ought to be done for the security of the northern frontiers? How were naval stores best procured from the colonies? Business of such consequence was not to be dispatched by only three caretakers, Stepney complained. He sent Blathwayt such materials as had been gathered for his evaluation and "correction," for "as wee are to stand & fall" together, it was fitting that the commissioners spoke as one. No "rash & indigested paper" ought to be submitted as the work of the Council of Trade, a report which "may prove hereafter a matter of Censure."[21]

After four years the commissioners of trade were still weak, hesitant, and uncertain of their position in the hierarchy of government. They had hardly been strong enough to carry through a program for the defense of America, for the enforcement of the navigation code in the colonies, or for the suppression of piracy in the Western Hemisphere.

Despite the assurances given by Increase Mather at Whitehall of the support of New England against the French and the expedient of allowing the governments of the provinces to retain their separate jurisdictions while providing quotas of militia to the governors of New York and Massachusetts, the English in northern America had remained militarily ineffective. Some men in the colonies, Stephen Sewall and John Usher, for example, had urged the appointment of a governor general.

In February 1697 the newly appointed commissioners of trade, Bridgewater, Tankerville, Meadows, Pollexfen, and Hill had come out for a unified military command, but emphasized that the different forms of government for the colonies rendered political union impractical. The provincial regimes had so little complied with the quotas of militia assigned them in 1694 that a more "vigorous" authority was now necessary. How to resolve the contradiction, the Commissioners of Trade did not state, except to observe that the provincial assemblies might be made to understand that it was to their own interest to support the king's captain general.

Such was the procedure followed. On 16 March 1697, Shrewsbury announced the king's decision: Bellomont was to be governor not only of Massachusetts but of New York and New Hampshire and, for the duration of the war, to have the command of the militia of Connecticut, Rhode Island, and East and West Jersey. But Fitzjohn Winthrop was able to have a clause added to Bellomont's commission, qualifying his authority over the militia of Connecticut. Moreover, New Hampshire was not annexed to the Bay colony. Bellomont, who favored such a merger, held Blathwayt responsible for the decision to maintain New Hampshire as a separate colony. The new captain general was particularly concerned over his personal finances. To satifsy his creditors, Bellomont prevailed on the Treasury to take over his debts, and he extracted a promise from Somers, Shrewsbury, and Romney: in case the New Englanders did not settle a yearly salary on him, the Whig lords would intercede with the king to allow him payment from England. Bellomont had wanted his friends among the Lords Justices to write to Boston about a permanent appropriation, but they declined to do so. It would be best for him to waive the matter. Upon so nice a subject one could hardly avoid saying either too little or too much.[22]

The Irish earl then sailed off, the king's captain general to organize the defense and security of the northern colonies. Some in England, certainly William III, had little faith that the peace signed with the French that year at Ryswick would resolve anything. By the seventh article of the treaty the status quo ante bellum was to prevail pending further negotiations. The king soon found the French claims for boundaries in North America pretentious.[23]

In America Bellomont served as captain general with little success until his death in 1701. After three years of fruitless haggling and bickering with the provincial assemblies, he came to view America with a jaundiced eye. The French had been active. After reinforcing Canada with a regiment from Europe they were able to maintain 1,400 men under arms, to fortify the frontiers, and to woo the Five Nations to adopt a neutral stance. The Iroquois seemed on the verge of defecting from the English interest. Bellomont needed money to hold them. With only 180 soldiers in the four companies of English troops stationed in America, he was also short of men. He blamed one bureaucrat, "a certain man in the world who is generally reputed an oracle for understanding the Plantations," an obvious reference to William Blathwayt. He had been responsible for reducing the number of royal troops stationed on the fontiers of New York from 400 to 200; he had so vigorously opposed uniting New York and New Hampshire with Massachusetts Bay.[24] In opposing such union Blathwayt, who served as secretary at war and auditor general of the plantation revenue as well as commissioner of trade, may well have sought to protect Samuel Allen and Benjamin Fletcher, but for years he had counseled against sending large numbers of royal troops to America as too expensive.

Bellomont was equally frustrated in fulfilling other tasks assigned him in America: to stamp out piracy and to put an end to the collusion practiced by local officials in the colonies with seaborne raiders. The number of buccaneers apparently had increased even before the cessation of hostilities with France. It was easy to slip from legal privateering into illegal piracy. Freebooters found it highly profitable to plunder rich merchantmen in the Indian Ocean, where vessels changed flags often. Maurauding ships, some outfitted in the American colonies, were later supplied at Madagascar by other colonial vessels. Plundered gold, silver, and East India goods exchanged there then found their way into American ports, where officials at times looked the other way or accepted bribes to allow them to be landed. If a pirate was unlucky enough to be charged and tried, he generally found juries sympathetic. Vice-admiralty courts gave judgments without juries, but these tribunals encountered strong resistance in America. In the chartered colonies they were ignored.

Edward Randolph's reports from America were revealing. Bellomont had secured the arrest of but a few of the more than two score pirates who had put in at Manhattan; the rest simply fled to Connecticut and East Jersey. Other vessels arriving from the Red Sea put in at Carolina. Randolph's deputy at Philadelphia, Robert Quary, had a similar tale. About sixty pirates, a party of Kidd's crew, arrived on the Delaware in a ship from Madagascar. When Quary called on William Markham, Penn's deputy, to raise a posse to seize them, Markham demurred. There were several thousand men capable of bearing arms in the colony, but no militia or other means of serving the crown. Civil authorities in Pennsylvania took no notice of complaints by royal officials of the affronts offered them or of the king's rights. Under the terms of an act passed by the Pennsylvania legislature, the local authorities had no power to call armed men to assist against pirates. If the Quaker magistrates "can preach the Pyrats into a Submission," all would be well; if not, the buccaneers simply went about unmolested. In West Jersey, the Quakers would not suffer the proprietary governor to apprehend piratical crews.

In response to these complaints, Sir Charles Hedges, judge of the

High Court of Admiralty in London, drafted and Parliament passed a bill to extend to the colonies uniform rules for trying pirates.[25]

Colonial commerce generally flowed legally within the requirements set by parliamentary statutes, in ships owned and manned predominantly by Englishmen and English colonists. Certain products of the colonies, those enumerated in parliamentary statutes, went first to an English port before shipment ot a foreign market. Most European imports found their way to the colonies via an English port. Some shippers, English and American, however, could not resist the temptation to avoid paying customs duties in England or to bring in European wares directly to America. During war with English vessels under restriction, it was particularly tempting in the colonies to allow foreign interlopers to take up the slack. The Commissioners of Trade, whatever their deficiencies in knowledge about conditions in America, were acutely aware of the role colonial commerce played in the overseas trade of the kingdom and in the finances of the administration.[26] With their colleagues in the London Customs House they were particularly concerned that the navigation code be followed.

The Commissioners of Customs singled out the governors in the proprietary colonies as having been especially remiss. They advocated erecting in each colony courts of admiralty staffed by men of known ability and integrity and empowered by commission from London to deal with all matters relating to the acts of trade and navigation. Randolph, the surveyor general of the customs for the American plantations, himself had a list of candidates to be commissioned as judges, registers, marshalls, and attorneys. On this issue he engaged in a running battle at Whitehall with William Penn and Fitzjohn Winthrop, agent for the corporation of Connecticut. He reported the Quaker proprietor incensed over the recent Act for Preventing Frauds. The law was made to ensnare honest people. He, Penn, had the "Regalia" and did not "value ye act." Winthrop was also outspoken: introducing the act had been "a barbarous thing."[27]

Agents and proprietors for Carolina, Pennsylvania, the Jerseys, and Connecticut petitioned to be heard before the king named attorneys for the chartered colonies. Such appointments were unnecessary; men well qualified and well affected to the royal interest already served. Nor was there any reason to establish courts of vice admiralty, for the common law courts had heard all suits relating to violations of the acts of trade and navigation.

The contest dragged on during the winter of 1697. To his friend, Sir William Trumbull, Penn warned that Randolph and the Customs Board were using the act for preventing frauds to set up an "imperium in Imperio." If they succeeded, separate and conflicting jurisdictions would exist in a colony, one established by the proprietor, the other a court of vice admiralty, set up under the king's authority. Such a situation would frighten and discourage people, putting a halt to commerce. Despite the opinion given by the English attorney general to the contrary, Penn argued that by granting a charter the monarch of England had excluded the crown from nominating governmental officials. Under the patent such authority belonged to the proprietor.

On this point, Penn, other proprietors, and the agent for Connecticut received a rude shock when they consulted counsel learned in the law: the charters granted them conferred no power of admiralty; the king, if he thought fit, might appoint officials to act for him. As Fitzjohn Winthrop explained it, the representatives of the chartered provinces now thought it best to submit on the legal point, but he and the proprietors for Carolina and the Jerseys petitioned the king to grant commissions of vice admiralty to the governors of the proprietaries and the corporations comparable to those issued the executives in the royal provinces.[28]

William Penn made the same plea in February 1697 in the House of Lords. Over the next few weeks the Quaker proprietor engaged in a spirited debate with Edward Randolph, Robert Southwell, and Samuel Clarke of the Customs establishment. In what became for a time an annual review of the state of English commerce, the Lords Spiritual and Temporal had called on the Commissioners of Trade for a report. Siding with the Customs Board, the commissioners for plantation affairs had suggested the crown establish courts of admiralty in the colonies to enforce the Act for Preventing Frauds and to put a halt to direct trade with Scotland and other illicit commerce. Randolph submitted evidence condemning Penn's officials: the acts of trade were not observed in his territory, nor could officials of the crown obtain justice in Pennsylvania and the Delaware counties for the king. Randolph and the proprietor continued to trade charges and countercharges over the enforcement of the navigation code in the ports along the Delaware River. Finally, on 3 March, the Quaker proprietor was asked point-blank: what objection had he to putting the government in the hands of the king? The proprietor's response was emphatic: the country was worth nothing to him—he would not be able to sell an acre of land—the moment he lost the government. Sensing that he must make some concession, Penn proposed that William Markham, his deputy in Philadelphia, obtain the approval of the king as governor and give security to fulfill his duties.

The view of the committee of the House of Lords considering the state of the nation's trade seemed conclusive: the governors of the chartered colonies should be subject to the same orders to observe the acts of trade as their counterparts in the royal provinces. The proprietors must assume responsibility for their deputies' observing regulations on navigation. For the committee the earl of Rochester issued a warning: further complaints might lead to a more drastic remedy.[29]

In the fall of 1697 Randolph departed for a tour of inspection in America. There he encountered strong resistance not only from proprietary and corporate officials but from royal officers as well. The king's servants in America did not always work together for the royal service. By the spring of 1698 Randolph reported that none of the governors in the chartered colonies had obtained the approval of the king to hold office, as required by law. Nor had the proprietors given security for them, as recommended by the House of Lords. In Rhode Island the management of public affairs was in the hands of Quakers and Anabaptists. Neither judges, juries, nor witnesses were under any obligation to swear an oath. The governor, Walter Clarke, a Quaker, had resigned rather than take the oath Randolph attempted to administer. When Colonel Peleg Sanford, the Royalist appointed judge of the court of vice admiralty, had appeared before Clarke to be sworn in office, the governor had refused him. Clarke affirmed before the assembly that to allow such a court would destroy the charter.

The surveyor general of the customs in America received little satisfaction in Pennsylvania, where by a "sham" law—the statute severely restricted customs officers, he charged—the provincial legislature had circumvented parliamentary intent in passing the Act to Prevent Frauds. Should this local statute be allowed to stand, it would become a precedent to be adopted in other colonies. Again Randolph warned: as long as the proprietary and other chartered governments remained, it would be impossible to suppress illicit trade.

Yet government under the immediate authority of the king did not necessarily ensure security for customs officials, as Randolph soon learned. In New York he suffered arrest for having seized a ship in Virginia. Bellomont intervened, ordering bond to be provided for him. In Bermuda Randolph was not as fortunate. Governor Samuel Day clapped him into jail after a dispute over naming a collector for the island. Day claimed to have found a letter among Randolph's papers in which he had supposedly railed against all of the governors, Bellomont among them, for conniving at unlawful trade. Day sent a copy to Governor Joseph Blake at Charles Town, who then passed it on to Bellomont's deputy at Manhattan, Captain John Nanfan. Randolph in a most scurrilous manner had written against Bellomont. Initially put out, the Irish earl soon realized the purported letter was only a ruse by Day to engage Bellomont and the other governors in his quarrel with the surveyor general. The Commissioners of Trade and the Lords Justices supported Randolph in his dispute with Day.[30] At least one royal governor, Francis Nicholson, had supported the charges Randolph had made against the proprietary governments.

Illicit trade continued. To make matters worse, the Scots threatened to siphon off commerce through a colony they planned at Darien. As revealed by the report Randolph submitted in 1700 after an extensive survey, the Scots were already active in the plantation trade, particularly in Pennsylvania and the Delaware counties. Illicit traffic in tobacco to the detriment of the royal customs was also carried on by New Englanders and Carolinians with Scots via Newfoundland.[31]

Little had been accomplished since 1696. The creation of the Plantation Board, the passage of the Act to Prevent Frauds in the colonial trade, and the establishment of courts of admiralty had failed to bring into line the proprietary and other chartered colonies or to check illicit commerce. An incident in Charles Town, South Carolina, illustrated the nature of the problem. Acting on information provided by the local collector of customs, the judge of vice admiralty, Joseph Morton, had condemned the *Cole and Bear* of London for want of proper registration as required by the Act to Prevent Frauds. The unfortunate collector was reviled and beaten before a hostile crowd by Nicholas Trott, who had defended the vessel although he was the proprietary attorney general and naval officer for South Carolina. "This is the informer, this is he that will ruin your Countrye," Trott had told the crowd. Shortly after, Governor Blake, Morton's brother-in-law, died. By proprietary regulations Morton claimed the post, but James Moore and others on the council voted him incapable of holding office because he had committed a breach of trust against the proprietors in accepting a commission as judge of admiralty, simply because he was in the king's service. With Moore as presiding officer, the local officials put through a bill for regulating the court of admiralty, designed, so Morton charged, to render ineffective the royal commission. This provincial statute was contrary to the laws of England. Morton had pressed the provincial council to repeal the measure, but to no avail. He had then put the case to the proprietors, but had received no satisfaction.[32]

Frustrated in the attempts to have the acts of trade enforced in the proprietary and corporate colonies by the privileges granted officials in the charters, the Board of Trade now turned to Parliament to take up the bothersome patents. Success would depend not so much on the force of argument as on the political influence of this junior board, the weight the contending sides would bring to bear, and the partisan alignment in Parliament.

CHAPTER 17

The Board of Trade, Parliament, and the Chartered Colonies, 1699–1703

For a quarter of a century, first as clerk of the Privy Council's Committee for Plantation Affairs and then as a commissioner for trade, William Blathwayt more than any other man had been concerned in the efforts of the English crown to bring the colonies across the Atlantic to a closer dependence on the royal government. It was with a note of anger, if not resignation, that he wrote to a principal secretary of state in 1700: "Give me leave to say, ye Security of our Colonies & rendring them more usefull to England etc. are common places that have entertain'd us these many years but the means which are very plain have always been opposed or not prosecuted."[1] Hitherto the politics of personal connection and private interest, as well as inefficiency, financial stringency, and preoccupation with other, seemingly more important matters than the overseas possessions, had all combined to put off the desired end.

To Blathwayt the solution seemed simple: bring the colonies directly under the monarchy by having the king appoint the provincial governors. So he had advocated for twenty years. But a more studied appreciation of the events occurring in Virginia, New York, and after 1691 even in Massachusetts would reveal that this solution was inadequate. Yet to Blathwayt it was axiomatic that an end had to be put to proprietary and other chartered regimes, for they hardly recognized the government of England, and by the advantages they enjoyed they prejudiced the other plantations, those immediately dependent on the crown.[2] Blathwayt and his colleagues on the Board of Trade at the outset of the eighteenth century made a determined effort to convince the members of Parliament to vacate the charters of the overseas provinces. It was to be the last major attempt to reduce the privileged colonies.

With the alterations in the ministry in 1700, Blathwayt was in a stronger position on the Council of Trade, but his new colleagues, Lexington and Stamford, had less influence in the House of Lords and in the administration than their predecessors, Bridgewater and Tankerville, and the Board of Trade still carried less weight than the senior governmental commissions.

The bureaucrats and politicians in the Plantation Office were not alone in their antipathy to the chartered colonies. John Usher, the Boston bookseller and former deputy governor of New Hampshire, following a tour of North America from New England to the Delaware, had written the Board of Trade strongly condemning the chartered provinces for inadequately supporting the common defense and allowing illicit trade. Parochial attitudes prevailing in the Jerseys and Pennsylvania threw the burden of securing the alliance with the Iroquois entirely on New York. The Quakers, governed by their own dictates, would not employ "carnal" weapons.[3] Robert Quary, Edward Randolph's deputy, supported Usher on these points. Quary's chief protagonist was William Penn. On behalf of the chartered colonies the proprietor would lead the fight against the Board of Trade.

Anitcipating a move in Parliament against the chartered regimes, early in 1699 Penn sought to gain as wide a political base as possible. He wrote Robert Harley, a member of an influential Nonconformist family who had succeeded Paul Foley as a leader among the country Whigs. In the political reorganization after 1696, this group emerged as one element of the new Tory party. Penn pleaded with Harley: let the proprietors be treated like Englishmen. They ought not to forfeit privileges enjoyed at home merely for cultivating the wilderness of America. The colonists had already suffered by the Act for Preventing Frauds, to say nothing of the blow given juries by the establishment of courts of vice admiralty. Should any "persecuting temper" manifest itself in the House of Commons, as Penn was certain it would, Harley must remember that liberty of conscience was one of the articles of the original contract by which the Protestant monarchy was established during the Glorious Revolution. A few envious, mercenary clergymen had combined to influence the administration to strike at Dissenters.[4] Thus Penn, a supporter of James II, sought to pose the issue in religious as well as constitutional terms.

Later that year Penn's administration of his colonial holdings came under strong attack from Francis Nicholson, Quary, the judge of the court of vice admiralty in Philadelphia; and Randolph, the surveyor general of the customs in America. Should not the crown remove William Markham, Penn's cousin, for acting as deptuy without the king's approbation, for countenancing illegal trade, for refusing to submit to the jurisdiction of the officers of the admiralty court, and for suffering a bill contrary to the laws of England to pass? So the Commissioners of Customs in London asked rhetorically.

Obstructions to the acts of trade appeared endemic in America, but the Commissioners of Trade stressed particularly the opposition to the courts of vice admiralty in the chartered governments, a point the Lords

Justices appreciated. The proprietary governments "being so intent on their own Profitts makes them altogehter regardless of the general concerns of England which is an inconvenience that begins to call for redress." The protection afforded pirates in Pennsylvania and the Jerseys confirmed this view. The attorney general was to consider whether Penn's officials had not exceeded the powers granted him in his charter. The Scots settled at Darien also posed a threat. Should they remain at their newly established colony at the isthmus, the governors appointed by the proprietors would "soon grow intimate with them." Sanction for Andrew Hamilton as governor of the Jerseys had already been denied for fear of the Scottish connection.[5]

During the first week in August 1699 the men at the Plantation Office occupied themselves chiefly with the affairs of Pennsylvania. Succumbing to their pressure, Penn committed himself to go to America. The Commissioners of Trade insisted that he turn out his deputy, as well as David Lloyd and the other offending justices, and ensure that for the future the provincial regime deal adequately with pirates and illicit traders. The failure to seize buccaneers had demonstrated the need for armed force on the Delaware. Penn must settle a militia according to the powers conferred on him in the royal patent.

Rhode Island and the Jerseys were also under scrutiny. In response to complaints that provincial officials had coddled pirates and openly challenged the court of vice admiralty, the governor of Rhode Island had merely transmitted to England what the secretary to the Board of Trade termed a "bland" copy of the provincial laws and "frivolous vindications" of the misdemeanors imputed to the Rhode Islanders. The Commissioners of Trade had returned a "very sharp answer." They then sounded out the crown law officers on the possibility of proceeding by writ of quo warranto against the recalcitrant provincial administration. The proprietors of East and West Jersey, unsure of their legal authority, were even then negotiating with the crown to surrender their claims in exchange for confirmation of their right to the soil.[6]

To avoid legal action against his charter, Penn that summer departed for America. Under great pressure from the Board of Trade, he dismissed those officials found offensive. Quary reported him zealous in all matters concerning the interests of the king, but others among the proprietor's opponents found his activities in Philadelphia distressing. Governor Francis Nicholson of Virginia, a strong adherent of the Church of England, reported to the archbishop of Canterbury that the proprietor "makes his braggs" of the strength of the Quaker interest in London, privately insinuating, no doubt, the weakness of the Anglican church. Nicholson was apprehensive, for he looked upon the majority of the

Commissioners of Trade as no friends of Anglicanism. Neither was their secretary, William Popple—rumored to have sheltered William Penn when the Quaker leader had been proscribed as a suspected Jacobite. None of the bishops, Nicholson complained, were taken notice of by the administration when considering American affairs.[7]

Nicholson's apprehensions, even if sincere, were not well founded, for whatever the political leanings of the religious sympathies of the Commissioners for Plantation Affairs, they were not favorably inclined toward the proprietaries.

An opportunity to attack the chartered colonies came in March 1700, when the House of Commons ordered the Commissioners of Trade to report on their achievements since 1696 in improving the trade of England. Stamford, Lexington, Blathwayt, Pollexfen, Hill, and Stepney—Locke was not then in London—singled out the proprietary governors for putting private above public interest in trials for violations of the navigation code. The requirements imposed by Parliament that the governors receive the sanction of the king and that proprietors give security for their deputies had gone unheeded. Nothing more could be done against the proprietary and other chartered regimes "without some further Provision by Parliament . . . to reduce them to a more Regular Conduct, and complyance with their Duty in reference to the trade of England."[8]

Before the session ended, Parliament passed two measures, one to suppress piracy in the colonies and the other to hold governors in the plantations responsible for the enforcement of the navigation code. Although far short of what the Commissioners of Trade wanted, these two measures, in the opinion of Attorney General Thomas Trevor, provided legal weapons against the chartered colonies. A refusal by a governor to obey parliamentary statute was grounds for forfeiting a charter.

If such was the case, the behavior of Governor Robert Treat placed the patent of Connecticut in jeopardy. The ministers of state in Whitehall took it as an inherent right of the crown to receive and hear appeals from subjects in the colonies. Treat and the assistants at Hartford had insisted on their right under the charter to determine all causes without admitting appeals from the provincial courts to the king, that is, the council or royal courts in England. In granting the charter in 1662 Charles II had not expressly reserved a right to hear appeals.[9]

By the close of 1700 Randolph had returned from an extended tour of America to find himself in a precarious position, the commissioners at the Customs House having learned that he had criticized their conduct of business. To reinstate himself in their good graces and to demonstrate his zeal, Randolph at the urging of his mentor, Blathwayt, submitted a journal recounting his trials and tribulations in America with supporting documents, among them a list of governors in the chartered colonies who had not secured the approval of the king to serve as required by the Act to Prevent Frauds. The list included Samuel Cranston of Rhode Island, Fitzjohn Winthrop of Connecticut, Andrew Hamilton of East and West Jersey, Henderson Walker and Joseph Blake of the Carolinas, and William Penn, governor and proprietor of Pennsylvania.[10]

From America, Penn fought back, orchestrating the theme of religious liberty to be sounded in political circles in London. He sought to condemn those who attacked proprietary governments—Randolph, Quary, and Nicholson—as Anglican bigots. It was never intended, he wrote Lord John Somers, that Pennsylvania "should be a Ch[urch] Plantation" or that the Quakers who founded the colony to accommodate their own circumstances, the men who had risked all to conquer the wilderness, should be imposed upon. Under the crown, the Friends had established a colony where all people owing God could live and those who confessed Jesus Christ savior of the world might share in the government. Not content with this, rude, factious, and troublesome men like Parson Edward Portlock, hiding behind the slogan of "king and church," sought to dominate the government and to oust the Quakers. Even while Portlock inveighed from the pulpit against the Friends for not taking up arms against pirates, he himself was not above buying 624 pieces of plundered coin brought in from the Red Sea. Penn saved his harshest words for Jeremiah Basse, a former Baptist preacher and arch-critic of the proprietary regimes in the Jerseys, and Edward Randolph, "Randal," as he referred to the customs official. Penn never got the name right. A scoundrel and a knave, Randolph had been the tool employed to plague the saints of Massachusetts. Even before leaving London in 1699 Penn had begun to undermine Randolph with Sir Robert Southwell at the Customs House. The chief man of business there was now Samuel Savage, a man who loved a token, Penn informed his English agent and solicitor, Charlwood Lawton. The proprietor would not begrudge Savage 20 pieces of eight or even five guineas.

Through Lawton and Edward Hastwell, a Quaker merchant in London, Penn now began to organize a lobby. He wrote to various noblemen and close acquaintances with influence: Somers, the earl of Romney, Sir John Holt (chief justice of the Court of King's Bench), John Thompson, Baron Havesham (a commissioner of the Admiralty), Robert Harley, Edward Seymour, Heneage Finch, and Sir James Lowther. Penn also urged Lawton and Hastwell to employ authorities on civil law from the Doctors Commons and to keep up the hearts of the Jersey proprietors not to relinquish their rights of government.

Such were the forces Penn hoped to marshal to counter the campaign against the proprietaries he assumed Quary, Nicholson, the bishop of London, and the latter's commissary for Maryland, Thomas Bray (a "Flanders camp parson," Penn called him) were mobilizing. A singular letter went out to Robert Harley, a leader of the country bloc in the House of Commons: "Methinks some of thy church acquaintances might moderate these follies a little."[11]

To blunt an attack upon proprietary charters in Parliament, Penn sought out men regardless of their party affiliation and religious sentiments. In January 1701 he sent off to his son, namesake, and heir in England the names of seventeen potential supporters with instructions to apprise them of Penn's position. The majority of the seventeen sat in the House of Lords; two—Harley and Sir Edward Seymour—carried great weight in the Commons. Eight were affiliated with the Tories, seven with the Whigs.[12] By this time in the reign of William III there had occurred a reordering of political factions. As a result the king's ministries were often coalitions of one party with a section of another. One element of the new Tory party consisted of former country Whigs now led by Harley. The new Whigs were essentially a court group. Party affiliation influenced the voting of members of Parliament on some, but not all, issues.[13]

The ministry was then disintegrating under pressure from the Parliamentary opposition, using, among other issues, the involvement of the Whig junta with Captain William Kidd. Impeachment of the ministers was the key issue for the members in the Commons. The resumption of the charters to the colonies did not become a party issue; it was a marginal, a relatively minor point for most of the politicians. Stamford, Lexington, Blathwayt, and the other commissioners of trade apparently did not have the active backing of the administration and were unable to arouse much sustained interest on the matter among the great majority of the members of Parliament.

The old Whigs in the first year or two of the new reign had objected to vacating of corporate charters by executive prerogative under Charles II and James II, but this procedure was not relevant if Parliament by statute sanctioned placing the chartered provinces directly under the king. Concern for the right of private property might have influenced the question. Some highly place men saw gain in the proprietary provinces. As late as 1698 Sir John Talbot and Lord Somers proposed giving New York, once the property of the duke of York, to the duke of Shrewsbury. The lord chancellor had gone as far as to draft letters patent and instructions to complete the transfer before Shrewsbury put a stop to the matter. The duke had judged it improper.[14]

The Commissioners for Trade and Plantations, confronted in 1701 by vested interests, the failure of a weak, disintegrating ministry to support them, and lack of interest among the rank and file of the Lords and Commons, had a difficult time marshaling support against Penn and the other proprietors of American colonies. Continued violations of the navigation code and the failure of the governments in the chartered provinces to adhere to the requirements of the Act to Prevent Frauds and subsequent parliamentary statutes had prompted the board to lay the matter before the legislature when the Lords and Commons requested the annual report on the nation's state of trade.

The report submitted by Blathwayt on 29 March 1701 contained a blanket denunciation of the proprietary and chartered colonies. Without discriminating one province from another, the Commissioners of Trade condemned all for failing to enforce the acts of trade, making laws contrary to the statutes of England, denying appeals from the local courts to the king in council, harboring pirates, and neglecting the defense of the English possessions in North America. The chartered colonies ought to be placed on the same footing as those whose governments depended directly on the king, but without prejudicing any man's property.[15]

The Commons ordered the report to lie upon the table to be perused by the members of the house. The affair of Captain Kidd, an element in the attempt to impeach the Whig ministers, had priority. When the house again took up the complaints lodged by the Board of Trade, it ordered the commissioners merely to hand in whatever information they had received relating to trade and the courts of justice in America. This Matthew Prior presented on 24 April. Again the commissioners urged resumption of the charters by legislative action, and again the Commons ordered their report to lie upon the table.[16]

That same day a bill for reuniting to the crown the government of several colonies in America was introduced into the House of Lords. It would void all clauses in the patents granted to Massachusetts, Rhode Island, Maryland, Connecticut, New Hampshire, the Jerseys, Carolina, Pennsylvania, and the Bahamas for governing English subjects and vest all authority granted in these charters to the king as if no such patents had been issued. Nothing in the bill was to be construed to abridge the right of property (governmental authority excepted) derived from any charter or to empower the king to govern the inhabitants of the colonies otherwise than by the statutes in force in the provinces, laws not repugnant to those of England.

Two days later, William Penn the younger, primed by his father, entered a spirited protest: despite the specific disclaimer protecting property, the proposed measure would deprive his father of his estate.

For almost a month the bill was before the Lords, but during this time they were engaged with the impeachment of Orford and Somers, two of the Whig peers involved in the Kidd affair. On twelve separate days during these four weeks the Lords received papers and heard witnesses, including such opponents of chartered governments as Joseph Dudley, Jeremiah Basse, and Jahleel Brenton, as well as members of the London mercantile community. Charles, Lord Baltimore, proprietor of Maryland, petitioned against the bill, as did the younger Penn, Sir Henry Ashurst (the Whig agent for Connecticut), and John, earl of Bath, for himself and the other proprietors of Carolina and the Bahamas. Four of the overlords of Carolina were peers, some underage. Bath claimed they stood to lose about thirty thousand pounds in property and trade.

Closely watching the situation at Westminster were the Quakers of London. Sensitive for years to any governmental action detrimental to their position, they had formed an effective organization to keep themselves informed of the voting records of members of Parliament and had developed a small corps of experienced lobbyists. In May 1701 they appointed a subcommittee with instructions to work for the defeat of the bill to place the governments of the chartered colonies directly under the king, a proposed law they viewed as a threat to the religious liberties of the Friends in America.

The measure did not pass the House of Lords. Why was not clear. Occupied with the impeachment of Somers and Orford, perhaps the peers did not get around to the bill for taking up the governments of the chartered colonies before the session came to an end. From America Penn wrote to seven peers who, he had been informed—perhaps by the Quaker lobbyists in London—had been helpful in his cause. They included men of various political factions. The influence of the Friends in London may have been one factor accounting for the failure to take up the bill, but probably the colonial issue was simply lost in the press of other business. Despite the plea made by the Board of Trade, the question of the chartered colonies in America was a minor affair. Lexington, Stamford, and their colleagues had "found it very difficult to make an issue of it at all."[17]

The confidence of the Commissioners of Trade was shaken. Stepney, for one, was thankful they had "rubbed through" the Parliamentary session. He now expected himself and his colleagues "to hold possession as the judges in Westminster unless the Ax . . . should chance to take off our Head; without which we might go forward without the miracle of St. Dennis."[18] (Saint Dennis, apostle to the Gauls, first bishop of Paris and patron saint of France, had been martyred by decapitation. Artistic works represented him carrying his severed head.)

Whatever the case with saints, men, including kings, could not so survive. More mundane business lay at hand for Stepney and the other commissioners. That year the earl of Bellomont, governor of New York, Massachusetts, and New Hampshire, died. With his demise, government by captain general came to an end. The appointment of Bellomont to joint governships had been in part, an attempt by the Whig ministers to endow him with a suitable, secure salary. With his death and the political decline of his patrons, the spoils of office could be divided. As with Bellomont's appointment, private interest and politics prevailed in the choice of his successors.

With the Whigs out of power, Joseph Dudley at last secured the post at Boston, despite the vociferous opposition of Sir Henry Ashurst, the New England agent who pushed the candidacy of Wait Winthrop of Massachusetts. For some years, Dudley had served John, Lord Cutts, as lieutenant governor of the Isle of Wight. With Bellomont dead and Cutts posted to the English army in Holland, Dudley became governor of Massachusetts and of New Hampshire. Blathwayt had supported Dudley's candidacy, but the two men had disagreed over a successor for Lieutenant Governor William Stoughton, who had died shortly after Bellomont. Dudley favored Nathaniel Byfield; Blathwayt, at the king's side in Holland, successfully advanced his cousin, Thomas Povey, an obscure army officer.[19]

The situation at Manhattan called for promptly filling the vacancy created by Bellomont's death. With deputy governor John Nanfan absent in Barbados, the councilors had begun squabbling among themselves, the majority refusing to recognize the authority of the president, William Smith. In London the choice fell on "poor" Edward Hyde, cousin to the princess Anne. As heir to the earl of Claredon he had the courtesy title of Lord Cornbury. Late in 1701 the Privy Council issued orders for transportation for Cornbury, his family, and their goods to America. But weeks passed without Cornbury's departing. He was jailed for debt, six hundred pounds owed to a mercer. Apparently neither the lord keeper nor the royal judges would take it upon themselves to discharge him. His creditor finally agreed to Cornbury's release for fear that he would be called to account when Parliament met for a breach of privilege in causing the arrest of a member. Still Cornbury delayed. September passed, as did October. Anticipating the governor would not arrive at his station that winter should he continue to delay, the Lords Justices finally issued him strict orders to depart.[20]

The military command in the northern colonies was now divided, Dudley having jurisdiciton over the militia of Massachusetts, New Hampshire, and Rhode Island, Cornbury over the forces of Connecticut, New

York, and the Jerseys as well as the four companies of royal soldiers in New York, units much depleted by desertion and now numbering fewer than two hundred men.

When the British proprietors of East and West Jersey finally decided to surrender their claims to government—by so doing, they hoped to nominate the first royal governor, so Jeremiah Basse thought—Cornbury's commission was enlarged to include these two jurisdictions now merged into a single colony of New Jersey.[21]

Encouraged perhaps by the decision of the Jersey proprietors, Stamford, Meadows, Abraham Hill, and Matthew Prior late in 1701 again took up the attack on the chartered governments in America. Lack of time and the press of other business, they conjectured, had prevented passage of the bill for the resumption of the charters the last parliamentary session. Seeking to bolster their case, they wrote to Francis Nicholson to procure information for them, at the same time enclosing a set of "observations" suggesting the nature of the intelligence they desired. Aiding the cause of the Commissioners for Plantation Affairs were the damaging assessments made by Jahleel Brenton, a collector of customs, and John Hawles, the solicitor general, of the several statutes enacted in Massachusetts Bay relating to navigation and the jurisdiction of the courts.[22] From America, word had also come from George Larkin and William Atwood (chief justice of New York and judge of the admiralty circuit from New Hampshire to the Delaware). Following a tour of the northern colonies from the Piscataqua to the Patuxent, Larkin had sent to Whitehall a strong condemnation of the proprietary provinces: they were prejudicial to the king's interest and a refuge for pirates and unlawful traders. None of the chartered governments had adequate defenses.[23]

From the Chesapeake, Governor Francis Nicholson was quick to take up the suggestions sent him by the Commissioners of Trade. For some years he had been in close touch with Anglicans in Philadelphia and the other ports on the lower Delaware, Englishmen unhappy with the rule of the Quakers. By the end of 1701 he had persuaded one of the churchmen, Robert Quary, a customs official and adversary of Penn, to cross the Atlantic "to do His Majesty and Old England a particular piece of Service." Fully primed, Quary carried a letter of recommendation from Nicholson to John Ellis, an undersecretary of state.[24]

The proprietor of Pennsylvania had not been idle. Through his son and his agent in London William Penn had again contacted several influential nobles and members of Parliament: the dukes of Devonshire and Somerset, the marquis of Normanby, Heneage Finch, Robert Harley, and the outspoken Tory, Jack Howe. His message to Howe was direct: if the charters were lost, security, liberty, and property would become precarious. Did not the proprietors of colonies deserve the same consideration as the municipal corporations in Old England? Penn's plea to the earl of Romney was both sentimental and mundane. The proprietor had received a charter from Charles II in compensation for a debt of sixteen thousand pounds owed his father. Penn had expended more than twenty thousand pounds on the province. He urged his old friend: "Possess the King of this usage[.] I cannot suffer myself to think he will be brought to Ruin Families[,] to Break Publick faith[,] to treat Merit in Guilt for Reasons of State."

Harley held a strategic place in the House of Commons. To him Penn sent a condemenation of royal officials in America—judges of admiralty courts, collectors, and governors—villains who sought to line their own pockets, not to serve the king's cause. Reasons of state ought never to be argued to justify violating property. "Let it not be said that a Parliament of England, the people's last resort for right[,]should ex parte, deprive whole provinces of their first and chief encouragement to planting them." Penn begged Harley to notify him, should a bill be introduced into Parliament in order that the proprietor might return in time to London.[25]

William Penn did not wait. For months he had been contending with the assemblymen in Philadelphia. He now agreed to a new charter—actually a provincial statute— of privileges granting separate legislative status for the lower counties and extensive powers to the provincial assembly. More than ever, the proprietor and the officials appointed by him would have a difficult time controlling the government of Pennsylvania in the face of demands by the royal authorities to enforce the parliamentary navigation code. On 3 November 1701 Penn took ship from Newcastle for England. He arrived in time to counter Quary's mischief, he thought, but the surrender of the British proprietors of the Jerseys he took to be "an ugly preface" to a larger matter. Yet he declared himself content to do his duty and "leave the Rest to God."[26]

At Westminster what had become for a time an annual ritual was repeated in January 1702. The Commons ordered the commissioners at the Plantation Office to lay before them an account of what they had done over the past year to improve trade, a report on the state of the colonies, and a list of the governors serving in the overseas plantations. Stamford, Meadows, Pollexfen, Blathwayt, and Prior were then drafting a representation to the king on the dangerous state of defenses in America and the West Indies. When submitting this report to William III on 24 January, they took the opportunity to attack the administrations of the chartered colonies, provinces in a wholly defenseless state. Further, these colonies provided a shelter for illegal traders, pirates, and deserters from the king's forces in the neighboring provinces, a situation perpetuated by maladministration of justice in the proprietary courts. Such independent governments were inconsistent with the welfare of England; they should be put into the same state of dependency as the other colonies by parliamentary statute.[27] Such also was the burden of the report Blathwayt presented to the House of Commons on behalf of his colleagues.

William III was evidently disturbed over the defenseless state of the colonies as described by the Board of Trade. He commanded the commissioners to advise what the monarch himself might undertake for the defense of the overseas possessions as well as what might be appropriate for Parliament.

Anticipating some unfavorable action, Penn submitted to the earl of Manchester—he had replaced Sir Charles Hedges as a principal secretary of state but would serve for only a few months—the heads of a bill to strengthen the English settlements in America. Penn proposed to vest authority over royal revenue in admiralty officials and military jurisdiction in a commander in chief appointed by the king. But civil authority and administration would remain as was, except that judicial proceedings would run in the name of the king. The monarch could also exercise a veto over bills passed in the colonies and hear appeals from provincial courts in cases involving over three hundred pounds. Unfamiliar with the situation in America, Manchester referred Penn's proposals to the Commissioners for Plantation Affairs. Did they suit all of the proprietary governments? Did they answer the ends of the representation the commissioners had recently submitted?[28]

The answer came the very next day, an emphatic no. Stamford, Pollexfen, and Prior judged Penn's proposals untenable. The bill the Commissioners of Trade had proposed to the House of Lords the previous session would better ensure the colonies' lending mutual assistance to each other, combat illegal trade and piracy, and prevent inhabitants running off to avoid military service.[29]

The previous year, time had run out on the Commissioners of Trade, but now changes in the domestic political scene coupled with a breakdown in relations with France altered the situation. William III died on 8 March 1701/2. By the terms Parliament had imposed in the Act of Succession, Anne became queen. But when Louis XIV recognized the Catholic son of James II as king of England, war broke out with France. Anne's participation in determining policy within the administration was limited. William Penn predicted: "Queens never read, as well as kings, what they sign."[30] Committees and secretaries of state would now predominate.

Initially the succession of the queen brought no significant change in personnel or policy. Manchester called for a meeting late in April at Vernon's office to consider a representation of the Commissioners for

Plantation Affairs on the state of defenses in the colonies. Agents of the various colonies and William Penn were invited to attend. But a reorganization of the administration intervened, Sir Charles Hedges and the earl of Nottingham becoming principal secretaries of state, the latter serving in the southern department. Nottingham dominated the administration of colonial affairs. As a condition of accepting office, he insisted that two of his kinsmen be appointed to the Board of Trade. Thomas Thynne, Viscount Weymouth, and William Legge, earl of Dartmouth, replaced Lexington and Stamford. Weymouth would have preferred a more thoroughgoing purge. Stepney, although he remained on the board, was then serving in Vienna.[31]

William Penn thought himself politically more secure by the alteration in the administration. Although the Church party, so he called it, had gained against the Whigs, he found good friends in the government. The wisest men in England, some of the greatest, and some who loved him were now advising him to remain in London and not to bargain away the government of the proprietary. Penn made himself useful to Sidney Godolphin, who now headed the Treasury, and to Nottingham. He acted as liaison for the lord treasurer in the prosecution of Daniel Defoe, accused of issuing a seditious libel.[32]

As had the proprietors of the Jerseys, Penn may have been willing to give up the government of his territories in America, provided the crown granted him sufficient concessions, among them the right to nominate the governor.[33] The preservation of his bargaining position required that Parliament not annex the chartered colonies. To this end Penn and the proprietors of the Carolinas employed William Wharton, son of a Massachusetts speculator and entrepreneur, then a lawyer living in London. So highly did Penn regard Wharton's abilities that the proprietor later recommended him to Governor Fitzjohn Winthrop to defend the Connecticut charter. During the summer of 1702 at London and at Bath, where the queen took up residence, Penn himself was busy, soliciting the governorship of New Jersey for Andrew Hamilton. The Commissioners of Trade had thought Hamilton unfit after Randolph had accused him of allowing Scottish ships to trade in New Jersey ports.[34]

In the fall the Commissioners for Plantation Affairs once more moved against Penn and the other proprietors. In response to an order from the House of Lords to report on the state of trade of the kingdom since the last session of Parliament, Dartmouth, Meadows, Blathwayt, Pollexfen, and Prior on 20 November condemned the chartered governments as "nurseries of illegal trade and guilty of other irregular practices, to the great prejudice of her Majesty's revenue and of fair traders." They now added complaints received from Dudley, the royal governor of the

Bay colony. The authorities of Rhode Island had refused him use of the provincial militia. He had found the colony in great disorder, a "receptacle for pirates," and a haven for illicit traders. Having obtained sole power, the Quakers and their supporters would admit no others to any place of trust. The Commissioners of Trade professed to see no other effective means than legislation by Parliament to bring Rhode Island and the other chartered provinces to an immediate dependence on the crown. Mutual assistance for the security and the trade of the American plantations required overall direction.

Apparently loath to conclude the obvious, the Lords Spiritual and Temporal merely asked the Board of Trade to submit an abstract of the most glaring irregularities and abuses prevailing in the chartered colonies and to suggest appropriate remedies. This was hardly necessary. Such recommendations had already been made, the commissioners replied, referring the peers to the reports and papers submitted earlier that year, among them the charges exchanged by Penn and Robert Quary. The protests and arguments of the Plantation Board came to naught. Other business the Lords and Commons thought more pressing.

Thirteen months passed before the House of Lords in December 1703 again routinely asked the Commissioners of Trade to report on the state of the commerce of the kingdom. Again the board cited the resistance Dudley of Massachusetts had encountered from the authorities of Rhode Island. They claimed the privileges granted them as a body politic by the charter. The Commissioners of Trade now referred to the opinion given almost a decade before in 1694 by the legal officers of the crown. If in a case of extraordinary exigency through default, incapacity, or neglect, proprietors or officials left a colony and its inhabitants unprotected or undefended, then the crown might constitute a governor. Such now appeared the situation in Rhode Island. A governor appointed by the queen already presided over New Jersey, the proprietors having surrendered their authority to the crown, and William Penn was then negotiating with the commissioners on terms for his territories. Penn's conditions were high: the right to veto provincial laws, confirmation of his privileges as lord of the soil, thirty-thousand pounds in compensation, and the right to submit a list of persons from whom the queen might select a governor.

These terms the Commissioners for Plantation Affairs found unacceptable and the sum Penn demanded exhorbitant. In reporting the status of their negotiations with Penn to Parliament, they again recommended legislation to vacate the colonial charters.[35]

As before, the recommendation was buried in an extensive, detailed survey of the general state of trade, one item among many. The administration did not press and Parliament did not act on the issue.

Penn spun out the negotiations for surrendering the government until an incapacitating stroke precluded any agreement during his life. In 1704, 1706, 1707, and again in 1715, members of the Board of Trade presumed to raise the question of the chartered colonies in Parliament, but with no success. The issue mattered neither to the administration nor the parties in Parliament.[36] The Commissioners of Trade simply did not carry enough political weight, and other boards and the higher ministers of state simply did not support them.

For decades bureaucrats in Whitehall had hoped to bring the colonies across the Atlantic to a closer dependence on the royal government, but their efforts had received an abrupt check and a massive reversal by the uprisings in Boston, Manhattan, and Saint Marys. They never recovered, could never overcome the operation of personal connections and private interests in London and the demands upon the administration of war with France and the vicissitudes of party politics. The logic of the revolution in England made it hazardous to undertake action against the privileged colonies in America through the royal prerogative or the royal courts at Westminster. Accepting the new constitutional arrangement, the Board of Trade beginning in 1701 made appeals to Parliament, but legislative supremacy would become a reality only if a majority in the legislature was disciplined in voting on issues by party loyalty. The resumption of the charters of the overseas plantations did not become a party matter in Parliament; it was a minor point for most of the members. Nor did the Commissioners of Trade have the active backing of the administration. With the Commons and the ministry occupied with seemingly more important partisan problems and the renewal of the war with France as well as Spain, the Board of Trade failed to countermand the influence of the proprietary interests, the Quaker lobby, and the indifference of the majority of the members.

Conclusion

With the failure of the Commissioners of Trade to persuade the Parliament of England to vacate the charters of the colonies, the political structure and governmental institutions prevailing in America—in great part, the consequence of the insurrections at Boston, Manhattan, and Saint Marys—remained intact. In the name of the Protestant religion and the rights fo Englishmen, the insurgents—led, in the main, by men displaced from authority or resentful over their failure to achieve political recognition commensurate with their social status—had seized power in New York, Massachusetts, and Maryland. Fear of Catholicism, social instability, too narrow a governmental base, ethnic animosities, and political immaturity had provided fruitful soil for the rhetoric of rebellion. The blunders of royal as well as proprietary officials had enhanced the insurgent cause.

The English in America remained divided among a dozen petty, local jurisdictions with three distinct governmental forms on the colonial level. Although the crown in 1719 sanctioned the overthrow of proprietary government in Carolina, in 1715 it had restored the political privileges of the Baron Baltimore. Maryland with Pennsylvania and the three lower counties on the Delaware River remained proprietary colonies. Connecticut, Rhode Island, and Massachusetts continued as chartered provinces, their governmental forms prescribed by their patents. Elsewhere in America, in the royal colonies, the forms of government followed the strictures contained in the commissions and instructions issued by the crown to governors, regulations easily circumvented, as events later proved.

In 1702 Joseph Dudley had returned to his native Massachusetts with a commission from the monarch of England as governor of the Bay colony. The charter granted by William III eleven years before and the instructions given to Dudley required him to call an elected assembly to enact laws for the populace of the Bay. Dudley's career over the previous seventeen years illustrated the struggles, the shifts and the turns at Whitehall. The political arrangement under which he served the monarch

260

and administered the provincial government in 1702 differed markedly from that of 1686, when he had received a commission from James II to preside over a council in Massachusetts, a board named by the king to govern the colony without the benefit of a locally elected assembly. Under his successor, Edmund Andros as governor of the Dominion of New England, this constitutional arrangement had been applied to all of the English settlements from the Penobscot to the Delaware.

The insurrections in Boston, Manhattan, and Saint Marys following the Protestant Revolution in England had overturned the administration James II and the earl of Sunderland had imposed on English America, but while William III, Shrewsbury, Nottingham, and the men who had driven out the Catholic king acknowledged certain rights for the English subjects in the colonies, particularly the privilege of an elected legislative assembly, they too held that the colonies must remain subservient to England, dependent on the crown. But if inclined to pursue this goal, they did so, not by exercising the prerogative of the monarch, but by the authority of Parliament. Thus they accepted the essential constitutional achievement of the revolutionary settlement. Whatever the political rhetoric of the revolution, freedom of religious conscience—at least for peaceable Protestants—was a goal common to the reigns of both James II and William III.

The onset of a long, protracted war with France, the nature of parliamentary politics, personal interest, and the preoccupation of men at Westminster and Whitehall with local concerns and European affairs precluded their adopting any systematic approach to governing the overseas colonies. This failure, one that William Blathwayt lamented in 1700, extended back over three or four decades. It prevailed as well into the eighteenth century. In the future some men in America continued to look to Whitehall and Westminster, but the more significant arenas for American politics were now Boston, Annapolis, Williamsburg, and the other provincial capitals where the more ambitious in the assemblies waged their battles not only with governors but with each other for power, influence, and status.

In following a simplistic formula, in seeking to render the chartered and proprietary governments in America immediately dependent on the crown by appointing a royal governor and mandating appeals from the provincial courts to Whitehall, successive English ministers of state had misunderstood the problem of administering the overseas colonies, of controlling political events in America. They assumed that an executive appointed and instructed by the crown would veto objectionable bills coming from a local assembly and implement decisions made in Whitehall for a colony. For a royal govenor to be free of local pressures, to be at liberty to execute policy made in England, he needed to be immune from financial pressure, to have his salary set and paid from England rather than by the local assembly. In the last year of the reign of William III, the king in council had noted the warning of the Commissioners for Plantation Affairs that the practice of having governors receive "presents" from the assemblies tended to "render them precarious and dependent" on the local populace. To enable them to support the dignity of government, they should receive adequate salaries.[1] The ministers of the crown never uniformly applied this recommendation. Of greater consequence during the coming decades, when war or the threat of international conflict was chronic, governors needed financing from England adequately to provide for military operations. Little was forthcoming for more than the next half-century. By leaving the representatives of royal authority in America financially dependent on the provincial assemblies, English authorities provided the mechanism for the rise to power of local politicians. Over the next sixty years, as war with France and Spain seemed always imminent and conflict with hostile Indians a constant threat, the chronic need of governors and military officials to provide for the security of English America served "as the stirrup by which the colonial assemblies mounted to the saddle."[2]

The ability of royal officials to end factional strife and discord and to achieve the goals desired by Whitehall in America depended not only on the formal governmental arrangements imposed by the crown on the colonies but also on the purposefulness, strength of personality, and integrity of the men sent out to preside over the provincial administrations.

No institutional reorganization, no simple constitutional formula—rendering the provinces immediately dependent on the crown—would suffice. Money and political talent liberally applied were the solution. For the seventy-five years remaining to the first British Empire, neither was forthcoming in adequate doses.

List of Abbreviations

Add. MSS Additional Manuscripts, British (Museum) Library, London
Adm.   Admiralty, Public Record Office, London
BL   British (Museum) Library, London
Bodl.   Bodleian Library, Oxford
CHSC   *Collections of the Connecticut Historical Society,* 31 vols.
          (Hartford: Connecticut Historical Society, 1860–1967)
CO   Colonial Office, Public Record Office, London
CW   Colonial Williamsburg, Williamsburg, Virginia
FDRL   Franklin D. Roosevelt Library, Hyde Park, New York
HL   Henry E. Huntington Library, San Marino, California
HMC   Royal Historical Manuscripts Commission, London
HMPEC   *Historical Magazine of the Protestant Episcopal Church*
HMSO   His (or Her) Majesty's Stationery Office
HSP   Historical Society of Pennsylvania, Philadelphia
LPL   Lambeth Palace Library, London
MHS   Massachusetts Historical Society, Boston, Mass.
MHSC   *Massachusetts Historical Society Collections,* 9 series, 79 vols.
          (Boston: Massachusetts Historical Society, 1792–1941)
NUL   Nottingham University Library, Manuscripts Department,
          Nottingham
PC   Privy Council, Public Record Office, London
PMHB   *Pennsylvania Magazine of History and Biography*
PRO   Public Record Office, London
SP   State Papers, Public Record Office, London
T   Treasury, Public Record Office, London
WMQ   *William and Mary Quarterly*

Notes

Chapter 1

1. Order in council, 6 February 1684/5, PC 2/71/p. 5.

2. William Penn to Thomas Lloyd, 16 March 1684/5, quoted in Samuel Mac. Janney, *The Life of William Penn: With Selections from His Correspondence and Autobiography*, 4th ed., rev. (Philadelphia, 1876), p. 264. See also James Reese Jones, *Country and Court England, 1658–1715* ([London]: Edward Arnold, 1978), p. 237.

3. C. D. Chandaman, *The English Public Revenue, 1660–1688* (Oxford: Oxford University Press, 1975), pp. 35, 255–59; Leo Francis Stock, ed., *Proceedings and Debates of the British Parliaments respecting North America*, 5 vols. (Washington, D.C.: Carnegie Institution of Washington, 1924–41), 1:423–31; John Reresby, *Memoirs of Sir John Reresby*, ed. Andrew Browning (Glasgow: Jackson, Son & Co., 1936), pp. 371–72; newsletters dated 2, 12 June, 28 July 1685, PRO, *Calendar of State Papers, Domestic Series, James II*, 3 vols. (London: HMSO, 1960–72), *1685*, nos. 763, 861, 1341; memoranda of the Common Council of Bristol, 4, 6 June 1685, *Records Relating to the Society of Merchant Venturers of Bristol in the Seventeenth Century*, ed. Patrick McGrath (Bristol: Bristol Records Society, 1952), pp. 251, 252–53; royal letter to the governors and proprietors of the American and West Indian plantations, 26 June 1685, PRO, CO 324/4/pp. 145–48; Francis, Lord Howard of Effingham (governor of Virginia) to the earl of Sunderland, 15 November 1685, CO 1/58/f. 309; address of the burgesses of Virginia to the king, 13 November 1685, CO 5/1357/pp. 77–79, with annexed reasons in CO 1/59/ff. 67, 69; and the report of the Commissioners of Customs, 1 February 1685/6, CO 1/59/f. 65.

4. Order in council, 7 February 1684/5, CO 324/4/p. 127; order in council, 1 April 1685, CO 1/57/p. 208; order in council, 29 April 1685, PC 2/71/p. 73; William Blathwayt to Henry Guy, with draft instructions for the colonial governors, 25 July 1685, CO 1/58/f. 35; Guy to William Bridgeman, 18 August 1685, SP 31/5/ff. 14, 62; and order in council, 18 December 1685, PC 2/71/pp. 177–78. The Tobacco Impost Act of 1685 (1 Jac. 2 c. 4), which raised the nominal duty from two to five pennies per pound, created some immediate and some unforeseen problems. The law sharply raised the domestic price for tobacco. It now became profitable to adulterate leaf for smoking by mixing it with stalks or stems. Merchants engaged in the tobacco trade particularly objected to the provision that the first buyer pay the duty in full and in cash. Many were small operators with

limited resources. In response, Lord Treasurer Rochester in a warrant issued on 31 July 1685 (CO 1/58/f. 39) allowed a rebate of 10 percent to merchants who paid the new duty in ready money. See Jacob M. Price, "The Tobacco Trade and the Treasury, 1685–1733," 2 vols. (Ph.D. diss., Harvard University, 1954), 2:549, 555, 751–52, 755–56, 817–51) and the proposals of ten of the larger merchants, among them Micajah Perry, John Cary, and Jeffrey Jeffreys of London (CO 1/58/f. 184). According to the accounts on tobacco shipped from London for 1689, at least seventy-seven merchants were involved in the export trade (CO 5/1305/ff. 79–86).

5. Francis Gwyn to John Ellis, 4 June 1686, John Ellis Papers, BL, Add. MSS 28875, f. 433; order in council, 19 June 1686, PC 2/71/p. 290; and order in council and annexed petition, 28 May 1686, SP 31/5/ff. 56–57.

6. Dongan to Sunderland, 31 October 1687, CO 1/63/ff. 267–268; memorial and report of the English commissioners, 16 November 1687, HL, Blathwayt Papers, BL 31, BL32; and Robert A Goldstein, *French-Iroquois Diplomatic and Military Relations, 1609–1701* (The Hague: Mouton, [1969]), p. 149.

7. Blathwayt to Sir Robert Southwell, 5 May 1688, NUL, MSS Department, Portland MSS, PwV53.

8. That it *was* a scheme to impose direct control and eliminate representative government institutions is the view of Philip S. Haffenden, "The Crown and the Colonial Charters, 1675–1688," *WMQ*, 3d ser. 15 (July–October 1958): 297–311, 452–66.

9. Minutes of the Lords of Trade and Plantations, 8, 22 November 1684, CO 391/5/pp. 21, 35.

10. Blathwayt to Lord Howard of Effingham, 6 March 1684/5, CW, Blathwayt Papers, vol. 14; Randolph to the Lords of Trade, with enclosures, 2 September 1685, CO 1/58/ff. 120, 124, 126; Randolph to Joseph Dudley, 9 January 1684/5, in Edward Randolph, *Memoirs of Edward Randolph, Including His Letters and Official Papers,* ed. Robert Noxon Toppan and Alfred T. Goodrich, 7 vols. (Boston, Mass.: Prince Society, 1898–1909), 4:12–13.

11. Blathwayt to Baron Howard of Effingham, 6 March, 2 July 1685, CW, Blathwayt Papers, vol. 14.

12. Randolph to Joseph Dudley, 9 January 1684/5, Randolph to the bishop of St. Asaph's, ? March 1685, Randolph to Sir Robert Southwell, 1 August 1685, *Randolph Letters,* 4:12–13, 15–18, 28–29; minutes of the committee for plantations, 5 May 1685, CO 391/5/p. 140. For an extended but unfavorable treatment of Randolph, see Michael G. Hall, *Edward Randolph and the American Colonies* (Chapel Hill: University of North Carolina Press, 1960).

13. Orders in council, 10, 15 July 1685, PC 2/71/pp. 115, 118–19; Randolph's petition and his charges against Connecticut and Rhode Island, CO 1/58/nos. 11, 11(I), 11(II); the addresses from New York City, CO 1/57/nos. 119, 119(I).

14. Randolph to Southwell, 30 July, 1 August 1685, *Randolph Letters,* 4:26, 28–30.

15. Randolph to the Lords of Trade, n.d., but read on 18 August 1685, CO 1/58/f. 71; Randolph to the Lords of Trade, with enclosures, 2 September 1685, CO 5/58/ff. 120, 122, 124–26.

16. Randolph to Southwell, 3 October 1685, *Randolph Letters,* 4:59. At the Plantation Office the following year John Povey, the undersecretary, reported that it was believed that James II "upon the private solicitation and complaint" of William Penn removed Richard Coney and named Sir Robert Robinson as governor of Bermuda (Povey to Southwell, 3 July 1686, NUL, Portland MSS, PwV60).

17. Povey to Southwell, 3 April, 26 May, 12 June, 3 July, 23 October 1686, NUL, Portland MSS, PwV60; Clarendon to Blathwayt, 15 May 1685, *The Correspondence of Henry Hyde, Earl of Clarendon, and of His Brother, Laurence Hyde, Earl of Rochester,* ed. Samuel Weller Singer, 2 vols. (London: Camden Society, 1929), 1:393. Ellipses (. . .) have routinely been omitted at the beginning and end of direct quotations and initial capitalization and final punctuation regularized accordingly.

18. Lords of Trade to the lord president of the council, 26 August 1685, CO 5/90/p. 251. On the role of Sunderland, see the discussion on Mather's source of information in Gertrude Jacobsen, *William Blathwayt, a Late Seventeenth Century English Administrator* (New Haven, Conn.: Yale University Press, 1932), pp. 134–35.

19. Memorandum of the Lords of Trade, 21 April 1686, CO 324/4/pp. 232–33; orders in council, 30 April, 30 May 1686, PC 2/71/pp. 258, 282; unsigned newsletter in a clerk's hand, Whitehall, 1 June 1686, King William's Chest, SP 8/1/f. 72.

20. Sunderland to the attorney general, 6 June 1686, SP 44/56/p. 337; Penn to the council of Pennsylvania, 25 September 1686, *PMHB* 33, no. 3 (1909): 305.

21. Shaftesbury to Craven, 7 July 1686, CO 1/59/f. 390; George Muschamp to the proprietors, 11 April 1687, CO 1/62/f. 90; Powis to the Lords of Trade, 7 July 1687, CO 1/62/f. 91; Carolina proprietors to the Lords of Trade, [August 1687], CO 5/288/f. 60; and order in council, 24 August 1688, PC 2/71/p. 728. The invasion by William of Orange that fall and the subsequent flight of James II may have put a halt to any proceedings against the charters.

22. See the order in council, 20 June 1686, transferring jurisdiction of Pemaquid on the far eastern frontier from New York to New England (PC 2/71/p. 291).

23. Randolph to [Blathwayt or John Povey], 27 June 1686, CW, Blathwayt Papers, vol. 1, no. 43; Randolph to Andros, two letters, both dated 28 July 1686, CW, Blathwayt Papers, vol. 1, nos. 48, 49; memorandum of the Committee for Plantation Affairs, 12 September 1686, CO 5/904/pp. 305–6, 307.

24. Order in council, 30 April 1687, CO 5/723/pp. 109–10; memorandum by the Lords of Trade, 18 May 1687, CO 5/723/p. 110; order in council, 28 May 1687, CO 5/723/p. 110 (also CO 324/4/p. 240 and PC 2/72/p. 467); order in council, 30 July 1687, CO 1/62/f. 363; order in council, 11 July 1687 (misdated 1677), SP 31/5/f. 29.

25. Randolph to Blathwayt, 23 November 1687, CW, Blathwayt Papers, vol. 1, no. 55.

26. Order in council, 27 January 1687/8, PC 2/72/p. 585; report of the English commissioners, 16 November 1687, H. L., Blathwayt Papers, BL33; and Dongan to Sunderland, 31 October 1687, CO 1/63/ff. 267–68.

27. Blathwayt to Randolph, 10 March 1687/8, in Randolph, *Randolph Let-*

ters, 4:216–17; order in Council, 23 March 1687/8, CO 1/64/no. 41; warrant for the commission annexing New York, 25 March 1688, CO 389/9/ff.467–68; Sunderland to Dongan, 20 April 1688, CO 389/9/ff. 469; and Godolphin to Dongan, 20 March 1687/8, PRO, T, 64/88/289.

28. G. F. Trevallyn Jones, *Saw-Pit Wharton: The Political Career from 1640 to 1691 of Philip, Fourth Lord Wharton* (Sydney: Sydney University Press, 1967), p. 257, thought it a moot point whether James II really wanted only toleration and equality for all religions. He concluded that the weight of opinion was that such equality would soon lead to the establishment of Catholicism with a diminishing hope of toleration or even survival for other faiths. Joseph E. Illick, *William Penn, the Politician: His relations with the English Government* (Ithaca, N.Y.: Cornell University Press, [1965]), p. 77, was even more emphatic: James's real policy was conversion of England to the Church of Rome. Maurice Ashley, "King James II and the Revolution of 1688: Some Reflections on the Historiography," in *Historical Essays 1600–1750 Presented to David Ogg*, ed. H.E. Bell and R.L. Ollard (New York: Barnes & Noble, [1963]), pp. 201–2, and in *The Glorious Revolution of 1688* (London: Hodder & Stoughton, [1968]), pointed out that historians have repeated completely false account of the character of the monarch and his policies. Ashley, while he doubted whether James could ever be exonerated, found it difficult to believe the king was the tool of Sunderland, his priests, or the French king, or that James was inconsistent in his attitude toward religious toleration. John Miller, *Popery and Politics in England, 1660–1688* (Cambridge: Cambridge University Press, 1973), pp. 197–222, was convinced that James's primary aim was to improve the position of Catholicism in England by peaceful means. There was not the slightest possibility of imposing Popery by force. The king directed all of his actions, condemned as arbitrary and illegal by later Whig historians, toward the single end of allowing greater liberty and civil rights for English Catholics and securing that freedom and those rights by parliamentary statute.

29. Richard E. Boyer, *English Declarations of Indulgence, 1687 and 1688* (The Hague: Mouton, 1968), pp. 68–71; royal warrants, 9, 25 March 1686, SP 44/336/pp. 385–86, 391; Maurice Cranston, *John Locke: A Biography* (London: Longmans, Green [1957], p. 260; order in council, 28 May 1687, PC 2/72/p. 461.

30. See their "An humble memorial . . . ," read before James II in July 1688, Leeds Papers, BL, Egerton MSS 3340, f. 179.

31. Gilbert Burnet, *History of His Own Times*, new ed. (London, 1838), p. 441. On the relations between Penn and James II, see John Carswell, *The Descent on England: A Study of the English Revolution of 1688 and Its European Background* (New York: John Day Co., [1969]), pp. 82–83.

32. Marriett to Penn, n.d., BL, Add. MSS 34727, f. 157; Jones, *Wharton*, pp. 257–58; Burnet, *History of His Own Times*, p. 441.

33. Blathwayt to Southwell, 19 January 1687/8, NUL, Portland MSS PwV53; Ashley, *Glorious Revolution of 1688*, p. 112; Robert H. George, "The Charters Granted to English Parliamentary Corporations in 1688," *English Historical Review* 55 (January 1940): 47–56; Jennifer Levin, *The Charter Con-*

troversy in the City of London, 1660–1688, and Its Consequences (London: Athlone Press, 1969), pp. 90–92.

34. Richard Jones to George Fox, 28 March 1688, London, Friends House Library, ARB I, no. 54; extracts of the memorial of Mather and Nowell, Leeds Papers, BL, Egerton MSS, 3340, f. 179.

Chapter 2

1. Quoted in Samuel Mac. Janney, *The Life of William Penn: With Selections from His Correspondence and Autobiography,* 4th ed., rev. (Philadelphia, 1876), p. 277, and in Bonomy Dobrée, *William Penn, Quaker and Pioneer* (Boston, Mass.: Houghton Mifflin, 1934), p. 203.

2. Archdale to George Fox, 25 March 1686, London, Friends House Library, ARB I, no. 68.

3. Henry Erskine, Third Baron Cardross, and others to the governor and council at Charles Town, 25 March 1685, CO 5/287/f. 67; Cardross to Quary, 17 July 1685, CO 5/287/f. 68; minutes of the palatine court, 6 October 1685, CO 5/287/f. 74; warrant dated 17 November 1685, CO 5/287/f. 75.

4. Proprietary instructions to James Colleton, 3 March 1686/7, CO 5/288/ff. 52–53; proprietors to Colleton, 3 March 1686/7, CO 5/288/ff. 53–54.

5. Muschamp to the [proprietors], 11 April 1687, with the opinion of the attorney general, Sir Thomas Powis, 7 July 1687, CO 1/62/ff. 90, 92; order in council, 30 July 1687, CO 324/5/p. 1; Blathwayt to the Carolina proprietors, 12 August 1687, CO 1/63/f. 72; Craven to the Lords of Trade, [August 1687], CO 1/63/f. 143; and the king to Craven, 26 May 1688, CO 389/9/p. 475.

6. Proprietors to Governor James Colleton, 3 March 1687, CO 5/288/ff. 54–55; The account of opponents who later assumed control of the government at Charles Town, n.d., CO 5/287/ff. 75–80; and Eugene Sirmans, *Colonial South Carolina: A Political History, 1663–1763* (Chapel Hill: University of North Carolina Press, 1966), pp. 44–46.

7. Spencer to Blathwayt, 22 December 1686, CW, Blathwayt Papers, vol. 16; minutes of the council of Virginia, 2 February 1687/8, CO 1/64/no. 16; James II to Lord Howard, 30 April 1688, CO 5/1357/p. 210; Byrd to Blathwayt, 21 June 1688, *The Correspondence of the Three William Byrds of Westover, Virginia, 1684–1776*, ed. Marion Tinling, 2 vols. (Charlottesville: University Press of Virginia, 1977), 1:84; royal warrant, 4 December 1687, T 64/88/p. 279; James II to Lord Howard, 4 December 1687, CO 5/1357/pp. 179–80. Byrd asked Blathwayt to offer Ayleway one hundred guineas to resign his commissions and promised John Povey, Blathwayt's assistant at the Plantation Office, a retainer of twenty pounds a year to do his "business" for as long as they kept their posts. (Byrd to Perry and Lane, 30 July 1688, 10 June 1689, *Correspondence of Byrd*, 1:86, 105.) Ayleway, when serving as commissary for the army in Ireland, later protested his suspension from the Virginia offices. See the Proceedings on his petition, 2 February 1691, SP 44/1/p. 297.

8. Lord Howard to the Lords of Trade, 10 February 1685/6, CO 1/59/ff. 87–89; Nicholas Spencer to the Lords of Trade, n.d., CO 1/59/ff. 153–54; Spencer to Blathwayt, 20 March 1685/6, CW, Blathwayt Papers, vol. 16.

9. Memorandum of the Lords of Trade, 10 May 1686, CO 5/1357/pp. 102-3; the king (countersigned by Sunderland) to Lord Howard, 1 August 1686, CO 5/1357/p. 119; Lord Howard to Sunderland, 22 February 1686/7, CO 1/61/ff. 247–48.

10. See the reference to the Treasury on the petition of Culpeper, 14 March 1686/7, SP 44/71/p. 321; Blathwayt's memorandum and report, 20 July 1688, T 64/88/pp. 303–4; order in council on the petition of Fairfax and the Culpepers, 21 May 1691, CO 5/1306/ff. 111, 114. During the reign of Queen Anne, the fifth Lord Fairfax petitioned to be allowed to exchange the grant for a lease of the Lot, Cape, and office of Bermaster of the Wapentake of Wirkworth, Derbyshire. At this time Blathwayt, the auditor general of the plantation revenue, estimated the returns from the Northern Neck to be three hundred pounds per annum (Blathwayt's memorandum and report, 22 January 1708/9, T 64/89/pp. 401–2.)

11. Royal circular to the governors, 26 June 1685, CO 324/4/pp. 145–48; address of the burgesses to the king, 13 November 1685, Co 5/1357/pp. 77–79; Lord Howard to Sutherland, 13 November 1685, CO 1/58/f. 309; Nicholas Spencer to the Lords of Trade, 2 February 1686/7, CO 1/61/f. 206; petition of the burgesses to the crown, with annexed paper, 13 November 1685, CO 1/59/ff. 67, 69; report of the Commissioners of Customs, 1 February 1685/6, CO 1/59/f. 65.

12. Fitzhugh to John Cooper, 18 April 1687, *William Fitzhugh and His Chesapeake World: The Fitzhugh Letters and Other Documents*, ed. Richard Beale Davis (Chapel Hill: University of North Carolina Press, 1963), p. 220.

13. Commissioners of Customs to the Treasury Board, 7 July 1687, CO 1/62/f. 295; petition of the London merchants, 13 August 1687, CO 1/63/ff. 74, 76–77; Commissioners of the Customs to the Treasury, 11 October 1687, CO 1/63/f. 230; Lords of Trade to the king, 25 October 1687, CO 5/1357/pp. 157–58; order in council, 28 October 1687, 5/1357/pp. 159–60; and Lords of Trade to Lord Howard, 4 November 1687, CO 5/1357/pp. 160–61.

14. Nicholas Spencer to Sunderland, 17 May 1688, CO 1/64/no. 68, ff. 321–23.

15. For a discussion of the religious affiliations and family connections of the Calvert circle, see David William Jordan, "The Royal Period of Colonial Maryland, 1689–1715," (Ph.D. diss., Princeton University, 1966), pp. 4–10; and Charles McLean Andrews, *The Colonial Period of American History*, 4 vols. (New Haven, Conn.: Yale University Press, 1934–38), 2:376–78.

16. David W. Jordan, "John Coode, Perennial Rebel," *Maryland Historical Magazine* 70 (Spring 1975): 1–28. See also Michael Kammen, "The Causes of the Maryland Revolution of 1689," ibid. 55 (Winter 1955): 293–333.

17. Order in council, 25 February 1684/5, CO 5/723/pp. 90–93; Lord Howard to Sunderland, [25 February 1685/6], CO 1/59/ff. 111a–b; proceedings of

the General Court at Jamestown, 20–24 April 1686, CO 1/59/ff. 254–55; royal warrant, 2 August 1686, SP 44/337/p. 81.

18. Lord Howard to Sunderland, 28 February 1686/7, CO 1/61/ff. 264–65; order in council, 28 May 1687, CO 324/4/p. 240; William Blathwayt to Baltimore, 12 August 1687, CO 1/63/f. 73; order in council, 28 October 1687, CO 1/63/f. 259.

19. Jordan, "Coode, Perennial Rebel," p. 15; "Royal Period of Maryland," pp. 11–12.

20. Mary Maples Dunn, *William Penn, Politics and Conscience* (Princeton, N.J.: Princeton University Press, 1967), p. 155; Penn's letter to Thomas Lloyd, 21 September 1686, *PMHB* 80 (April 1956): 239–47; Edwin B. Bronner, *William Penn's "Holy Experiment": The Founding of Pennsylvania, 1681–1701* (New York: Temple University Press, 1962), pp. 39–41, 88, 99.

21. Janney, *Life of Penn*, p. 277; Bronner, *Penn's Holy Experiment*, p. 98; Penn to the council, n.d., HSP, Letters and Papers of Penn, Dreer Collection.

22. Royal warrants, 9 March, 15 March 1685/6, SP 44/336/pp. 385–86, 391; Sunderland to the attorney general, 6 June 1686, SP 44/56/p. 337; and Penn to the president and council of Pennsylvania, 25 September 1686, *PMHB* 33, no. 3 (1909): 305.

23. Penn's instructions, dated 1 February 1686/7, Janney, *Life of Penn*, pp. 288–89; Gary B. Nash, *Quakers and Politics: Pennsylvania, 1681–1726* (Princeton, N.J.: Princeton University Press, 1968), pp. 81–86, 97–114.

24. Blackwell to Penn, 13 January 1689/90, 25 February 1689/1690, HSP, Blackwell Letters to Penn; W. L. Nuttall, "Governor John Blackwell: His Life in England and Ireland," *PMHB* 88 (April 1964): 157–59; Bronner, *Penn's Holy Experiment*, pp. 111–20; Dunn, *Penn*, pp. 157–59; Nicholas B. Wainwright, "Governor John Blackwell," *PMHB* 74 (October 1950): 457–72.

Chapter 3

1. For the very complicated details relating to West New Jersey, see John E. Pomfret, *The Province of West New Jersey, 1609–1702: A History of the Origins of an American Colony* (Princeton, N.J.: Princeton University Press, 1956), pp. 112–59; "The Proprietors of the Province of West New Jersey, 1674–1702," *PMHB* 75 (April 1951): 117–46; and Frederick R. Black, "The Last Lords Proprietors of West Jersey: The West Jersey Society, 1692–1702," (Ph.D. diss., Rutgers University, 1964), pp. 11–35.

2. John E. Pomfret, "The Proprietors of the Province of East New Jersey, 1682–1702," *PMHB* 77 (July 1953): 251–93; "The Apologia of Governor Lawrie of East New Jersey, 1688," *WMQ*, 3d ser. 14 (July 1957): 344–57.

3. James II to the proprietors, n.d., CO 389/9/p. 202; Blathwayt to Dockwra, 5 May 1685, CO 1/57/f. 272; Dyer to the Commissioners of Customs, 30 June 1685, CO 1/57/f. 417; order in council, 11 October 1685, PC 2/71/p. 143 (also in CO 1/57/f. 288); Spragge to Sunderland, 25 November 1686, CO 1/61/f. 33.

4. Petitions of the East Jersey proprietors, 30 May, 12 July 1687, CO 1/62/ff. 220–21, 331–32; order in council, 14 August 1687, PC 2/74/p. 498; commission

for Plowman, 4 November 1687, T 64/88/pp. 260–61; Dongan to Sunderland, 19 February 1687/8, CO 1/64/ff. 74–75.

5. Petition of the proprietors and a schedule of their rights, CO 1/64/ff. 182, 184–85; the attorney general, Sir Thomas Powis, to the Lords of Trade, 6 July 1688, CO 1/65/f. 35.

6. Order in council, 20 June 1686, PC 2/71/p. 291.

7. Dongan to James II, 30 September 1685, CO 1/58/f. 188; minutes of the provincial council, 13 December 1686, CO 1/61/f. 89; commissions for Plowman and Van Cortlandt, 4, 10 November 1687, T 64/88/pp. 260–61, 267–69; Sidney Godolphin to Dongan, 20 March 1687/8, T 64/88/p. 289; Blathwayt to Andros, 4 May 1688, T 64/88/p. 295.

8. Like Dongan, Plowman later complained that he had never been repaid the money, about six-hundred pounds, he had expended for provisioning the garrison at Albany (Secretary of State Charles Hedges to the Commissioners for Trade and Plantations, 1 November 1704, SP 44/105/p. 149).

9. Dongan to Sunderland, 22 February 1686/7, CO 1/61/f. 247; Dongan to James II, 24 October 1687, CO 1/63/ff. 249–50; Dongan to Blathwayt, 11, 22 August, 24 October 1687, CW, Blathwayt Papers, vol. 11.

10. A Scottish immigrant who had married a well-to-do widow from the Schuyler clan, Livingston had established commercial connections with Stephanus Van Cortlandt at Manhattan and Jacob Harwood in London. See Harwood to Livingston, 2 August 1687, FDRL, Livingston Family Papers, Robert Livingston General Correspondence. See also in the Livingston Papers the order in council, 16 January 1695/6, for the statement of Dongan's debt and John Povey's report on Dongan's petition to the crown, 23 September 1692, T 64/88/pp. 446–47. Dongan, who did not leave America until the summer of 1692, had also borrowed money from two other New York traders. When he could not pay, they had him arrested. Lawrence Leder, "Dongan's New York and Fletcher's London: Personalities and Politics," *New-York Historical Society Quarterly* 55 (January 1971): 28–37, suggested that Andros and Edward Randolph were using Livingston in an effort to force Dongan to leave New York for London to have his accounts audited in order to remove the popular governor as a figure about whom elements discontented with Andros might rally. See also Leder's *Robert Livingston, 1654–1728, and the Politics of Colonial New York* (Chapel Hill: University of North Carolina Press, 1961).

11. Robert A. Goldstein, *French-Iroquois Diplomacy and Military Relations, 1609–1701* (The Hague: Mouton, [1969]), p. 163; Dongan to James II, 2 March 1686/7, CO 1/61/ff. 270–71; Dongan's report to the Lords of Trade, ? March 1687, CO 1/67/ff. 273–312; Dongan to Sunderland, 25 October 1687, CO 1/63/ff. 251–53; and Dongan to Sunderland, 19 February 1687/8, CO 1/64/ff. 74–75.

12. Blathwayt to Edward Randolph, 10 March 1687/8, in Edward Randolph *Memoirs of Edward Randolph, Including His Letters and Official Papers*, ed. Robert Noxon Toppan and Alfred T. Goodrich, 7 vols. (Boston: Prince Society, 1898–1909), 4:216; memorandum of the Lords of Trade for the Lord President

Sunderland, [early April 1688], CO 1/67/f. 222; James II (countersigned by Sunderland) to Dongan, 22 April 1688, CO 5/1113/p. 187.

13. Randolph's petition and annexed charges, CO 1/58/ff. 18, 20–22; order in council, 17 July 1685, CO 5/904/245–46.

14. James Mark Poteet, "Preserving The Old Ways: Connecticut, 1690–1740," (Ph.D. diss., University of Virginia, 1973), pp. 10–13; " 'What Interest Has Governed Mr. Allyn?': John Allyn and the Dominion of New England," *Connecticut Historical Society Bulletin* 39 (January 1974): 1–9; Richard S. Dunn, *Puritans and Yankees: The Winthrop Dynasty of New England, 1630–1717* (Princeton, N.J.: Princeton University Press, 1962), p. 238.

15. Allyn to Fitzjohn Winthrop, 7 January 1686/7, *MHSC*, 6th ser. 3:478; Fitzjohn Winthrop to Allyn, 13 January 1686/7, ibid., 5th ser. 8:300–302.

16. Robert Treat and the General Court to Sunderland, 26 January 1686/7, CO 5/904/pp. 342–45 (also in CO 1/62/f. 81); the governor and council of Connecticut to Andros, 6, 26 January, 17 March 1686/7, and the General Court to Andros, 26 January 1686/7, CO 1/62/ff. 74, 77, 79, 82; Randolph to the Lords of Trade, 25 March 1687, CO 5/904/pp. 342–43 (also CO 1/64/f. 171).

17. Whiting to Allyn, 12 March 1686/7, "The Wyllys Papers," *CHSC*, 2:22; Saffin to Allyn, 14 June 1687, *Public Records of the Colony of Connecticut (1636–1776)*, ed. J. H. Trumbull and C. J. Hoadly, 15 vols. (Hartford, Conn., 1850–90), 3:382.

18. Order in council, 28 May 1687, CO 324/4/p. 240; Whiting to Allyn, 11 June, 9 August, 21 September 1687, *Records of the Colony of Connecticut*, 3:384, 385, 386; order in council, 18 June 1687, on a report of the Committee for Plantation Affairs of 15 June 1687, PC 2/72/p. 467; James II (countersigned by Sunderland) to Andros, 18 June 1687, CO 389/9/pp. 438–39.

19. The official account of the annexation recorded by the secretary of the Dominion of New England is printed in Albert C. Bates, "Expedition of Sir Edmund Andros to Connecticut in 1687," *Proceedings of the American Antiquarian Society*, n.s. 48 (October 1938): 286–88. Andros enclosed a copy of this account in a letter to the Lords of Trade, 28 November 1687, CO 1/63/f. 316. Randolph also sent an account to Blathwayt in a letter dated 23 November 1687, CW, Blathwayt Papers, vol. 1, no. 65. According to Bate's interpretation, Andros attempted unsuccessfully to secure the charter. There is no contemporary evidence that he tried to secure the patent or for the popular tale printed by Benjamin Trumbull in 1797 that, during the meeting with Andros, with the charter lying on the council table, someone extinguished the lights and Captain Joseph Wadsworth (allegedly) seized and carried off the document, concealing it in a large oak tree, the "Charter Oak." Bates, *Proceedings of the American Antiquarian Society*, n.s. 48 October 1938): 298–99, further assumed that the journey Andros undertook was unsuccessful as it related to receiving the charter and that he must have known that as long as the patent remained in the possession of the principal officers and no vote to vacate or annul it had been passed by the General Court, the chartered government was merely dormant and the patent itself still valid. Bates was correct, in part. The charter was still valid because it had not been

vacated by the Court of King's Bench in Westminster, the crown not having prosecuted the writ of quo warranto. Consequently, after the overthrow of James II, when officials of the corporation of Connecticut resumed their offices, the Protestant monarchy allowed them to function as before.

20. Petition of Culpeper, Wharton, and others, CO 1/57/f. 178 referred to the Lords of Trade by the king in council, 24 March 1684/5; address of the proprietors of the Narragansett country to the king, received 15 July 1685, CO 1/58/f. 17; petition of Randolph with annexed charges against Rhode Island, read on 15 July 1685, CO 1/58/ff. 18, 20; order in council, 17 July 1685, CO 5/904/pp. 245–46; Randolph to John Povey, 27 June 1686, CW, Blathwayt Papers, vol. 1, no. 48; petition of the inhabitants of Rhode Island, 28 October 1685, CO 1/58/f. 297; protest of Hutchinson, Saffin, and Wharton, 22 March 1685/6, CO 1/59/f. 146.

21. Governor and Company of Rhode Island to the king, 3 July 1686, CO 1/59/ff. 368–69; Walter Newberry to George Whitehead, 3 July 1686, CO 1/59/f. 367; the petition of Richard Smith and other inhabitants, 18 July 1686, CO 1/60/f. 7; Edward Randolph to Andros, 28 July 1686, CW, Blathwayt Papers, vol. 1, no. 48; John Greene to Dongan, 5 August 1686, CO 1/60/f. 50; address of the Quakers, 25 August 1686, CO 1/60/ff. 68–69.

22. Memorandum of the Lords of Trade, 12 September 1686, CO 5/904/pp. 305–6; order in council, 27 May 1687, CO 324/4/p. 240; James II to Andros, 11 March 1686/7, CO 389/9/p. 421.

23. Order in council, 8 April 1685, CO 5/940/pp. 138–39; Robert Mason to the Lords of Trade, 20 August 1685, CO 1/58/ff. 78–79; report of the Lords of Trade, 6 November 1686, and order in council, 4 December 1686, CO 5/904/pp. 156–57, 160–61; petition of the townsmen of New Hampshire, CO 1/59/ff. 360–66.

24. Navy Commissioners to Samuel Pepys, 15 May 1686, PRO, Adm. 1/3555/p. 731.

Chapter 4

1. Clarendon to Rochester, 15 May 1686, *The Correspondence of Henry Hyde, Earl of Clarendon, and of His Brother, Laurence Hyde, Earl of Rochester*, ed. Samuel Weller Singer, 2 vols. (London: Camden Society, 1928), 1:393.

2. Nowell to Richards, 28 March 1683, "The Winthrop Papers," *MHSC*, 5th ser. 1:434–35.

3. Theodore B. Lewis, "Land Speculation and the Dudley Council of 1686," *WMQ*, 3d ser. 31 (April 1974): 255–72.

4. Randolph to the Lords of Trade, 2 September 1685, with enclosed proposals, CO 1/58/ff. 120, 122, 124, 126; Lords of Trade to Sunderland, 26 August 1685, CO 5/904/p. 251; royal commission for Dudley and the councilors, 27 September 1685, CO 5/904/pp. 252–58; order in council, 27 October 1685, PC 2/71/p. 329.

5. Proceedings of the General Court, 18 March 1684/5, *Records of the Gov-*

ernor and Company of the Massachusetts Bay in New England, ed. Nathaniel B. Shurtleff, 5 vols. in 6 (Boston, 1853–54), 5:469; William Dyer to William Blathwayt, 16 November 1685, CW, Blathwayt Papers, vol. 4; entries for 21, 23 July, 19 November 1685, 1 April 1686, in Samuel Sewall, *Diary of Samuel Sewall*, ed. M. Halsey Thomas, 2 vols. (New York: Farrar, Straus, Giroux, 1973), 1:71, 72, 85, 103.

6. Shurtleff, *Records of Massachusetts Bay*, 5:515–16, 517; Sewall, *Diary of Samuel Sewall*, 1:112–15; Randolph to Blathwayt, 29 May 1696, CW, Blathwayt Papers, vol. 1, no. 40. The letter from the General Court to Dudley, 20 May 1686, is CO 1/59/f. 314 (printed in Shurtleff, *Records of Massachusetts Bay*, 5:515–16.)

7. Dudley to Blathwayt, 31 July 1686, CW, Blathwayt Papers, vol. 1, no. 50; Benjamin Bullivant to Randolph, 11 September 1686, CO 1/60/f. 151.

8. Randolph to Archbishop Sancroft, 7 July 1686, *A Collection of Original Papers Relative to the History of Massachusetts Bay*, comp. Thomas Hutchinson, 2 vols. (Boston, 1769), 2:291; Randolph to Sancroft, 2 August 1686, Bodl., MS Tanner 30, ff. 97, 98; the Council of New England to the Lords of Trade, 21 October 1686, CO 1/60/ff. 234–35.

9. Randolph to Blathwayt, 12, 28 July 1686, CW, Blathwayt Papers, vol. 1, nos. 47, 49; Randolph to the Lords of Trade, 23 August 1686, CO 1/60/ff. 62–63; Theodore B. Lewis, "Massachusetts and the Glorious Revolution, 1660–1692" (Ph.D. diss. University of Wisconsin, 1967), pp. 178–93.

10. Povey to Sir Robert Southwell, 12 June, 24 July 1686, NUL, Portland MSS PwV60; Blathwayt's draft, "Reflections on a Paper Concerning America," n.d., HL, Blathwayt Papers, BL416, possibly written in 1686 but perhaps early in 1689, for on 23 March 1688/9, Southwell wrote to the earl of Nottingham (HL, Blathwayt Papers, BL418) that Blathwayt was sending him a paper on colonial administration.

11. Povey to Southwell, 20, 25 May 1686, NUL, Portland MSS PwV60; memoranda in the Plantation Office entry book for New England, 24 March, 25 May 1686, CO 5/904/pp. 270, 282; Lords of Trade to Sunderland, 26 August 1685, CO 5/904/p. 251; Blathwayt to Southwell, 22 May 1686, NUL, Portland MSS PwV53; James II to Andros, 19 October 1686, T 64/88/pp. 206–8.

12. Blathwayt to Southwell, 8 February 1686/7, NUL, Portland MSS PwV53.

13. Sewall, *Diary of Samuel Sewall*, 1:127–31. Lewis, "Massachusetts and the Glorious Revolution," pp. 215–16 considered that by this action Andros was violating his instructions relating to religious toleration and was planning to promote the Church of England at the expense of the Congregational churches.

14. Sewall, *Diary of Samuel Sewall*, 1:130; Fitzjohn Winthrop to John Allyn, 13 January 1686/7, "The Winthrop Papers," *MSHC*, 5th ser. 8:300; Wait Winthrop to Fitzjohn Winthrop, 20 December 1686, MHS, Winthrop Family Papers; minutes of the Council of New England, 30, 31 December 1686, 3, 4, 31 January 1686/7, "The Andros Records," ed. Robert N. Toppan, *Proceedings of the American Antiquarian Society*, n.s. 13 (Worcester, Mass., 1899): 242–46.

15. Randolph to Blathwayt, 3 February 1686/7, CW, Blathwayt Papers, vol. 1, no. 58; Andros's report on the Narragansett country, enclosed in his letter to

the Lords of Trade, 31 August 1687, CO 1/63/ff. 105, 109–10; Randolph to Blathwayt, 21 May 1687, CW, Blathwayt Papers, vol. 1, no. 60; Lewis, "Land Speculation and the Dudley Council," pp. 266–68.

16. The objectionable statement was also later attributed to Robert Mason and to Joseph Dudley. See George Allan Cook, *John Wise: Early American Democrat* (New York: King's Crown Press, 1952), pp. 50–53 and Lewis, "Massachusetts and the Glorious Revolution," pp. 230–36. The evidence for such a statement given at the time of the trial was secondhand and was based apparently on the word of John Wise. Evidence later given was also ex parte, gathered to support the charge that Andros and the councilors had governed illegally and to justify the partisans who had overthrown his government.

17. Andros to the Lords of Trade, 28 November 1687, CO 1/63/f. 316, with enclosed proceedings of the meetings at Ipswich and Topsfield, CO 1/63/ff. 325, 326; and the proceedings against Wise and others of Ipswich, CO 1/63/f. 373.

18. Povey to Southwell, 13 October 1687, NUL, Portland MSS PwV61; Richard Wharton to Wait Winthrop, 17 November 1687, 10 March 1687/8, 26 April 1688, "The Winthrop Papers," *MHSC*, 6th ser. 5:9–10, 14, 16; order in council, 10 February 1687/8, on the petition of Wharton, Shorter, Coxe, and others, PC 2/172/p. 609; order in council, 13 January 1687/8, on the petition of Lord Culpeper and Wharton, CO 1/64/ff. 5, 6; memorandum of the Lords of Trade on mines in New England, 10 October 1686, CO 1/60/f. 198; and report of the Lords of Trade, 10 April 1688, CO 5/905/pp. 8–9.

19. Lewis, "Massachusetts and the Glorious Revolution," pp. 251–62, saw in this policy adopted by Andros a threat to property, but in attacking the governor on this issue as well as on his efforts to obtain some place of worship for Anglican communicants in Boston, Lewis cited ex parte rationalizations published by opponents of Andros's regime after the fact in an effort to prove that the governor had ruled illegally and thus to justify a coup d'etat they had carried out against him. See also Dunn, *Puritans and Yankees*, pp. 248–50, and Sewall, *Diary of Samuel Sewall*, 1:172.

20. Sewall, *Diary of Samuel Sewall*, 1:171.

21. Increase Mather, "The Autobiography of Increase Mather," ed. Michael G. Hall, *Proceedings of the American Antiquarian Society*, n.s. 71, pt. 2 (Worcester, Mass., 1961): 320–21.

22. Randolph to John Povey, 19 October 1688, with enclosures, CO 1/65/ff. 322, 325–30. Mather financed his stay in London—it was to be a long one—in part by borrowing several hundred pounds from the Company for Propagating the Gospel in New England, a society for converting Indians consisting mainly of Dissenting merchants of London, and from a London barrister, the Boston-born Thomas Lake. Mather later married Lake's sister, Anne.

23. Blathwayt to Sir Robert Southwell, 19 June 1688, NUL, Portland MSS PwV53.

24. Mather, "Autobiography of Mather," pp. 325–26, 329–30. See also the extract of a paper by Mather, Samuel Nowell, and Elisha Hutchinson read before the king in July 1688, Leeds Papers, vol. 17 BL, Egerton MSS 3340 f. 179. This

memorial made substantially the same charge against Andros as that related by Mather in his autobiography.

25. Petition of Mather, Nowell, and Hutchinson, n.d., CO 1/65/ff. 162, 163.

26. Petition of Mather, Nowell, and Hutchinson, 10 August 1688, with enclosed proposals, CO 1/65/ff. 90–91, 92.

27. As related in a pamphlet entitled *A Narrative of the Miseries of New-England* issued in London in 1688 and then reprinted in Boston, the clerk of the council board, William Blathwayt, sent to Powis a copy of the petition and proposals submitted by Mather and his colleagues, a copy in which the project for an assembly was omitted. On being asked about this, Blathwayt, according to Mather, replied that Sunderland had affirmed to the clerk that it was by his advice that James II had given a commission to Andros as governor to rule without an assembly and that he, Sunderland, knew that the king would never consent to an alteration of the government for New England. Nor would Sunderland propose it to the monarch. See the version printed in William Henry Whitmore, ed., *The Andros Tracts: Being a Collection of Pamphlets and Official Papers Issued during the Period between the Overthrow of the Andros Government and the Establishment of the Second Charter of Massachusetts*, 3 vols. (Boston, 1868–74), 2:10.

28. Mather, "Autobiography of Mather," p. 331; memorandum of the Lords of Trade, n.d., CO 1/65/f. 165; minute of the Lords of Trade, 17 October 1688, CO 5/905/pp. 76–77; Richard Wharton to Wait Winthrop, 17 October 1688, MHS, Winthrop Family Papers.

Chapter 5

1. Edward F. Carpenter, *The Protestant Bishop: Being the Life of Henry Compton, 1632–1713,. Bishop of London* (London: Longmans, Green, 1956), pp. 154–68, 192.

2. Edward Randolph later reported a rumor circulating in Boston that Increase Mather, Samuel Nowell, and Elisha Hutchinson, with the assistance of Robert Brent, the Catholic solicitor of the king's confessor, Father Petrie, had induced the attorney general, Sir Thomas Powis, to report to the Lords of Trade and Plantations that the Massachusetts charter had been illegally vacated (Randolph to the Lords of Trade, 29 May 1689, CO 5/855/no. 8 [also CO 5/905/pp. 130–41]). The letter was printed in William Henry Whitmore, ed., *The Andros Tracts: Being a Collection of Pamphlets and Official Papers Issued during the Period between the Overthrow of the Andros Government and the Establishment of the Second Charter of Massachusetts*, 3 vols. (Boston, 1868–74), 3:226. There appears to be no other evidence for such a report; indeed, all parties concerned subsequently acted to the contrary. Mather sought to have the charter restored through legislation by Parliament. Viola Barnes, *The Dominion of New England: A Study in British Colonial Policy* (New Haven, Conn.: Yale University Press, 1923), pp. 234, 238, citing only Randolph's letter and an anonymous pamphlet concluded that Powis did so report, that Mather so wrote to Boston, and that his letter arrived there on 10 January 1688/9, when a plot to overthrow Andros was formed. Charles McLean Andrews, in a note to his edition of *Narratives of the*

Insurrections (New York: Charles Scribner's Sons, 1915), p. 254, wrote that Andros—perhaps a slip for Randolph—believed the report had been obtained from Powis. Some persons in New England, learning of James's concession in October 1688 to restore the municipal charters in England, may have believed this applied to the patents of the colonial corporations in New England. See Richard Wharton to Wait Winthrop, London, 18 October 1688, MHS, Winthrop Family Papers. Powis was involved with two New England charters in the summer of 1688, one for the mining company headed by Richard Wharton, the other for Harvard College.

3. On Hampden, Wharton, and the others among the Dissenting political faction, see Douglas R. Lacey, *Dissent and Parliamentary Politics in England, 1661–1689: A Study in the Perpetuation and Tempering of Parliamentarianism* (New Brunswick, N.J.: Rutgers University Press, 1969), pp. 400–402.

4. Leo Francis Stock, ed., *Proceedings and Debates of the British Parliaments Respecting North America,* 5 vols. (Washington, D.C.: Carnegie Institution of Washington, 1924–41), 2:1, 8.

5. The prince of Orange to the colonial governors, 12 January 1688/9, Plantations General entry book, CO 324/5/pp. 34–35; memorandum in the New England entry book, CO 5/905/pp. 41–42; Increase Mather, "The Autobiography of Increase Mather," ed. Michael G. Hall, *Proceedings of the American Antiquarian Society,* n.s. 71 pt. 2 (Worcester, Mass., 1961): 322.

6. See his memorial dated 22 January 1688/9, endorsed in Edward Randolph's hand as transcribed from a printed copy brought over from Holland, CO 5/855/f. 1. Kick later sought a position as consul or purchasing agent for the English army in Europe (Kick to Blathwayt, 4 April, 19 May [n.s.] 1692, BL, Add. MSS 9723, ff. 47, 117).

7. Order in council, 16 February 1688/9, CO 391/6/pp. 195–96; Mather to Sir Henry Ashurst, 18 February 1688/9, "The Mather Papers," *MHSC,* 4th ser. 8:117; petition of Phips and Mather, n.d., with order in council, 18 February 1688/9, CO 5/751/f. 3 (also in Co 5/905/pp. 77–78); order in council, 19 February 1688/9, CO 324/5/p. 36.

8. Minute of the Lords of Trade, 22 February 1688/9 and report of the Lords of Trade to the king, 22 February 1688/9, CO 5/905/pp. 78–80; order in council, 26 February 1688/9, PC 2/73/p. 21.

9. Mather, "Autobiography of Mather," p. 332.

10. Southwell to [Nottingham?], 23 March 1688/9, HL., Blathwayt Papers, BL 418. It might have been at this time that Blathwayt drew up his reflections concerning America (HL, Blathwayt Papers, BL 416). He advised against sending military forces to New England as too expensive.

11. Order in council, 18April 1689, PC 2/73/p. 77.

12. Samuel Sewall, *Dairy of Samuel Sewall,* ed. M. Halsey Thomas, 2 vols. (New York: Farrar, Straus, Giroux, 1973), 1:212–13.

13. Minute of the Lords of Trade, 26 April 1689, CO 391/6/p. 209; memorandum of the Lords of Trade, 26 April 1689, CO 5/723/f. 117; order in council, 2 May 1689, CO 5/1/ff. 4–5.

14. Orders in council, 6, 12 May 1689, PC 2/73/pp. 98, 108, 112; Sewall,

Diary of Samuel Sewall, 1:215–17. The Privy Council Register records no discussion or action on colonial affairs on 18 May.

15. See the reasons alleged in the writ of scire facias for vacating the charter of Massachusetts under date of 29 May 1689 and the memorandum of the Lords of Trade, CO 5/855/ff. 14–15; Lords of Trade to the king, 16 May 1689, CO 324/5/pp. 50–51; memorandum of the Lords of Trade, 16 May 1689, and Lords of Trade to the King, 29 may 1689, CO 5/723/ff. 118, 119.

Chapter 6

1. David S. Lovejoy, *The Glorious Revolution in America* (New York: Harper & Row, 1972), and to a lesser extent Timothy H. Breen, *The Character of a Good Ruler: A Study of Puritan Ideas in New England, 1630–1730* (New Haven, Conn.: Yale University Press, 1970), both stress republican ideology and Puritan commonwealth thought, the former by accepting rationalizations, the latter by an analogy with American revolutionary thought almost a century later. Breen saw the sermons preached by Puritan ministers opposed to the regime of Andros as an honest reflection of contemporary thought about the nature of civil government, yet he offered no standard by which to judge either the sincerity or the representative nature of this thought. He criticized Viola Barnes for her work, *The Dominion of New England,* as having too little sympathy with Puritanism, accusing her of treating the Puritan defense of the revolt as disingenuous propaganda. By viewing the published tracts attacking the Andros regime "as sincere expressions of political beliefs, no matter how outrageous they may now appear," Breen claimed to establish the importance of the revolution in Boston to the development of political ideas (pp. 135–36). Yet the possible future effects of Puritan beliefs, more properly, Puritan charges, does not speak to the motivation of the men who penned them; nor are they necessarily a reflection of what men believed as distinct from what they professed to believe. Ideas familiar to all within a society are not accepted by all within that community. Why do some individuals accept these ideas, find them suitable? Why do others not?

2. Cotton Mather, a principal in the momentous events that spring, apparently destroyed his correspondence with his father in London for this period. His diary over the same span of time seemingly met the same fate. See Theodore B. Lewis, "Massachusetts and the Glorious Revolution, 1660–1692" (Ph.D. diss., University of Wisconsin, 1967), p. 290. Wait Winthrop also played a large role in the overthrow of Andros. Up to January 1689 he wrote frequently from Boston to his brother in Connecticut. But no letters from January through 18 April 1689 seem to have survived in the Winthrop Family Papers.

3. Whatever the validity of the arguments Bernard Bailyn presented respecting the political ideology expressed in the pamphlet literature of the American Revolution, his earlier comments about the rebellion in Massachusetts in 1689 have great merit. See his "Communications and Trade: The Atlantic in the Seventeenth Century," *Journal of Economic History* 31 (Fall 1953): 386.

4. Wait Wintrhop to Fitzjohn Winthrop, 5 January 1688/9, "The Winthrop Papers," *MHSC,* 5th ser. 8:489; John Allyn to Wait Winthrop, 15 April 1689, ibid., 6th ser. 5:19; Richard Wharton to Wait Winthrop, 18 October 1688, MHS, Winthrop Family Papers.

5. John West to Fitzjohn Winthrop, 23 February 1688/9, MHS, Winthrop Family Papers.

6. See the depositions and testimony in James P. Baxter, ed., *Documentary History of the State Maine,* ser. 2 of the *Collections of the Maine Historical Society,* 24 vols. (Portland, 1831–1906), 4:446–47, 5:28–29, 6:472–73.

7. See Richard S. Dunn, *Puritans and Yankees: The Winthrop Dynasty of New England, 1630–1717* (Princeton, N.J.: Princeton University Press, 1962), pp. 254–55. G. B. Warden, *Boston 1689–1776* (Boston: Little Brown, 1970), pp. 8–10, appreciated that the precision and timing of the events of that day are suspicious and acknowledged the possibility of a planned effort against Andros, but, he speculated, since the Bostonians were a resourceful people who could be expected to act appropriately at a moment's notice, the uprising "may indeed have been a purely spontaneous act."

8. There are several analyses of the coup. Lewis, "Massachusetts and the Glorious Revolution," pp. 290–325 is generally favorable to the insurgents. Viola Barnes, *The Dominion of New England: A Study in British Colonial Policy* (New Haven, Conn.: Yale University Press, 1923), pp. 239–44, is skeptical. Dunn, *Puritans and Yankees,* pp. 254–56; Guy Howard Miller, "Rebellion in Zion: The Overthrow of the Dominion of New England," *Historian* 30 (May 1968): 441–57; and Jeanne Gould Bloom, "Sir Edmund Andros: A Study in Seventeenth Century Colonial Administration," (Ph.D. diss., Yale University, 1962), p. 138 are generally balanced.

9. The declaration is printed in William Henry Whitmore, ed., *The Andros Tracts: Being a Collection of Pamphlets and Official Papers Issued during the Period between the Overthrow of the Andros Government and the Establishment of the Second Charter of Massachusetts,* 3 vols. (Boston, 1868–74), 1:13–19.

10. Bradstreet and the revolutionary council to William III, 20 May 1689, CO 5/855/ff. 8–9.

11. See those printed in Whitmore, *Andros Tracts,* and Charles McLean Andrews, *Narratives of the Insurrections* (New York: Charles Scribner's Sons, 1915). For a rebuttal to these accounts, see *The Revolution Justified,* in *Tracts and other Papers Relating Principally to the Origin, Settlement, and Progress of the Colonies in North America . . . to . . . 1776,* comp. Peter Force, reprinted from the 1836–46 ed., 4 vols. (Gloucester, Mass.: Peter Smith, 1963), vol. 4, no. 9.

12. Randolph to Blathwayt, 4 June 1689, CW, Blathwayt Papers, vol. 1, no. 83. See also the printed sheet, *The Case of Massachusetts Colony Considered in a Letter to a Friend in Boston, May 18, 1689,* CO 5/855/f. 5; Captain John George's report to Samuel Pepys, secretary to the Navy Board, 12 June 1689, CO 5/855/ff. 10–13; and the narrative submitted by John Riggs, a messenger employed by Andros, 16 July 1689, CO 5/855/ff. 35–36.

13. See Bernard Bailyn, *The New England Merchants in the Seventeenth*

Century (Cambridge, Mass.: Harvard University Press, 1955), p. 176, and the paper signed by C. D., "An Answer to the Account of the Revolution at Boston," CO 1/67/ff. 263–65.

14. "A Short Account of the Loss of Pemaquid Fort," 3 August 1689, CO 5/855/ff. 75–76.

15. Memorandum of the Lords of Trade, 16 July 1689, Co 5/905/pp. 81–85; Jephson to Blathwayt, 23 July 1689, CO 5/855/f. 64; order in council, 25 July 1689, and the letter from the king to Massachusetts, 30 July 1689, CO 5/905/pp. 107–8; and the royal letter to those administering the government in Boston, countersigned by Shrewsbury, 12 August 1689, CO 5/751/f. 4.

16. See the reports of Edward Randolph to Francis Nicholson, 29 July 1689, CO 5/855/f. 70; Randolph to Blathwayt, 30 July 1689, CW, Blathwayt Papers, vol. 1, no. 86; and Randolph to the lord privy seal, 23 July 1689, CO 5/855/f. 51.

17. Declaration of the convention, 24 May 1689, and the answer of the governor and council, CO 5/855/ff. 44, 45; the declaration by the gentlemen of Boston for preserving order, 25 May 1689, "The Winthrop Papers," *MHSC*, 5th ser. 8:491–92; the addresses to the crown, 20 May, 6 June 1689, CO 5/855/ff. 24–25, 77–78; Lewis, "Massachusetts and the Glorious Revolution," pp. 327–34; and Dunn, *Puritans and Yankees*, pp. 255–57.

18. See Richard C. Simmons, "The Massachusetts Charter of 1691," in *Contrast and Connection: Bicentennial Essays in Anglo-American History*, ed. H. C. Allen and Roger Thompson (Athens: Ohio University Press, 1976), pp. 2–4.

19. Resolutions of the Massachusetts convention, CO 5/855/ff. 55, 56.

20. Randolph to Blathwayt, 28 October 1689, CW, Blathwayt Papers, vol. 1, no. 92.

21. James Lloyd to Thomas Brinley, 10 July 1689, CO 5/855/f. 33; extracts of Francis Brinley to Thomas Brinley, 16 July 1689, Benjamin Davis to Edward Hull, 31 July 1689, John Legg to John Browne, 14 August 1689, CO 5/855/f. 80; Bradstreet to the Lords of Trade, 26 October 1689, CO 5/855/f. 113; and the extract of a letter sent from Boston to John Usher, 10 July 1689, CO 5/855/f. 33.

22. The pamphlet was printed with a short introduction and notes by C. J. Hoadly in *CHSC*, 3:79–269. See also Bulkeley to Robert Treat and the other justices, 8 May 1689, H. L., Blathwayt Papers, BL285.

23. Address of the colony of Connecticut to the king, 13 June 1689, and Whiting to Treat, 12 August 1689, *Public Records of the Colony of Connecticut (1636–1776)*, ed. J. H. Trumbull and C. J. Hoadly, 15 vols. (Hartford, Conn., 1850–90), 3:463–66, 469.

24. James Porter to Robert Treat, 8 May 1690, *CHSC*, 24:29–30.

25. Address of the General Court of New Plymouth, 6 June 1689, CO 5/855/ff. 26–27.

26. Brinley to Wait Winthrop, 6 May 1689, "The Winthrop Papers," *MHSC*, 6th ser. 5:20–21. See also Sidney V. James, *Colonial Rhode Island: A History* (New York: Charles Scribner's Sons, 1975), pp. 109–10; and the extract of an unsigned letter from Newport, dated 7 July 1689, transmitted to the Committee for Trade and Plantations by John Usher of Boston, CO 5/855/f. 34.

Chapter 7

1. William J. Eccles, *Frontenac, the Courtier Governor* (Toronto: McClelland and Stewart, 1959), pp. 192–203; *Canada Under Louis XIV, 1663–1701* (New York: Oxford University Press, 1964), pp. 161–64; and Robert A. Goldstein, *French-Iroquois Diplomatic and Military Relations, 1609–1701* (The Hague: Mouton, 1969), pp. 163–67.

2. J. P. Kenyon, *The Popish Plot* (London: Heinemann, 1972), p. 151.

3. Charles Howard McCormick, "Leisler's Rebellion," (Ph.D. diss., American University, 1971), p. 11, and to some extent, Philip Haffenden, *New England in the English Nation, 1689–1713* (New York: Oxford University Press, 1974), p. 16, argue that men genuinely believed, sincerely feared, the threat from Catholicism and the French monarchy. But what must be explained is why, if such ideas were known to all men within English society, they were "believed" or accepted by some and not others.

4. For an example of the charges made against Nicholson, Bayard, Van Cortlandt, and Philipse, see "The Case of Cap[tain Jacob] Leisler Deceased and Others," submitted by his son of the same name and by Abraham Gouverneur to the English authorities, (Portland Papers, BL, Loan 39/289). The case for their opponents is discussed in this chapter. See also Charles McLean Andrews, *Narratives of the Insurrections* (New York: Charles Scribner's Sons, 1915), pp. 315–400.

5. The following account is based mainly on the journal of Stephanus Van Cortlandt for the period 1 March to 2 July 1689, CO 5/1183/pp. 148–60; Nicholas Bayard's journal, 11 June to 5 July 1689, CO 5/1183/pp. 134–46; and the documents individually cited in the notes below.

6. Declarations, dated 3, 10 May 1689, CO 5/1081/f. 3.

7. Declaration of Bartholomew le Roux, 26 September 1689, CO 5/1081/f. 164.

8. Nicholson and the council to the Lords of Trade, 15 May 1689, CO 5/905/pp. 81–84.

9. Another member of Cuyler's company, Gilbert Bosch, *later* deposed that during the alleged incident, he was outside the window of Nicholson's room and heard him say, "If they should any more so trouble him he would sett ye town a fire." The printed manifesto is in CO 5/858/f. 256; a manuscript version of Cuyler's deposition is in CO 5/1081/f. 53; Bosch's deposition, dated 10 June 1689, is in CO 5/1081/f. 58.

10. Declaration of 31 May 1689, CO 5/1081/f. 14; deposition of Dischington, 5 June 1689, CO 5/1081/no. 16 (vii); and the deposition of Philip French, 7 June 1689, CO 5/1081/no. 16(viii).

11. Address of the militia of New York to William and Mary, ? June 1689, CO 5/1018/no. 31.

12. Bayard's journal, 10 June–5 July 1689, CO 5/1183/pp. 134–46; Van Cortlandt's narrative in his letter to Andros, 9 July 1689, Co 5/1183/pp. 148–60.

13. See the abstract of the proceedings of the committee of safety, 27 June–15 August 1689, CO 5/1081/no. 46.

14. See the Albany convention to [Colonel Henry Sloughter], 20 January 1689/90, in the hand of Robert Livingston, FDRL, Livingston Family Papers, Robert Livingston General Correspondence.

15. George McKenzie to Francis Nicholson, 19 August 1689, CO 5/1081/f. 142; deposition by Lodowyck, 25 July 1689, CO 5/1081/f. 87; Nicholas Bayard to ———, 23 September 1689, CO 5/1081/ff. 161–62; depositions of Mollenax, Shute, Witt, and Browne, CO 5/1081/ff. 99, 159.

16. Leisler to William and Mary, 20 August 1689, CO 5/1081/f. 143; abstract of the proceedings of the committee of safety, 15 August 1689, CO 5/1081/no. 46.

17. Memoranda of the Committee for plantation Affairs, 3, 16 July 1689, CO 5/1/f. 16, CO 5/905/p. 81; William III to Nicholson, 20 July 1689, CO 5/1081/f. 88. (The copy of the entry book, CO 5/1113/pp. 194–95, is dated 30 July 1689.)

18. Pass for Riggs, 6 August 1689, CO 5/1113/pp. 195–96; draft letter by the Lords of Trade, 29 July 1689, with the proclamation to be sent to New York, CO 5/1113/pp. 192, 194; order in council, 8 August 1689, PC 2/73/p. 208.

19. Council of New York to Shrewsbury, 10 June 1689, Co 5/1081/ff. 27–28; memorandum of the Committee for Plantation Affairs, 31 August 1689, CO 5/1113/pp. 202–3; and warrant dated 1 September 1689, CO 324/22/pp. 123–24.

20. Reasons offered for preserving New York, presented by Sloughter, CO 5/1081/f. 171.

21. Representation given to Shrewsbury by Stoll, 16 November 1689; account by Stoll, 16 November 1689, CO 5/1081/ff. 182–85; petition by the merchants, with annexed paper of reasons, CO 5/1081/ff. 207, 209; and the lists of the names of the men nominated by Sloughter for the council, CO 5/1081/ff. 215–16.

22. See the information gathered on him, Bodl., Rawlinson MSS A, vol. 175, f. 83.

23. The best factual account of the revolt in New York in McCormick, "Leisler's Rebellion." The best analysis is Lawrence H. Leder, "The Glorious Revolution and the Pattern of Imperial Relationships," *New York History* 46 (July 1965): 203–11. In a valuable article, Milton Klein, "Politics and Personalities in Colonial New York," *New York History* 47 (January 1966): 3–16, agreed that Leisler was no proletarian, that he represented the men of moderate wealth who aspired to a place in the provincial political hierarchy as against those already entrenched in positions of power. But Klein also argued that the frustrated ambitions of the insurgent leaders do not fully explain the Leislerian movement. In this chapter I have suggested that there may well not have been an extensive movement, that opposton to the dominion did not mean support for Leisler, and that many men in the province did not accept Leisler until compelled to do so.

24. Van Cortlandt to [Nicholson] 18 December 1689, CW, Blathwayt Papers, vol. 9.

25. John E. Pomfret, *The Province of West New Jersey, 1609–1702: A History of the Origins of an American Colony* (Princeton, N.J., Princeton University Press, pp. 162, 170; and H. Clay Reed and George J. Miller, eds., *The Burlington Court Book: A Record of Quaker Jurisdiction in West New Jersey, 1680–1709*, (Washington: American Historical Association, 1944), p. xxxiii.

Chapter 8

1. See the minutes of the council of Pennsylvania, 29 June 1689, in *Pennsylvania Archives*, ed. Samuel Hazard et al., 119 vols. in 9 series (Philadelphia and Harrisburg: State of Pennsylvania, 1852–1935), 4th ser. 1:138–39; and the deposition of John Forat, justice at Newcastle, 4 October 1689, CO 5/1081/f. 168.

2. Blackwell to Penn, 13 January 1689/90, HSP, Blackwell Letters; and Edwin B. Bronner, *William Penn's "Holy Experiment": The Founding of Pennsylvania, 1681–1701* (New York: Temple University Press, 1962), pp. 109, 112, 113.

3. Blackwell to Penn [25 February 1688/9], HSP, Blackwell Letters.

4. Growdon, Simcocke, and others to Penn, [9 April 1689], HSP, Penn MSS, Official Correspondence, 1:11; Bronner, *Penn's Holy Experiment*, pp. 120–23; Roy N. Lokken, *David Lloyd: Colonial Lawmaker* (Seattle: University of Washington Press, 1959), pp. 29–36.

5. Penn to the council, 12 August 1689, Penn to Blackwell, 25 September 1689, HSP, Dreer Collection, Penn Letters and Papers; Blackwell to Penn, 13 January 1689/90, HSP, Blackwell Letters.

6. See the unsigned, undated account presented to Sothell by the opponents of Colleton, CO 5/287/ff. 75–80.

7. Hugh Rankin, *Upheaval in Albemarle: The Story of Culpeper's Rebellion* (Raleigh: North Carolina Charter Tercentenary Commission, 1962), pp. 58–59.

8. Proprietors to Sothell, 2 December 1689, instructions to Ludwell, 5 December 1689, CO 5/288/f. 80.

9. William Byrd to ———, 10 June 1689, *Virginia Magazine of History and Biography* 24 (January 1918): 27.

10. See the petitions by Ludwell, CO 5/1305/ff. 21, 51–52; and his particulars of grievances, CO 5/1305/f. 50. The governor's defense is in his letters to the Lords of Trade, 23 May, 16 October 1689, CO 5/1305/ff. 36–38, 56–61.

11. Spencer to Blathwayt, 1 March, 10 June 1689, CW, Blathwayt Papers, vols, 16, 18; Spencer to the Lords of Trade, 29 April 1689, CO 5/1305/ff. 30–31; William Fitzhugh to George Duke, 27 October 1690, *William Fitzhugh and His Chesapeake World, 1676–1701: The Fitzhugh Letters and Other Documents*, ed. Richard Beale Davis (Chapel Hill: University of North Carolina Press, 1963), pp. 287–88; W. Stitt Robinson, *The Southern Colonial Frontier, 1607–1763* (Albuquerque: University of New Mexico Press, 1979), pp. 70–71. Philip Haffenden, *New England in the English Nation, 1689–1713* (New York: Oxford University Press, 1974), p. 27, concluded that the Indian who brought the news of the alleged Catholic plot to light was killed before he could be questioned, but as evidenced by Spencer's letter to Blathwayt of 10 June 1689, the provincial secretary was able to question the native.

12. Council of Virginia to the Lords of Trade, 22 October 1689, CO 5/1305/ff. 63–64; order in council on a draft of a commission to Nicholson, 14 November 1689, and instructions to Nicholson, CO 5/1357/pp. 302–3, 305. See also the instructions to Lord Howard of Effingham, 9 October 1689, CO 5/1357/pp. 319–39. From the petition Ludwell submitted on 20 November 1689

(CO 5/1305/f. 66), it is clear the crown had ignored his complaints against the governor.

13. Lorena S. Walsh, "Charles County, Maryland, 1658–1705: A Study of Chesapeake Social and Political Structure," (Ph.D. diss., Michigan State University, 1977).

14. Richard A. Gleissner, "Religious Causes of the Glorious Revolution in Maryland," *Maryland Historical Magazine* 64 (Winter 1969): 329–30, and especially, Lois G. Carr and David Jordan, *Maryland's Revolution of Government, 1689–1692* (Ithaca, N.Y.: Cornell University Press, 1974).

15. Report of the Maryland committee of secrecy, 4 September 1689, with memorandum of the Lords of Trade, CO 5/718/f. 9.

16. See the entry book of the Lords of Trade for Maryland under dates of 30 August, 12 September 1689, CO 5/723/pp. 121, 123–24.

17. Declaration of Jowles and others, [27 March 1689], CO 5/718/f. 7. For the rumors in Maryland as they reached Virginia and Pennsylvania, see Nicholas Spencer to William Blathwayt, 10 June 1689, CW, Blathwayt Papers, vol. 18, and the minutes of the governor and council of Pennsylvania, 29 June 1689, *Pennsylvania Archives*, 4th ser. 1:138–39.

18. See the letter sent from the Patuxent River by Paul Bertrand to the bishop of London, 12 September 1689, CO 5/718/ff. 44–45; and David Jordan, "John Coode, Perennial Rebel," *Maryland Historical Magazine* 70 (Spring 1975): 15.

19. The declaration is printed in Charles McLean Andrews, *Narratives of the Insurrections*, (New York: Charles Scribner's Sons, 1915), pp. 305–13. See also Richard A. Gleissner, "The Establishment of Royal Government in Maryland: A Study of Crown Policy and Provincial Politics, 1680–1700," (Ph.D. diss., University of Maryland, 1968), p. 48. Another version of the insurgents' complaints, "Mariland's Grevances Wiy The[y] Have Taken of Arms," ed. Beverly McAnear, is printed in the *Journal of Southern History* 8 (August 1942): 396–409.

20. Address of the Protestants to William and Mary, 3 August 1689, CO 5/718/f. 16.

21. Declaration of Calvert County, 20 August 1689, CO 5/718/f. 12.

22. See the analysis in David William Jordan, "The Royal Period of Colonial Maryland, 1689–1715," (Ph.D. diss., Princeton University, 1966), pp. 22–26.

23. See the copy of the report in CO 5/718/f. 9 with the comment by Baltimore made before the Lords of Trade.

24. Hill to Baltimore, 20 September 1689, Smith and Taney to Paul Bertrand, 10 September 1689, in Bertrand to the bishop of London, 12 September 1689, Richard John to Samuel Groome, 27 September 1689, and Carroll to Baltimore, 25 September 1689, CO 5/718/ff. 34–37, 44–45.

25. See the memorandum of Smith's case and his statement, 16 December 1689, the narrative of his wife Barbara Smith, 30 December 1689, and Darnall's narrative, 31 December 1689, CO 5/718/ff. 29–33, 48.

26. Peter Sayres to Baltimore, 31 December 1689, CO 5/718/ff. 46–47.

27. The loyalist petitions are in CO 5/718/ff. 67–70, 77; those favoring the insurgents in CO 5/718/ff. 58, 61–66.

28. Coode to the Lords of Trade, 17 December 1689, CO 5/718/f. 59.

Chapter 9

1. Order in Council of 26 February 1688/9 on the report of the Lords of Trade of 22 February 1688/9, PC 2/73/p. 21. See also the entries for 19, 21, 26 February 1688/9, in Edward Southwell's book of Privy Council memoranda, BL, Add. MSS 38861, ff. 33, 35, 37, 38.

2. Increase Mather, "The Autobiography of Increase Mather," ed. Michael G. Hall, *Proceedings of the American Antiquarian Society*, n.s. 71, pt. 2 (Worcester, Mass., 1961): 332–33; Samuel Sewall, *Diary of Samuel Sewall*, ed. M. Halsey Thomas, 2 vols., (New York: Farrar, Straus, Giroux, 1973), 1:215.

3. See the reasons for vacating the Massachusetts charter, 29 May 1689 and the attached memorandum on the other colonies, CO 5/855/ff. 14–15.

4. Thomas, *Diary of Samuel Sewall*, 1:224, 232; Hall, "Autobiography of Mather," pp. 332–33; Mather to Governor Thomas Hinckley of Plymouth, 12 September 1689, "Hinckley Papers," *MHSC*, 4th ser. 5:209–10.

5. Orders in council, 25, 30 July 1689, CO 5/905/pp. 107, 108; printed addresses of 20 May and 6 June with annotations of 7 August 1689, CO 5/855/ff. 77–78; royal letter of 12 August 1689, CO 5/751/f. 4; Hall, "Autobiography of Mather," pp. 340–41; and Mather to Baron Wharton, 11 September 1689, Bodl., MS Rawlinson, 51, f. 329.

6. Presentments of the Customs Board, 23 August, 2 October 1689, CO 5/855/ff. 83, 93; minute of the Treasury Board, 21 October 1689, T 29/7/126; and minutes on the exemplification, CO 5/905/pp. 42–75.

7. Leo Francis Stock, ed., *Proceedings and Debates of the British Parliaments respecting North America*, 5 vols. (Washington, D.C.: Carnegie Institution of Washington, 1924–41), 2:8; Halifax's notes of his conversation with William III, in Helen Charlotte Foxcroft, ed., *The Life and Letters of Sir George Savile, Bart., First Marquis of Halifax*, 2 vols. (London, 1898), 2:244; HMC, *The Manuscripts of the House of Lords*, 1st ser., vol. 2, *Twelfth Report* (London: HMC, 1889), app., pt. 6, pp. 442–49.

8. Proceedings on the petition of Mather and Sir William Phips, 18 February 1689/90, SP 44/235/p. 53; Mather to Thomas Hinckley, 24 May 1690, *MHSC*, 4th ser. 5:254–55. The attempt to link the restoration of the provincial charters with those of the English boroughs inspired a pamphlet debate. See the printed piece, *Considerations Humbly Offered to the Parliament*, CO 5/856/ff. 460–63; the memorandum on the bill for restoring charters, CO 5/856/f. 485; the reasons against restoring the several charters, CO 5/856/f. 483; and the *Reasons for the Confirmation of the Charters*, CO 5/856/ff. 470–72.

9. See the paper lising objections against Andros, 14 April 1690, with memorandum, CO 5/855/f. 198 and CO 5/905/pp. 194–95.

10. Minute of the Lords of Trade, 17 April 1690, CO 391/6/p. 323; order in council, 24 April 1690, CO 5/905/pp. 188–89; Increase Mather's notes on the hearing and Thomas Brinley to Francis Brinley, 28 May 1690, in Theodore B. Lewis, ed., "Sir Edmund Andros's Hearing before the Lords of Trade and Plantations, April 17, 1690: Two Unpublished Accounts," *Proceedings of the American Antiquarian Society* n.s. 83, pt. 2 (Worcester, Mass., 1974): 243–50; and

Elisha Cooke to Simon Bradstreet, 16 October 1690, *Proceedings of the Massachusetts Historical Society*, 2d ser. 45 (Boston, 1912): 644–50. The crucial aspect of the proceedings was the failure of the agents to take responsibility for highly improbable charges made against Andros. Theodore B. Lewis, "Massachusetts and the Glorious Revolution, 1660–1692" (Ph.D. diss., University of Wisconsin, 1967), p. 351, thought that Somers, although counsel for the agents, was acting in collusion with Treby, who represented the officials of the dominion. For this he offered no evidence. In the account Cooke sent Bradstreet, it was Humphreys, the solicitor employed by the agents, not Somers, who advised there was no need for anyone to sign the accusations against Andros.

11. Address of various gentlemen, merchants, and others, 25 January 1689/90, CO 5/855/f. 153; the address from Maine, 25 January 1689/90, CO 5/855/ff. 151–52; address of the Anglicans of Boston, CO 5/855/ff. 156–57; address from Charleston, CO 5/855/ff. 158–59.

12. Paper by Andros, 27 May 1690, CO 5/855/ff. 265–68.

13. Blathwayt to Sir Robert Southwell, 2 August 1690, Greenwich, National Maritime Museum, Southwell Papers, Phillips MSS Sou 1/93–94.

14. The opinions of Ward, Somers, and Treby, 2 August 1690, "The Trumbull Papers," *MHSC*, 5th ser. 9:175–77.

15. Nottingham to Sir Robert Southwell, 26 August 1690, National Maritime Museum, Phillips MSS, Southwell Papers, Sou 13; Hall "Autobiography of Mather," p. 328.

16. Proposals by the Massachusetts agents, 1 January 1690/1, CO 5/855/f. 354 (also in the Massachusetts Bay entry book, CO 5/905/p. 258); abstract of the Massachusetts charter and of further powers desired, CO 5/856/f. 513; and heads of the charter granted to Ferdinando Gorges in 1639, CO 5/856/ff. 487–90.

17. Petition of Samuel Allen, 30 March 1691, CO 5/914/f. 5; copy of the opinion of chief justices Rainsford and North, 17 July 1676, CO 5/914/ff. 10–11; and Ashurst, Mather, Cooke, and Oakes to the Lords of Trade, 4 May 1691, CO 5/924/f. 13.

18. Undated extract of a letter to John Usher, CO 5/856/f. 377; address presented by Temple to the secretary of state on 9 April 1691, CO 5/856/ff. 387, 398; the petition in manuscript and in print, CO 5/856/ff. 391–93, 395; undated letter from Boston received at the Plantation Office on 27 May 1691, CO 5/856/f. 533.

19. Account of persons who signed the Boston and Charleston addresses, CO 5/856/ff. 414–15; the agents to the Lords of Trade, [21 April 1691], CO 5/856/ff. 404–5; and the list of persons to be consulted on New England, CO 5/856/f. 523.

20. Increase Mather, "The Autobiography of Increase Mather," ed. Michael G. Hall, *Proceedings of the American Antiquarian Society*, n.s. 71, pt. 2 (Worcester, Mass., 1961): 333–35.

21. Minute of the Lords of Trade, 22 April 1691, CO 5/856/f. 406; memorandum of the Lords of Trade for the lord president, CO 5/905/p. 269; and Hall, "Autobiography of Mather," pp. 335–36.

22. Order in council, 30 April 1691, PC 2/73/p. 161; Mather, "Autobiography of Mather," p. 336.

23. See the documents included in CO 5/856/no. 158, especially no. 158(xxx), the paper labeled, "Powers Wanting in the Massachusetts Charters." On the objections to the proposed franchise, see CO 5/856/f. 450.

24. See the heads of a charter for Massachusetts, CO 5/856/no. 158(xxxv), f. 521 and the minute for the draft charter, CO 5/905/p. 273.

25. Proposals offered by the New England agents, CO 5/856/f. 578.

26. Observations on the draft charter, CO 5/856/ff. 580–86.

27. Minutes of the Committee for Plantation Affairs, 9, 17 July 1691, CO 5/905/pp. 274–75, 276; minute on the abstract of the charter, 29 July 1691, minute of the Committee for Trade, 29 July 1691, CO 5/856/ff. 596, 598; order of the Queen in council, 30 July 1691, PC 2/73/pp. 220–21 (also in CO 5/905/pp. 279–81).

28. Nottingham to William III, 31 July 1691, in HMC, *Report on the Manuscripts of the Late Allan George Finch*, 4 vols. (London: HMC, 1913–65), 3:187. Ironically, years later Mather wrote to the Tory earl thanking him for the kindness he had shown him when agent for Massachusetts (Mather to [Nottingham], 8 December 1703, Hatton-Finch Papers, BL. Add. MSS 29549, f. 111.)

29. Sydney to Nottingham, 10 August 1691, Nottingham to Sydney, 18 August 1691, minutes of the cabinet council, 18 August 1691, HMC, *Finch Manuscripts*, 3:199, 217, 405.

30. Minutes of the Lords of Trade, 20 August, 2 September 1691, CO 5/905/pp. 293, 295; petition of Mather and Ashurst, 27 August 1691, CO 5/856/f. 612.

31. Three petitions of Samuel Allen, one dated 7 September 1691, two undated, CO 5/924/ff. 23, 28, 32; order of the king in council, 21 January 1691/2, CO 5/924/f. 34; minute of the Lords of Trade, 11 January 1691/2, CO 5/940/p. 182.

32. Draft charter by Treby, 6 September 1691, CO 5/856/ff. 622–60.

33. Order in council, 17 September 1691, PC 5/1/p. 170; "Concerning the Draught . . . ," n.d., but endorsed as received from Mather on 15 September 1691, CO 5/856/f. 664; and the names of the officials submitted on 18 September 1691, CO 5/856/f. 666.

34. Wiswall to Hinckley, 17 October 1690, Hinckley to Wiswall, 17 October 1691, Wiswall to Hinckley, 5 November 1691, "The Hinckley Papers," *MHSC*, 4th ser. 5:276–78, 293, 299.

35. G. B. Warden, *Boston, 1689–1776* (Boston: Little, Brown, 1970), pp. 37–40. Warden also saw a narrow favoritism in Mather's selections for the council: six of the eleven councilors from Boston belonged to Mather's own church, two others lived in the North end, and another was Cotton Mather's father-in-law. This and the apparent resentment of the voters in the South end over the selections notwithstanding, the slate nominated by Mather for the most part constituted a good cross-section of the revolutionary group in the colony.

36. Lewis, "Massachusetts and the Glorious Revolution," pp. 329–31, perhaps did not emphasize this, choosing instead to stress the support for the governmental institutions of the old charter. Yet the shift in the qualifications for the franchise struck at the crux of the old religious bias. Warden, *Boston,* p. 35, remarked that by the property restrictions for voting in the new charter, only fifty

Bostonians on the basis of the tax lists for 1687 could qualify and that the number of eligible voters in Boston was reduced by at least 85 percent. Warden did not specify whether the reduction was in the number of voters for provincial, as distinct from town, elections. Moreover, as Warden himself realized, what was critical was the method used in assessing the value of property. Since property before 1691 was assessed not so much to determine voting eligibility as to fix a tax liability, it was grossly undervalued. A ratable estate was the amount of property local officials chose to evaluate. Previous assessments had been made "not on the full value of property but only on its annual income or rent, perhaps a quarter or a sixth of the full value." When Elisha Cooke became tax commissioner in Boston after 1692, the number of voters doubled, "nearly equal to the number of town voters under the old charter" (Warden, *Boston,* p. 42–43). Boston under the old charter probably had a much higher percentage of voters than any other town in the colony.

37. Mather, "Autobiography of Mather," pp. 336–37. From the letter Blathwayt sent to Joseph Dudley, 2 February 1692/3, CW, Blathwayt Papers, vol. 4, it is clear Blathwayt had little to do with, and even disapproved of, the appointments to the council of Massachusetts.

38. The commission to Phips and the additional clauses approved on 27 November 1691, CO 5/856/no. 207, f. 700.

39. The lords justices of the council bitterly complained almost four years later that since the commissioning of Phips, it could hardly be said that a governor in Massachusetts had been of the king's appointment, it having been thought fit in 1691 "to gratify them with a governor of their own nomination who was sent only with a provision to be granted by the assembly" (report of the Lord Justices, 16 July 1695, Southwell Papers, BL, Add. MSS 21494, f. 37).

40. Increase Mather to Nottingham, 23 June 1692, CO 5/751/f. 12; Nottingham to Blathwayt, 9 August 1692, National Maritime Museum, Southwell Papers, Phillips MSS, Sou/14; and Phips to Nottingham, 12 October 1692, CO 5/751/f. 21.

Chapter 10

1. Circular letter of 1 February 1688/9, Plantations General entry book of the Committee for Trade and Plantations, CO 324/22/pp. 205–6; Jephson to William Blathwayt, 23 July 1689, CO 5/855/f. 64.

2. James Rees Jones, *The Revolution of 1688 in England* (New York: Norton, 1972), pp. 322–25; George Stepney to Baron Lexington, 13/23 February 1694/5, BL, Add. MSS 46535, f. 11.

3. See, for example, the problem of the Whigs in filling the Customs Board: Somers to the king, 15 June 1694, SP 8/15/no. 22, ff. 62–64; and Shrewsbury to the king, 15 June 1694, SP 8/15/no. 29, ff. 66–68.

4. See Southwell's book of Privy Council memoranda and his Privy Council notes, BL, Add. MSS 38861, f. 125 and Add. MSS 34349, ff. 14, 19; and the second volume of the establishment and accounts of the committee for Plantation Affairs kept by Blathwayt, BL, Add. MSS 9767, pp. 1–2.

5. Robert Southwell, a veteran clerk at the council, drew up a memorandum

on 6 March 1688/9 on the functions of the office when Nottingham became secretary of state. While in this office Nottingham should think of "Spys and Intelligence" where needed abroad and "the like more specially at Home, in several ports of the kingdom and in particular to know what passed in London and at the Royal Exchange," where merchants congregated. To this end a secretary of state ought to cultivate substantial merchants in each of the trades to learn not only the state of affairs at home but in the several countries where they maintained commercial correspondents (BL, Add. MSS 38861, f. 47).

6. See Stephen B. Baxter, *William III and the Defense of European Liberty, 1650–1702* (New York: Harcourt, Brace & World, 1966), pp. 285–326, and Gertrude A. Jacobsen, *William Blathwayt, a late Seventeenth-Century Administrator* (New Haven, Conn.: Yale University Press, 1932), p. 255, as correctives to Stephen Saunders Webb, "William Blathwayt, Imperial Fixer: Muddling Through to Empire, 1689–1717," *WMQ,* 3d ser. 26 (July 1969): 378. There was no such position as secretary of war and plantations. Blathwayt held the post of ordinary clerk of the council assigned to the committee for plantation affairs and the office of secretary at war, a position he purchased in 1683 from Matthew Locke. The latter position was purely administrative, not political in any sense.

7. See, for example, the efforts to find employment for George Stepney, a minor English diplomat, in Stepney to Blathwayt, 10/20 July 1694, Stepney to Charles Montagu, 11/21 October 1695, SP 105/54; and Jacobsen, *Blathwayt,* pp. 142–43, 307.

8. Tucker to Ellis, 28 March 1694, John Ellis Papers, BL, Add. MSS 28878, f. 170.

9. Mulgrave's memorandum for the king, n.d., SP 8/13/no. 7, f. 10; George Stepney to ———, 30 October/9 November 1694, SP 105/55.

10. Henry Horwitz, *Revolution Politicks: The Career of Daniel Finch, Second Earl of Nottingham, 1647–1730* (London and New York: Cambridge University Press, 1968), pp. 86–93; Edward F. Carpenter, *Thomas Tenison, Archbishop of Canterbury: His Life and Times* (London: Society for Promoting Christian Knowledge, 1948), pp. 97, 113, 164; George Every, *The High Church Party, 1688–1715* (London: Society for Promoting Christian Knowledge, 1956), pp. 31–61; and Norman Sykes, *From Sheldon to Secker: Aspects of English Church History, 1660–1768* (Cambridge: Cambridge University Press, 1959), pp. 85–92. On support in the House of Commons for the maintenance of Anglican privileges, see the debate on the bill sent down from the House of Lords for allowing Quakers to substitute a solemn declaration for an oath, in Narcissus Luttrell, *The Parliamentary Diary of Narcissus Luttrell, 1691–1693,* ed. Henry Horwitz (Oxford: Oxford University Press, Clarendon Press, 1972), p. 198.

11. Instructions to Sydney, 3 March 1691/2, *Calendar of State Papers, Domestic Series, of the Reign of William and Mary, 1689–1695,* 5 vols. (London: HMSO, 1895–1906), *1691–1692,* p. 169.

12. John Taylor to Charles Montagu, 2 July 1695, BL, Add. MSS 10120, f. 77; John J. Murray, *George I, the Baltic, and the Whig Split of 1717: A Study in Diplomacy and Propaganda* (Chicago: University of Chicago Press, 1969), pp. 36–37.

13. Proceedings on the petition of Phips and Evance, 31 August 1691, SP 44/235/pp. 170–71.

14. Commissioners of Customs to the Treasury, 6 February 1692/3, PRO, T 1/21/75; memorial of Taylor, 25 January 1693/4, CO 323/1/ff. 135–36; proposals and memorandum of Bernon, CO 323/1/ff. 162, 163.

15. Proposals by Dudley, ? January 1693/4, CO 5/858/f. 62; and memorandum of Allen and Evance, 2 February 1693/4, CO 324/1/f. 162.

16. Reports of the Admiralty Board, 16 March 1693/4 and order of the Lords of Trade, 16 March 1693/4, CO 323/1/ff. 155, 159, 161; license to Taylor, 26 March 1696, SP 44/346/p. 347.

17. Report of the Navy Commissioners, 5 June 1696 with report of the surveyors, 2 June 1696, T 1/38/ff. 124, 126; Navy Commissioners to the Treasury, 10 June 1696, CO 5/859/f. 54; minutes of the Lords Justices of the Council, 29 June 1696, SP 44/271/p. 190. For a discussion of problems in the trade, see J. J. Malone, *Pine Trees and Politics* (Seattle: University of Washington Press, 1964).

18. Carmarthen to William III, 28 August 1691, SP 8/9/no. 161, f. 283; Nottingham to Viscount Sydney, 11 September 1691, *Report on the Manuscripts of the Late Allan George Finch,* 4 vols. (London: HMC 1913–65), 3:260. See also the proceedings at Whitehall on the petition of the merchants and planters trading to the Chesapeake and the West Indies, 7 August 1691, SP 44/235/p. 168.

19. Minute of the Privy Council, 15 April 1689, PC 2/76/pp. 393–94; order in council, 27 June 1689, PC 2/73/p. 158; Leo Francis Stock, ed., *Proceedings and Debates of the British Parliaments respecting North America,* 5 vols. (Washington, D.C., Carnegie Institution of Washington, 1924–41), 2:3, 4, 7, 31; presentment of the Commissioners of Customs, 21 March 1691/2, with petitions of the merchants, CO 5/1306/ff. 402, 404–7.

20. Journal of the Lords of Trade, 4 September 1690, CO 324/5/pp. 119–20; petition of the New England merchants, 11 September 1690, CO 1/68/f. 14; Carmarthen to Blathwayt, 22 September 1690, CO 1/68/ff. 24–25.

21. See the lists of the Londoners in the Chesapeake trade and the number of vessels allowed each, CO 1/68/ff. 206, 235A; the case of the London merchants, CO 1/68/f. 241; order in council, 15 October 1691, PC 2/74/p. 260; and Francis Nicholson to the Lords of Trade, 26 February 1691/2, CO 5/1306/f. 378.

22. Lords Justices of Ireland to Shrewsbury, 13, 18 April 1695, SP 63/357/ nos. 18, 20, ff. 30, 34.

23. Minute of the Lords Justices, 21 May 1696, James Vernon Papers, BL, Add. MSS 40728, f. 81; the protest of the London merchants, 11 September 1696, CO 5/1309/ff. 11–12; and order in council, 22 October 1696, CO 5/1309/f. 14.

24. Nicholson, Philipse, Van Cortland, and Bayard to the Lords of Trade, 15 May 1689, CO 5/905/pp. 81–84; James Lloyd to Thomas Brinley (extract), 10 July 1689, CO 5/855/f. 33; Bradstreet to the Lords of Trade, 26 October 1689, CO 5/855/f. 113; [John Usher] to ———, 24 October 1689, CO 5/855/f. 104; Randolph to the Lords of Trade, 5 September 1689, CO 5/855/f. 88.

25. Memorandum of the Lords of Trade, 31 August 1689, CO 5/1113/pp. 202–3; Nicholson to the Lords of Trade, 20 August 1690, CO 5/1305/ff. 109–10; Nicholson to William Blathwayt, 10 June 1691, CW, Blathwayt Papers, vol. 15.

26. Sloughter to the duke of Bolton, 7 May 1691, CO 5/1037/f. 47; Van Cortlandt, Bayard, and William Nicolls to Blathwayt, 11 January 1691/2, CW, Blathwayt Papers, vol. 7.

27. Vaughan and Waldron to William Wallis, 21 October 1691, CW, Blathwayt Papers, vol. 11; order in council, 11 February 1691/2 approving the recommendation of the Lords of Trade, PC 2/74/p. 328.

28. See the account of the King's reasons for the appointment of Fletcher in Blathwayt to the Lords Justices, 6 August 1695 (n.s.) BL, Add. MSS 9722, f. 89.

29. Blathwayt to Nicholson, 5 January 1691/2, CW, Blathwayt Papers, vol. 15.

30. See the Privy Council Register, PC 2/73/pp. 98, 108, 112.

31. Order in council, 22 May 1690, PC 2/73/p. 441. In this connection, see the strongly anti-Leslierian letter, or narrative, from New York dated 10 December 1689 and endorsed by William Balthwayt as received on 14 April 1690, CW, Blathwayt Papers, vol. 7.

32. Stock, *Proceedings of Parliaments,* 2:i, 8; and [Sir Robert Southwell to Nottingham?], 23 March 1688/9, HL, Blathwayt Papers, BL418.

Chapter 11

1. Minute of the Lords of Trade, 26 April 1689, CO 391/6/p. 209 (also CO 5/723/f. 117); memorandum of the Lords of Trade, 25 May 1689, CO 5/723/f. 119; orders in council, 2 May 1689, CO 5/1/ff. 4, 5.

2. A copy of his will dated Albemarle, 20 January 1689/90, is in the John Archdale Papers, no. 26, Library of Congress, Washington, D.C. He left his plantation and other property to Francis Hartley, Anna Blount Sothell (his wife), William Duckenfield, William Wilkinson, Henderson Walker, and Edward Wade.

3. Proprietors to Sothell, 2 December 1689, CO 5/288/f. 80; instructions to Ludwell, 5 December 1689, CO 5/288/f. 80; proprietors to Sothell, 12 May 1691, CO 5/288/ff. 89–90.

4. Proprietors to Ludwell, 28 June 1695, CO 5/289/f. 14; proprietors to Harvey, 10 September 1696, CO 5/289/f. 14; Marrie Erma Edwards Parker, ed., *North Carolina Higher Court Records, 1670–1696* (Raleigh: North Carolina State Department of Archives and History, 1968), pp. lx, lxii.

5. "Letters from John Stewart to William Dunlop," *South Carolina Historical and Genealogical Magazine* 22 (January 1931): 3–4.

6. Proprietors to Sothell, 12 May 1691, CO 5/288/ff. 88–89; warrant to the grand council, 13 May 1691, CO 5/288/f. 86; proprietors to their deputies, 13 May 1691, CO 5/288/f. 88; proprietors to the governor and magistrates, 22 September 1691, CO 5/288/f. 94.

7. Instructions to Ludwell, 8 November 1691, CO 5/288/ff. 94–97; private instructions to Ludwell, 8 November 1691, CO 5/288/ff. 98–99; and additional instructions, 8 November 1691, CO 5/288/f. 99.

8. Proprietors to Ludwell, 10, 12 April 1693, CO 5/288/ff. 114–18.

9. John Stewart to William Dunlop, 20 October 1693, *South Carolina Historical and Genealogical Magazine* 30 (April 1931): 170–71; the proprietors' letter to Smith, 24 April 1694, CO 5/289/f. 7, with reference to his of 12 October 1693.

10. Archdale's commission, 28 November 1694, John Archdale Papers, no. 16, Library of Congress, Washington, D.C.; instructions to Archdale, 31 August 1694, CO 5/289/f. 10; proprietors to Archdale, 27 March 1695, CO 5/289/f. 13.

11. H. Boyd to Lord Ashley, n.d., John Archdale Papers, no. 30. According to M. Eugene Sirmans, *Colonial South Carolina: A Political History, 1663–1763* (Chapel Hill: University of North Carolina Press, 1966) p. 62, the Huguenots refused to swear allegiance to the king of England. Many of them, he speculated, hoped to return to France.

12. Proprietors to Archdale, 23 August 1695, CO 5/289/f. 15; Archdale to the proprietors, 19 October 1695, Archdale Papers, no. 35, Library of Congress, Washington, D.C.

13. Proprietors to Archdale, 29 January, 27 June 1696, CO 5/289/ff. 15, 16; Sirmans, *Colonial South Carolina*, pp. 62–66, and "Masters of Ashley Hall: A Biographical Study of the Bull Family of Colonial South Carolina," (PhD. diss., Princeton University, 1959), pp. 105–7.

14. William Cole to the duke of Shrewsbury, 1 August 1690, enclosing the minutes of the council of Virginia, 26 July 1690, CO 5/1305/ff. 104–5; Lord Howard of Effingham to Blathwayt, 7 November 1691, CO 5/1306/f. 335; Nicholson to Blathwayt, 10 June 1691, CW, Blathwayt Papers, vol. 15; Byrd to Blathwayt, 1 November 1692, and Robinson to Blathwayt, 6 July 1692, CW, Blathwayt Papers, vols. 13, 16.

15. Bradford Spangenberg, "Vestrymen in the House of Burgesses: Protection of Local Vestry Authority during James Blair's Term as Commissary (1690–1743)," *HMPEC* 32 (June 1963): 77–100; George McLaren Brydon, *Virginia's Mother Church* (Richmond: Virginia Historical Society, 1947), pp. 279–87; Blair to Nicholson, 3 December 1691, 27 February 1691/2, CW, Francis Nicholson Papers. See also *A Supplement to Burnet's "History of My Own Time,"* ed. Helen C. Foxcroft (Oxford: Oxford University Press, 1902), pp. 389–90.

16. Memorial presented by the Virginia agent, Jeffrey Jeffreys, CO 5/1306/f. 353. Apparently opposition to Nicholson—resentment over his support of Blair and his alleged influence in the House of Burgesses—was already manifest in the council. See the certificate of Christopher Robinson and Henry Hartwell, 7 July 1692, CO 5/1306/ff. 45–52.

17. Blathwayt's report on the revenue, 22 February 1691/2, CO 5/1358/pp. 183–85; Commissioners of the Customs to the Treasury, 30 June 1692, CO 5/1358/pp. 186–89; Treasury report of 15 July 1692, CO 5/1306/no. 16; two memorials on the quitrents, CO 5/1306/ff. 461–64; order in council, 1 September 1692, CO 5/1358/pp. 202–3; William III to Andros, 25 February 1692/3, CO 324/24/p. 117.

18. Petition of the clergy of Virginia, 25 June 1696, CO 5/1307/ff. 230–31.

19. Blathwayt to William Cole, 4 June 1691, CW, Blathwayt Papers, vol. 17; order in council, 25 January 1692/3, CO 5/1358/pp. 219–21 on the report of the attorney general, 11 January 1692/3.

20. Richard Beale Davis, ed., *William Fitzhugh and His Chesapeake World, 1676–1701: The Fitzhugh Letters and Other Documents* (Chapel Hill: University of North Carolina Press, 1963), pp. 43–45; Shrewsbury to Andros, 30 November 1694, Sir William Trumbull to Andros, 5 May 1696, CO 324/26/pp. 2, 36; Robert

294 *Notes (pp. 168–70)*

Beverley, *The History and Present State of Virginia,* ed. Louis Wright (Chapel Hill: University of North Carolina Press, 1947), p. 94.

21. Byrd to Perry and Lane, 19 July 1690, *Virginia Magazine of History and Biography* 26 (April 1918): 133; Byrd to Blathwayt, 30 August 1690, 8 January 1692/3, 23 June 1696, CW, Blathwayt Papers, vol. 13.

22. In 1691 the Virginia legislature passed two measures, one to encourage manufacturers and another for ports where warehouses would be established for collecting and shipping tobacco. The first allowed colonial debtors to make payment either in money or produce at about one-third more than the market value and often in commodities of no use to the London creditor. The act for ports, unrealistically, some thought, limited to certain locations the collecting, storing, and lading of tobacco for shipment and imposed an excessively high duty on the export of hides. The tax was designated for the support of the ministry and for learning. See Blathwayt to Nicholson, 5 January 1691/2, CW, Blathwayt Papers, vol. 15; report of the Commissioners of Customs, 15 March 1691/2, T 1/17/ 240–41; and Commissioners of Customs to the Lords of Trade, 15 March 1691/2, CO 5/1306/ff. 384–85. There was strong resentment against the London traders in the colony. Writing to a friend in England, John Ming referred to "our poverty," our "predominant Vertue[,] a Rx prescribed us by our learned Physicians[,] the merchants of London." (Ming to _____, 30 June 1692, Portland MSS, BL, Loan 29/285).

23. Presentment of the Commissioners of Customs, 21 March 1691/2, T 1/17/249; order in council, 28 April 1692 with report of the Treasury, 22 April 1692, CO 5/1358/pp. 173, 174; minute of the Lords of Trade, 27 June 1692, CO 5/1358/p. 176; John Povey to the secretary of the Treasury (Henry Guy), 6 September 1694, T 1/29/69.

24. Randolph to the Commissioners of Customs, 27 June 1692, *Memoir of Edward Randolph: Including His Letters and Official Papers,* ed. Robert Noxon Toppan, 7 vols. (Boston: Prince Society, 1898–1909), 7:367–68; Randolph to Blathwayt, 21 April 1692, CW, Blathwayt Papers, vol. 2; Treasury to the governor of Maryland, 15 November 1692, T 64/88/pp. 430–31; Customs Board to the Treasury, 27 October 1694, T 1/30/f. 59; memorial of Sir Thomas Lawrence, 25 June 1695, CO 5/713/ff. 304–6.

25. For a statement of the amount, sources, and disbursement of the revenue, see the memorandum for 1692–93 submitted to the Lords of Trade, 11 June 1694, CO 5/1358/pp. 253–54.

26. Nicholson to the Lords of Trade, 4 November 1690, CO 5/1305/ff. 158–60 enclosing the journal of Cuthbert Potter, CO 5/1305/ff. 174–77; minutes of the council of Virginia, 15 January 1690/1, CO 5/1306/ff. 14–15; representation of Nicholson and the council, read at the Committee for Trade and Plantations, 27 April 1691, CO 5/1306/ff. 98–99.

27. Minute of the Treasury on the proposal by Andros, 8 April 1692, T 1/18/32; Andros to the Lords of Trade, 22 July 1693, 5 January 1693/4, CO 5/1308/ff. 122–23, 174; Andros to Shrewsbury, 4 June 1695, CO 5/1308/f. 240; Secretary Cole to the Lords of Trade, 10 June 1695, CO 5/1308/f. 242; and Ordnance Board to John Povey, 10 August 1695, CO 5/1308/f. 250.

28. Andros to the Lords of Trade, 27 June 1696, CO 5/1309/ff. 5–6.

Chapter 12

1. Nicholas Sewall and Richard Hill escaped, but after a protracted controversy with the government of Virginia the insurgent junta brought to trial three of the crewmen who, it claimed, acted on the specific orders of Sewall. John Woodcock, George Mason, and William Burley were tried, convicted, and sentenced to death to set an example of "terror" to "like evil doers." Woodcock was executed after confessing that he alone was guilty. Execution of the sentences against the other two men was deferred until the pleasure of the king was known (the Associators to the king and queen, 25 April 1690, CO 5/713/ff. 154–55; Coode to Nottingham and Shrewsbury, 24 March 1689/90, SP 42/1/no. 10; order in council, 19 November 1691, PC 2/74/p. 277). Four years later the assembly of Maryland voted to reprieve Mason and Burley. Shrewsbury, on behalf of William III, signed a warrant for their pardon.

2. Smithson to the Bishop of London [?June 1690], CO 5/713/f. 51. Other petitions by Protestants opposing the Association are in CO 5/713/ff. 73, 75.

3. The best treatment is David William Jordan, "The Royal Period of Colonial Maryland, 1689–1715," (Ph.D. diss., Princeton University, 1966), pp. 30–49.

4. Coode to Shrewsbury, 14 May 1690, CO 5/713/f. 31; committee of safety to the king, 11 July 1690, CO 5/713/ff. 54–55.

5. Minutes of the Lords of Trade, 30 August, 13 September 1689, CO 5/723/pp. 121, 123–24.

6. Memorandum of the Lords of Trade, 7 January 1689/90, CO 5/723/pp. 146–47; memorial of Baltimore, 7 January 1689/90, CO 5/718/ff. 55–56.

7. Proposals by Baltimore, read 14 January 1689/90, CO 5/718/f. 53; order in council, 30 January 1689/90 and royal letter of 1 February 1689/90, CO 5/723/pp. 147, 148–50; petition of William Payne, report of the Lords of Trade, and order in council, 24 April 1690, CO 5/723/pp. 163–64, 170–72.

8. Copley's memorandum, [?June 1690], CO 5/713/f. 53; Heath's demands, 2 June 1690, and the answer of the revolutionary government, 18 June 1690, CO 5/713/ff. 40, 41.

9. Holt to Carmarthen, 3 June 1690, CO 5/713/f. 44; order in council, 21 August 1690, CO 5/719/f. 4; report by Treby, 1 September 1690, CO 5/713/f. 61.

10. Petition by Baltimore, read 30 October 1690, CO 5/713/f. 77; orders in council, 30 October, 20 November 1690, PC 2/74/pp. 35, 56; Bacon to the Lords of Trade, 11 March 1689/90, CO 5/1305/ff. 90–92; and the petitions by Coursey, Hill, and others, CO 5/713/ff. 73, 75.

11. Declaration of Anne Arundel County, CO 5/718/f. 206; three sets of articles submitted by Coode and Cheseldyne, CO 5/713/ff. 78–83; and the answer of Coode and Chesldyne to the petition of Coursey and Hill, CO 5/713/ff. 88–90.

12. Depositions made before John Paige, mayor of Plymouth, 13 November 1690, CO 5/713/f. 92.

13. Narcissus Luttrell, *A Brief Historical Relation of State Affairs from September 1678 to April 1714*, 6 vols. (Oxford, 1857), 2: 40; order in council, 1 January 1690/1, CO 5/723/p. 207; minute of the Lords of Trade, 3 January 1690/1, CO 5/723/p. 207.

14. Baltimore's answer to the draft commission, 15 January 1690/1, CO 5/713/f. 97; orders in council, 15, 29 January, 12 February 1690/1, CO 5/719/ff. 10, 12, 14; royal warrant, 14 February 1690/1, CO 324/23/pp. 1–11; report of the Lords of Trade, 23 February, and the order in council, 27 February 1690/1, CO 5/723/pp. 217–20; Henry Guy to Blathwayt, 11 January 1690/1, HL, Blathwayt Papers, BL42.

15. See the anaylsis in Jordan, "Royal Period of Maryland," pp. 53–65. The various lists for the council submitted by Copley, Baltimore, Hammond, and Perry are in CO 5/713/ff. 158–66. The final slate is in CO 5/713/f. 168.

16. Minute of the Lords of Trade, 15 December 1691, CO 5/713/f. 186; memorandum by Lawrence, 15 November 1691, CO 5/713/ff. 174–75; Copley to the Lords of Trade, n.d., CO 5/713/f. 180; and the royal letter to a later governor, John Seymour, 15 January 1707/8, in response to a petition from Lawrence, CO 5/210/ff. 38–39.

17. Jordan, "Royal Period of Maryland," pp. 78–81; Copley and the council to the Lords of Trade, 9 July 1692, and the address of the council to the king, CO 5/713/ff. 199, 201–2; and Bernard C. Steiner, "The Royal Province of Maryland in 1692," *Maryland Historical Magazine* 15 (June 1920): 130.

18. John H. Seabrook, "The Establishment of Anglicanism in Colonial Maryland," *HMPEC* 39 (September 1970): 287–94.

19. Randolph to John Povey, 12 May 1692, Randolph to Blathwayt, 28 June 1692, CW, Blathwayt Papers, vol. 2; Copley to Blathwayt, 21 June 1692, Blathwayt to Copley, 28 February 1692/3, CW, Blathwayt Papers, vol. 18.

20. Randolph to Blathwayt, 7, 13, 28 July 1692, 1 January 1692/3, CW, Blathwayt Papers, vol. 2; Randolph to the Commissioners of Customs, n.d., but received at the Plantation Office 6 September 1692, CO 5/1306/f. 496; Copley to the Lords of Trade, 29 July 1692, CO 5/713/ff. 206–7; Treasury Board to Copley, 15 November 1692, T 64/88/pp. 430–31.

21. Representation and petition of the assembly, both presented at the Committee for Trade, 15 September 1692, CO 5/713/ff. 203, 208; address of the council and assembly, received at the Committee for Trade 19 September 1692, CO 5/713/f. 218; Trevor's report to the Lords of Trade, 2 November 1692, CO 5/713/f. 226; order in council, 23 February 1692/3, PC 2/75/pp. 99–101.

22. Petition of Lawrence to the king, with order in council of 26 January 1692/3, CO 5/713/ff. 244, 245; Copley and the Maryland council to the Lords of Trade, 24 October, 21 December 1692, CO 5/713/ff. 224–25, 239–40.

23. Copley and the Council to the Lords of Trade, 11 April 1693, with heads of charges against Lawrence, CO 5/713/ff. 254, 256–57; Jordan, "Royal Period of Colonial Maryland," pp. 113–14.

24. Order in council, 28 September 1693, on the report of the Lords of Trade of 15 September 1693, CO 5/719/f. 34.

25. Blathwayt to Blair, 13 March 1692/3, CW, Blathwayt Papers, vol. 13; Blair to [Nottingham], 29 March 1693, CO 5/1307/ff. 22–23.

26. Andros to the Lords of Trade, 23 October 1693, CO 5/1308/ff. 163–63; Andros to the Lords of Trade, 4 May 1694, CO 5/713/f. 287; Plater to Blathwayt, 27 January 1693/4, CW, Blathwayt Papers, vol. 12. The harpies in Whitehall were no less rapacious for colonial patronage. An erroneous rumor reached London

late in March 1694 of the death of Sir Thomas Lawrence. Since the provincial secretary's post was worth about three hundred pounds a year, one undersecretary of state wrote to a colleague employed by the duke of Ormonde to have his patron solicit the post from the king. He should act immediately, otherwise Blathwayt might be "too nimble for us both" (John Tucker to John Ellis, 28 March 1694, John Ellis Papers BL, Add. MSS 28878, f. 170).

27. Royal warrant for a commission for Nicholson, 23 January 1693/4, CO 324/24/pp. 170–82; memorandum by Nicholson, n.d., CO 5/713/f. 285.

28. Anglican clergy of Maryland to Bishop Compton, 14 May 1698, LPL, Fulham Palace Papers, American Colonial Section, vol. 2, ff. 100–103; Nicholson to the Lords of Trade, 11 June 1695, CO 5/713/f. 300.

29. Order in council, 4 January 1695/6, CO 5/724/ff. 106–7; (also in Fulham Palace Papers, American Colonial Section, vol. 2, f. 48); Nicholson to Tenison, 12 June, 14 July 1696, Fulham Palace Papers, American Colonial Section, vol. 2, ff. 53, 76. A compromise was finally worked out by the Commissioners of Trade and Plantations and adopted by the provincial legislature in 1702. Every Anglican congregation was considered part of the established church, and every Anglican priest received his salary from the levy of forty pounds per tithable, but the religious rights of Protestant Dissenters were safeguarded. See Seabrook, "Establishment of Anglicanism in Colonial Maryland," pp. 287–94.

30. Jordan, "Royal Period of Colonial Maryland," pp. 145–82; Nicholson to the Lords of Trade, 18 March 1695/6, CO 5/714/f. 1.

31. Nicholson to the Lords of Trade, 11 June 1695, CO 5/713/f. 300; Nicholson to the duke of Shrewsbury, 14 June 1696, CO 5/719/ff. 36–37; memorial by Lawrence, 25 June 1695, CO 5/713/ff. 304–6; Copley to Nottingham, n.d., but received at the Plantation Office, 15 September 1692, CO 5/713/ff. 214–15.

Chapter 13

1. Blackwell to Penn, 13 January 1689/90, HSP, John Blackwell Letters; W. L. F. Nuttall, "Governor John Blackwell: His Life in England and Ireland," *PMHB* 88 (April 1964): 141; Nicholas B. Wainwright, "Governor John Blackwell," ibid. 74 (October 1950): 472.

2. Entry for 24 June 1690, diary of Henry, earl of Clarendon, in *The Correspondence of Henry Hyde, Earl of Clarendon, and of His Brother, Laurence Hyde, Earl of Rochester,* ed. Samuel Weller Singer, 2 vols. (London: Camden Society, 1928), 2:319; Penn to [Sydney], 31 July 1690, in HMC, *Report on the Manuscripts of the Late Allen George Finch*, 4 vols. (London: HMC, 1913–65), 2:391; Nottingham to William III, 26 June 1691, ibid., 3:128; minutes of the cabinet council, 24 July, 11 August 1691, ibid., 3:401, 404; Penn to [Sydney?], [12 June], 21 November 1691, ibid., 4:506, 507.

3. Penn to the councilors, 13 June, 11 September 1691, HSP, Dreer Collection, Letters and Papers of Penn.

4. Gary B. Nash, *Quakers and Politics: Pennsylvania, 1681–1726* (Princeton, N.J.: Princeton University Press, 1968), pp. 143–59, saw the conflict in social, economic, and political terms with the theological arguments as semiconscious rationalizations. Jon Butler, " 'Godpel Order Improved': The Keithian Schism

and the Exercise of Quaker Ministerial Authority in Pennsylvania," *WMQ*, 3d ser. 31 (July 1974): 431–52, viewed it in religious and doctrinal terms. The two views are not necessarily incompatible. See also John Kendall Nelson, "Anglican Missions in America, 1701–1725: A Study of the Society for the Propagation of the Gospel in Foreign Parts," (Ph.D. diss., Northwestern University, 1962), pp. 79–117; and Edwin B. Bronner, *William Penn's "Holy Experiment": The Founding of Pennsylvania, 1681–1701* (New York: Columbia University Press for Temple University Press, 1962), pp. 134–53, 283.

5. Order in council, 10 March 1691/2, on a report of the Lords of Trade, CO 5/1236/ff. 12–13; memorandum of the Lords of Trade, 2 May 1692, CO 5/1236/f. 13; order in council, 12 May 1692, CO 5/1037/f. 209; draft commission of 27 June 1692 with minute by the attorney general and order in council, 21 July 1692, and instructions to Fletcher, 28 October 1692, CO 5/1113/ff. 403–22; warrant for Fletcher's commission, 29 June 1692, CO 324/24/pp. 7–16.

6. Penn to Fletcher, 5 December 1692, CO 5/1038/f. 128; Penn to ———, extract, n.d., CO 5/1038/f. 129; Bronner, *Penn's Holy Experiment*, p. 75.

7. Fletcher to Blathwayt, 15 August 1693, CO 5/1038/f. 147; Fletcher to Blathwayt, 18 August 1693, CW, Blathwayt Papers, vol. 8; Fletcher to Nottingham, 18 August, 5 October 1693, CO 5/1082/nos. 35, 36.

8. Minute of the Lords of Trade, 4 February 1693/4, CO 5/1114/p. 88; order in council, 8 February 1693/4, PC 2/75/p. 334; and report by Trevor and Ward, CO 5/1236/f. 22.

9. Minutes of the Lords of Trade and Penn, 1, 3 August 1694, agreement between the Lords of Trade and Penn, 3 August 1694, CO 5/1236/ff. 25, 27–29; orders in council, 9, 20 August 1694, CO 5/1236/ff. 29–30, 33–34; and ——— to Robert Harley, 18 August 1694, in HMC, *Report on the Manuscripts of the Duke of Portland, Fourteenth Report*, app., pt. 2 (London, 1894), p. 553.

10. Penn to the Friends of Philadelphia, [24 November 1694], printed in Samuel Mac. Janney, *The Life of William Penn: With Selections from His Correspondence and Autobiography*, 4th ed. rev. (Philadelphia, 1876), pp. 396–97.

11. See Bronner, *Penn's Holy Experiment*, pp. 176–80; Nash, *Quakers and Politics*, pp. 192–201; and Roy N. Lokken, *David Lloyd: Colonial Lawmaker* (Seattle: University of Washington Press, 1959), pp. 70–72.

12. Fletcher to the Lords of Trade, 10 June 1696, enclosing Markham to Fletcher, 26 May 1696, CO 5/1039/ff. 173–74, 192–93.

13. Dudley to Blathwayt, 28 November 1690, CO 5/1081/f. 425.

14. Petition of Coxe and order in council, 25 February 1691/2, CO 5/1037/ff. 164, 165; memorandum of the Lords of Trade, 18 April 1692, CO 5/1037/f. 198; and Frederick Reeves Black, "The Last Lords Proprietors of West Jersey: The West Jersey Society, 1692–1701," (Ph.D. diss., Rutgers University, 1964), pp. 171–72.

15. Order in council, 10 March 1691/2, CO 5/1236/ff. 12–13; West Jersey proprietors to Fletcher, 1 June 1692, CO 5/1037/ff. 217, 219; instructions of the proprietors, CO 5/1037/ff. 221, 223–24.

16. Black, "West Jersey Society," pp. 82–83.

17. Eugene R. Sheridan, "Politics in Colonial America: The Career of Lewis Morris, 1671–1746," (Ph.D. diss., University of Wisconsin, 1972), pp. 32–35.

18. Brooke to Blathwayt, 23 November 1694, CW, Blathwayt Papers, vol. 11; Fletcher to Blathwayt, 19 November 1694, HL, Blathwayt Papers, BL191.

19. Hamilton to Fletcher, 26 June, 28 August 1696, CO 5/1039/ff. 196, 229.

Chapter 14

1. Order in council, 22 May 1690, PC 2/73/p. 441.

2. For alternative views to the thesis of ethnic conflict posed by Thomas J. Archdeacon in his "The Age of Leisler—New York City, 1689–1710: A Social and Demographic Interpretation," in *Aspects of Early New York Society and Politics,* ed. Jacob Judd and Irwin H. Polishook (Tarrytown, N.Y.: Sleepy Hollow Restorations, 1974) and Archdeacon's *New York City, 1664–1710: Conquest and Change* (Ithaca, N.Y.: Cornell University Press, 1976), see Lawrence H. Leder, *Robert Livingston 1654–1728, and the Politics of Colonial New York* (Chapel Hill: University of North Carolina Press, 1961), pp. 59–60; James A. Leamon, "War, Finance, and Faction in Colonial New York: The Administration of Governor Benjamin Fletcher, 1692–1698," (Ph.D. diss., Brown University, 1961), pp. 21–23; and, especially, Joyce Diane Goodfriend, " 'Too Great a Mixture of Nations': The Development of New York City Society in the Seventeenth Century," (Ph.D. diss., University of California, Los Angeles, 1975), pp. 164–75, 257–64. The best factual account of the Leislerian insurgency, although it uncritically accepts the sincerity of the belief in a Catholic conspiracy, is Charles Howard McCormick, "Leisler's Rebellion," (Ph.D. diss., America University, 1971).

3. Leisler and others to Gilbert Burnet, 7 January 1689/90, CO 5/1081/ff. 233–34; protest of the inhabitants of Albany, 3 January 1689/90, CO 5/1081/ff. 222–29; the Albany convention to Slater [Sloughter], 20 January 1689/90 (in the hand of Livingston), FDRL, Livingston Family Papers, Robert Livingston Correspondence; Livingston to Robert Ferguson, 27 March 1690, Robert Livingston Correspondence; Livingston to Andros, 19 April 1690, CO 5/855/ff. 200–201; and the revolutionary council to the governor of Connecticut, 1 March 1689/90, CO 5/1081/f. 247.

4. Livingston to Andros, 19 April 1690, CO 5/855/ff. 200–202; Bayard to John West, 14 January 1690, CO 5/1081/f. 239; William Nicolls to George Farwell, 14 January 1689/90, CO 5/1081/ff. 240–41; Van Cortlandt to Andros, [May 1690], CO 5/1081/ff. 306–8. For Blackwell's assessment, see the report of his comments in the journal of Benjamin Bullivant, entry for 27 March 1690, CO 5/855/ff. 244–59.

5. Address of 19 May 1690, CO 5/1081/ff. 304–5; Lawrence H. Leder, " '. . . Like Madmen Though the Streets': The New York City Riot of June 1690," *New-York Historical Society Quarterly* 39 (October 1955): 405–15; John Clapp to one of the principal secretaries of state, 7 November 1690, CO 5/1081/f. 416; information of Henry Greverat, received at the Plantation Office, 23 March 1690/1, CO 5/855/f. 351.

6. For evidence that the Leislerian council knew of Ingoldsby's commission, see its proclamation, 5 March 1690/1, CO 5/1037/ff. 1–2.

7. See Chidley Brooke to Sir Robert Southwell, 5 April 1691, CO 5/1037/ff. 13–14; Sloughter to Blathwayt, 7 May 1691, CO 5/1037/ff. 43–44; Sloughter to Nottingham, 27 March 1691, CO 5/1081/no. 3. A sympathetic treatment of

Leisler, one accepting his delusions and rationalizations, is in McCormick, "Leisler's Rebellion," pp. 370–79.

8. Sloughter to the Lords of Trade, 7 May 1691, CO 5/1037/ff. 42–44; trial of Leisler and others, 31 March 1691, CO 5/1037/ff. 7–11; Sloughter to Nottingham, 6 May 1691, CO 5/1082/f. 2; unfinished letter from Sloughter to Blathwayt, enclosed in the council of New York to the Lords of Trade, 29 July 1691, CO 5/1037/ff. 89–90; William Nicolls to Francis Nicholson, 1 May 1691, CW, Blathwayt Papers, vol. 10; Van Cortlandt to Nicholson, 6 April 1691, CW, Blathwayt Papers, vol. 9. For a detailed analysis of the judicial proceedings, see McCormick, "Leisler's Rebellion," pp. 425–52.

9. Memorial of William Van Breen and others, 15 October 1691, CO 5/1082/no. 16; order in council, 7 January 1691/2, and petition by Leisler, CO 5/1037/ff. 148, 149–50.

10. Memorandum of the Lords of Trade, 11 March 1691/2, orders in council, 17 March, 7 April, 13 May 1692, CO 5/1113/pp. 383, 384, 386–87, 390–91; minute of the Lords of Trade, 8 July 1692 and order in council, 15 July 1692, CO 5/1037/ff. 244, 246.

11. See the list of the council with marginal notes, CO 5/1037/f. 190; the petition of the landowners and merchants of New York, CO 5/1037/f. 185; instructions to Fletcher, 17 March 1691/2, CO 5/1113/pp. 340–61.

12. See Lawrence Leder, "The Politics of Upheaval in New York, 1689–1709," *New-York Historical Society Quarterly* 44 (October 1960): 414–17; Leamon, "The Administration of Fletcher," pp. 77–78, 145–53.

13. Certified copy of an English translation from the Dutch of Gouverneur's letter to his parents, 12 October 1692, CO 5/751/f. 23; Fletcher to Dudley, 7 January 1692/3, CO 5/1038/f. 1; Gouverneur to Fletcher, 20 January 1692/3, CO 5/751/f. 24; James Graham to Blathwayt, 1 February 1692/3, CW, Blathwayt Papers, vol. 10; Fletcher to Nottingham, 14 February 1692/3, CO 5/1082/no. 27; and Phips to Nottingham, 20 February 1692/3, CO 5/751/f. 40.

14. Fletcher to Blathwayt, 5 October 1693, CO 5/1038/f. 183; and Fletcher's comments on the council, 18 April 1693, CO 5/1038/f. 109.

15. Leamon, "The Administration of Fletcher," pp. 151–52 and Sung Bok Kim, *Landlord and Tenant in Colonial New York: Manorial Society, 1664–1775* (Chapel Hill: University of North Carolina Press, 1978), pp. 60–62.

16. Povey's report on Dongan's petition, 23 September 1692, Treasury warrant, 12 April 1693, T 64/88/pp. 289, 446–47; Chidley Brooke to [Blathwayt], 24 November 1694, CO 5/1038/ff. 421–22; Fletcher to Livingston, 26 October 1692; Harwood to Livingston, 22 August 1693; Livingston's case with Harwood, 11 November 1694, and Livingston's journal, all in FDRL, Robert Livingston Correspondence.

17. Order in council on the petition of Leisler and Gouverneur, 28 February 1694/5, CO 5/1031/f. 1; "The Case of Capt. Leisler . . . ," and power of attorney to Leisler and Gouverneur, BL, Portland Papers, Loan 29/289/nos. 31, 32.

18. Leo Francis Stock, ed., *Proceedings and Debates of the British Parliaments respecting North America*, 5 vols. (Washington, D.C.: Carnegie Institution, 1924–41), 2:113–15, 120–31; *The Manuscripts of the House of Lords,* n.s., 10

vols. to date (London: HMC, 1900–), 1:540. For arguments against the bill, see CO 5/1039/ff. 7–8, 9, 13–14.

19. Such was also the conclusion of John C. Rainbolt, "The Creation of a Governor and Captain General for the Northern Colonies," *New-York Historical Society Quarterly* 57 (April 1973): 103–5, and James Leamon, "Governor Fletcher's Recall," *WMQ*, 3d ser. 20 (October 1963): 527–31.

20. Delanoy to ———, 13 June 1695, CO 5/1039/ff. 66–69. Penn later turned over this letter to the Plantation Office.

21. Address dated 6 August 1691, CO 5/1037/ff. 110–13.

22. Commission to Winthrop, 2 September 1693, CO 5/1038/f. 176; Fletcher to Nottingham, 10 December 1693, 22 January 1693/4, CO 5/1082/nos. 38, 39.

23. Order in council, 29 Januay 1693/4, and petition of Winthrop, CO 5/1038/ff. 293, 295–96; order in council, 19 April 1694, and the queen to the governor of New York, 21 June, 21 August 1694 with memorandum, CO 5/1114/pp. 116–26, 127–30, 142–45, 150–51; Winthrop's petition, CO 5/1039/f. 154; Winthrop's reasons for the failure of Connecticut to comply, CO 5/959/ff. 89–90; Andrew Hamilton to Fletcher, 16 June 1696, CO 5/1039/f. 196; and Fletcher to Blathwayt, 30 May 1696, CO 5/1039/ff. 173–74.

24. Fitzjohn Winthrop to Wait Winthrop, 13 July 1695, *MHSC*, 5th ser. 8:324.

25. Shrewsbury to William III, 1/11 June, 12/23 July 1695, *Private and Original Correspondence of Charles Talbot, Duke of Shrewsbury, with King William . . .* , ed. William Coxe, (London, 1821), pp. 40, 94; the account by James Vernon, Shewsbury's secretary, of the minutes of the Lords Justices, 12 July 1695, Vernon Papers, BL, Add. MSS 40782, f. 36; and the minutes of the Lords Justices, 12 July 1695, SP 44/274/p. 40.

26. Blathwayt to the Lords Justices, 8 August 1695 (n.s.), BL, Add. MSS 9722, f. 89.

27. Graham to Blathwayt, 29 May 1695, CW, Blathwayt Papers, vol. 10.

28. In February 1696 Kidd and Livingston sold to Sir Richard Blackburn one-third of their interest in the venture for £396.13.11, promising to reimburse him if Kidd did not encounter pirates. See the articles of agreement, 7 February 1695/6. FDRL, Robert Livingston General Correspondence.

29. See Livingston's journal for the period 9 December 1694–3 October 1695, FDRL, Robert Livingston General Correspondence, and the undated letter from either Povey or Blathwayt to Fletcher, HL, Blathwayt Papers, BL215.

30. Heathcote to Povey, 31 August 1695, CO 5/1039/f. 83; Narcissus Luttrell, *A Brief Historical Relation of State Affairs from September 1678 to April 1714*, 6 vols. (Oxford, 1857), 3:520; minutes of the Committee for Trade and Plantations, 14 September 1695, CO 391/8/pp. 111–14.

31. Memorial by Heathcote, 17 February 1695/6, CO 5/1039/f. 145; Blathwayt to Fletcher forwarding a copy of the testimony presented against Fletcher, 17 February 1695/6, CO 5/1114/p. 251; copy of order in council, 16 January 1695/6, in FDRL, Robert Livingston Correspondence.

32. Fletcher to William Blathwayt, 13 July 1695, CO 5/1039/ff. 198–99; Fletcher's answers to the depositions made against him, CO 5/1039/ff. 221–22;

council of New York to the Lords of Trade, 2 August 1696, CO 5/1039/ff. 250–51.

33. John Palmer to ———, 23 April 1696, Robert Harley Papers, Portland MSS, BL, Loan 29/289/no. 33; James Graham to Blathwayt, 31 May 1696, CW, Blathwayt Papers, vol. 10.

34. Statement by Gouverneur and Leisler, CO 5/1039/ff. 266–68; statement of grievances from 1 September 1692 to 31 October 1695, CO 5/1039/ff. 270–73 (also in the Portland MSS, BL, Loan 29/289 with remarks on a memorial presented by Brooke and Nicholls).

35. Fletcher to the Council for Trade and Plantations, 24 December 1698, CO 5/1041/ff. 395–410. It is difficult to establish the truth of the partisan, ex parte charges against Fletcher of graft and corruption. It may well have been that after 1695, realizing that his days as governor were numbered, Fletcher began to line his pockets by accepting bribes from privateers and issuing extravagant land grants—seven in number—for manors in New York.

36. Shrewsbury to the king, 15 August 1696, *Correspondence of Shrewsbury,* p. 136.

37. See Robert Blackborne (secretary to the East India Company) to William Popple (secretary to the Council of Trade), 18 December 1696, with enclosures, CO 323/2/ff. 112, 113, 119–22.

Chapter 15

1. See the address of the "freeholders" of Connecticut to the crown, 16 September 1692 and "Some Objections against the Pretended Government of Connecticut," CO 5/1037/ff. 263–74.

2. See the opinion of Sir George Treby, Sir John Somers, and Edward Ward, 2 August 1690, Hartford, Connecticut Archives, Foreign Correspondence, 2d ser.; Increase Mather to Governor Robert Treat, 19 August 1690, *CHSC,* 24:37–38; and William Whiting to Treat, 8 November 1690, ibid., p. 40.

3. Bulkeley to Fletcher, 5 April 1693, with address to the crown, CO 5/1038/ff. 94, 95–100; Fletcher to Blathwayt, 8 March 1692/3, CO 5/1038/f. 45; Fletcher to Nottingham, 13 August, 5 October 1693, CO 5/1082/nos. 34, 36; Bulkeley to Fletcher, 15 September 1693, CO 5/1038/f. 193. The most extensive treatment of local conditions is James Mark Poteet, "Preserving the Old Ways: Connecticut, 1690–1740" (Ph.D. diss., University of Virginia, 1973), pp. 57–81.

4. Wyllys to Fitzjohn Winthrop, ? September 1693, *MHSC,* 6th ser. 3:16–17.

5. Address of Bulkeley and others, 3 April 1694, CO 5/1038/ff. 332–33; petitions by Winthrop, 29 January 1693/4, 23 April 1696, CO 5/1038/ff. 295–96 and CO 5/1039/f. 152.

6. Fitzjohn Winthrop to Robert Treat and the council, Winthrop to John Allyn, 13 July 1695, *CHSC,* 24:105—6, 107—8; Wait Winthrop to [Allyn], 22 September 1696, *MHSC,* 5th ser. 8:522.

7. Wyllys to Fitzjohn Winthrop, 25 December 1697, *MHSC,* 6th ser. 3:31–32.

8. Coggeshall and others to the king, 30 January 1689/90, CO 5/855/f. 162; Francis Brinley to Thomas Brinley, 31 March 1690, CO 5/855/f 189; John Easton

to Henry Sloughter, 6 May 1691, CO 5/1037/f. 33; and Sydney V. James, *Colonial Rhode Island: A History* (New York: Charles Scribner's Sons, 1975), pp. 109–11, 187–98, 234–35.

9. Greene to Blathwayt, 19 December 1692, and Brinley to Blathwayt, 29 December 1692, CW, Blathwayt Papers, vol. 11.

10. Order in council, 24 August 1693, with petition and address from Rhode Island, CO 5/857/ff. 226, 227; memorandum of Almy, n.d., CO 5/857/f. 242.

11. Report by Trevor, 28 October 1696, CO 5/859/f. 125.

12. Weare to Robert Pike, 15 March 1689/90, in *Documents and Records Relating to the Province of New Hampshire*, ed. Nathaniel Bouton et al., 40 vols. (Concord: New Hampshire Historical Society, 1867–1943), 2:43–45: Pickering to the governor of Massachusetts, 19 March 1689/90, ibid., 2:40–41; David E. Van Deventer, *The Emergence of Provincial New Hampshire 1623–1741* (Baltimore, Md.: Johns Hopkins University Press, 1976), pp. 136–37; Gary Thomas Lord, "The Political and Social Structure of Seventeenth-Century Portsmouth, New Hampshire," (Ph.D. diss., University of Virginia, 1976), pp. 262–65; and Peter Ralph Barry, "The New Hampshire Merchant Interest," (Ph.D. diss., University of Wisconsin, 1971), pp. 216–21.

13. Petition of the inhabitants of Great Island, 15 May 1690, CO 5/855/ff. 250–51; and extract of a letter from John Bullivant to John Usher, 10 July 1690, HL, Blathwayt Papers, BL242.

14. Order in council, 30 March 1691, and the legal opinions, CO 5/914/ff. 5, 9, 10–11, 30.

15. The Massachusetts agents to the Lords of Trade, 4 May 1691, CO 5/924/f. 13; petitions of Allen, CO 5/856/f. 604, CO 5/924/ff. 23, 25–26.

16. Minute of the Lords of Trade, 11 January 1691/2, CO 5/940/p. 182. Several years later Allen wrote to Blathwayt acknowledging the intercession of the secretary to the committee in obtaining the governorship for him (Allen to Blathwayt, 23 September 1698, CW, Blathwayt Papers, vol. 12).

17. Usher to the Lords of Trade, 29 October 1692, 31 January 1692/3, CO 5/924/ff. 42–43, 47–48; two addresses to the crown, CO 5/924/ff. 56, 58; Phips to Nottingham, 20 February 1692/3, CO 5/751/f. 42; and Usher to Nottingham, 31 January 1692/3, CO 5/751/f. 25.

18. Usher to the Lords of Trade, ? November 1694, and the assembly to Usher, 14 November 1694, CO 5/924/ff. 138, 141.

19. Minute of the Lords Justices, 9 July 1695, James Vernon Papers, BL, Add. MSS 40782, f. 34; minute of the Lords of Trade, 24 September 1695, CO 5/940/pp. 270–75.

20. Usher to the Lords of Trade, 26 October, 12, 15 November 1695, CO 5/940/pp. 275–81, 282; orders in council on the petition of Allen and Partridge, 30 April, 18 June 1696, PC 2/76/pp. 414, 446, 448; minute of the Lords Justices, 16 June 1696, James Vernon Papers, BL, Add. MSS 40782, f. 101. See also Allen to Edward Flower, 31 March 1696, CW, Blathwayt Papers, vol. 12.

21. Usher to the Lords of Trade, 23 October 1696, CO 5/759/f. 123; Usher to the Lords of Trade, 5 October 1696, CO 5/859/f. 115; Usher to Blathwayt, 23 October 1696, CW, Blathwayt Papers, vol. 6.

22. George D. Langdon, Jr., *Pilgrim Colony: A History of New Plymouth, 1620–1691* (New Haven, Conn.: Yale University Press, 1966), pp. 228–33, 242–43.

23. Viola F. Barnes, *The Dominion of New England: A Study in British Colonial Policy* (New Haven, Conn.: Yale University Press, 1923), p. 259.

24. Journal of Benjamin Bullivant, CO 5/855/ff. 255–59; address of the Royalists of Boston, 25 January 1689/90, CO 5/855/f. 153; address of the Royalists of Charleston, CO 5/855/ff. 158–59. See also extracts, Elizabeth Usher to John Usher, n.d., Edward Randolph to Usher, 16 October 1689, CO 5/855/f. 99; Randolph to Blathwayt, 30 December 1689, CW, Blathwayt Papers, vol. 1, no. 96; and extract, Bullivant to Usher, 10 July 1690, HL, Blathwayt Papers, BL242.

25. Extracts of two letters by Myles, 29 November, 12 December 1690, CO 5/855/ff. 343, 349; Samuel Sewall, *Diary of Samuel Sewall*, ed. M. Halsey Thomas, 2 vols. (New York: Farrar, Straus, Giroux, 1973), 1:268, 275. The Royalist view can be found in the extract of a letter to the Lords of Trade, 27 May 1691, CO 5/856/f. 533.

26. On this point see Blathwayt to Joseph Dudley, 2 February 1692/3, CW, Blathwayt Papers, vol. 4.

27. G. B. Warden, *Boston, 1689–1776* (Boston: Little, Brown, 1970), pp. 42–43.

28. Nottingham to Blathwayt, 9 August 1692, Greenwich, National Maritime Museum, Southwell Papers, Phillips MSS Sou/14.

29. Chidley Brooke to Benjamin Fletcher, 2 August 1693, CO 5/1038/f. 146.

30. Phips to Nottingham, 21 February 1692/3, CO 5/751/f. 47.

31. Stoughton to Blathwayt, 24 October 1693, CW, Blathwayt Papers, vol. 5; Cutts to Dudley, 31 May 1695, MHS, Winthrop Family Papers.

32. Phips to Blathwayt, 12 October 1692, CW, Blathwayt Papers, vol. 5; Sewall *Diary of Samuel Sewall*, 1:310. For the list of councilors elected in 1693, see CO 5/857/f. 208.

33. Byfield to Dudley, 12 June 1694, CO 5/858/ff. 102–3.

34. Short to the Admiralty Board, 24 April 1693, CO 5/857/ff. 191–92; minute of the Lords of Trade, 19 January 1693/4, CO 5/858/ff. 16–17.

35. Order in council on the petition of Brenton, 22 December 1692, PC 2/75/p. 59; Cutoms Commissioners to the Treasury with a petition by Brenton, 22 November 1693, CO 5/857/ff. 264, 266; order in council, 7 December 1693, PC 2/75/pp. 293, 294; Customs Commissioners to the Treasury, 9 December 1693, CO 5/858/f. 1.

36. Jackson's petition, 5 January 1693/4, CO 5/858/f. 3; another petition, undated, and minute of the Lords of Trade, CO 5/859/ff. 16–17, 60–61; report of the Lords of Trade, 2 February 1693/4; William III to Phips, 15 February 1693/4, CO 5/858/ff. 67, 69–71; William III to Stoughton, 22 February 1693/4, CO 324/24/pp. 183–87.

37. Address of the council and assembly, 31 October 1694, CO 5/858/ff. 121–22; *A Letter from New England*, CO 5/858/ff. 123–26. The previous fall Phips had written to Blathwayt with a proposal for the trade in pelts with the eastern tribes. Blathwayt would procure a patent from the crown for a company

with each man contributing five hundred pounds. The profits would return Blathwayt his investment, Phips claimed, allowing the remaining five hundred pounds with which to carry on the business. Thereafter the partners could expect a return of 50 percent annuallly on their investment. Phips sent his personal secretary to give Blathwayt further details (Phips to Blathwayt, 11 September 1693, CW, Blathwayt Papers, vol. 5).

38. Stoughton to Sir John Trenchard, 15 November 1694 with sworn evidence and articles by Brenton, CO 5/858/ff. 127, 129–240, 255.

39. Fitzjohn Winthrop to Wait Winthrop, 13 July 1695, *MHSC*, 5th ser. 8:324; undated letter from either John Povey or Blathwayt to Benjamin Fletcher, HL, Blathwayt Papers, BL215.

40. James Vernon's minutes of the Committee for Plantation Affairs, 4 July 1695; minutes of the Lords Justices on the report of the Committee for Trade, 12 July; and minutes of the Lords Justices, 16 July 1695, BL, Add. MSS 40777, ff. 14, 15 (also SP 44/274/p. 49 and Southwell Papers, BL, Add. MSS 21494, f. 37).

41. Blathwayt in a letter to the Lords Justices, 8 August 1695 (n.s.), Blathwayt Papers, BL, Add. MSS 9722, f. 89, set out the king's response to the proposal to appoint Bellomont governor of both Massachusetts and New York. See also the minutes of the Lords Justices, 12, 26 August 1695, BL, Add. MSS 40782, ff. 49, 52.

42. Bellomont to [Vernon], 12 December 1696, SP 63/358/no. 75; Trumbull to Blathwayt, 7 July 1696, in HMC, *Report on the Manuscripts of the Marquis of Downshire*, 4 vols. in 5 (London: HMC, 1924–40), 1, pt. 2:677.

43. Commissioners of Trade to the king, 25 November 1696, CO 5/907/p. 51; address by Stoughton and the council, 24 September 1696, CO 5/859/ff. 136–37; Stephen Sewall to Edward Hill (merchant of London), 2 November 1696, CO 5/859/ff. 127–28.

Chapter 16

1. T. C. Barker; "Smuggling in the Eighteenth Century: The Evidence of the Scottish Tobacco Trade," *Virginia Magazine of History and Biography* 62 (October 1954): 391; Lords Justices of Ireland to Secretary Trenchard, 3 April 1965, SP 63/356/no. 43, f. 104; Edward Randolph to the Commissioners of Customs, 27 June 1692, CO 5/1306/ff. 439–44; Randolph to William Blathwayt, 21 April 1692, CW, Blathwayt Papers, vol. 2.

2. Edward Southwell's memoranda of council affairs, 1 May 1693, BL, Add. MSS 34250, f. 5; minute of the Lords of Trade, 12 June 1693, CO 5/1114/p. 43; Customs Board to the Treasury, 2 August 1693, T 1/23/f. 123; Lords of Trade to the governors of Connecticut and Rhode Island, 8 September 1693, CO 5/906/pp. 64–66; petitions of Perry, Lane, and others to the Commissioners of Customs, 3 February 1693/4, T 1/26/ff. 211, 212; Customs Board to the Treasury, 22 March 1693/4, T 1/27/f. 87; order in council, 9 August 1694, and Treasury to Governor Edmund Andros, 15 November 1694, CO 5/1358/pp. 267–68, 290–91.

3. Cary and Edward Hackett to Day and Yate, 2 December 1695, John Cary Papers, BL, Add. MSS 5540, f. 78; minutes of the Bristol committee of trade, 15 January 1695/6, Add. MSS 5540, f. 101; Day and Yate to William Snyder, 23 December 1695, Add. MSS 5540, f. 88.

4. Report of the Customs Board to the House of Lords, 3 January 1695/6, T 1/36/f. 9; order in council, 13 January 1695/6, and presentment of the Customs Board, CO 324/5/pp. 348–49, 350–52; Customs Board to the Privy Council, 17 January 1695/6, CO 324/5/pp. 365–71.

5. Minutes of the Lords of Trade, 28 January, 10 February 1695/6, circular latter to the governors, 13 February 1695/6, CO 324/5/pp. 371–73, 375, 376–77.

6. The passage of the act may be followed in Leo Francis Stock, ed., *Proceedings and Debates of the British Parliament respecting North America*, 5 vols. (Washington D.C.: Carnegie Institution of Washington, 1924–41), 2:132–71, and in HMC, *The Manuscripts of the House of Lords*, n.s., 10 vols. to date (London: HMC, 1900–), vol. 2, no. 1047. See also ibid., no. 955, for a discussion of general trade concerns, and Michael G. Hall, "The House of Lords, Edward Randolph, and the Navigation Act of 1696," *WMQ*, 3d ser. 14 (October 1957): 494–515; and Charles McLean Andrews, *The Colonial Period of American History*, 4 vols. (New Haven, Conn.: Yale University Press, 1934–38), 4:157–60.

7. Hall, "House of Lords, Randolph, and the Navigation Act," pp. 502–5; Andrews, *Colonial Period*, 4:160–69; and Thomas G. Barrow, *Trade and Empire: The British Customs Service in Colonial America, 1660–1775* (Cambridge, Mass.: Harvard University Press, 1967), pp. 53–58.

8. For the various proposals, see Ian K. Steele, *The Politics of Colonial Policy: The Board of Trade in Colonial Administration, 1689–1720* (Oxford: Oxford University Press, 1968), p. 11; and minutes of the Lords Justices, 26, 27 September 1695, James Vernon Papers, BL, Add. MSS 40782, ff. 67, 68.

9. The Bristol committee to Day and Yate, 16, 21 December 1695, John Cary Papers, BL, Add. MSS 5540, ff. 84, 87; Day and Yate to Alderman William Swimmer, 31 December 1695, Add. MSS 5540, f. 92.

10. Gilbert Burnet, *History of His Own Times*, new ed. (London, 1888), p. 621; John Ellis to Baron Lexington, 3 January 1695/6, BL, Add. MSS 46525B, no. 63; Blathwayt to Lexington, 3/13 January 1695/6, Add. MSS 46528B, no. 10.

11. Stock, *Proceedings in Parliament*, 2:156–58; John Ellis to Lexington, 31 January 1695/6, BL Add. MSS 46525B, no. 65. For the political background on the question of the Council of Trade, see Dorothy H. Somerville, *The King of Hearts, Charles Talbot, Duke of Shrewsbury* (London: Allen & Unwin, 1962), pp. 108–9; Henry Horwitz, *Revolutionary Politicks: The Career of Daniel Finch, Second Earl of Nottingham, 1647–1730* (New York: Cambridge University Press, 1968), p. 155; John P. Kenyon, *Robert Spencer, Earl of Sunderland* (London: Longmans, Green, 1958), pp. 276–78. The best work on the founding of the Council of Trade is Steele, *Politics of Colonial Policy*, pp. 10–18, 178–79, which argues for the influence of Shrewsbury rather than John Locke, whose influence was stressed in Peter Laslett, "John Locke, the Great Recoinage, and the Origins of the Board of Trade: 1695–1698," *WMQ*, 3d ser. 14 (July 1957): 370–402. See also R. M. Lees, "Parliament and the Proposal for a Council of Trade," *English Historical Review* 54 (January 1939): 36–66; Andrews, *Colonial Period*, 4:272–90; and Maurice Cranston, *John Locke: A Biography* (London: Longmans, Green, 1957), pp. 399–403.

12. Locke to James Blair, 16 October 1699, CW, Francis Nicholson Papers, Emphasis added.

13. Povey to Francis Nicholson, 4 July 1696, LPL, Fulham Palace Papers, American Colonial Section, 2, f. 67; Robert Henley to Blathwayt, 3 July 1696, BL, Add. MSS 9729, f. 140; Charles Montagu to Blathwayt, 17/27 July 1696, Add. MSS 34355, F. 15.

14. Robert Henley to Blathwayt, 9 June 1696, BL, Add. MSS 9729, f. 143; Blathwayt to George Stepney, 18 February 1697/8, SP 105/51.

15. Montagu to Blathwayt, 17/27 July 1696, Add. MSS 34355, f. 15; Stepney to Mantagu, 13/23 August, 31 August/9 September 1696, SP 105/56; Methuen to Robert Harley, 1/11 June 1696, in HMC, *Fourteenth Report*, app., pt. 2 (London: HMC, 1894), p. 576; James Vernon to Matthew Prior, 24 July 1696, in HMC, *Report on the Manuscripts of the Marquis of Bath, Preserved at Longleat, Wiltshire*, 3 vols. (London: HMC, 1904–1908), 3:82.

16. Stepney to Robert Sutton, Baron Lexington, 15/25 June 1697, BL, Add. MSS 46535, f. 240; Stepney to John Ellis, 5/15 September 1699, John Ellis Papers, Add. MSS 28904, f. 39.

17. John Nelson to Blathwayt, 29 October 1698, CO 5/860/f. 80; Blathwayt to Stepney, 24 June 1698, SP 105/51; Stepney to John Ellis, 4/14 March 1698/9, Add. MSS 28903, f. 33; James Vernon to Blathwayt, 8 June 1697, Add. MSS 34348, f. 45; Shrewsbury to the Treasury, 11 April 1697, SP 44/100/p. 281; minute of the Lords Justices, 22 June 1697, Add. MSS 40782, f. 208.

18. Stepney to John Ellis, 27, 31 December 1698, Add. MSS 28902, ff. 212, 230; Viscount Villars to Richard Hill, 26 November 1697, Middlesex Record Office, London, Jersey MSS, vol. 2, 131/1.

19. Blathwayt to Stepney, 30 December 1698, 23 May 1699, Stepney to Blathwayt, 6 June 1699, Stepney to John Ellis, 6 June 1699, SP 105/53; Vernon to Shrewsbury, 31 May, 3 June 1699, *Letters Illustrative of the Reign of William III from 1696 to 1708 Addressed to the Duke of Shrewsbury . . . by J. Vernon, Secretary of State*, ed., G. P. R. James, 3 vols. (London, 1841), 2:298, 300; Blathwayt to Stepney, 12/22, 17/27 September 1699, SP 105/53; Blathwayt to Lexington, 18/28 June, 4/14 August, 18/28 September 1698, Add. MSS 46542, ff. 2, 4, 6, 9.

20. So it appears from a later letter, Lodowyck to the earl of Oxford, 4 June 1711, Portland MSS, BL, Loan 29/45c/no. 18, f. 145.

21. Stepney to Blathwayt, 9 July 1700, BL, Add. MSS 9719, ff. 165–66.

22. Council of trade to the king, 25 February 1696/7, CO 5/907/pp. 134–39; Shrewsbury to the council of trade, 16 March 1696/7, SP 44/100/p. 275; Shrewsbury to Blathwayt, 13 July 1697, Blathwayt to Shrewsbury, 19/29 July 1697, in HMC, *Report on the Manuscripts of the Duke of Buccleuch and Queensbury . . . Preserved at Montagu House*, 3 vols. (London: HMC, 1899–1926), 2:492; William Popple to Bellomont, 14 April 1697, CO 5/907/p. 153; Council of Trade to the king, 15 April 1697, CO 5/907/p. 154; Vernon to Shrewsbury, 10 May 1697, *Letters to Shrewsbury*, 1:229; minutes of the Lords Justices, 13, 22, 27 July, 12 August 1697, SP 44/100/pp. 126, 137, 151–52, 179; Bellomont to Somers, 16 October 1697, Kingston, Surrey Record Office, Somers Papers, ACC 775 G1/1. See also Bellomont to Bridgewater, 22 June 1700, HL, Bridgewater Americana, 9782.

23. Blathwayt to Matthew Prior, 9/19 August 1697, in HMC, *Manuscripts of*

the Marquis of Bath, Longleat, 3:148; Vernon to the Commissioners of Trade, 9 January 1698/9, SP 44/99/p. 578.

24. Bellomont to Bridgewater, 22 June 1700, HL, Bridgewater Americana, 9782; and the memorial of the Commissioners of Trade on Bellomont's dispatches, 24 April 1700, T 1/68/165.

25. Randolph to William Popple, 25 April, 12 May 1698, CO 323/2/ff. 302, 318; Quary to the Commissioners of Trade, 1, 6 June 1699, CO 5/1258/ff. 152–53, 155–56; Steele, *Politics of Colonial Policy*, pp. 44–48, 55–57.

26. See the general review of trade since 1670 in the report of the Board of Trade, 23 December 1697, Abraham Hill Papers, BL, Sloan MSS 2902, ff. 171–80, particularly the section on colonial commerce, f. 173 (also in CO 389/15/pp. 265–82); Sir Philip Meadows's general estimate of the state trade, 7 April 1697, CO 389/15/pp. 126–30; and the general estimate, dated 14 January 1697/8, in the Hill Papers, BL, Sloan MSS 2902, f. 115.

27. Presentment of the Commissioners of Customs, 17 July 1696, SP 32/6/no 47; order of the Lords Justices, 23 July 1697, CO 323/2/f. 13; Randolph's lists and proposals, CO 323/2/ff. 19, 23, 26, 33–34; and copy by Francis Nicholson of a memorandum by Randolph, 18 January 1697/8, HL, Bridgewater Americana, no. 9593.

28. Petition of the proprietors and agents, CO 5/1/f. 74; memorial of the proprietors and agents, CO 5/1/f. 87; Attorney General Thomas Trevor to William Popple, 4 December 1696, CO 5/1/f. 84; Penn to Sir William Trumbull, 4 January 1696/7, in HMC, *Report on the Manuscripts of the Marquess of Downshire*, 4 vols. (London: HMC, 1924–40), 1, pt. 2:727; Winthrop to the governor and magistrates of Connecticut, 8 February 1696/7, *CHSC*, 24:132; and petition by Coxe, 21 January 1696/7, CO 5/1/f. 93. The role of Blathwayt, who might well have been expected to attack the chartered governments, is uncertain. When Winthrop returned to Connecticut, he wrote Blathwayt thanking him for his aid when Winthrop was attending court as agent for the colony. "I remember with a great deale of thankful[l]nes[s] yor. favourable interpretation of some complaints against this gouvermt., & we owe much to yor. justice & inquiry into them for our vindication, wcͪ set us right in the opinion of the Court" (Winthrop to Blathwayt, 1 July 1698, *MHSC*, 5th ser. 8:344–45.

29. Stock, *Debates in Parliament*, 2:191–207; HMC, *Manuscripts of the House of Lords*, n.s. 2:411–504, no. 1115.

30. Randolph to the Commissioners of Trade, 26 April, 30 May, 25 August 1698, CO 323/2/ff. 304, 320, 374; Bellomont to the Commissioners of Customs, 27 May 1698, T 1/56/272; Bellomont to William Popple, 6 November 1699, CO 5/861/f. 75 enclosing Blake to Nanfan, 22 July 1699, CO 5/861/f. 76; order of the Lords Justices, 31 August 1699, Edward Southwell's book of Privy Council memoranda, 1660–1708, BL, Add. MSS 35107, f. 52; William Popple to John Sansom, 19 July 1700, CO 324/7/pp. 307–8.

31. Randolph's papers submitted to the Commissioners of Trade, 5 November 1700, CO 323/3/ff. 231–34; and the narrative of Randolph's survey from 8 November 1697 to 1 July 1700, CO 323/3/ff. 235–41.

32. Morton to the Admiralty Board, 28 August 1701, John Ellis Papers, BL, Add. MSS 28887, ff. 244–55.

Chapter 17

1. Blathwayt to James Vernon, 17 September 1700 (n.s.), Vernon Papers, BL, Add. MSS 40774, f. 305.

2. Blathwayt to the earl of Bridgewater, 18 October 1697 (n.s.), HL, Elsmere Collection, Bridgewater Papers, EL8741.

3. Usher to the Commissioners of Trade, 29 October 1698, CO 5/860/f. 78.

4. Penn to [Harley], 30 January 1698/9, in HMC, *Fourteenth Report*, app., pt. 2 (London, 1894), pp. 601–2.

5. Customs Board to the Treasury, 24 May 1699, T 1/64/234; draft circular of the Lords Justices, 6 July 1699, CO 324/7/pp. 60–61; Stamford, Lexington, Locke, and Hill to the Lords Justices, 13 July 1699, CO 5/908/pp. 156–61; William Popple to William Blathwayt, 4 August 1699, Blathwayt Papers, BL, Add. MSS 9747, f. 21; Vernon to William III, 21, 25 July, 4 August 1699, Vernon Papers, BL, Add. MSS 40774, ff. 112, 116, 130.

6. Popple to Blathwayt, 4, 11, 22 August 1699, Blathwayt Papers, BL, Add. MSS 9747, ff. 17, 19, 21–22.

7. Quary to the Commissioners of Trade, 6 March 1699/1700, CO 5/1260/f. 100; Nicholson to the archbishop of Canterbury, 23 July 1700, *Historical Collections Relating to the American Colonial Church*, ed. William Stevens Perry, 5 vols. (Hartford, Conn.: 1870–78), 1:222.

8. Copies of the report to the House of Commons, 22 March 1699/1700 are in CO 389/17/pp. 32–39; Locke Papers, Bodl., MS Locke, c. 30, ff. 122–23; Abraham Hill Papers, BL, Sloane MSS 2902, f. 8.

9. Trevor to the king, 19 June 1700, CO 5/1260/f. 217; William Popple to the attorney general and solicitor general, 18 December 1700, CO 5/1288/f. 202.

10. Randolph to Blathwayt, 23 November 1700, CW, Blathwayt Papers, vol. 2; Randolph's list, CO 5/1260/f. 248.

11. Penn to Somers, 22 October 1700, Penn to the Commissioners of Trade, 31 December 1700, Penn to Lawton, 21 December 1700, HSP, Penn Letterbook, 1699–1700; Penn to Lawton [December 1700], *Pennsylvania Archives*, ed. Samuel Hazard et al., 119 vols., in 9 series (Philadelphia and Harris burg: State of Pennsylvania, 1852–1935), 1st ser., 1:139–42; Penn to Harley, n.d., in HMC, *Fifteenth Report*, app., pt. 4 (London, 1897), pp. 30–32.

12. The best analysis is in Ian K. Steele, "The Board of Trade, The Quakers, and the Resumption of Colonial Charters, 1699–1702," *WMQ*, 3d ser. 23 (October 1966): 596–619, and *Politics of Colonial Policy*, pp. 71–75, correctives to Alison Gilbert Olson, "William Penn, Parliament, and Proprietary Government," *WMQ*, 3d ser. 18 (April 1961): 176–95. Gary B. Nash, *Quakers and Politics: Pennsylvania, 1681–1726* (Princeton, N.J., Princeton University Press, 1968), pp. 242–43, follows Penn's line that Henry Compton, bishop of London, Thomas Bray, and other Anglicans were behind the push by the Commissioners of Trade to have Parliament take up the proprietary charters. As Steele points out, despite the charges of Penn and the Quaker community in London, there is no evidence of organized support by the Anglican societies or that Compton and his commissary, Bray, sought to arouse such support (Steele, *Politics of Colonial Policy*, pp. 76–77, and Samuel Clyde McCulloch, "The Foundation and Early

Work of the Society for the Propagation of the Gospel in Foreign Parts," *Huntington Library Quarterly* 8[May 1945]: 241–58). William III during his reign appointed twenty-one bishops. He favored Latitudinarians because of their greater sense of toleration and political trustworthiness. Only three of the appointees were moderate High Churchmen, none real Highflyers (that is, extremists).

13. Henry Horwitz, *Parliament, Policy, and Politics in the Reign of William III* (Manchester: Manchester University Press, 1977); Ian F. Burton, P. W. J. Riley, and E. Rowlands, *Political Parties in the Reigns of William III and Anne: The Evidence of the Division Lists, Bulletin of the Institute of Historical Research*, special supplement, no. 7 (London: University of London, 1968); and Geoffrey Holmes, *British Politics in the Age of Anne* (London and New York: Macmillan and St. Martin's Press, 1967), p. 265.

14. Somers to Shrewsbury, 26 May, 9, 23 June 1698, Coxe, *Letters Illustrative of the Reign of William III from 1696 to 1708 Addressed to the Duke of Shrewsbury . . . by J. Vernon, Secretary of State*, ed. G. P. R. James, 3 vols. (London, 1841), pp. 539, 540, 638.

15. Commissioners of Trade to Bellomont, 29 April 1701, CO 5/1118/pp. 252–66; report of the Board of Trade, 27 March 1701, CO 389/17/pp. 159–80 (copy in the Lexington Papers, BL, Add. MSS 46542, ff. 37–48; Commissioners of Trade to the king, 26 March 1701, CO 5/1289/ff. 6–9.

16. Board of Trade report, 23 April 1701, CO 324/7/pp. 424–25 (also in Lexington Papers, BL, Add. MSS 46542, ff. 62–73.)

17. Leo Francis Stock, ed., *Proceedings and Debates of the British Parliament respecting North America*, 5 vols. (Washington, D.C.: Carnegie Institution of Washington, 1924–41), 2:382–415; HMC, *The Manuscripts of the House of Lords*, n.s., 10 vols. to date (London: HMC, 1900–), 4:314–55; Steele, *Politics of Colonial Policy*, pp. 61, 70–71, 76. Steele thought that the Quakers provided "an effective lobby" against the bill, but aside from the claims of the Friends themselves, there is no evidence to show how many votes they swayed.

18. Stepney to Blathwayt, 25 June 1701, Blathwayt Papers, BL, Add. MSS 9712, f. 23.

19. John Ellis to Stepney, 20 June, 8 July 1701, Stepney Papers, BL, Add. MSS 7074, ff. 31, 37; James Vernon to Blathwayt, 22 August 1701, Vernon to the earl of Rochester, 6 September 1701, Vernon Papers, BL, Add. MSS 40775, ff. 91, 132–33; Ashurst to Wait Winthrop (two letters), 10 June 1701, *MHSC*, 6th ser. 5:88, 89–91.

20. John Ellis to Stepney, 20 June 1701, Stepney Papers, BL, Add. MSS 7074, f. 31; order in council, 28 June 1701, CO 5/1046/f. 241; James Vernon to William III, 20, 26 August 1701, Vernon to Blathwayt, 8 July, Vernon to Rochester, 30 October 1701, Vernon Papers, BL, Add. MSS 40775, ff. 6, 85, 93, 318–19.

21. Basse to [Blathwayt], 20 August 1701, Blathwayt Papers, BL, Add. MSS 9747, f. 38.

22. Commissioners of Trade to Nicholson, 22 July 1701, with observations, CO 5/1360/pp. 86–90; Hawles to the Commissioners of Trade, 9 August 1701,

CO 5/862/ff. 6–7, 10–11; Brenton to the Commissioners of Trade, n.d., but received 4 October 1701, CO 5/862/f. 38.

23. Larkin to the Commissioners of Trade, 5 December 1701, CO 5/715/f. 230; and Barrow, *Trade and Empire*, pp. 61–62.

24. Nicholson to Ellis, 2 December 1701, Ellis Papers, BL, Add. MSS 28887, f. 396.

25. See Penn's letters to various English peers and politicians, dated 25 August 1701, HSP, Penn Letterbook, 1699–1703; and Penn to Harley, 27 August 1701, in HMC, *Fifteenth Report*, app., pt. 4, pp. 19–21.

26. Penn to James Logan, [3 February 1701/2], *The Correspondence of William Penn and James Logan*, ed. Edward Armstrong, 2 vols. (Philadelphia, 1879–80), vols. 9–10 of the *Memoirs of the Historical Society of Pennsylvania*, 14 vols. (Philadelphia, 1826–95), 1:78.

27. Commissioners of Trade to the earl of Manchester, with representation to the king, 24 January 1701/2, CO 324/8/pp. 36, 37–63.

28. Manchester to the Commissioners of Trade, 2, 17 February 1701/2, SP 44/101/pp. 184, 185, 196. The heads of the bill are in CO 5/1261/f. 229.

29. Commissioners of Trade to Manchester, 18 February 1701/2, CO 5/1289/f. 192; report of the Board of Trade, 16 February 1701/2, in HMC, *Manuscripts of the House of Lords*, n.s. 4:462–64.

30. Penn to James Logan, [4 December 1701], *Correspondence of Penn and Logan*, 1:247.

31. Weymouth to Nottingham, 2, 5 June 1702, Hatton-Finch Papers, BL, Add. MSS 29589, ff. 39, 47; Stepney to John Ellis, 5, 12 July 1702, Ellis Papers, BL, Add. MSS 28911, ff. 263, 281.

32. Penn to James Logan, [21 June 1702], *Correspondence of Penn and Logan*, 1:112, 116; Godolphin to Nottingham, 17 July 1703, Hatton-Finch Papers, BL, Add. MSS 29589, f. 28; and John Robert Moore, *Daniel Defoe, Citizen of the Modern World* (Chicago: University of Chicago Press, 1959), pp. 133–36.

33. In hearings conducted before the Board of Trade later that spring, Penn denied that in 1694 he had promised as a condition of having the government restored to him to settle a militia in Pennsylvania, but said he had merely promised to use his influence to produce a quota of men to assist in the defense of New York (minutes of the Board of Trade, 1 June 1702, CO 391/15/pp. 53–60). He had also contested the jurisdiction of the vice-admiralty courts vis à vis the powers of the courts established under the proprietary charter. After reviewing the provisions of the Act to Prevent Frauds, the attorney general and the advocate general of the Admiralty, Sir Edward Northy and Sir John Cooke, concluded by implication that both the Court of Vice Admiralty and the common law courts were competent to try violations of the navigation acts. Cooke may have come to this conclusion after consultation with Northy. See his report, 23 July 1702, CO 5/1261/ff. 452–53; and Northy to the Commissioners of Trade, 21 August 1702, CO 5/1261/ff. 491–92.

34. Penn to Fitzjohn Winthrop, [27 July 1703], *MHSC*, 6th ser. 3:103; Penn to Logan, [6 September 1702], *Correspondence of Penn and Logan*, 1:133, 136.

35. Stock, *Proceedings in Parliament*, 3:1, 6, 33–35; HMC, *Manuscripts of*

the House of Lords, n.s. 5:66–100, 311–55 (nos. 1829, 1951).

36. See the discussion in Steele, *Politics of Colonial Policy*, pp. 79–80. Steele established that the Quakers worked against the bill in the House of Lords. Whether their influence was decisive is not known.

Conclusion

1. Representation of the Commissioners of Trade, 29 April 1701, CO 324/7/pp. 454–55; minute of the king in council, 30 April 1701, CO 323/3/f. 278.

2. Douglas Edward Leach, *Arms for Empire: A Military History of the British Colonies in North America, 1607–1763* (New York: The Macmillan Co., 1973), p. 508.

Index

313

DATE DUE

JUN 28 84			
DEC 2 0 1993			
NOV 2 9 1993			